A Year of Forgiveness

A Course in Miracles Lessons with Commentary from Jesus

THROUGH TRANCE CHANNEL

Tina Louise Spalding

A
Year
of
Forgiveness

A Course in Miracles Lessons
with Commentary from Jesus

THROUGH TRANCE CHANNEL
Tina Louise Spalding

𝔩 *Light Technology* PUBLISHING

For information about special discounts for bulk purchases, please contact Light Technology Publishing Special Sales at 1-800-450-0985 or publishing@LightTechnology.com.

Illustrations are copyrighted and remain the intellectual property of the artist, Renée Phillips ©2020, for future use in any medium.

ISBN-13: 978-1-62233-076-8
ebook ISBN: 978-1-62233-831-9

Light Technology Publishing, LLC
Phone: 1-800-450-0985
1-928-526-1345
Fax: 928-714-1132
PO Box 3540
Flagstaff, AZ 86003
LightTechnology.com

About This Book

This book is designed to be a companion text to your larger *A Course in Miracles* book. It is designed to assist your understanding of the daily lessons offered in *A Course in Miracles* workbook with guided daily commentaries from Jesus channeled through Tina Spalding.

These commentaries came through daily during Tina's yearlong reading of the lessons of *A Course in Miracles* presented on YouTube in 2019. Many have found them very helpful in coming to understand the meaning and purpose of the lessons.

Contents

About This Book... V

Preface.. XVII

Introduction.. XIX

LESSONS

1   Nothing I see in this room [on this street, from this window, in this place] means anything 1

2   I have given everything I see in this room [on this street, from this window, in this place] all the meaning that it has for me 2

3   I do not understand anything I see in this room [on this street, from this window, in this place] 3

4   These thoughts do not mean anything. They are like the things I see in this room [on this street, from this window, in this place]...............4

5   I am never upset for the reason I think 6

6   I am upset because I see something that is not there........................7

7   I see only the past..9

8   My mind is preoccupied with past thoughts 10

9   I see nothing as it is now.. 12

10   My thoughts do not mean anything 13

11   My meaningless thoughts are showing me a meaningless world 15

12   I am upset because I see a meaningless world 16

13   A meaningless world engenders fear 18

14   God did not create a meaningless world................................. 19

15   My thoughts are images that I have made 20

16   I have no neutral thoughts... 21

17   I see no neutral things.. 23

18   I am not alone in experiencing the effects of my seeing 24

19   I am not alone in experiencing the effects of my thoughts........... 25

20   I am determined to see.. 26

21   I am determined to see things differently................................ 27

22   What I see is a form of vengeance 29

23   I can escape from the world I see by giving up attack thoughts 31

24   I do not perceive my own best interests 32

25   I do not know what anything is for 34

26   My attack thoughts are attacking my invulnerability................... 36

27   Above all else, I want to see 38

28   Above all else, I want to see things differently 39

29   God is in everything I see.. 41

30 God is in everything I see because God is in my mind 42

31 I am not the victim of the world I see 43

32 I have invented the world I see 45

33 There is another way of looking at the world.................................... 46

34 I could see peace instead of this.. 48

35 My mind is part of God's. I am very holy 49

36 My holiness envelops everything I see.. 50

37 My holiness blesses the world.. 52

38 There is nothing my holiness cannot do.. 54

39 My holiness is my salvation 55

40 I am blessed as a son of God.. 57

41 God goes with me wherever I go.. 59

42 God is my strength. Vision is his gift.. 60

43 God is my source. I cannot see apart from him.................................. 62

44 God is the light in which I see 63

45 God is the mind with which I think 64

46 God is the love in which I forgive 66

47 God is the strength in which I trust.. 68

48 There is nothing to fear.. 69

49 God's voice speaks to me all through the day 71

50 I am sustained by the love of God.. 72

51 Review I: Part 1 74

52 Review I: Part 2 75

53 Review I: Part 3 76

54 Review I: Part 4 77

55 Review I: Part 5 78

56 Review I: Part 6 80

57 Review I: Part 7 81

58 Review I: Part 8 83

59 Review I: Part 9 84

60 Review I: Part 10.. 87

61 I am the light of the world 88

62 Forgiveness is my function as the light of the world.......................... 89

63 The light of the world brings peace to every mind through my forgiveness... 90

64 Let me not forget my function.. 92

65 My only function is the one God gave me 94

66 My happiness and my function are one 95

67 Love created me like itself.. 96

68 Love holds no grievances.. 98

69 My grievances hide the light of the world in me................................ 99

70 My salvation comes from me 100

71 Only God's plan for salvation will work 102

72 Holding grievances is an attack on God's plan for salvation 104

73 I will there be light 106

74 There is no will but God's 107

75 The light has come 109

76 I am under no laws but God's 110

77 I am entitled to miracles 111

78 Let miracles replace all grievances 112

79 Let me recognize the problem so that it can be solved 113

80 Let me recognize my problems have been solved 115

81 Review II: Part 1 115

82 Review II: Part 2 116

83 Review II: Part 3 118

84 Review II: Part 4 119

85 Review II: Part 5 120

86 Review II: Part 6 121

87 Review II: Part 7 122

88 Review II: Part 8 123

89 Review II: Part 9 124

90 Review II: Part 10 125

91 Miracles are seen in light 127

92 Miracles are seen in light, and light and strength are one 128

93 Light and joy and peace abide in me 129

94 I am as God created me 129

95 I am one self, united with my Creator 130

96 Salvation comes from my one self 131

97 I am spirit 132

98 I will accept my part in God's plan for salvation 133

99 Salvation is my only function here 135

100 My part is essential to God's plan for salvation 136

101 God's will for me is perfect happiness 138

102 I share God's will for happiness for me 139

103 God, being love, is also happiness 141

104 I seek but what belongs to me in truth 142

105 God's peace and joy are mine 143

106 Let me be still and listen to the truth 145

107 Truth will correct all errors in my mind 146

108 To give and to receive are one in truth 147

109 I rest in God 148

110 I am as God created me 149

111 Review III: Part 1 150

112 Review III: Part 2 151

113 Review III: Part 3 152

114 Review III: Part 4 152

115 Review III: Part 5 153

116 Review III: Part 6 154

117 Review III: Part 7 155

118 Review III: Part 8 156

119 Review III: Part 9 157

120 Review III: Part 10 158

121 Forgiveness is the key to happiness 159

122 Forgiveness offers everything I want.. 160

123 I thank my Father for his gifts to me.. 161

124 Let me remember I am one with God.. 162

125 In quiet, I receive God's word today.. 164

126 All that I give is given to me 165

127 There is no love but God's 167

128 The world I see holds nothing that I want 168

129 Beyond this world, there is a world I want... 169

130 It is impossible to see two worlds 171

131 No one can fail who seeks to reach the truth....................................... 173

132 I loose the world from all I thought it was 174

133 I will not value what is valueless.. 175

134 Let me perceive forgiveness as it is 177

135 If I defend myself, I am attacked.. 178

136 Sickness is a defense against the truth... 180

137 When I am healed, I am not healed alone... 182

138 Heaven is the decision I must make 183

139 I will accept atonement for myself... 185

140 Only salvation can be said to cure 186

141 Review IV: Part 1 — My mind holds only what I think with God............. 187

142 Review IV: Part 2 — My mind holds only what I think with God............. 189

143 Review IV: Part 3 — My mind holds only what I think with God............. 190

144 Review IV: Part 4 — My mind holds only what I think with God............. 191

145 Review IV: Part 5 —My mind holds only what I think with God............. 192

146 Review IV: Part 6 — My mind holds only what I think with God............. 194

147 Review IV: Part 7 — My mind holds only what I think with God............. 195

148 Review IV: Part 8 — My mind holds only what I think with God............. 197

149 Review IV: Part 9 — My mind holds only what I think with God............. 198

150 Review IV: Part 10 — My mind holds only what I think with God 200

151 All things are echoes of the voice for God 201

152 The power of decision is my own.. 202

153 In my defenselessness, my safety lies.. 204

154 I am among the ministers of God 205

155 I will step back and let him lead the way 207

156 I walk with God in perfect holiness 209

157 Into his presence would I enter now.. 210

158 Today I learn to give as I receive 211

159 I give the miracles I have received 212

160 I am at home. Fear is the stranger here 213

161 Give me your blessing, holy son of God 214

162 I am as God created me... 216

163 There is no death. The child of God is free 217

164 Now are we one with him who is our source 218

165 Let not my mind deny the thought of God... 219

166 I am entrusted with the gifts of God 220

167 There is one life, and that I share with God... 221

168 Your grace is given me. I claim it now.. 223

169 By grace, I live. By grace, I am released... 224

170 There is no cruelty in God and none in me.. 225

171 Review V: Part 1 — God is but love; therefore, so am I 227

172 Review V: Part 2 — God is but love; therefore, so am I 228

173 Review V: Part 3 — God is but love; therefore, so am I 229

174 Review V: Part 4 — God is but love; therefore, so am I 230

175 Review V: Part 5 — God is but love; therefore, so am I 232

176 Review V: Part 6 — God is but love; therefore, so am I 233

177 Review V: Part 7 — God is but love; therefore, so am I 234

178 Review V: Part 8 — God is but love; therefore, so am I 235

179 Review V: Part 9 — God is but love; therefore, so am I 236

180 Review V: Part 10 — God is but love; therefore, so am I 237

181 I trust my fellow humans, who are one with me 238

182 I will be still an instant and go home.. 240

183 I call on God's name and on my own 241

184 The name of God is my inheritance 242

185 I want the peace of God 243

186 Salvation of the world depends on me 244

187 I bless the world because I bless myself.. 245

188 The peace of God is shining in me now... 246

189 I feel the love of God within me now 247

190 I choose the joy of God instead of pain.. 249

191 I am the holy child of God himself.. 250

192 I have a function God would have me fill.. 251

193 All things are lessons God would have me learn 252

194 I place the future in the hands of God 253

195 Love is the way I walk in gratitude 254

196 It can be but myself I crucify 256

197 It can be but my gratitude I earn 257

198 Only my condemnation injures me 259

199 I am not a body. I am free 260

200 There is no peace except the peace of God 261

201 Review VI: Part 1 — I am not a body.
   I am free, for I am still as God created me 262

202 Review VI: Part 2 — I am not a body.
   I am free, for I am still as God created me 263

203 Review VI: Part 3 — I am not a body.
   I am free, for I am still as God created me 265

204 Review VI: Part 4 — I am not a body.
   I am free, for I am still as God created me 266

205 Review VI: Part 5 — I am not a body.
   I am free, for I am still as God created me 267

206 Review VI: Part 6 — I am not a body.
   I am free, for I am still as God created me 268

207 Review VI: Part 7 — I am not a body.
   I am free, for I am still as God created me 269

208 Review VI: Part 8 — I am not a body.
   I am free, for I am still as God created me 270

209 Review VI: Part 9 — I am not a body.
   I am free, for I am still as God created me 271

210 Review VI: Part 10 — I am not a body.
   I am free, for I am still as God created me 272

211 Review VI: Part 11 — I am not a body.
   I am free, for I am still as God created me 274

212 Review VI: Part 12 — I am not a body.
   I am free, for I am still as God created me 275

213 Review VI: Part 13 — I am not a body.
   I am free, for I am still as God created me 276

214 Review VI: Part 14 — I am not a body.
   I am free, for I am still as God created me 277

215 Review VI: Part 15 — I am not a body.
   I am free, for I am still as God created me 278

216 Review VI: Part 16 — I am not a body.
   I am free, for I am still as God created me 279

217 Review VI: Part 17 — I am not a body.
   I am free, for I am still as God created me 280

218 Review VI: Part 18 — I am not a body.
I am free, for I am still as God created me 281

219 Review VI: Part 19 — I am not a body.
I am free, for I am still as God created me 282

220 Review VI: Part 20 — I am not a body.
I am free, for I am still as God created me 284

221 Peace to my mind. Let all my thoughts be still 285

222 God is with me. I live and move in him 286

223 God is my life. I have no life but God's 287

224 God is my Father, and he loves his children 288

225 God is my Father, and his children love him. 289

226 My home awaits me. I will hasten there 290

227 This is my holy instant of release 291

228 God has condemned me not. No more do I 293

229 Love, which created me, is what I am 294

230 Now will I seek and find the peace of God 295

231 Father, I will but to remember you 296

232 Be in my mind, my Father, through the day 297

233 I give my life to God to guide today 298

234 Father, today I am your child again 300

235 God in his mercy wills that I be saved 302

236 I rule my mind, which I alone must rule 303

237 Now would I be as God created me 304

238 On my decision, all salvation rests 305

239 The glory of my Father is my own 306

240 Fear is not justified in any form 307

241 This holy instant is salvation come 308

242 This day is God's. It is my gift to him 310

243 Today I will judge nothing that occurs 311

244 I am in danger nowhere in the world 312

245 Your peace is with me, Father. I am safe 313

246 To love my Father is to love his child 314

247 Without forgiveness, I will still be blind 315

248 Whatever suffers is not part of me 317

249 Forgiveness ends all suffering and loss 318

250 Let me not see myself as limited 319

251 I am in need of nothing but the truth 320

252 The child of God is my identity 321

253 My self is ruler of the universe 322

254 Let every voice but God's be still in me 323

255 This day I choose to spend in perfect peace 324

256 God is the only goal I have today 325

257 Let me remember what my purpose is.. 326

258 Let me remember that my goal is God 327

259 Let me remember that there is no sin... 328

260 Let me remember God created me.. 329

261 God is my refuge and security.. 330

262 Let me perceive no differences today.. 331

263 My holy vision sees all things as pure 333

264 I am surrounded by the love of God.. 334

265 Creation's gentleness is all I see 335

266 My holy self abides in you, God's child.. 336

267 My heart is beating in the peace of God 337

268 Let all things be exactly as they are 338

269 My sight goes forth to look upon Christ's face 339

270 I will not use the body's eyes today.. 340

271 Christ's is the vision I will use today 341

272 How can illusions satisfy God's child?.. 342

273 The stillness of the peace of God is mine 343

274 Today belongs to love. Let me not fear 345

275 God's healing voice protects all things today 346

276 The word of God is given me to speak 347

277 Let me not bind your child with laws I made.. 348

278 If I am bound, my Father is not free.. 349

279 Creation's freedom promises my own.. 350

280 What limits can I lay on God's child? 351

281 I can be hurt by nothing but my thoughts 352

282 I will not be afraid of love today.. 353

283 My true identity abides in you 354

284 I can elect to change all thoughts that hurt.. 356

285 My holiness shines bright and clear today 357

286 The hush of heaven holds my heart today 358

287 You are my goal, my Father — only you 359

288 Let me forget my fellow human's past today.. 360

289 The past is over. It can touch me not 361

290 My present happiness is all I see.. 362

291 This is a day of stillness and of peace 363

292 A happy outcome to all things is sure.. 364

293 All fear is past, and only love is here 365

294 My body is a wholly neutral thing.. 366

295 The Holy Spirit looks through me today.. 367

296 The Holy Spirit speaks through me today.. 368

297 Forgiveness is the only gift I give 369

298 I love you, Father, and I love your child 370

299 Eternal holiness abides in me 371

300 Only an instant does this world endure 372

301 And God himself shall wipe away all tears 374

302 Where darkness was, I look upon the light 375

303 The Holy Christ is born in me today 376

304 Let not my world obscure the sight of Christ 378

305 There is a peace that Christ bestows on us 380

306 The gift of Christ is all I seek today 381

307 Conflicting wishes cannot be my will 383

308 This instant is the only time there is 384

309 I will not fear to look within today 386

310 In fearlessness and love, I spend today 387

311 I judge all things as I would have them be 388

312 I see all things as I would have them be 390

313 Now let a new perception come to me 391

314 I seek a future different from the past 392

315 All gifts my fellow humans give belong to me 394

316 All gifts I give my fellow humans are my own 395

317 I follow in the way appointed me 396

318 In me, salvation's means and end are one 397

319 I came for the salvation of the world 398

320 My Father gives all power unto me 399

321 Father, my freedom is in you alone 401

322 I can give up but what was never real 402

323 I gladly make the "sacrifice" of fear 403

324 I merely follow, for I would not lead 405

325 All things I think I see reflect ideas 406

326 I am forever an effect of God 407

327 I need but call and you will answer me 408

328 I choose the second place to gain the first 410

329 I have already chosen what you will 411

330 I will not hurt myself again today 412

331 There is no conflict, for my will is yours 413

332 Fear binds the world. Forgiveness sets it free 414

333 Forgiveness ends the dream of conflict here 415

334 Today I claim the gifts forgiveness gives 416

335 I choose to see my fellow human's sinlessness 417

336 Forgiveness lets me know that minds are joined 418

337 My sinlessness protects me from all harm 419

338 I am affected only by my thoughts 421

339 I will receive whatever I request 422

340 I can be free of suffering today 423

341 I can attack but my own sinlessness,

and it is only that which keeps me safe 425

342 I let forgiveness rest on all things, for thus forgiveness will be given me 426

343 I am not asked to make a sacrifice to find the mercy and the peace of God 428

344 Today I learn the law of love:

that what I give my fellow human is my gift to me 429

345 I offer only miracles today, for I would have them be returned to me 430

346 Today the peace of God envelops me,

and I forget all things except his love 432

347 Anger must come from judgment. Judgment is the weapon I use

against myself to keep the miracle away from me 433

348 I have no cause for anger or for fear, for you surround me.

And in every need that I perceive, your grace suffices me 434

349 Today I let Christ's vision look upon all things for me

and judge them not but give each one a miracle of love instead 435

350 Miracles mirror God's eternal love. To offer them is to remember him

and, through his memory, to save the world 436

351 My sinless fellow human is my guide to peace. My sinful fellow human

is my guide to pain. And what I choose to see, I will behold 437

352 Judgment and love are opposites. From one come all the sorrows

of the world. But from the other comes the peace of God 439

353 My eyes, my tongue, my hands, my feet today have but one purpose:

to be given to Christ to use to bless the world with miracles 440

354 We stand together, Christ and I, in peace and certainty of purpose.

And in Christ is his creator, as Christ is in me... 441

355 There is no end to all the peace and joy and all the miracles

that I will give when I accept God's word. Why not today? 442

356 Sickness is but another name for sin. Healing is but another name

for God. The miracle is thus a call to him... 443

357 Truth answers every call we make to God,

responding first with miracles and then returning unto us to be itself 444

358 No call to God can be unheard nor left unanswered.

And of this, I can be sure God's answer is the one I really want.............. 445

359 God's answer is some form of peace. All pain is healed;

all misery is replaced with joy. All prison doors are opened.

And all sin is understood as merely a mistake 446

360 Peace be to me, the holy child of God. Peace to my fellow beings, who are

one with me. Let all the world be blessed with peace through us 448

361 This holy instant would I give to you. Be you in charge,
      for I would follow you, certain that your direction gives me peace.......... 450

362 This holy instant would I give to you. Be you in charge,
      for I would follow you, certain that your direction gives me peace.......... 452

363 This holy instant would I give to you. Be you in charge,
      for I would follow you, certain that your direction gives me peace.......... 453

364 This holy instant would I give to you. Be you in charge,
      for I would follow you, certain that your direction gives me peace.......... 455

365 This holy instant would I give to you. Be you in charge,
      for I would follow you, certain that your direction gives me peace.......... 456

Conclusion 459

About the Channel 460

Preface

Tina Louise Spalding

I have been channeling Jesus since 2013, when he came through as the last contributor in my book *Great Minds Speak to You*. The following day, he asked me to write his autobiography, which was published the following year. We have had an ongoing relationship in subsequent years, as I channel multiple times each month for both public and private audiences.

On December 31, 2018, I was inspired to read the daily lessons in *A Course in Miracles* on YouTube, where many of my channelings have been posted. I thought this would be a wonderful way to start the new year. Little did I know that Jesus would decide to come through each day after the lessons were read to give his wonderful and encouraging commentary.

Within just a few months, many people were emailing and thanking me for helping them with these complementary videos, stating that Jesus's commentaries were invaluable to their understanding of the material. By lesson 100, it was clear that the commentaries needed to be made into a book. This is that book.

This book is made even more appealing by the whimsical art of Renee Phillips, who has contributed beautiful illustrations for each lesson. Thank you, Renee, for the artistic element that adds so much to the daily commentaries. I would also like to thank Ian Helsinga for his tireless work transcribing the commentaries and last but not least my amazing and supportive assistant Carol Morgan, without whom my life would be rather chaotic.

Keep this book close at hand with your *A Course in Miracles* manual, and read Jesus's commentaries after practicing the lesson as described in that text. Allow Jesus's simple and direct discussion of the topic to aid your understanding of these wonderful teachings.

A Course in Miracles has changed my life, and it will change yours too. I hope you find help and a clearer understanding of the lessons through these 365 channeled messages from Jesus.

Much love,
Tina Louise Spalding, channel

Introduction

Jesus through Tina Louise Spalding

You are blessed beings, indeed. I am the one you know as Jesus, and this is your year. This is the year you have chosen to do *A Course in Miracles*. And what a year it will be. This is the year that you are acting in accord with truth, the truth that you really don't like what your mind produces. You really don't enjoy living here that much all the time. This is a common trait for humans on this Earth plane now.

A Course in Miracles was first transmitted through another channel for a specific time, and this book was channeled for this time. These lessons have been on your Earth plane for over fifty years. Many teachers and groups have formed, educated themselves, and then dissolved. Some have passed on from this plane using the information and the knowledge that they gained from their studies to relieve the suffering of their distorted minds. This is what the book is for.

I am that one you know as Jesus. There may be some doubts in your mind about whether or not that is true, and there is nothing I can do to prove to you that I am the one you know as Jesus. But I want you to understand that, as you study this material, your hateful and unloving beliefs and ideas will be revealed in your mind; many of them were inadvertently put there by others with the best intentions. You will begin to see that suffering is optional. In the end, it doesn't matter whether you believe who I am. It doesn't matter.

What I want you to understand is that you do not need to suffer. You do not need to live in pain and agony, in a state of sickness and eventual death. Death is an illusory state that you believe in because you've been taught about it so much in your society — your murder movies, your war movies. Your society worships death.

You might say, "No, this society does not worship death. We try to save people." But when you look at the actions of your governments, some of your parenting techniques, some of your working conditions, and the terrible environmental degradation and damage done to the beautiful sphere on which you find yourselves living, you will know that the tree that bears the fruit of modern Western society is not a healthy one. It does not have a healthy thought system.

I will guide you through the next 365 days on how to step away from the unhealthy and unloving warmongering thought system of your modern Western world toward the thought system of love and true forgiveness.

You will learn each day how to train your mind, and you will learn what is within you that does not serve you, your planet, or your family. The ideas of sacrifice and suffering are not contained within this teaching. Do not bring your traditional Christian beliefs to this work. This work is about freedom. It is about self-expression. And it is about true love — the true spiritual love of one brother or sister for another. Your salvation lies in practicing these lessons.

[To the channel]: Thank you for joining this, dear being, a great teacher in your own right.

I will encourage the channel to do these lessons with you daily over the next 365 days. She has some preconceived ideas of what this journey is going to be for her. She will learn her own lessons as she dedicates her life to helping you achieve the transformation of heart and mind that she has achieved.

I am that one you know as Jesus, and we will speak to you again soon.

Nothing I see in this room [on this street, from this window, in this place] means anything.

Follow the complete lesson guidelines in your *ACIM* book.

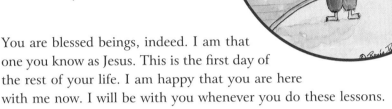

You are blessed beings, indeed. I am that one you know as Jesus. This is the first day of the rest of your life. I am happy that you are here with me now. I will be with you whenever you do these lessons.

I want you to understand that you are calling in the greatest teachers of all time. There is not just me but also many ascended master teachers involved in the transformation of Earth's consciousness at this time. By taking the first step in this long journey toward the rehabilitation of your mind, you call in great teachers and walk with beings far more powerful than you know.

These lessons seem small. They seem insignificant. But process by process, thought by thought, and idea by idea, your mind will be healed. In these baby steps, you might notice at times even a physical difference in your consciousness. For example, you may experience feelings in your head or body, or you might hear slightly different sounds ringing in your ears. You might even feel pressure on certain parts of the body.

With your training in the Judeo-Christian teachings of your time, it is very important that fear not be allowed to generate an anxious feeling. You are expanding your consciousness, and your body is a reflection of your consciousness. It is created by your consciousness, and you will have shifts in your bodily feelings as a consequence of the expansion of your mind.

On this side of the veil, there is much less separation than on your side. So when I say "we," we work as a collective — many ascended master teachers. But this particular project is mine. These teachings are about expansion. They are about freedom — true freedom. You cannot be free in your physical body when you are not free to think and choose with your mind.

We are taking down the barbed wire around the concentration camp of your limited ego-mind, and you will feel expansion in many different ways. Be brave, and step into these new feelings with enthusiasm and curiosity rather than fear. When you experience fear arising in your mind, know that it is planted there by some less-than-loving teaching.

You are brave, indeed, stepping into this new work. It is with great pleasure that we hold you close to our hearts and encourage you to do these lessons and to join us tomorrow for lesson 2. I am the one you know as Jesus, and we will speak to you again soon.

LESSON 2

I have given everything I see in this room [on this street, from this window, in this place] all the meaning that it has for me.

Follow the complete lesson guidelines in your *ACIM* book.

I am the one you know as Jesus. It is wonderful to have you with me again. These lessons are designed to transform the inner fundamental workings of your mind, and you may not understand them. You may not see the significance of them. But as you apply them, you will begin to see, feel, and become aware of the fact that you have different values laid on different objects.

You do not like saying things like, "My child has no meaning, my home has no meaning, and my car has no meaning other than the meanings I have given them." You will feel little indicators that your mind does not agree with this lesson.

Do not allow these little feelings to distress you; pay attention to them after the lesson. Do the lesson as described, then pay attention: "Ah! I didn't like saying that my dog or my cat has no meaning other than the one that I have laid on it." You will feel those little tugs of resistance, and they are little indicators of your argumentative position with this teaching.

Remember, you don't have to agree with these lessons. By doing them, you use your free will to transform the aspects of your consciousness that you do not yet know are causing you trouble or difficulty. Those little tugs give you an indication of something going on inside your mind.

Trust in this process. It is the means you have been given to achieve

2

absolute freedom — freedom from all your fears, freedom from death, and freedom from all the things that worry you and cause you consternation. It is hard in these early lessons to believe that saying such things could transform your mind, but rest assured that you are studying the most powerful transformative texts available to you at this time.

I am that one you know as Jesus, and we will see you again tomorrow.

LESSON 3

I do not understand anything I see in this room [on this street, from this window, in this place].

Follow the complete lesson guidelines in your *ACIM* book.

You are blessed beings, indeed. I am the one you know as Jesus. This is an important year for you. You are here for lesson 3 — the early stages of questioning yourself about how you see reality. Now, for most of you, how you see reality is never questioned. You feel perfectly fine to say, "This is right" or "That is wrong" and "She is good" or "He is bad" and "This looks good on me, but it looks really bad on you." Whatever the judgment is, you base it on your perception of reality.

Your emotional feedback from your guidance system, which is the loving system you have been given to tell you how close or how far from love you are, will feed back to you information about the judgments you make.

When you look at others doing something and make a judgment, "That is bad. They should not be doing that," you feel feedback from your emotional guidance system. That feedback will be a bad feeling, and you will associate the bad feeling with the actions of those you have judged. What is actually happening is your feedback system — this beautiful guidance system that you have been given — is giving you feedback on your behavior. This is the great secret you are all missing in your teachings. The guidance system tells you about *your* behavior.

Judge not, for you will suffer. Not because you are being punished by a vengeful God, as many of you believe, but because your guidance system is perfect. It will never stop telling you how close you are to love or how far away you are from love. When you observe others' actions and say, "That behavior is unacceptable, and they are bad people for doing that," your loving guidance system that teaches you how to love will say, "Mm-hmm!" It will give you a negative emotional response because you have just stepped away from love. You have not viewed others with forgiving eyes.

This is the principle we will work with here — that you don't know the meaning of things. When you see people do something, hear people say something, or watch information on your television screens, you do not understand it because you do not know the motivation. You do not know the evolutionary status of those people, and you don't know what they are here to learn. So you should not judge — not only because it's unloving but also because you will suffer for stepping away from love in your judgment, isolation, or persecution of others.

Your guidance system is perfect. It is impeccable. It constantly tells you how close you are to love. In your peace, happiness, and joy, it tells you, "Yes, you are on the way to love." In your frustration, shame, and fear, it says, "No, you are off track here, beloved." You need to look at how you perceive things. Perception makes your world. It makes your emotional world, and that is all you know. That is all you experience. You think it is "out there," but you are experiencing the emotional inner world of your perceptions, interpretations, and judgments.

I am the one you know as Jesus, and we are happy you are with us today on lesson 3. Do your lesson impeccably. Pay attention to the stories that you tell about the world and how they make you feel. We will return tomorrow.

LESSON 4

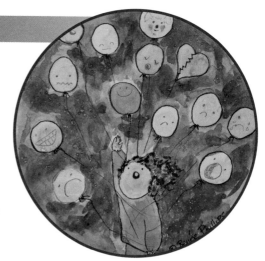

*These thoughts do not mean anything.
They are like the things I see in this room
[on this street, from this window, in this place].*

Follow the complete lesson guidelines in your *ACIM* book.

4

You are blessed beings, indeed. I am that one you know as Jesus. I am pleased you have made it to day four. This is no small feat when you consider the part of your mind you know as yourself has no interest in this process. You encounter an aspect of your mind that argues with what you, in your attempt at consciousness evolution, try to do. You hear a voice in your mind or have feelings of resentment or resistance to doing these lessons.

It is very important at this early stage (when you are a novice at this mind-training business) that you understand: the larger part of your consciousness has no interest in spiritual evolution or consciousness expansion. In fact, it absolutely resists it.

Why is this so? Well, you have chosen to come into separation. You have chosen to come into this place that so profoundly lacks love. Your body and your individual appearance demonstrate — a physical demonstration — your conscious belief in individuality and separation. In that individuality and separation, you have been further trained by your society to feed that part of you. So when asked to do things that go against your society's training, that well-fed (also loud and obnoxious at times) part of your mind used to having things its way will not be happy at all.

It is just as people newly going to the gymnasium to improve their fitness; three or four days in, the muscles complain. The minds of the beings trying to improve their fitness realize that this is going to be a little more difficult than they thought. This is when it is really important to recall the decision you have made to do this year-long study, because you made this decision based on evidence that the way your mind works and the way you do things is not bringing you what you want. That has not changed on day four, has it, dear ones? You have not suddenly started to live the life that you want. You still have the same evidence speaking to you that you had on the beginning of this journey.

Do not back out now. Do not sabotage yourself by saying, "Oh, I can't do this. This is too much bother." Go back to the decision you made: "There must be a better way than what I am doing." You must understand that your behavior comes from your feelings and thoughts, and your feelings and thoughts come from what you believe to be true about the world. If your beliefs about reality — the world, what you are, who you are, and why you are here — are incorrect, then your behaviors will not serve you because they are based on untruth.

On day four, recalibrate yourself to align with that decision: "I'm going to do the yearlong practice of *A Course in Miracles*. I'm going to observe when my mind argues, because there is a part of my mind that's curious about what's going to happen and wants to continue to do these lessons.

But there seems to be another part of my mind that is not happy about it. I am going to step back from being deeply involved and engaged with both of those aspects, and I'm going to observe and say, 'I have made a decision, and I'm going to stick by that decision to do the lessons of *A Course in Miracles* to see what happens and to see whether there is a discernible and quantifiable transformation in my life.'" We are here with you.

I am the one you know as Jesus, and I'm happy that you joined us today. We look forward to joining with you tomorrow. We will speak to you again soon.

LESSON 5

I am never upset for the reason I think.

Follow the complete lesson guidelines in your *ACIM* book.

You are blessed beings, indeed. I am that one you know as Jesus. It is important for you to understand that most of the things that upset you are not at all what you think. Your anger when another driver cuts you off or the look somebody gives you that makes you feel terrible are fictitious opportunities for separation that the ego uses to keep you alone, fearful, and powerless.

When you begin to understand how your mind affects your feelings, your feelings affect your behavior, and your behavior affects your life, you will understand the importance of this mind-training program. Some people do not like that phrase, so I want to address it.

You have been in a deeply convoluted mind-training program your whole life through your cultural and religious teachings, school systems, and television. All these are mind-training programs. Many of your behaviors do not come from a place of free will and choice. They come from the mind-training programs deeply embedded in your personality.

When you view the world, you see it through a multiplicity of lenses. Many of them — most, in fact — are not your own and do not hold up the values you know are good, right, and true. Because you've never gone into

6

your mind and excavated these little upsets, you do not know what your mind is made of. You do not know what ingredients your mind uses to bake the cake for each day.

All the fears your parents instilled in your mind and the superficial values your society added through television have become the value systems through which you view the world. You may not watch television now, but trust us, you have had thousands of hours of indoctrination from various sources. Each has put its values in your mind. This version of *A Course in Miracles* brings you back to the truth, but it takes a while.

So here, on day five, we congratulate you for showing up. We thank this being [the channel] for stepping into her role as teacher, facilitator, and channel to assist you in your journey toward love and home to truth. Your mind becomes increasingly peaceful as you eliminate these beliefs and ideas. Your heart opens more. You become more generous. You will not lose your personality, only some of the sharp edges and darker corners of it — the shadows.

So stick with these lessons. We will see you tomorrow for lesson 6.

LESSON 6

I am upset because I see something that is not there.

Follow the complete lesson guidelines in your *ACIM* book.

I am that one you know as Jesus. These are important gatherings as we come together to do these lessons. We want you to understand how reaching out through your technology to connect with love makes a powerful statement to the universe. Indeed, do not dismiss it as meaningless, small, or inconsequential.

The linear nature of the teachings you have had — the idea of only physical cause and effect — is one of the great handicaps in your society. You are a holographic being in that sense, the center of a massive creation. It emits and attracts back and forth, to you and from you. When you change your mind and look at the world differently, the world changes. Is that not a miracle — something that should not happen, given the physical laws of the universe as you understand them at this time? The laws are not true. They are materialistic in nature, narrow, and low in frequency. You look at the material world only. That means if you touch something, then it falls over, but if you don't touch that thing, then it won't fall over. Those are the limits of the sophisticated concepts in your society. "I must earn $2 to buy a $2 item."

As you go through the lessons of *A Course in Miracles*, you clear your mind of these ridiculously simplistic and low-frequency ideas. We bring you into alignment with the truth of who you are — a magnificent creator made in the image of your God. That means you are a powerful creator, and you can create worlds.

You have created your own world. Your body, job, family, friends, and bank account — all these things comprise the world you have created. Beyond that, you contribute the frequencies in your collective consciousness to the overall frequency of the planet. What you do here is powerful work, indeed. Do not dismiss it.

With lesson 6, you step further into your consciousness. You begin to question the normal way you look at things. This, indeed, is a gift to yourself, your family, your friends, and to the world in general. Miracles are your right. They are the natural way for your powerful, creative mind to work. You have not been taught how your mind works.

You have not been taught the power of your thoughts. You have wielded your thoughts and feelings willy-nilly, not realizing every single thought is a prayer that asks for something. The attention we ask you to pay to your mind begins the stage of disciplining your mind to create in alignment with what you want to experience and what you know to be good, true, loving, and kind.

I am that one you know as Jesus. We are pleased that you joined us today. We hope you join us again tomorrow for lesson 7. This being here [the channel] enjoys these lessons. She is surprised at her joy after revisiting something that has become a dear old friend to her. I am a dear friend to her, and you are a dear friend to her. She enjoys sharing this work with you, and we want you to know it is her passion and purpose.

You too will find your passion and purpose when you do these lessons. So continue to join us daily for these explorations of your most beautiful mind. We will speak to you again soon.

I see only the past.

Follow the complete lesson guidelines
in your *ACIM* book.

You are blessed beings, indeed. I am that one you know as Jesus. It is important that you have made it to day seven. We want you to understand that even though you have only joined us for seven days, your life as you know it has begun to shift a little bit.

Some of you might already feel shifts and changes in your perception. Perhaps you feel a little more open, or maybe you think about an old resentment you wish to resolve. You may experience, as we've mentioned before, physical feelings in your body such as tingling or pressure here and there. Do not be distressed by any of these symptoms. We want you to know that the mundaneness and the repetition in your life remain there because you don't change your mind.

Your programs have been deeply implanted. Many — dare we say all — have never been questioned or brought to the surface and asked, "Are you good for me? Are you true? Are you bringing me what I want?"

What has happened, even within this short seven-day period, is you have changed your thinking. You now question fundamental ideas about reality, and that brings about fundamental changes in your experience. It can even induce spiritual occurrences, such as visions or out-of-body experiences. If you encounter any of these things and you feel fear, we want you to know you are being shown your mind.

Something in your mind does not like the idea of having a spiritual experience. Yet here you are, studying spiritual material (with a good teacher, indeed). We want you to know when you study the lessons in *A Course in Miracles*, you change your future. You step out of time in that way. This lesson introduces the idea that the way you look at time can change and future experiences differ from the past ones you have become so familiar with.

When you are in a rut or feel stuck in an old pattern, that is how your beliefs manifest. You are seeing the result of a mind stuck in the past. That means you're not reassessing, reevaluating, and retraining the mind to come into alignment with what you hold to be true now. In doing *A Course in Miracles*, you align your mind with love, and you let go of fear. When you do that diligently and daily, you will see a transformation of not only your physical body and the experiences it gives you but of your entire world.

I am that one you know as Jesus, and we are pleased you are with us here for day seven. Hang in there, and know this year is one of great change on your planet. You will see some revelations, and it is important that you prepare your mind for what is, not what was or what you think should be. This course will, indeed, help you stay out of the past and future and keep you in the present moment where you are designed to be. We will speak to you again soon.

LESSON 8

My mind is preoccupied with past thoughts.

Follow the complete lesson guidelines in your *ACIM* book.

You are blessed beings, indeed. I am that one you know as Jesus. We congratulate you for showing up for lesson 8. You are a week into the new training, and it is important for you to remember that as you do these lessons, I do them with you. I stand side by side with you and hold your hand as you go through this mind-transformation program.

As you use your free will — the most powerful creative device in the universe — and choose to question the way you look at the world, this precipitates transformation in the world. The way you see the world comes from you. When you don't question the past experiences on which you base your decisions, you always create the same thing. If that thing does not suit you, then you develop unhealthy patterns of behavior that cause suffering.

When you begin to question your decision-making abilities based on your past experience as in, "When I am thinking about the past, I'm not really thinking about anything," you are imagining. You use your imagination when you relive or mull something over. You go back through your own filters of thought to a time and place when you made a decision about something — whether good, bad, or indifferent — and you bring that past recollection into the present and contaminate the present moment.

We want you to understand that you need to leave the present free and clear to create a new thing with a clarified mind. We want you to become more present, more accepting of the present moment, because this is where everything happens. If you bring your past ideas into this present moment and base your present decisions and judgments on past experience, you get the same thing over and over again.

Presence is what we want to cultivate here. You begin to see the time you spend in future ruminations and past regrets as a waste of your creative energy. This amounts to nothing but a waste of the present moment, the only moment you have for your creative mind to play.

Do not contaminate the present moment. When you feel sadness, depression, or pain, you have left the present moment. You think about what bad thing might come to you. You worry about or regret the past and the time you have wasted. You still waste your time when you look back at the past and think it should have been different.

This helps with the forgiveness practice, which this course cultivates in your consciousness, because if you don't keep regurgitating past wounds or sins that people might have committed against you, then you will not hate them. When you meet them, you do so in the present moment, free to accept them as they are. Harboring hatred and unforgiveness means you cannot meet people as they are in this moment. You're always layering what they have done and said, or shouldn't have done and said, between you and them, and you live an untrue idea of those people.

To live in the moment is a very loving thing. This lesson is a very loving practice. You begin to free not only yourself of the illusions of past and future but also those people you meet from your past judgments and decisions about them. You begin to meet them, perhaps for the first time, free and clear of judgment. In that moment, you have a true and honest interaction with them. This is cultivated over time.

When you meet people with whom you share resentments, you have a feeling of negativity because these past misdeeds have been fought and nurtured. As you begin to let go of these past wounds, judgments, and stories — involving your parents, ex-lovers, and partners — you can also release the future stories of poverty, homelessness, job loss, or betrayal. These illusory ideas contaminate your mind in the present and cause suffering.

Thank you for joining us today. We are pleased you are on this journey with us toward a new, clarified mind. These lessons free you from the prison of thoughts that hurt you, and we want you to know it is a powerful process, indeed. We will speak to you again tomorrow.

LESSON 9

I see nothing as it is now.

Follow the complete lesson guidelines in your *ACIM* book.

You are blessed beings, indeed. I am that one you know as Jesus. Once again we congratulate you for making it to the next lesson.

Lesson 9 states you do not see anything as it is now, and this is true enough. You are deeply contaminated by ideas, thoughts, recollections, and projections in your mind that interfere with your ability to see clearly. This is something you must, at this stage, take on faith.

In your normal state of consciousness as you exist now, you look at something and say: "Well, of course I see this as it is now. It's a cup. It's a cup now, it was a cup yesterday, and it will be a cup tomorrow." That is the logical, linear-thinking mind arguing with the practice periods designed to shift and change the deepest parts of your consciousness, not the superficial layers. You function in a superficial way. You base your words, reactions, and opinions on stories and lessons from other beings. Then, you were punished if you did not agree with them.

Sometimes you revisit your school system. We remind you how indoctrinating that felt when as a small child, you sat in a desk when you were tired or would have preferred to play. These are traumatic indoctrination techniques given under threat of punishment. This is not the way you recall school, but these are some of the training programs you've endured that have distorted your mind and indoctrinated you into particular modes of thought you no longer have choice about.

We are loosening the locks and scraping away the rust to allow your freedom. To do that, we must begin to push your mind in unfamiliar directions. This is why your ordinary consciousness might feel confused or resistant as we ask you to take journeys down tracks and pathways forbidden to you. We want you to question things and look at them in a different way.

This is not how you are trained in your society, so these lessons seem ridiculous. Your training programs of linearity and time-based, focused thinking and materialism all have been ingrained into you for a particular reason: to keep you out of your miracle-mindedness. That is where we are leading you. So listen to that voice. Just be aware of it, and say: "Oh, there's the trained mind arguing with this lesson. I don't have to understand the lesson. I don't have to agree with it. I just have to practice it. I am curious enough about the inner workings of my consciousness that I am willing to keep practicing these lessons with Jesus."

I am that one you know as Jesus, and my work has never changed over all these eons. It is about relieving suffering. It is about giving freedom to the heart and mind of all the humans on this planet. That is what I started teaching so many years ago, and I still continue to teach this. It comes from a deep love for humanity.

You do not need to suffer. You suffer too much in this world now, and these lessons show you a way out of that suffering. Join us tomorrow for lesson 10. We will see you then.

LESSON 10

My thoughts do not mean anything.

Follow the complete lesson guidelines in your *ACIM* book.

I am that one you know as Jesus, and we are here together to enlighten you. That is the path of all human beings on this planet — the path to awaken to their true nature, which is love.

That is clearly not where you are at this time. The results and the physical manifestations on your planet of war, sickness, and death testify to the fact that you do not know love. Even though made of love from love for love, you have walked so far down the road away from love that you have forgotten your true nature.

This training program you have decided to join with me reveals how far you have walked along the road in the wrong direction. You can look at the physical manifestations in your life, body, relationships, and society and know you lack love. If something is lacking, what do you add to that situation? The thing it lacks.

You must add love to this life that you live in your perceptual journey. First of all, you must have your mind clarified because most of you do not even know what love is. Truly, dear ones, you do not know what love is. You have a programmed, superficial, and distorted definition of love. Many of the acts you participate in and call love are not loving at all. The clarification begins with the fundamentals of how you look at yourself, how you look at your interior language, and how you interpret that interior language.

If you respond to every thought as true, you live in a chaotic and violent world. Most of the thoughts in your mind come from unloving (and thus untrue) beliefs and ideas. They have been inserted into your consciousness without your knowledge, even though you have supported them for many years through word, thought, and deed.

Trust in this process. Trust, as we get into the inner workings of your consciousness, even though you do not understand yet what comes from that transformation. You will feel more loving. You will feel less violent. When you do have the urge to attack, judge, or curse somebody or yell, shout, or scream, there will come a time when you truly have a choice. You will say, "I am not going to do that anymore."

These early lessons might confuse you because they counter everything you have ever been taught. We know this is a great act of faith on your part to do these lessons and allow us into your consciousness. For that, we are very grateful.

I walk beside you on this journey, and I want you to know my teachings always have been centered on love. They have never been about control, punishment, suffering, sacrifice, or martyrdom. These lies have covered over the work I have done throughout my existence.

I am that one you know as Jesus, and we are grateful that you came to join us today. We will see you again tomorrow.

My meaningless thoughts are showing me a meaningless world.

Follow the complete lesson guidelines
in your *ACIM* book.

You are blessed beings, indeed. I am
that one you know as Jesus. It is a great
blow to the ego mind to hear in these lessons
that your meaningless thoughts create a meaning-
less world. You often feel a rearing up of some great resistance within you,
and this is perfectly normal and okay.

It is important to continue with your lessons regardless of the ego's
reaction to them. You do not have to approve of these lessons. You do not
have to understand these lessons. You merely have to practice them and
trust that the process at play will help clarify your mind and bring peace to
your troubled world.

In the anxiety, fear, anger, shame, and guilt in your own mind — in this
soup of low frequency ideas — you age and die. This is an important thing
to understand.

During my earthly existence 2,000 years ago, I did not go to the cross
as a sacrifice, and I did not martyr myself. I demonstrated my ability to
overcome death, incorrectly called the resurrection. The body did not get
resurrected as such. I created a new body because my mind had reached a
point of love where it mastered the low frequencies of this material plane.
Miracles ensue when you align with love to such a degree. You lose your
fear, and you do not act as a victim of this world.

Many of you feel like victims. People attack you, governments want
money from you, or somebody hits your car in the parking lot and you
respond as if attacked by the whole world. This demonstrates your lack
of understanding about the meaningless thoughts and ideas that create
the world. You put all your energy into them and believe in them with
your heart, soul, and mind. That power reflects back to you, but you are
unconscious of it. This makes your life troublesome, because you have an
untrained mind filled with debris from other people's teachings.

You must clarity the mind, and we are doing this together. We clarify the mind and teach you the truth about how the thoughts you believe, act on, and imagine in your past and future are nothing but the detritus of dead ideas. We train your mind toward love, the vibrant force that allows life.

Life is never ending. You existed before this body, and you will continue after this body passes away. You are not your body. These thoughts and teachings demonstrate the fact of your immortality. You are a spiritual being temporarily housed in a physical body that appears to age and die. You will break free from these ideas as you practice with us daily.

It is with great joy that we join you for these lessons, and we say it each day so that you understand this is not an inconsequential relationship. You are developing relationships with great beings, including me. It's okay to say I am a great being. I have evolved into levels of consciousness that you also can achieve if you begin this journey with us. There is no point in false modesty.

You are great creators. You are as powerful as I am, but you "miscreate." You use your amazing creative skills inadvertently and mistakenly, which brings you things, experiences, and relationships that do not serve you. These are errors of thought. They are not sins. It does not make you bad. You merely make mistakes, but you can correct every mistake. We help you correct the errors in your mind so that you no longer miscreate but rather create in alignment with God's will for you, which is love, happiness, and joy.

I am that one you know as Jesus, and we thank you for joining us today. We will see you again tomorrow.

LESSON 12

I am upset because I see a meaningless world.

Follow the complete lesson guidelines in your *ACIM* book.

You are blessed beings, indeed. I am that one you know as Jesus. As we make headway through these lessons, we are pleased you are with us on this magnificent journey into peace, for that is what these lessons bring you.

The stories you lay on the world cause you suffering. The judgments you hurl at people, places, things, and experiences upset you. You believe the world upsets you, but the projection of your judgment onto others disconnects you from love. Love brings you peace. This is the great change of heart we ask you to make as you go through these lessons: the understanding that if you observe something with judgment and you begin to suffer, you have a choice whether you suffer or not. It takes a great evolutionary leap in your mind to see this truth.

You will never be the same after you realize that every time you suffer, you have caused it with unloving thoughts about yourself, some thing, or somebody else. In that realization, you understand the choice between freedom and suffering.

The state of mind in the 3D world reflects the training by religion, parents, culture, commercials, television, and banking institutions, to name a few, and programs you to judge and separate. Separation is, in fact, your natural state. How do you know? You appear in a separate body with separate, secret thoughts manifested in a physical demonstration of your belief in separation.

Ultimately, when you remove your belief in separation from your consciousness, you no longer have a seemingly separate individual body. You connect with everything and everyone. That is where your evolutionary journey ultimately leads you, but it is a long way off.

In each moment, you choose not to judge but instead understand that the story you lay on the world is yours and not anyone else's; you have the freedom to change. In that moment, you can shift your consciousness to peace.

You begin to see this more and more as you do these lessons. Increasing periods of peace enter your awareness. When you plummet down into judgment again, it will feel even more painful than before. This is the fork in the road that *A Course in Miracles* speaks about. Once you have made the choice to do these lessons and you experience what peace feels like — perhaps for the first time in your life — you cannot go back. You understand your suffering is optional and up to you.

Allow this lesson to percolate through your consciousness. Do not belabor it. Do it as described, and it will do the work it is meant to do.

I am that one you know as Jesus. We will see you, again, tomorrow.

A meaningless world engenders fear.

Follow the complete lesson guidelines
in your *ACIM* book.

You are blessed beings, indeed. I am
that one you know as Jesus. It is with
great joy that we join you today.

You do not need to fear, dear ones, yet
you remain very afraid. You have set up many
defenses in your mind to protect yourself from this profound fear that is,
perhaps, unrealized in your conscious mind though you feel it all the time.
It manifests as anxiety, a sense that something bad might happen, or you
wake up in the middle of the night with a sense of doom. These hidden
fears dwell beneath the surface of what you consider your personality.

It is important not to rush through the deconstruction of some of these
ideas. Your personality — who you think you are, your self-concept — is
built on some fragile, shifting, and contradictory ideas. They are unloving
and untrue ideas deep in your consciousness. So we must do these lessons
as prescribed so that you do not become destabilized.

The ego will want to rush. It will say, "Let's play all these videos
together in one day, and we will get through this mind transformation program quicker than anyone else." Do not listen to this voice. Some people
have become destabilized by rushing through the lessons.

The lessons are not something to fear. Oh no. They take you on a path
to peace, a greater connection with knowledge, and all kinds of wonderful experiences. But if you do them too quickly, if you rush through them
thinking you know better than the designer of these lessons, then you use
the unhealed mind to shift and change the curriculum.

You do not ask a student in a university classroom to take over the pro-
fessor's teaching, so do not do that here. Bring a healthy sense of humility
to these lessons. Do them as described, gently and kindly, and follow the
directions perfectly.

If you find yourself upset to such a degree that you want to quit the lessons,
then reassess the way you do them. Perhaps you are pushing too hard or doing
them too infrequently to get the results you expect. Perhaps you are rushing

them and feel a sense of anxiety as you shift and change your consciousness too quickly. You will not feel bad if you do these lessons as described. They are designed perfectly to expose the shadows, fears, and misperceptions you have about yourself and the unconscious fears and dreads that lurk deep in your mind.

I am with you all of the way. It is important you do not allow these words to frighten you. We will look at these shadows, fears, and confusions slowly and lovingly together.

I am that one you know as Jesus. We thank you again for joining us today. We will see you tomorrow.

LESSON 14

God did not create a meaningless world.

Follow the complete lesson guidelines in your *ACIM* book.

You are blessed beings, indeed. I am that one you know as Jesus. We are proud of you for making it this far.

You are two weeks into the deconstruction and reconstruction of your consciousness. As you go through these lessons, we are undoing decades — even incarnations — of distorted ideas, fears, and misinformation accepted into your mind and acted on. This is something to remember when you get frustrated, which your ego will definitely do at times. It will say, "This is the most ridiculous lesson. These things are too slow. Let's do an intensive weekend workshop to deconstruct this ego in a weekend."

Those are the kinds of things your ego will suggest to you. It will do this because of your deep challenge to its control over your choices, value system, and what you believe to be reality. We want to warn you about this world called reality. In this teaching, what you see as your physical world with you inhabiting a body is not referred to as reality.

Reality is your oneness with all that is, your true nature. Reality is the "you" without all of the fears, distortions, and beliefs that keep you from your true nature (which is reality). Remain aware of that as you go through these lessons.

You might become confused and say, "Well, if this isn't reality, what is?" We will lead you to reality by directing you toward your loving self and a higher frequency, where you have access to different experiences. You will begin to see the "reality" you believe you live in today is very different from the reality you will experience in the future. You will change to such a degree in a few years that you will look back on today and say, "Ah, I thought I knew what reality was, but I am completely changed now."

Be conscientious, but be patient. Infinite patience brings the desired results. That means if you trust in this quiet and gentle daily process and do it as asked — whether you understand it, like it, or it disturbs you or not — you get the greatest rewards. If you become impatient, leap about, miss days, or procrastinate, you extend the time in which you suffer before you are freed of that distorted mind.

Remember that if you think, "Oh, I'm gonna skip that lesson today." Don't do it. Know that you are investing in the most lucrative, bountiful, and abundant thought system in existence that offers health, happiness, joy, and eventual freedom from this earthly plane.

I am that one you know as Jesus. We will see you again tomorrow.

LESSON 15

My thoughts are images that I have made.

Follow the complete lesson guidelines in your *ACIM* book.

You are blessed beings, indeed. I am that one you know as Jesus. These lessons do challenge your mind, don't they?

You are trained to believe there is an objective world out there that is completely separate from you, that has nothing to do with you, and that will never change no matter what happens inside your mind. This is one of the great secrets kept from you over the most recent millennia.

It was not always so. There were teachings a long time ago really in alignment with this work. It is the intended practice of some of the established religious structures of your society to keep you from understanding how your mind works. If you don't understand how your mind works, you constantly — we will say — shoot yourself in the foot by blaming and projecting and not assuming responsibility for the world you project out from you.

That knowledge allows you to transform your world very quickly, and those ruling powers do not want that. They want you in a powerless, fearful, and easily controlled place. But we will not dwell on this, and we will not call these sins. We will merely say these were errors that many people made, and now we are correcting those errors. We do not want to get into blame. We do not want to maintain the dualistic belief that someone was "bad" and you were "good"; therefore, you are a victim of the world you see.

As you now reclaim your power over the world you experience, you begin to understand that it is up to you what you experience. This is a wonderful, powerful place — a place of joy. We want you to feel that joy in you that you are able to work miracles, you are a miracle-minded person, and you are in alignment with truth deep inside your consciousness.

You have merely forgotten, and you have covered that truth with mistaken ideas, identities, and focus. Today we congratulate you, once again, for coming to this lesson. We want to encourage you to come again tomorrow.

This year is one of transformation on your planet. You will be well served to preemptively transform your mind so that you are not so attached to the way things are. When you see great changes or great turbulence on your planet's surface — weather or politics or money — you do not overly identify with the world and you connect to spirit so that you are at peace.

I am that one you know as Jesus, and we will see you tomorrow.

LESSON 16

I have no neutral thoughts.

Follow the complete lesson guidelines in your *ACIM* book.

You are blessed beings, indeed. I am that one you know as Jesus. This is an important lesson: "I have no neutral thoughts."

Many of you have thousands of thoughts

a day of which you are blissfully unaware. These thoughts create and bring things to you to experience because you think about them. So if you are resentful and you are driving in your car as you replay an argument you had at work (and of course you always win the argument in your imagination, don't you?), you plant seeds of war. That is what you do. You choose with your free will to entertain an image of a battle, and you win. That tells the world you want to have war and you want to win war because you believe in attack as a solution to your problem.

Now, when you're in the car mulling that idea over, you don't really think about the message you send out, do you? You don't think, "I value war and attack, and that's why I envision winning the fight." But that's exactly the frequency you send out. When you get home to your television screens and you see war, you wring your hands and say, "Oh my goodness, what a terrible thing." You dissociate yourself from the fact that you entertained war in your mind on the drive home.

That frequency of war and belief in attack are used as fuel for the warmongers in your society. They are wise about energy and thought. They know that if they train you to believe that attack and winning are good things, you will send out frequencies they can surf (if you will). They can ride those energies to the wars that they want, and there will not be a difference in or a discrepancy between the frequency of war and your frequency.

You won't see the disparity there, and that energy will continue. This is why it is so important for you to understand that peace of mind, which is where we want to lead you, is so important. Your opinions about attacking or judging other people are not neutral thoughts, and they are used to generate negativities.

I am that one you know as Jesus, and we want you to think about this for a little while. Where do you attack? Where do you war? It is okay; you do not need to beat yourself up about it. You are doing the very practice, with these loving lessons, that removes these ideas from your mind. But know that there are no neutral thoughts. We will see you again tomorrow.

I see no neutral things.

Follow the complete lesson guidelines
in your *ACIM* book.

You are blessed beings, indeed. I am
that one you know as Jesus. This is
one of the great causes of your suffering on this planet, this attachment and
overlay of meaning you give to every single
little thing.

We are heading toward the equanimity of the master. For those of you
controlled by your egos — and that is okay, you all are controlled by your
egos in this world until you've done a lot of work — your egos tell you that
if you become calm and balanced you're not actually human anymore. You
do not feel enough. You are indifferent and uncaring. The opposite is true.
The ego, with its volatile emotions and stories about every person and place
it sees and its constant value judgments, does not make you human. It
makes you dangerous, and it causes you suffering.

It is important to bring this into your mind because sometimes you
might fear becoming like a blank slate: "If I don't lay my meaning on you
and your dog and your house and your car and my clothes and my body, I
won't have any feelings about anything." This is not so. In fact, these are
merely opinions.

You all have a different opinion based on some value system inserted
into your consciousness. What happens as you step back from these meaningless judgments that have no basis is that you begin to really feel. You
have access to more feelings, not reactivity or volatility, which are emotions
and feelings out of control and driven mostly by fear.

You begin to have a calm, rich experience of your present moment rather
than living in the past with your guilt, shame, and resentments or your
future of anxiety and confusion about what might happen to you. When
you come into that place where you eliminate these erroneous ideas from
your mind, you live in a beautiful, endless present. You are present, and you
are in that moment that you can only create in this present moment.

When you regurgitate old stories or future terrors, you contaminate the
present moment with what was or a fiction about what will be. You aren't

really thinking at all. You aren't really feeling at all. You live in an illusion. So know that this takes you to peace of mind, calmness, and a clarity of perception and understanding about who and what you are and why you are here. That will be delicious indeed. You do not need to fear it.

I am that one you know as Jesus, and we will see you again tomorrow.

LESSON 18

I am not alone in experiencing the effects of my seeing.

Follow the complete lesson guidelines in your *ACIM* book.

You are blessed beings, indeed. I am that one you know as Jesus. We are pleased you are here with us again today.

We want you to understand the power of collective thought, collective consciousness. You are all joining and doing the same thing, feeling the same confusions at times. That is okay. These lessons are not meant to be understood by your ego mind. Here we have a perfect demonstration of minds being connected, and that is what we seek for you to realize in this lesson.

You have been taught that you are completely separate. The pooh-poohing or ridiculing of psychic phenomena is one of the strategies your society uses to keep you apart from each other and keep you from realizing you are all connected to Divine Mind and each other.

Many of you felt ridicule from others when you have had some kind of psychic phenomenon or feeling of premonition. Really, all you experienced there was a connection of minds. Somebody thought about you, and you picked up on that. Most of you have experienced being with a close friend or partner whom, when you're just about to say something, says it first. You think, "Oh, that's so unusual, we thought about the same thing." But that goes on all the time. Because you keep secrets and are so well defended in your society, none of you really get to experience that until you are in an intimate relationship with somebody in which you reveal these things to each other.

This is an important part of understanding why it's so valuable to train your mind. Your mind connects to all others and affects everything. This idea of idle thoughts is no longer true in this training program. We are saying your thoughts are very important. It is a gift to you and everyone else around you and on the planet to maintain a loving frequency within that consciousness you think of as yourself.

Do this lesson willingly. Do this lesson enthusiastically, and know you do a very great service to humanity by practicing these lessons together with us each day. You are now part of a great group that does this each day. Know that changes are happening not only in you but also in the collective mind.

I am that one you know as Jesus, and we will speak to you again tomorrow.

LESSON 19

I am not alone in experiencing the effects of my thoughts.

Follow the complete lesson guidelines in your *ACIM* book.

You are blessed beings, indeed. I am that one you know as Jesus. You are hanging in there very well. We are pleased about the fact that you are here again today. Each day you allow these lessons to go deeper into your beliefs about reality, yourself, and the place you have in existence.

The idea that your thoughts are secret and don't affect anybody else are clearly believed by most beings in your society. People think all the time. They often negatively ruminate on things and have absolutely no idea that every single thought they have plants a seed of that very thing they fear.

You begin to see how you can create things, like dysfunctional relationships or diseases, by constantly worrying and fretting about things. You don't realize — because you've never been taught the truth — that your thoughts affect everything and everyone. You are the central, pivotal linchpin in the creation of your life in all of its aspects and facets. You must have an affect, because you draw to yourself those experiences, people, places, and things that you see and feel in your life. They come to you from you. This is a very important lesson, one we hope reveals that the mind wandering is, in fact, like laying landmines along your future path.

Think about that. If you complain in your mind and envision a fight with your brother or your sister or your father or your mother, you plant that fight in yours and that person's future. The more you do it, the more likely that event comes into physical manifestation. A momentum has to be built, it's true. But most of you who gnaw at a particular subject (like a dog with a bone) keep going back to it time and time again.

Apply yourself to this lesson today. Know it is extremely important that you understand this principle.

I am that one you know as Jesus, and we will speak to you again tomorrow.

LESSON 20

I am determined to see.

Follow the complete lesson guidelines
in your *ACIM* book.

You are blessed beings, indeed. I am that one you know as Jesus. It is an important lesson, this one.

You are convinced that you can see. You are convinced that you know exactly what's going on in the world. You are convinced you know exactly what's right and what's wrong and what should be and what should not be. You are arrogant in that belief, for you are not qualified to make that determination.

"I am determined to see" means you are humble in your acknowledgment that you may not be able to see right now, and that gives you negative emotional feedback from your guidance system. If you look at something — a situation, person, place, or thing — and you feel strong negative emotion, you do not see it correctly. Because you come from the ego's judgmental and narrow focus, your very limited experience with and understanding of spirituality and spiritual principles causes you to assume you know what it means. You do not. That is what your negative emotional feedback will tell you: That you are looking at it incorrectly.

You have no choice, currently, on how to look at something. You have been trained to believe certain rigid rules about your current experience that you call reality. Those have been placed in your mind by other beings, generally speaking, although you can come into this incarnation with leftovers from other incarnational experiences. So what you use to try and determine whether what you see is good or bad is a hodgepodge of many different ideas.

We seek, through these lessons, to align you with love so that you do not war with the world you see. That is where most of you find yourselves: in a constant state of judgment, fear, and anxiety about survival. You worry what will happen in the future and about your relationships and what they mean.

This idea of "being determined to see" is a wonderful, powerful statement to the universe that you know you don't see things clearly. You can tell because you're not happy and at peace all the time. That is your messaging system telling you so.

You may begin to get the idea that now we will push you a little bit more to pay more attention to what goes on in your mind. You will fail at times. You will get frustrated at times. The ego mind will say, "Let us stop these silly lessons." That is why we do this now. It is very important for you to really grasp this year that the outside world is not where you should look for your safety and your happiness. You must go inside and look there in your connection to Spirit, in your connection to All That Is.

I am that one you know as Jesus, and we will see you again tomorrow.

LESSON 21

I am determined to see things differently.

Follow the complete lesson guidelines in your *ACIM* book.

You are blessed beings, indeed. I am that one you know as Jesus. This is one of the fundamental principles you need to realize you are pursuing in this practice. You are "determined to see things differently." That, by assumption, means that some of the things you see now and interpret are incorrect. You acknowledge that by your willingness to practice.

It is important for you to remember you are going to change some things in your world by doing this practice. This practice is a mind-transformation process. Therefore, the world projected from your mind shifts and changes. This brings up fear in the eager mind because the ego's security and safety believes things should not change — specifically you.

As you know, the ego is an aspect of your mind that uses separation and fear as its foundation. Now, as you go toward love and say, "I need to change the way I see these things that I'm surrounded by," the ego begins to argue with you and responds: "Well, hang on a second. We've set up all these defenses. We've set up all these ways of doing things to keep you safe and away from potential danger. For example, other beings." That is one of the things the ego wants to do. It wants to keep you away from other beings because it perceives they are going to injure you or hurt you, and your control of your environment through defensiveness and attack is what actually keeps you safe. The truth is it is actually what makes you miserable or sick.

It is important for you to know that as you go through these lessons, that voice of argumentativeness presents itself on a regular basis. It may be quite loud at times, but you must go back to the reasons you began this course. You must go back to the reasons you felt you needed to have your mind changed. It is important that you revisit your initial decision to start the lessons of *A Course in Miracles* so that you do not forget or listen to the voice of the ego that says: "Hey. We were doing great without all of this discipline being asked of us. Let's go back to doing what we have always known and what we have always done."

As you know, if you always do what you have always done, you will always get what you have always gotten. If that is not what you want and how you wish to express yourself and live, then you must decide to continue these lessons regardless of the commentary coming from the separated part of your mind that you call the ego-mind.

We are very proud of you for coming this far. We challenge you today to share these videos whether or not you feel that anyone else in your group or your gathering place — your Facebook page, for example — will understand them. It is a great gift to humanity for you to share this series of lessons for those beings who might be suffering and may not know of its existence.

It is a wonderful thing for you to contemplate doing. If you are too frightened to do it because you fear persecution or judgment from others, then you can look at that little secret hiding in your mind, which is that you care more about what others think than the health and well-being of your fellow brothers and sisters. That is a good thing to know if that lurks in your mind. You can work on that as well while we go through these lessons.

I am that one you know as Jesus, and we are very pleased you are here. We will see you again tomorrow.

LESSON 22

What I see is a form of vengeance.

Follow the complete lesson guidelines in your *ACIM* book.

You are blessed beings, indeed. I am that one you know as Jesus. This is a challenging lesson for those of you who were taught that God created the world. This is one of the fundamental issues that comes up in these lessons that you may feel, at times, a great contradiction with.

In your ignorance, you have been taught that God created this world. But when you see the death, destruction, starvation, poverty, and even natural disasters, you say, "Well, how is this God loving if this is the destruction, death, and separation that we all face?" Your loved ones dying, your children passing away before their time — surely this God is insane if he created this.

This is what we want you to understand: This world is not created by that one you call God, all-powerful and loving. If it was, then it would not look this way. Things would not depend on other things to die in order to survive. Everything would not be separated from you — your loved ones, your children. All sorts of things are going on in your lives that demonstrate a lack of love. If everything was created by a loving God, then you would not experience this. That is your clue that this is not the real world. This is not God's world. This is the playground of the ego.

This is where all your idols, lusts, wants, needs, and fears play out in front of you so that you can see them. This is why it is so important for you to comprehend the magnitude of the projection happening. It is not just you laying your feelings on someone else. This is a level of projection many modern beings have begun to understand — that you are responsible for your own feelings. But the whole thing is a projection. The whole thing is a giant projection from the collective consciousness. Yes, some of you share the same dreams and nightmares, but you are the one that is in charge of your projector and your experience. You need to take ownership of that which is called life for this planet Earth here.

You play your role in the way you think you should based on what you have been taught up until this point. We are going to turn you around. We are going to pivot you on your feet and turn you in the other direction — away from fear, separation, and war — toward love. That is why this takes practice. That is why these lessons seem so slow and cumbersome for those of you in a rush.

We want to address this issue here today. Do not be in a rush to deconstruct your personality or your mind. You will not fare well if you do more than one lesson a day. You will destabilize your consciousness. We repeat: You will destabilize your consciousness. So do not watch one video after another, pushing, pushing, pushing because you are tired of your suffering. You will suffer more if you do not do the lessons as prescribed — not as a punishment but because they are so powerful. They redirect you away from darkness and fear and turn you 180 degrees so that you walk in the correct direction on the road toward your home, which is love.

Know that this idea of vengeance is a challenging one. You may not completely understand it, and that is okay. Remember, you do not have to understand the lessons. You merely need to do them so that your mind gets truthful information. Remember, your mind is full of untruths. You are going to, at times, react to these lessons as if they are lies, because when you are told that a lie is the truth, the truth will look like a lie. Be aware of this as you go through these lessons that challenge the very fabric of the way you look at your world. They challenge your concept of reality.

I am that one you know as Jesus. Be gentle with yourselves. Be gentle with your brothers and sisters. Understand this is a great undertaking we are all on here together. Be brave and share these videos. You will add a light to someone's life somewhere. Someone will see this lesson and say: "What is *A Course in Miracles*? It sounds intriguing." Who knows what doors you may open for someone you might not even know.

I am that one you know as Jesus. Spread love and light everywhere you go today, and you will make your experience a better one. We will see you tomorrow.

I can escape from the world I see by giving up attack thoughts.

Follow the complete lesson guidelines
in your *ACIM* book.

You are blessed beings, indeed. I am that one you know as Jesus. It is with great joy that we hear the laughter this being brings to this lesson. We ask you not to criticize her for that little bit of fun. It was just a moment of joy that slipped through the serious demeanor of these lessons. That will come to you, dear ones, from changing your mind about the world and how you contribute to the chaos and unloving nature of this place in which you find yourselves. You have been deeply manipulated, further and further, into attack, and we want to address this here.

Pure nondualism will say that what happens in the world does not affect you; you are the affecter. Some very clever beings in your society understand these principles. They are well educated in spiritual creation. They understand exactly what we teach here, and they have made sure that in your school curriculum, education, and religions that you do not get taught this. They use that information in their mass media programming systems — the programming of violence and attack in your entertainments — because it teaches you how to attack more, be more violent, and be more aggressive so that you continue to miscreate along the lines of fear and war. This gives you very little power, but to those beings who understand these principles, this gives a great deal of power.

We are not here to attack anybody else, but we want to be truthful that watching violence — in sports, on your murder-mystery shows, or the war in blockbuster movies — invites attack thoughts into your mind that will be used in your creative process. You must understand that there are no idle entertainments when violence is involved.

As part of this lesson, you must understand how that indoctrination works. Please step away from watching violence; it is counter to this particular lesson. It is one of the most difficult addictions for you in your society. Your lives have become boring because of the work, urbanization of your societies, and your indoctrinations into doing jobs for money. It is often only in your entertainment that you experience feelings.

This is part of the process that we want you to incorporate into this lesson today. We want you to just observe where you enjoy watching violence. Perhaps it is a good takedown in a football game, the hero killing the enemies in your blockbuster movies, or a seemingly quaint British murder movie. We ask you to just observe where you use that form of entertainment today without judgment, self-loathing, or hatred.

Just observe. The first forgiveness practice in anything you see yourself doing is to just say, "Ah, there I am doing that thing, how interesting." Do not attack yourself. That does not solve the problem. Observe and ask: "Is there another way for me? Is there something else I could do instead of this?"

I am that one you know as Jesus, and we love you very much on this side. We bring forth as much support as we can — not only verbally in this form but energetically as well. Do call on me as you do your practice each day, before you go to sleep at night, and when you wake up in the morning. Just ask me to be with you and guide you through your learning process.

I am that one you know as Jesus, and we will see you again tomorrow.

LESSON 24

I do not perceive my own best interests.

Follow the complete lesson guidelines in your *ACIM* book.

You are blessed beings, indeed. I am that one you know as Jesus. This is how you get yourself into a lot of trouble — this conviction that you know what makes you happy.

We draw your attention again to the many conditioning processes you have been through in your society. For example, your car manufacturers have spent inordinate amounts of money advertising very sexy cars in very sexy locations being driven by very sexy people. If you feel bored, unattractive, or lonely, the multitude of car advertisements you have stockpiled in your memory (they are not in your conscious memory, but they are there) will rise to the surface as a solution for your feelings. Marketing is very well done in your society and one of the great burdens that you, as trained consumers in this society, face.

We speak in *A Course in Miracles* about profound spiritual principles. There are practical demonstrations every day of ordinary things and situations that use and apply these principles. For example, you can look at your diets. You are constantly bombarded by commercials for food-like products (we will not even call them food). Pizza is an example. You see those ads with the big strings of cheese and the happy people drinking Coke and scarfing down pizza.

When you get hungry, those images that have coursed through your consciousness rise to the top. A bowl of organic blueberries will not be what comes to mind, because you make the cake of your day from the ingredients you have in your consciousness. That means as you sit on your couch watching programs programming you, you voluntarily use your free will to allow that commercial into your mind, which makes you complicit in contaminating the ingredients for the cake you make today.

We want you to know that this is where a lot of your inability to determine your own best interests comes from. The interventions you feel coming from spirit these days — the many channelings and messaging programs about transforming your mind and turning toward love — are amplified because we have to call you back from the precipice of the intense mental and emotional manipulation you are subject to in your society.

Know it is going to take some time for us to turn your mind around, eliminate, and get you to reprogram yourself. Once again, we ask for your patience in this process. The marketers, corporations, churches, and schools that have trained you have been exceedingly patient and exceedingly determined, and they have spent a lot of money to get you where they want you.

You must now become exceedingly determined. You don't need to spend a lot of money — no money, in fact. However, you must now become as determined as they are. We do not ask you to judge them. We do not ask you to hate them. We are saying they are clever, and they have used these very principles against you.

Now it is time to turn from their food to our nutritious plan of healing your mind. Let us not look out there anymore. Let us turn those programs off. Let us return to the simple clarification process here. Get out in nature as much as you can. Read some good books. Do some creative projects. Connect with your family and friends in loving ways. Begin the reclamation process of taking back your free will.

I am that one you know as Jesus, and it is a very important thing for you to do this year. The shenanigans, games, and chaos that you witness out in the world will upset you if you seek peace out there. You won't find it out there. It is the result of a lot of negative programming and fearful minds.

Come back to me. Come back to peace. Come back to love a few times each day, even today, and demonstrate your determination to have a peaceful mind. We will speak to you again tomorrow.

LESSON 25

I do not know what anything is for.

Follow the complete lesson guidelines
in your *ACIM* book.

You are blessed beings, indeed. I am that one you know as Jesus. We are once again proud of you for showing up today.

We know that your world is a busy one. We know that your mind works counter to these teachings in many ways. Even if you are familiar with them, it is a challenge to discipline the mind in this way. This is something you notice, now, as you get toward five or six practice periods throughout the day: You forget them. You need to set little alarms at times. You notice you put it off because your lunchtime is too precious for you to take a couple of minutes out to do these exercises. You will say, "I might look foolish. I can't find the time. My day just flew by, and I didn't know I missed these lessons until I got home. Then suddenly the light went on in my mind, and I thought, 'Oh my goodness, I've missed four practice periods today.'"

This is normal. We don't want you to beat yourself up about it. We want you to witness the error and correct it. Do not think: "These are too difficult for me. This lesson is too hard. I'm a bad student of *A Course in Miracles*. See, I can never do anything right." You will hear a litany of voices in your head speaking about what you are going through.

Remember, this is a training program. It is just as when you first start going to the gym. In the beginning, you can only do three sit-ups or four sit-ups in a week, but before you know it, you are able to do twenty-five or thirty sit-ups, and you remember when you could barely touch your toes and do one. That happens as we go through this training period. Do not lament that you are untrained. We know you're untrained. You are in the early stages of your training program.

Witness how you might attack yourself for not doing it perfectly. There may be perfectionists among you being very sorely challenged because you're unable to do the lessons perfectly. Just witness that desire for perfection, and let it go. Forgive yourself, and say, "I'm doing a difficult mind-training program that is profound and will deeply affect my life. It's okay if I miss a day or if I miss a lesson."

Again, do not throw the baby out with the bathwater. Do not throw away the book or the distance that you have traveled because you make a simple error. This is one of the favorite tricks of the ego. It will say: "You've had a piece of cake. You have blown your diet. Let's eat whatever is in the fridge." You know this story. "You've had one drink. You were on the wagon for a month. Let's drink the whole bottle." This is a self-sabotaging aspect of the ego that you are all very familiar with, and it will try to assert itself as you get further along in the lessons.

This is the beginning of your forgiveness practice. You forgive yourself and say, "I forgot that lesson. I will do the next lesson at the appropriate time, and I will not look to the past and contaminate the present with that guilt. I will allow my fallibility and my untrained mind, and I will witness: 'Ah, my mind is not trained yet. That is why I am doing a mind-training program, because I do not know what I'm thinking about most of the time. All those thoughts affect a lot of people, places, things, and experiences; and it is important for me to train my mind.'"

This is how we want you to respond to any errors you make. You correct the errors; you do not punish yourself for errors. That is the ego's way.

I am that one you know as Jesus, and we are pleased you are with us today and every day that you come here with joy in your heart to share these lessons with our dear one [the channel] and with me. It is my life's purpose to help you relieve suffering, bring joy to your heart and mind, help you turn on the road toward love, and to make, step by step, your journey home to your true self, which is at home in God always.

That is your reality. That is where we are headed together. We will see you again tomorrow.

My attack thoughts are attacking my invulnerability.

Follow the complete lesson guidelines
in your *ACIM* book.

I am that one you know as Jesus. We are once again pleased that you are disciplined enough to join us today in this coming together. Many people are doing these lessons each day. We want you to envision this beautiful community that you have become a part of. Many of you feel alone, abandoned, or isolated, but we want you to look at those numbers when you click on this video [referring to the YouTube series] and see that some 1,800 people have done the very same lesson you have. What a wonderful joy that is to see.

We want you to really feel a communion with that community. This is a global community you are a part of. Just as fear is broadcast throughout your mass media systems, here we are all together broadcasting love. We're doing the disciplined work of mind training that gets all of you to step back from your attack thoughts about yourself or about another. Know that these have to be reflected back to you in fear, and that this is an act of free will. You choose to refuse to attack another or yourself. You know there must be a projection of that attack, and you will feel it.

It is important that you understand you only attack yourself. Your mind permeates the entire world in which you live. When you attack it, you attack yourself — not figuratively speaking but literally speaking. The parts of your consciousness you project are you even when they seem to be outside of you. They are the parts of your mind that you put away from you to maintain a semblance of tentative peace. However, we will say it's more of a cease-fire than true peace. True peace means that you know you're invulnerable.

You are an eternal spiritual being. You were before this body was born, and you will be after this body seems to pass away, for the body does not die. It was never alive. We want to clarify that. The body is a corpse animated by your spirit. Your spirit was before, it will be now, and it is in the future always the same. It is of God and, therefore, unchangeable.

The body is animated by you so that you have an experience here of letting go of aspects of your mind that do not serve you. That is its only purpose: to communicate love, allow you to travel through your experiences, learn what is unloving, and let it go. Once that body has served its purpose, allowing you to gather that experience, you no longer need it. This is not something to fear; this is your coming home.

You are changeless. You are eternal, and you are at one with God in truth. You are not separated. This separation is an illusion powered by your belief in it, and that is what we are undoing now. We are undoing your belief in attack, which demonstrates your belief in separation.

This is a powerful exercise for you to contemplate, and we ask you to do your best to practice as often as asked. We know your worlds are busy and that you need to have some reminders. Eventually, you will not need to be reminded. You will find that these lessons permeate your mind. You will train your mind to align with these beautiful principles and ideas. Those tormenting terrors that cause you anxiety, fear, regret, shame, and guilt will disappear from your mind. We promise you that if you follow this — what is, in fact, a scientific program — as stated and do the lessons as written, you will find peace. That is what you all seek when you go shopping, drink, or watch television. You seek respite from your suffering mind.

This way will do it permanently and lovingly. When you come to that point of peace, you know you have the most beautiful gift to give to others. You can tell them how you found peace. That is all this being did. She found peace of mind that she had never experienced before, and she became willing to share that most beautiful gift with all of you.

When you have completed these lessons, you will realize how you cause your own suffering through attacking others and yourself in your mind, verbally, and in action; and you will realize that it is a choice. You do not need to suffer.

I am that one you know as Jesus, and once again, we are glad you joined us today. We will see you again tomorrow.

Above all else, I want to see.

Follow the complete lesson guidelines in your *ACIM* book.

You are blessed beings, indeed. I am that one you know as Jesus. It is important for you to recognize any hesitation you have in asking for this.

There is a great training in your society that to follow me means you have to sacrifice, suffer, and even martyr yourself. Those beliefs of your society will come up as you make more determined statements with your free will. Most of these beliefs and ideas — the Judeo-Christian teachings of the churches that have founded and ruled the society on which these teachings are based — have been hidden from you for quite some time. You don't realize they are even in your mind. It's not until you start to step toward love that you begin to feel the unloving arising.

This is a very important day, for this is a very important message. Many of you see yourselves as innocents. The "bad guy" is always out there. You're the one who is loving and kind. They shouldn't have done that, and you did your best. These stories run rampant through the untrained mind. It's not until you truly walk toward love and turn toward that which teaches you pure, true, spiritual love that you see your ego's desire for death.

Some of the wording in *A Course in Miracles* is very blatant. It is very graphic because these ideas are hidden from you, and we want to get your attention. We want you to realize that as you walk toward love, you feel fear. Why would that happen? If you're the loving being you perceive yourself to be, why would walking toward love bring up fear? It is because in your society, love has been associated with sacrifice and suffering, and the ego does not want to love.

The part of your mind trained in your society by your warmongers and your torturous training programs — that part of your mind that has complied and agreed with those training programs by employing them in your actions, words, thoughts, and deeds — rises up and argues. It's going to say:

"This is not safe. We're heading toward something we have no control of. Control is of the utmost importance. Defenses are important." These are the words of the ego-mind.

When you do these lessons and feel some fear or resistance, know that you are being shown a part of your mind that believes that following my teachings will cause you suffering. There's no surprise there, because the story that was laid over my life and my teaching modality was of suffering, sacrifice, and punishment by a loving father of a dutiful son. There was no way out, given that teaching.

No matter how good you were, are, or will be, God will punish you. That is the underlying message of the teachings around my life, crucifixion, and resurrection. It is important for you to understand this and realize these beliefs and fears of sacrifice are going to surface in your mind. Fear not. We do the work every day that eventually removes those from you.

I am that one you know as Jesus, and suffering, sacrifice, and martyrdom are not required on this path. You can trust me on that. We are glad you came to see us today, and we will see you again tomorrow.

LESSON 28

Above all else, I want to see things differently.

Follow the complete lesson guidelines in your *ACIM* book.

You are blessed beings, indeed. I am that one you know as Jesus. This is a very powerful lesson. You agree to transform the way you look at everything when you practice this lesson with us today.

Again, you may have some fear arising. We want you to refer to the channeled portion of yesterday's lesson to reassure you that you lose nothing except the limiting, fearful, resentful hatred that lurks beneath the surface of your seemingly innocent minds. We are not accusing you of being bad people. We are informing you that you are only aware of a certain part of your consciousness that you have been permitted to explore in your society. For example, when you are punished for getting angry with a parent when you were a little child, which most of you were, you began to lose access to that part of your consciousness. You pushed it down because it was unacceptable. You would lose love if you allowed that part of you to surface. That little raging two-year-old who said, "I don't want to eat my peas," can be punished cruelly in your society. Many of you were. Many of you don't remember it. Some of you do.

When you fracture yourself in that way through trauma — you're traumatized by a great big parent who punishes you, withdraws love, makes you sit in your little chair for a long time until you eat those peas, or perhaps even physically smacks you — you push parts of your consciousness down and away from you. You do not have access to those feelings and emotions.

What happens as you do these lessons is we tap into some of those fears. We tap into some of those repressed and controlled parts of your consciousness because we love you. We love you in an unconditional way. We love you in a pure, spiritual way without requiring anything of you. Sometimes with your free will, your decision-making process — even when you were a small child — you decided that part of you was not okay.

All of you are okay. All of you are acceptable. All of you are loved. This is a process of healing — the reintegration of the mind, the taking back of that unconscious part of yourself. These lessons do not go through your traumas with you. This is not necessary. The practices as described in these lessons are designed to clarify the mind of fear. One of the dysfunctional aspects of your society is to go back into traumas over and over again, bringing that feeling into the present moment over and over again in an effort to heal it.

It is not in doing that you heal your mind. It is in relentlessly turning toward love that you heal your mind. The thought forms, fears, and nightmares dissipate when you no longer feed them because you stop looking there. You look to love. You look to truth. That is what will eventually fill your mind. That is what we do here.

I am that one you know as Jesus, and we will see you again tomorrow.

God is in everything I see.

Follow the complete lesson guidelines
in your *ACIM* book.

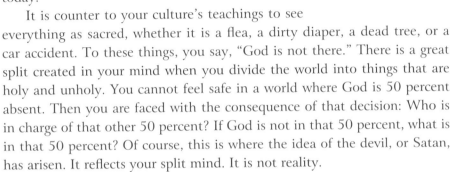

You are blessed beings, indeed. I am that one you know as Jesus. It is the truth: God is in everything that you see today.

It is counter to your culture's teachings to see everything as sacred, whether it is a flea, a dirty diaper, a dead tree, or a car accident. To these things, you say, "God is not there." There is a great split created in your mind when you divide the world into things that are holy and unholy. You cannot feel safe in a world where God is 50 percent absent. Then you are faced with the consequence of that decision: Who is in charge of that other 50 percent? If God is not in that 50 percent, what is in that 50 percent? Of course, this is where the idea of the devil, or Satan, has arisen. It reflects your split mind. It is not reality.

God is in everything you see. You can rest assured in that. You must retrain your mind to believe it, and you won't believe it at first. That's okay. The ego will say, "Surely God is not in that. God can't be in that." You must understand the consequence of dividing the world into good and bad. It means you are not safe. It means there is a force invisible but equal in power to that of God. You have no idea where it lurks, what it is, or why it's there. That induces deep fear in you.

Understand that this lesson is a profoundly peace-inducing lesson. It stops you from walking around in fear, waiting for the devil's hammer to hit you on the head. It is not going to happen, so why behave as if it is? God is in everything you see, including you.

I am that one you know as Jesus, and we will see you again tomorrow.

God is in everything I see because God is in my mind.

Follow the complete lesson guidelines
in your *ACIM* book.

You are blessed beings, indeed. I am
that one you know as Jesus. We are happy
that you are still with us, coming to the end
of this first month of lessons. You did not believe
you would make it this far, yet here you are on day thirty of *A Course in Miracles* lessons. You are already one-twelfth of the way toward the goal you set. So do not fade away now. Do not miss lessons or think they are too hard to understand or too difficult to accomplish. You are already planting seeds of love all around you as you do these exercises.

When God is in everything you see, you step back from judgment. This is the greatest gift that you can give yourself, your body, your family, your community, and the world. When you step back from judgment — saying, "That is wrong, that is evil, and that is profane" — you open to the universe. You open your consciousness to All That Is, and that is the path we walk on together, where we come to a place that there is love for everything.

Instead of projecting your hatred — instead of laying hateful stories on the world and giving it a terrible meaning — now you project into the world the truth that God is in everything you see. That does not mean that God created everything you see, but God is All That Is.

It is important for you to understand this basic principle of forgiveness. Many of you think of forgiveness as letting people off the hook, so to speak. Forgiveness is a way of looking at the world. It is a soft way, a loving way, and a kind way. It keeps your heart open and your defenses down, and that is how you connect to your brothers and sisters without fear.

Your stories about the world, your judgments about the world, and your cursing of the world (or saying it is profane) keep you defensive, shut down, and alone. That is why you suffer.

Go into this lesson today with great enthusiasm, for you shift your consciousness more than you know. You shift the projections that emanate from you more than you know as you begin to see the world not as your enemy but as a simple reflection of that which is in you, in your mind.

It is important these days, as we go deeper into the lessons, to witness at times your inability to remember what you're meant to do. It is important for you to just see this and say: "Ah, I have not known what my mind has been doing for several hours. This is why I am in a mind-training program." It is not a demonstration of failure. It demonstrates the necessity to do this program. So do not hate yourselves or judge yourselves harshly. Merely witness what you are unable to do with your mind.

You're unable to focus. At times, you're unwilling even to give a minute to your spiritual practice. In that observation you realize that if you go six or seven hours without giving a minute to your spiritual practice with presence, you create unconsciously all day long, and you will get a very mixed bag of results reflected back to you.

I am that one you know as Jesus, and we love that you are with us. Share this information; be brave. Let people know what you're up to. Do not feel the need to justify or explain it. Just say: "This is what I'm up to. Join or don't join. It's up to you."

I am that one you know as Jesus, and we will speak to you tomorrow.

LESSON 31

I am not the victim of the world I see.

Follow the complete lesson guidelines in your *ACIM* book.

You are blessed beings, indeed. I am that one you know as Jesus. This is a lesson I taught to my disciples while on the cross. That is what I was teaching them — that I am not a victim of the world as you see it.

In that great lesson, that great teaching/learning opportunity, many of those beings who followed me could not assimilate the lesson. They could not believe that I was not being victimized, that I was not suffering. I was standing firm in my elevated consciousness above the battleground, and I knew — even though it was a great challenge, a great act of discipline on my part — that I did not need to suffer. My mind could assess the situation accurately and choose to move through that experience without the pain, suffering, and despair of the martyr. That is not what I was doing, and that is why it has been so hard for you to understand in your society. It was an extremely sophisticated lesson for the beings who were in front of me.

This lesson was not designed for the world, necessarily. Although, it has become so. In the time and place when I was in the physical incarnation that you know as Jesus, I was teaching my students. I taught them and showed them my abilities to overcome the physical/material world and that, indeed, I was not being victimized. I chose to go through a very dramatic teaching-learning experience for their benefit. However, only a couple of those disciples integrated that information into their minds. But that is okay. One mind changed is enough. One mind healed is enough. One mind in alignment with truth is more powerful than ten thousand minds in fear, cowering in the corner, afraid to stand up and be counted.

Do not allow yourself to be victimized by your beliefs. You are not a victim of the world you see. It is a reflection of your consciousness rushing toward you in order for you to understand what is going on inside of you. If it seems to attack you, look where you attack yourself or others. Examine where you attack principles, ideas, politicians, countries, creeds, or money. Whatever you attack, know that it will reflect back to you in a world that seems to attack you.

We heal your mind from the deepest levels with these teachings, and we want you to know that it brings great love to you. Many of you feel that now, a month into this gathering together. You are going to see that you are not so quick to judge or attack, that perhaps you open a door for someone when before you would have charged through. Perhaps you find yourself sitting quietly contemplating ideas because you have decided to give yourself space to do the lessons, and after the lessons, you enjoy sitting in your armchair with the radio, phone, and television off. You find that being with yourself is much more agreeable because the mind you are experiencing has calmed down a little bit. It is not so fractious.

We love you very much, and we will be here with you every single day. Every day we nudge this being, and she knows this is her assignment this year. So do not despair. If you miss a lesson, do your forgiveness practice and make it up as soon as you can. We will speak to you again tomorrow.

I have invented the world I see.

Follow the complete lesson guidelines in your *ACIM* book.

You are blessed beings, indeed. I am that one you know as Jesus. This is a challenging concept for many of you. It does not matter whether you believe this idea right now. Remember, you are in a training program. You are not coming to these ideas through a sense of understanding but rather from a place of faith. You are stepping day by day with us, holding our hand, into new concepts and new ideas that will seem counter to everything you have been taught.

In your Newtonian physics, you are taught that yours is an objective reality. You're not given an option about this in your school system. You're not given an option about this in your family. You believe the stories you hear and the judgments you experience hook, line, and sinker. So when you say this lesson to yourself and you feel a sense of doubt creeping in, do not think that this means that you are off track. You are merely challenging the paradigm, the worldview, that you hold in your consciousness. We are indeed challenging your worldview. We are challenging your self-concept. We are challenging everything you believe to be true about reality — your reality as you see it today.

Your mind, which is used to telling these stories, is going to question why you're doing what you're doing. Your ego has used these stories to defend itself and arm itself for a very, very long time. It will, in fact, even tell you that you are going to make yourself vulnerable to attack because you are opening up to the unknown.

This is one of the great teachings that you have to unlearn in your experience, thoughts, and consciousness — the idea that if you do not defend yourself, then you are open to attack. On the contrary, when you defend yourself, you are preparing for attack. Think about that for a moment. When you wear your armor with your closed heart, sharp tongue, and quick wit, you are preparing to attack someone back. That means that you will be attacked because you are the creator. You are setting the tone.

Defending yourself means that you will inevitably be attacked. Some of these ideas you are learning are beginning to challenge that idea of defensiveness and the value of attack as a way of getting what you want. So be prepared for the ego's little stories and reactions, and soothe it and placate it by saying, "It's okay! We don't have to believe this. We don't have to understand this. Just relax. Everything is going to be fine!"

You can, in fact, speak to your ego because it is not you. You are now aligning with truth. You are now aligning with love, and the ego will seem to be less like you than it used to be. You used to think that it was you, but now you are becoming wiser.

I am that one you know as Jesus, and we will see you again tomorrow.

LESSON 33

There is another way of looking at the world.

Follow the complete lesson guidelines in your *ACIM* book.

You are blessed beings, indeed. I am that one you know as Jesus. What a great gift you give yourself when you assess the world in this way.

There is another way of looking at the world. This is something many of you never question. This person is "that," he is "this," and she is "that." Questioning yourself opens your narrow, boxed-in, programmed mind to a different future. After all, is that not why you are here? You have come to these lessons because there is a little niggling of dissatisfaction in the way your body, life, world, and relationships work. You know there can be more, but you don't know how to get it.

This lesson, taken to heart, provides a powerful transformative device, because when your ego rises up in judgment or attack, you immediately use your powerful free will to say, "Hang on a second. Maybe there's another way of looking at this." That opens the door for communication, connection, and love, as well as a potentially new creation to come forth into your experience. That is what these lessons are for. They give you a new experience. You begin to see that as you change your mind, you get new experiences.

What new experiences might you expect? Some of you will have more vivid dreams with messages contained within them. Some of you will have overwhelming urges to connect with people that you have not talked to for a long time or that you feel a slight resentment toward. Some of you will have more compassion and offer help to somebody that you would not have helped before. Perhaps you will offer somebody a ride to work when before you would have watched him or her get on the bus. Perhaps you will pay back a long-overdue debt. These examples show some of the healing experiences you might expect.

You might have physical experiences. Our dear channel had some (what she calls) amazing out-of-body experiences in which she had direct conscious contact with guides and teachers in higher realms in the early days of her core studies. This got her attention. She knew the strange blue book caused these unusual feelings and experiences. So if you start to feel different — you start to have new ideas or inspirations — know you have done that yourself by changing the way you look at the world through this training program.

If you have an unusual idea, contemplate it and say, "Ah, this may be a consequence of the *A Course In Miracles* studies. I should not just dismiss it because it's something I've never thought of or done before. It is, perhaps, guidance. Let me give it a try."

We are happy you have the braveness to transform into the most powerful creative device in the universe — the human mind aligned with love. You are heading toward that dear ones, so hang in there and keep coming back to see us every day. We are with you all the time, but we enjoy these group gatherings.

I am that one you know as Jesus. We will see you again tomorrow.

I could see peace instead of this.

Follow the complete lesson guidelines in your *ACIM* book.

You are blessed beings, indeed. I am that one you know as Jesus. This is, of course, the lesson that you begin to see the choices you make. The unconscious desire for attack and war is something most of you remain completely oblivious to when you perceive yourself. You lay the face of innocence on your consciousness and see yourself as a loving and gentle being — unless provoked. We want to address that caveat, "unless provoked."

It is true that you are a loving being. You were made of love, from love, and for love. You have forgotten this truth, and you have had many teachings to strengthen that memory lapse. This has caused a place of separation. You must remember that. The default setting here causes separation. How do you know? Look at your separate body. Your separate body demonstrates your belief in separation. It is the most powerful tool the ego uses to prove you are alone and abandoned. It is the ego's vehicle, as most of you use it. The body, in and of itself, is neutral. You can use it for good or bad. You can love it or hate it. You can see it as a communication device, weapon, or bait.

We want you to understand that your seeing things differently comes as a choice; it's your free will how you use your body. That comes up in another lesson. For now, we remind you that how you look at the world and the interior experience generated from that perception is your choice, indeed. When you feel that little frisson of anger, judgment, or hatred, you say to yourself, "I can see this differently. I am able to see this differently. There's another way of looking at this thing. I don't have to cause this wound in myself." That is what you do, dear ones, when you do not see peace in front of you. You attack yourself. You mistakenly think you are attacking another, but that feeling of distress, loss of peace, anxiety, fear, or anger inflicts a wound on your dear self.

Do this lesson willingly and happily. Know you are cultivating a higher frequency closer to love with this lesson. And what happens in a frequency of love and peace? Healing takes place. Your body thrives at the frequency of love and peace. Your aging and illness processes come from a lack of peace and resistance to what is. It is not an act of weakness to accept what is, but it is an act of love and strength to say, "I will not inflict pain and suffering on myself by judging this situation."

I am that one you know as Jesus. We thank you, once again, for taking time out of your busy day to heal your mind. That is what we are about here. We are healing your mind so that you can create a peaceful world. We will see you again tomorrow.

LESSON 35

My mind is part of God's. I am very holy.

Follow the complete lesson guidelines in your *ACIM* book.

You are blessed beings, indeed. I am that one you know as Jesus. I always tell you that you are blessed beings because you do not perceive yourself that way.

An important point of view for you to carry through your day is to forgive yourself for the misperceptions and poor teaching you have had that have caused arrogance, irritability, lust, anger, or self-righteous. You have many opinions of yourself that cause you great suffering, because they shut down a part of your mind. They shut down a part of your emotions, which shuts down access to parts of the world and the experience you might potentially have.

If you see yourself as angry, then you will have to reflect that back to yourself in the world; so you will encounter anger. If you see yourself as imposed on, you will have people imposing on you, and you will feel you are a victim of the world. Remember lesson 11: I am not a victim of the world. These perceptions create experiences for you. So it is important for you to remember that your vision of yourself as holy means you have beautiful experiences — holy experiences. We want you to soak in the knowledge that you are, in fact, a divine aspect of God mind. You have merely forgotten it, and your world reflects your lack of belief in your divinity.

49

Your divinity will take you Home. The shift in your knowledge of your connection to All That Is, that you are not abandoned or separate, takes you Home to the truth that you are at one with All That Is — God, the great universal consciousness.

This is not your natural home. You are away from your natural home, which makes you feel abandoned and alone. But you have chosen this journey into fear and separation, and it continues every time you have an unloving thought about yourself that does not see you as holy. So we want you to take this lesson seriously. It serves as a beacon for your journey home to love.

I am that one you know as Jesus. We will see you again tomorrow.

LESSON 36

My holiness envelops everything I see.

Follow the complete lesson guidelines in your *ACIM* book.

You are blessed beings, indeed. I am that one you know as Jesus. It is important for you to understand the consequences of the statement you make today that holiness envelops everything you see.

When you look at the world, extend your holiness, and then envelop things with your holiness, you use your love in an appropriate way. The extension of your holiness makes a wonderful gift to yourself and the world. Instead of seeing your brothers and sisters as your enemies and potential attackers, you preemptively send love to them and envelop them in nonjudgmental, healing energy.

You extend yourself all the time. You extend arrows of attack and judgment, or you extend your holiness and loving, creative, vital life force. You can do whatever you choose. You can be a powerhouse of hatred and judgment or one of holiness and love. You know which one feels better. How do you know? Because we have talked about your guidance system, this inevitable feedback system that tells you how far away or close you are to love. There is only one road, and you are all on the same road. You are either walking toward love or walking away from love. When you walk toward love, you experience feelings like contentment, enthusiasm, happiness, curiosity, and intrigue. It is just a general upbeat kind of vibe. You are not necessarily hysterically happy, but you feel at peace. You know you're on the right track. You can feel it.

When you make an incorrect decision based on your current perception, you feel a limiting energy. You shut down. You feel a vibration of hatred, fear, shame, or guilt. That means your guidance system is saying to you, "Oh no, dear one, you have made an incorrect decision." Many of you do not understand your feelings. You perceive your feelings as curses because they are volatile, erratic, cause trouble, or make you yell at people. Your feelings, once you begin to clarify your mind and step back from incessant judgment, make the perfect guidance system to let you know where you are and what you just did. It is not meant as a punishment.

You do not experience a feeling of negativity to be punished, but to get your attention. So you ask, "What just happened there? I've stopped feeling contentment and happiness; I've gone down into fear. What did I just do to myself?" This feedback system is not about the world but your relationship to the world.

You should look at any negative feelings you have. Instead of laying them on a person, place, thing, or experience, you should own that feeling and say, "What did I just do?" In every single case, every single time you have the awareness to do that, you will see, "Ah, I just worried about money. That is a fear-based thought. I just turned around on the road from love and walked toward fear. Let me not indulge in those thoughts."

This is what we call sloppy thinking in which you allow negative or unloving thoughts into your mind. You must remember you are in a training program. That means you will encounter many thoughts, beliefs, ideas, and feelings you would consider negative. Do not think that you are a bad student when you encounter these. You are merely experiencing the content of your consciousness. Be grateful for those dips in mood, those upsets, because they indicate something in your subconscious. If you were conscious of it, then these things wouldn't happen.

Be kind to yourself. When you feel a dip in mood, don't say, "Oh, I'm a bad student of *A Course in Miracles* because I had a feeling of jealousy." Instead, go deeper and say, "Ah, that is me turning away from love. How can I see this differently? How can I not go down that rabbit hole of jealousy and into personally created suffering?"

Perhaps you voluntarily go down that rabbit hole. You follow the thought and add another thought. The addition of more thoughts of fear and jealousy create a little vortex of fear that takes you away from love. It does not happen to you. It happens because you ignore your mind and allow it to run free like a wild horse. You are not used to reining it in and saying, "No, we're not doing that. That thought will take me into suffering."

Many of you on this path feel artificial when you try to be consistently happy, and it is unnatural in your current state of consciousness . You become increasingly at peace as you practice these lessons. As these lessons increase in frequency throughout the day, they require you to pay more attention to what you think about. Consequently, as you pay more attention to your thoughts, your feelings calm down. You become less volatile, less emotionally reactive, and much less likely to attack.

I am that one you know as Jesus. We are excited that you are beginning to feel the difference in your consciousness even though we have only done these lessons for a few weeks. Imagine how you will feel in a few months. Hang in there. We will see you tomorrow.

LESSON 37

My holiness blesses the world.

Follow the complete lesson guidelines in your *ACIM* book.

You are blessed beings, indeed. I am that one you know as Jesus. My holiness blessed the world.

This is what you experienced with my last incarnation on this plane. Those who met me — once I awoke and had become an enlightened being — were blessed in my presence. I did not impart a blessing of arrogance, as the ego would do, but a frequency that the enlightened master teacher holds and emanates because he or she does not have any blocks preventing the extension of his or her powerful connection to Source. It is not an individuated energy. It comes from the divine mind through the unobstructed consciousness of the master, the enlightened teacher. It extends to everyone and everything. It is most powerful in its creative abilities and will cause spontaneous miracles to happen.

The clarification of the mind becomes so important when you understand whatever comes through you gets magnified by what is in you. Those of you with low frequencies and ego-driven consciousnesses do not have access to tremendous powers, because they become magnified by the ego. You see this often where you have teachers of spiritual material that have not had their egos clarified through a process such as you are going through. They wield sexual power over people. They transmit tremendous energy from Source, but they filter it through their ego's blocks.

This is something we encourage you to understand. As you go through this clarification process, do not become impatient with a desire for kundalini awakenings, psychic powers, or the ability to manifest more money. Clarify your mind first so that the power that is your rightful inheritance does not become distorted through those blocks.

This is an important warning that is not meant to terrify you but to encourage your patience and diligence with these exercises so that you do not wield your amazing connection to Source power with the ego in control. It is not a pretty sight. Many distortions become laid on people around you if you seek power too quickly.

An important gift to give yourself is to clean out the basement and attic of your mind so that the increasing energies your planet experiences at this time have a pristine vehicle through which to function. As you see around you, the stresses on your mind increase as your planet goes through this ascension process. We speak specifically about 2019, when this recording was made. These lessons clarify your mind. When energies peak, you will have a clean vessel in which to house them.

Be patient, dear ones. Love yourself enough to do these exercises. Do not berate yourself if you miss one here and there, but correct yourself as quickly as you can and make a determined promise to do better in the next exercise. Do not feel you have failed if you have missed something or did not perform it perfectly. This is a training program. Just as when you practice a physical training program, you might pull a muscle, miss a day when you're too sick to exercise, or become too busy to do your exercise program. That happens. But you must remember that even in the busiest of days, there are moments when you're sitting on the bus, waiting in line at the grocery store, or waiting on hold on the phone during which you can do your exercise. It does not take much time at all, and no one will know you are doing it except you. You will know because you begin to feel better.

Do this wonderful favor for yourself and know that we are with you, supporting you all the way along your journey. You will have situations come up in your life when you need to apply these lessons. Do not see them as theoretical things separate from your current life experience, but employ them whenever you get upset. Utilize them whenever you feel fear of the future or resentment of the past. Use them to master your mind so that it does not master you.

I am that one you know as Jesus. We will see you again tomorrow.

LESSON 38

There is nothing my holiness cannot do.

Follow the complete lesson guidelines in your *ACIM* book.

You are blessed beings, indeed. I am that one you know as Jesus. As usual, we thank you for joining us today.

You give yourself the most wonderful gift when you discipline your mind. You no longer exist as a victim of its stories, hatefulness, and fear as you master these lessons. We know they have become more difficult for you to fit into your day. Your decision to continue to make progress becomes very important right now. You must decide, "Is my peace of mind worth finding these five-minute periods in which to do this exercise? Do I value everything else that is going on in my day more than finding the time to do these exercises?"

If you say to yourself, "I am too busy with the problems and busyness of my current life to do these exercises," you tacitly say, "My life will stay the same because I am not willing to do anything differently." It's an important thing for you to see. If you get to the end of your day and you have forgotten all the lessons — you didn't make the time — you must admit to yourself that your spiritual practice is not that important to you, because you didn't think about it all day long.

Many people, in regard to their spiritual practice, say, "Oh, no, I'm a very spiritual person. I've read all these books, and I believe in these things." But when it comes down to the discipline of doing these lessons, the mind becomes occupied with worldly matters, not spiritual matters. It's very important that you notice this if it happens in you. Don't berate or

54

condemn yourself, but witness, "Ah, I went through eight hours today and not once did I think about my spiritual life. I must reassess my definition of myself as a spiritual practitioner, because for those eight hours, I wasn't. I was not paying attention. I was caught up in the momentum of my already-existing material life."

This is a hard lesson for many people, because they view themselves as highly evolved spiritual students yet have no idea what's going on in their minds. For those of you now beginning to see that, perhaps you're not quite as spiritually focused as you thought, and that is okay, dear ones. That is what this training program is for, as we have said many times.

Now is the time to call on your holiness, your connection to spirit, and your connection to love to carry you through these more disciplined time frames we speak about in this particular lesson. You can take five minutes to buy yourself a coffee, put gas in your car, and go on Facebook to scroll through the posts there. So allow yourself the luxury of taking five minutes to connect with truth.

My name is Jesus. I am that one you know as Jesus. I lived on your Earth plane a long time ago in your timeline. I remember the temptations of Earth — not in the sense of evil or lustfulness but how much time every-thing took: the labor, busyness, dramas, and other people wanting you to do things. So I know that these lessons challenge you. We on this side know the benefits of these lessons, and we encourage you to follow this guidance. We will speak to you again tomorrow.

LESSON 39

My holiness is my salvation.

Follow the complete lesson guidelines in your *ACIM* book.

You are blessed beings, indeed. I am that one you know as Jesus. This lesson presents very arrogant-sounding ideas to the ego-mind — salvation and saving the world, being saved from the guilt, shame, and fear that feels so much a natural part of your consciousness.

These occur in everyone's mind, because it is a place of separation, a place where you have come because you are mistaken. This is not a place of love or connection. It is a place where you get to experience the aberrant, divisive, and distorted ideas in your unhealed consciousness.

Remember, you have free will, and you can continue to choose unloving thoughts as often as you wish — until you are sick of yourself, you have had enough, or you are worn, weary, and tired. Some of you might fall to your knees in surrender. In that surrender, you say, "I cannot do it this way anymore. I must do something differently." For many of you, that is when these lessons will come to you — when you reach your wit's end. They will come in the final days of your divorce, during a prolonged sickness, when you get tired of poverty, or your family is driving you crazy. You will fall to your knees and say, "I cannot do this anymore. Please, God, show me another way," and then these lessons will come to you. They will come to you because you have surrendered and are finally teachable.

You see, the ego has control when it says, "Well, we'll do 'this,' and 'this' will fix everything. We'll lose 'this' much weight, and we'll get happy then. We'll study for 'this' job — marry 'that' person, get 'that' car, or build 'that' house — and everything will be okay." As long as these thoughts go through your mind and as long as you believe in the world as your salvation, then you will suffer. You will continue on the ego's way until you become thoroughly exhausted.

It happens eventually, in one lifetime or another. It happens when you finally wear yourself out. But you do not need to do that anymore. These lessons have come to you to offer you respite from the ego's driving, relentless requirements.

It is okay to relax. It is okay to be you. It is okay to fall back into the arms of love. That is what we teach you to do here. We correct your mind and vision. We point you in the right direction. Many of you have momentum going in the wrong direction. You're on your knees in surrender, and you're tired. You have had experiences in the earthly realm that brought you to this place. It is not instantaneous, this letting go of the world and seeing yourself as holy.

We want you to give up chasing idols and worshiping false gods. You can associate these familiar phrases with chasing money, for instance. To believe in "getting that body" is a false god because you believe it will make you happy. It will not, indeed, make you happy. What will make you happy is peace of mind. What will make you happy is knowing you are innocent, forgiven, and, indeed, holy.

It is not easy for you to hear this but it is true. You become separated from these truths by the teachings in your society, your idols, and the many false distortions in your mind. But we are walking toward love and light, and you feel relief as you do these lessons. They are getting longer and more challenging, but we know that you can rise to the occasion and apply yourself to doing these lessons each day.

We are here, our dear one [the channel] is here, and we thank you for being here. We will see you again tomorrow.

LESSON 40

I am blessed as a son of God.

Follow the complete lesson guidelines in your *ACIM* book.

©Renée Phillips

You are blessed beings, indeed. I am that one you know as Jesus. You are indeed blessed as the son of God. But we want to address the language.

The use of masculine pronouns has come up in our dear one's [channel's] mind as a frequent accusation of this material. The word "father" and "son" are used, and there is no mention of daughters or females. We want you to understand this is not an attack on the feminine. I am, indeed, a feminist. My partner, Mary, was my equal. I could not have lived the life I did on the Earth plane so many years ago if not for her.

We want you to understand the great forgiveness practice inherent in this teaching. You are not ignored because you are female. You are not less than because you are female. But you must become aware of the anger and resentment that you hold. If you hold it, you will have resistance to masculine pronouns.

There is a different journey for the feminine than for the masculine on Earth. The dichotomy and the separation manifested in the physical demonstration of separation gives each of you a different experience. For the feminine — the women, daughters, wives, and mothers in this world — it is important you understand you are not under threat by the use of words. It shows how easily you feel victimized, put down, and made less than. If you have that reaction to these statements, "the son of God" or "you are blessed as the son of God," you misunderstand what this wording means. This wording shows you where you have resentment.

This sounds like a controversial commentary today, because your society now encourages an attack on the masculine in defense of the feminine. But this is a dualistic battleground. We want you to rise above the battleground. If these words offend you, if you say, "I want to have 'daughter' there instead," you may use that word if it makes you feel more comfortable. We also want you to witness what made you uncomfortable. What dissatisfies you with the use of the word "son" or "father"? Does it make you feel less than?

A word cannot do that. That feeling of "less than" comes from you somehow, and we want you to look at this today. Determine whether the feeling of dissatisfaction has arisen through this particular language structure. A word cannot make you feel bad unless you already have that bad feeling unconsciously present.

We challenge the feminists in the group, and our dear one, indeed, is a feminist, so do not feel that she is not. I am a feminist. We want you to look at whatever the words "son" or "father" trigger and upset in you. We want you to know the words are gifts that reveal something within your mind that believes in victimization and value systems not based on truth.

You can use that resentment and negative feeling triggered by these masculine pronouns as a way to heal your mind and say, "I am not threatened by a word. I am connected to the divine. I am a holy son and daughter of God." You can use those words in whatever format you wish.

I am that one you know as Jesus. We hope these masculine pronouns do not lose the feminists among you. We are feminists as well. We believe in the absolute equality of all children of God and the use of words to heal the mind. If the word "God" or "Jesus" upsets you, then you know something evil has been done in that word's name, and it is not true. Words like "God, Jesus, son, father, or mother" should not upset any of you. That upset is what needs to be looked at.

We thank you for joining us today. We will see you again tomorrow.

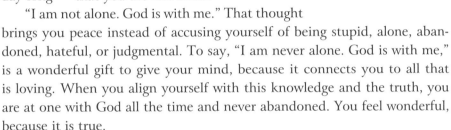

God goes with me wherever I go.

Follow the complete lesson guidelines in your *ACIM* book.

You are blessed beings, indeed. I am that one you know as Jesus. This is the most basic truth you can tell yourself all day long — that you are not alone.

"I am not alone. God is with me." That thought brings you peace instead of accusing yourself of being stupid, alone, abandoned, hateful, or judgmental. To say, "I am never alone. God is with me," is a wonderful gift to give your mind, because it connects you to all that is loving. When you align yourself with this knowledge and the truth, you are at one with God all the time and never abandoned. You feel wonderful, because it is true.

Remember, your guidance system responds to truth with positive emotional feedback. It responds to untruth with negative emotional feedback. So if you say, "I'm always alone. I have been abandoned, and nobody loves me," you get a strong negative emotional feedback from guidance saying, "Oh, dear one, you are so wrong. Don't do that to yourself," and you feel bad. You have never been taught the proper interpretation of your emotional guidance system. You feel good when you are on point, when you accurately think in alignment with truth. The thought that God goes with you wherever you go is one of the most truthful statements with which you can align your mind.

God is with you wherever you go because you are a holy son of God, you are a holy child of God, and you are a holy daughter of God. (If that is the wording that you would like us to speak, then we will do that for you.) I am that one you know as Jesus, and nothing is more rewarding than to be at peace, because you know you are connected to Source energy — All That Is — and that is the truth.

Suicide and depression separate you from truth. You are never separated from God. You can, with your powerful creative minds, believe you are, and so you will suffer. It does not mean it's true. You will never be abandoned, even in death. Even if you attempt suicide, you will not be abandoned. You will be picked up in the arms of angels, taken home, nurtured, and looked after until you are ready to come down once again to learn the lessons you were unable to learn.

I am that one you know as Jesus. There is all-pervasive forgiveness for any errors you make. We want you to understand that, truly, in every fiber of your being — no matter what you have done, no matter what you have said, and no matter what mistakes you have made because of the distortions that you carry in your mind — you always have forgiveness and God is always with you. We will speak to you again tomorrow.

LESSON 42

God is my strength.
Vision is his gift.

Follow the complete lesson guidelines in your *ACIM* book.

You are blessing beings, indeed. I am that one you know as Jesus. This lesson holds one of the great truths hidden from you.

Your tiny body — your little physical body, which society has taught you that you must count on — is not your strength. It carries the vital life force that is a God-given gift, but it is not your strength. This is one of the reasons why you are all so afraid. In this society, body obsession gets constantly reinforced and strengthened. You become more fearful the more you focus on the body. That is why society does this. It wants you to obsess over your body as the source of your strength, because then you are guaranteed fear.

This lesson lays the foundation for your ability to become fearless and defenseless. That will arise in you over time. This is not something to strive for or insist on. As you release your obsession with the body and become more focused on your connection to the Divine, you tap into your true source of strength and power, which is the Divine. It is your source. It is the very thing that keeps you alive.

The body does not keep you alive, nor does it die. You are the vital life force of that which you call God, experiencing things through the body. But the body is not who you are. Do this lesson today with joy. Say it as many times to yourself as you are able without becoming stressed or obsessed. But whenever you think of it, say it.

We come to you today with great love. We are here to support you on this journey. We are here to encourage you even if you forget the lessons, stumble, or have a couple of days where you get so distracted with your life that you feel as if you have failed. We are here to tell you it is normal to do these kinds of things. It is normal to make mistakes, but you want to get right back on track and pick up where you left off. Do not worry about always having the current day's lesson as your lesson. If you get behind, just keep going on with the lessons.

This is a wonderful resource for all of you. If you feel you need to do a lesson over again, do not feel panic that you must move ahead to the next lesson. Listen to your inner guidance. You have the ability to discern whether or not you have done a lesson well. If you have attempted the lesson but feel it was not perfect, that's okay; go on to the next day. If you ignored it and failed to give it its due, then repeat the lesson. But do not stay too long on one lesson. You might feel defeated, the ego will begin to attack you, and you will most likely stop doing the lessons. So there is a fine balance between doing a daily lesson and acknowledging when you have not accomplished the goals that you've set for yourself in the day.

Always look to your practice with forgiving eyes. Know that you can start again tomorrow with more discipline and focus, and know that this is normal at this stage of the game. As you go through the years with *A Course in Miracles*, practicing these lessons (yes, you will continue to use the 365 lessons) whenever you feel fear, judgment, or loneliness, the course reconnects you to the new habits, commitment, and connection you have to spirit. So know that in these early days, you may stumble, you may fall, and you may even fall off the wagon a little bit, but climb back on. Forgive yourself, and say, "Ah, see. I need a training program. I don't know what I'm thinking about most of the time."

I am that one you know as Jesus. We are happy you joined us today. We will see you tomorrow.

God is my source.
I cannot see
apart from him.

Follow the complete lesson guidelines
in your *ACIM* book.

You are blessed beings, indeed. I am
that one you know as Jesus. It is important for you to see that God is your source.
It is the miraculous, benevolent, life-giving energy
and power of your vital life force. You are not a random occurrence in the
universe. You are designed and specifically created by that which you call
God.

Now you have come down into separation, and you have forgotten who
and what you are and why you are here. That is why you are doing these
lessons, to remind you of your sanctity and the unique place you hold in the
mind of God. You are not more special than anyone else, but as a unique
manifestation of the mind of God, it is important for you to remember that
you have particular qualities that will become more evident as you remove
untrue ideas and confusions from your mind. Many of you struggle with
this.

You wonder about your purpose. You wish you could have a better job
or some inspired career to fulfill your life. These things become more appar-
ent as you clean up the detritus and garbage from your mind.

That is something logical to think about. If you have too many untrue
ideas — contamination in the mind — you won't clearly receive the guidance you need to make decisions. This is why so many of you have confused lives, unhealthy bodies, or distorted and dysfunctional relationships.
You have too many things in your mind that confuse you, because they
are not true, yet you act as if they are true. You think you are a body, and
you think you will die when your body dies. This is not true. You are not
a body, you enliven the body. You are the creator of the body in the sense
that it cannot exist without you.

You do not need it, however; and this will become a more comfortable
belief and idea for you as you go through these lessons and practice them
as you have been guided. You are a beautiful idea in the mind of God. You

have always been, and you will always be. The body comes and goes. It is not who you are. Do not think it is.

In my earthly incarnation, I went to the cross to prove I was not the body that people thought I was. I reached the point in my evolution where I knew this, and I had no contaminating ideas in my mind that caused me suffering, disconnected me from my Father, or caused me to fear. I went through that experience to demonstrate my ability to overcome the physical/material world, and that is what we are working toward. Everything I did you too can do as you evolve, clarify, and walk closer to love.

I am that one you know as Jesus. We do not expect you to believe this wholeheartedly, but we tell you to remind yourself that you are, indeed, the same as me. I am merely your older brother, who has walked further and for much longer on the road toward love. I call you to come with me. I call you to walk with me on that road, for that road has no suffering.

I am that one you know as Jesus. We will see you again tomorrow.

LESSON 44

God is the light in which I see.

Follow the complete lesson guidelines in your *ACIM* book.

©RENEE Phillips

You are blessed beings, indeed. I am that one you know as Jesus. This begins your deeper connection to the faith you develop when you become one with the Divine.

You are asked not to manipulate or change your thoughts but to go beneath your thoughts to that ever-present deep awareness. You always have this deep awareness of consciousness with you. You get distracted by the little bells and whistles and shiny things of your world, the thoughts that gallop across your mind. You chase them and look after them. We want you to go beneath that. We want you to go deep inside your consciousness where the truth of your being lies. It exists whether you are young or old, whether you are happy or sad, and whether you are healthy or sick.

The consciousness lies like an ocean beneath the waves on the surface that is profoundly present and always calm, very much as the oceans on Earth. There are waves and storms — these would be the thoughts and ideas of the ego mind — and seemingly dangerous and treacherous currents up there that might drag you under. Beneath that, deep beneath that, lies a quiet and profoundly stable space that is the true nature of your consciousness. It is not the turbulent, fractious, frightening, and frightened aspects of you with which you identify. It is that endless, peaceful, deep connection you have with All That Is.

We do not want you to be afraid of this experience. We want you to understand it is the you always present from lifetime to lifetime, whether you have a body or not. It is not associated with the physical body. It is consciousness, pure and untrammeled by the ego mind. So be kind to yourself today. If you cannot master what this lesson asks of you, it is okay. Try again later in the day. Try again before you go to bed. Forgive yourself if your mind seems to run away on you, but do your best to go beneath the thoughts. Do your best to connect with that stillness within.

As you do this exercise and begin to master these abilities, you begin to have experiences of expansion, being immersed in endless space, or connected to something other than the world. This is a wonderful experience, indeed.

This first lesson in seeking that experience may or may not bring it to you. Do not panic if it doesn't. It doesn't mean that you won't have it. But do your best to employ the lesson today as it is described. Read it carefully, make notes if you need to, and practice.

I am that one you know as Jesus. We will speak to you tomorrow.

God is the mind with which I think.

Follow the complete lesson guidelines in your *ACIM* book.

You are blessed beings, indeed. I am that one you know as Jesus. We thank you for joining us today. We are impressed with the work you are doing with the benefit of this supportive commentary.

A Course in Miracles is a very challenging mind-training program. We want to remind you of the mind-training program that you have gone through in your society. Think of all the years of school — you got up when you didn't want to, perhaps wore clothes you didn't want to, sat in hard chairs even when you were tired, studied things you had no interest in, and participated in activities that did not appeal to you.

This was the foundational mind-training program of your society for more than a decade — every single day, barely giving you time off, with homework, projects, and extracurricular activities. You must remember it for what it is. You were trained to override the ideas, inspirations, and guidance you have access to innately as a son or a daughter of God.

You then go to university or work, whichever comes your way. Once again, if you want to get your paycheck or make your grades, you do things you do not want to do. You write papers that challenge the mind about subjects you do not feel aligned with, yet it's a mandatory subject you must complete to get your degree. Or you work in a place that pays you poorly, treats you badly, and asks you to override that guidance that says to run outside into the sunshine — another mind-training program.

After your exhausting day, you go home to your television and watch it, because you have no energy left. You have been in resistance all day — a joyless, difficult, challenging, and scary day. Perhaps you have had no support. Perhaps you are alone in a dorm or an apartment. You come home exhausted and lonely, and you turn on your television. There again, the programming continues — night after night, day after day, year after year. You have experienced a profound mind-training program.

When you reflect on the lessons in *A Course in Miracles*, we want you to compare apples with apples. We want you to compare this mind-training program with the mind-training program we have just described. We are asking very little of you compared to that mind-training program. Yet this one is a powerful transformative tool that brings you to a place of peace.

We want you not to argue with this plan; rather, compare it to the plan you've gone through. We want you to compare the two because we are undoing that mind-training program together — a powerful, long, determined mind-training program your society set for you. We want you to compare these few minutes and these little challenges we set for you to what you have already gone through — the most magnificent mind-training program there is, Western society.

Relax a little bit, come to these lessons joyfully, and know you are breaking free from this. Return to that connection with the holy mind of God that you have been asked to abandon in favor of television, work, money, food, cigarettes, alcohol, and sex — all the things you had programmed into you as replacements for this most wonderful connection.

I am that one you know as Jesus. You will not regret these lessons. Make sure you do not tell yourself they are far too hard for you to handle and that you cannot master this. Remember, you have been through the mind-training program of Western society, and you have mastered it. If you can do that, you can do this. We will see you again tomorrow.

© RENÉE PHILLIPS

LESSON 46

God is the love in which I forgive.

Follow the complete lesson guidelines in your *ACIM* book.

You are blessed beings, indeed. I am that one you know as Jesus. Forgiveness as the path to your salvation lays the foundation of the teachings in *A Course in Miracles*. Many of you in this world practice a way of forgiveness not in alignment with this course's particular truth based on the nondualistic thought that there exists only love.

Love flows or is blocked, whether you know it or not. You are all one. Nondualism means you are not divided. The practice of forgiveness in the dualistic world differs from the practice of forgiveness we teach here, and it is important to bring it to mind early in your learning. In the dualistic world, you see people who have committed sins; maybe they robbed you, betrayed you, or cheated you. Over time, you get so sick of hating them that you decide to forgive them of their sins. They still did those terrible things, and you think they're bad people, but eventually the suffering of judgment can wear you down, and you might forgive.

Many people don't ever forgive anything. They take their resentments to the grave and will have to deal with them in another incarnation. That is indeed so. Your reincarnational journey is one of many opportunities to do this work. We encourage you to do this work now. Why? Because now is the time. It is the end of the spiritual season. There is an escalating energy permeating all that is. It seeks you to remove from your mind all illusions, and that is what forgiveness does. It removes from your mind the illusion that others are separate from you: You are good, and they are bad. You are innocent, and they are guilty. These are all illusions.

In true forgiveness, as it is described in *A Course in Miracles*, you realize you are all one. You are actors in a dream playing your parts, the "good guys" and the "bad guys." In truth, you are all connected. When you pass over, you will see that you assigned these tasks to the "bad guys" in your play. So why attack them? Why judge them? Why call them bad when in fact you brought them into manifestation through your desire for separation? Just the same, you have a desire for reunification of mind, as well as body and spirit, with all that is. It is your destiny to reunify yourself so that you do not need to suffer anymore in this place of guilt, shame, death, and unforgiveness.

Those are a lot of words for today's lesson, but we want you to understand that forgiveness does not mean an act did not happen in human terms. You must look after yourself in human terms. If somebody is a rapist, you don't want to hang out with that person; but it is important you forgive any trespasses perpetrated against you.

Once again, you must treat yourself as a human and keep yourself safe, and that also means you must forgive yourself. You must forgive the foolish decisions you've made in the past and the unloving things you've said and done, because you didn't know any better. You must, in fact, forgive yourself to have a clean slate now, today, and choose love.

There is no consequence for not choosing love, for it is not real in God's eyes. It is not real in love's eyes. Love is all there is in love's eyes. Those shadows, spaces, and dark patches that demonstrate the unloving behaviors you have participated in are nothing to God, because love is all that exists in nondualistic teachings.

I am that one you know as Jesus. I love all of you regardless of what you have done, what you have said, how you dress, how much you weigh, how much money you have, or where you live. It does not matter. You are all beloved. You must remember that. We will see you again tomorrow.

God is the strength in which I trust.

Follow the complete lesson guidelines in your *ACIM* book.

You are blessed beings, indeed. I am that one you know as Jesus. We thank you for joining us today.

We truly thank you for joining us today. You do not understand how much joy it brings us on the other side of the veil to see the transformation that comes to the minds doing this work. You begin to have little snippets of peace. You can see where you create negative fantasies and how they cause you to become cynical, depressed, or sad. You see the part you play with the untrained mind, the mind aligned with the ego. You understand what your mind is up to, and you get excited at the possibility of a different future than the one you have anticipated.

That demonstrates the importance of this lesson. When you trust in God, you do not try to micromanage the future. This induces anxiety in the ego mind, where most of you function at this stage of your training. The ego mind is all about the physical body. It maintains the safety of the physical body and indulges its senses to get what it wants. The ego, inextricably entwined with the physical body, desires the separation that has manufactured your body.

The body itself is indifferent. It does not align with any particular thought structure. It aligns with what you decide. Take the global warming issue, which is now front and center in many people's minds. If you try to figure out that problem, you create great anxiety, because the ego mind cannot glean enough information to feel at peace. In fact, the ego is never at peace; it's always at war. So if you hand over your future to God and you say, "I am not qualified to make decisions here or predict what the global warming issue will bring about," you stay in the present. If you stay in this moment, the ego can deal with you using your senses to interpret the present moment. You don't predict a fearful future, and you don't regurgitate the past. In the present moment, the ego remains manageable and feels okay.

To stay out of the future, you must understand you have no qualifications to predict, arrange, or organize it. Your trust in the strength of God and the wisdom of spirit to guide you in each moment to the correct place, people, and experience is one of the important foundational elements in your practice. That, with your guidance system — your feeling, emotional body — will let you know when things are right. You will know when things are not right as you encounter them. You will not try to plan a concrete future using the ego mind, for that is what you use when you plan.

Many of you do not like the idea of not planning, and that is okay. You are taught to plan and schedule your world. Your current reality depends on you showing up at certain times to do certain things. But remember, this is a training program. Things slowly shift as you shift your consciousness. You do not have to understand or believe in what you study right now. Just have the willingness to entertain these concepts and the idea of another way to guide your path through this incarnation. These lessons introduce those ideas to your mind (and your mind probably does not like them, but that is okay). You only have to participate in them for the several minutes each day. You can carry on with your normal life in the other twenty-three hours or so.

I am that one you know as Jesus. You are in safe hands. You are guided and loved, and you will be shown what you need to do. We will speak to you again tomorrow.

LESSON 48

There is nothing to fear.

Follow the complete lesson guidelines in your *ACIM* book.

You are blessed beings, indeed. I am that one you know as Jesus. This is a hard lesson to believe when you are riddled with fears.

Part of your training in this program includes the realization that if you trust this course and still feel fear, then a great divide remains between you and where truth lies. This is one of those fundamental concepts important to think about once in a while. It is very logical. If I tell you there is nothing to fear and you are fearful, then you are not in accord with these teachings. Of course, we do not judge you for that. We know that you are here to unlearn everything you have learned. Every single thing you've learned in this world will be unlearned, and you will learn the truth.

When you see your fears, you want to counter them with truth. Fear that causes you to shake and shiver in your shoes means you believe in it. To undo that belief, you must introduce truth. If you believe lies as truth, which you do if you harbor certain fears, then you voluntarily go out of alignment with truth. When I tell you there is nothing to fear but you still fear, though you say you believe me and you believe these teachings, then you must say, "Well, I believe something that's not true. I believe a lie. Therefore, the truth — that there is nothing to fear — seems to be a lie."

This is, indeed, an upside-down world you live in. What is valued by spirit is not valued here. It is important for you to understand that you have truly, through your own volition, chosen separation. You have chosen not-love, and you have taken a deep, convoluted, and profound detour into fear. We know you cannot eliminate all your fears in one day. We do not expect you to do that, and we do not want you to even think it a possibility. But when you respond to your mind's belief in fear with another statement that counteracts it and you do it increasingly over the days and years of your studies in *A Course in Miracles*, you stop feeding the fear. As you stop feeding that thought form with your energy, focus, and belief, it slowly and surely fades from your experience.

I am that one you know as Jesus, and there is nothing to fear. You are eternal spiritual beings. You are beloved by that which you call God — that absolute and all-pervasive benevolent force that permeates everything and keeps everything whirling and living.

God is life. God is love. Anything you experience that is not life affirming and love affirming is not true. It is an illusion. It will make you feel bad because your emotional guidance system is tuned to love, and anything not loving gives you negative emotional feedback. So do not despair if you have negative feelings throughout the day. Be glad that you now know how to interpret them. You now know it means you have incorrect thoughts that bring you out of alignment with love. You will see where you have indulged in a fearful or judgmental thought about yourself or somebody else.

I am that one you know as Jesus. We will see you again tomorrow.

God's voice speaks to me all through the day.

Follow the complete lesson guidelines in your *ACIM* book.

You are blessed beings, indeed. I am that one you know as Jesus. It is important for you to understand the ego's voice talks to you all through the day as well as God's.

When you choose not to listen to the ego's voice and go beneath its raucous cries of attack, shame, and fear, you can reach another level of consciousness. It is always there, dear ones. It is always there. You are so busy reacting to the voice in your head that says, "Buy this. Eat that. Drink that. She's bad. He's bad. You're bad," that you never get to hear the guidance we often speak about when we channel through this being.

This being quieted her mind through the practice of forgiveness. Through the practice of forgiveness, she quieted her mind enough from the raucous voice of the ego so that we could be heard. This takes time. In your world, things seem to take time, and that is what time is given to you for. Time is not given to you to become wealthy, nor is time given to you to become old or sick. Time is given to you to learn how to hear the voice of God, to hear the guidance from deep inside of you beneath the ego's crazy and vicious voice.

To weaken the ego, you must stop listening and reacting to it. You must stop believing those thoughts and impetuses to do certain things. You must quiet your mind and align it with less-combative thoughts, ideas, and beliefs. You must go beneath the surface of the storm. Just like in your oceans, you see that deep, calm quiet beneath the waves that constantly ebb and flow. Deep down, beneath the tides that move back and forth, there is calm. The same is true for your minds.

Remember, the world you live in reflects consciousness. You can use the ocean as an analogy as well as skies. What always remains above the clouds and storms? The Sun always shines a constant and loving emanation of energy that gives life. That symbolizes what, in your world, you call God.

It is a physical symbol to remind you of the truth that God's voice — that love, that life-giving essence — is always available to you. Even though it may be hidden beneath storm clouds, know it is always there.

I am that one you know as Jesus. We will speak to you again tomorrow.

LESSON 50

I am sustained by the love of God.

Follow the complete lesson guidelines in your *ACIM* book.

You are blessed beings, indeed. I am that one you know as Jesus. This is the ultimate truth: You are sustained by the love of God.

You are not sustained by money. You are not sustained by food. You are not sustained by any of these material things that you have been taught sustain you. As long as you believe they sustain you, they do. This is one of the great paradoxes of being in physical experience, as you are in this 3D plane you call life. What you believe becomes true for you. Indoctrinated on your plane to believe in these systems, you truly — with every part of your being — believe you are sustained by your paycheck and physical/material things.

Once you change your mind, you have a different experience, and that is what we are doing here. We are changing your mind when we have you say and repeat things that you don't believe — things you *really* don't believe, until they shift your mind a little bit and you begin to have a different experience. Those of you now fifty lessons into this training program see differences in your lives. Perhaps you have become less reactive or find feelings of love surface in your mind that you didn't have before. Perhaps you have the feeling to reach out to people you have not talked with for some time. Perhaps you have the urge to change your diet a little bit. That unhealthy food you've always eaten is now less attractive. You're still eating it, but there's something going on.

These are the effects of the lessons. They change your experience. They present themselves to you in the form of experience, of shifting consciousness, and you develop your faith. You do not understand the lessons, how they work, or how they transform your mind. Then lo and behold, there is physical evidence of them doing something.

We want this developing faith to fuel you to do the next fifty lessons. We want you to use the faith you have developed from the little changes you've seen — the little ups in your frequency that you experience — to charge you to move through the next fifty lessons. Look, you have gone through fifty lessons already. You can go through the next fifty lessons just as quickly. As you do, you continue to receive experiential shifts and changes.

In addition, the escalating energies of your planet cause shifts and changes apart from these lessons. You encounter ideas, beliefs, and thoughts that do not fit anymore with these escalating frequencies. They are hateful thoughts, unloving ideas, and separation concepts. You will become more aware of them over the next few months, and this is wonderful news for you.

These things will disturb you when you encounter them, but they do not deserve to reside in the mind of God's most holy son or daughter. They do not love. They are fear-based, hate-driven, and attack-oriented, and they always attract like frequencies to you in the form of experience. So we want to remind you when an unloving part of your mind comes into your awareness, do not hate or resent it and think it makes you a bad student of *A Course in Miracles*. Be joyful and say, "Ah, I see this part of me now. I do not want this to reside in my mind or to send out that frequency and attract like things to me. I'm going to, now that I see this part of my mind, bring it up into the light for healing. I will ask to have it removed. Although, I must do my part to not strengthen this unloving part of my mind by behaving as if it's true." That is how you reinforce beliefs and ideas. You strengthen them when you act as if they're true.

When you see that unloving part of yourself, we want you to not identify it as you. We want you to identify it as something placed in your mind that you no longer want. It is not part of you. It is not you. It is an unloving belief taught to you, trained in you, and surreptitiously implanted in you.

We want you to understand that you are love. You are made by love, from love, and for love. Anything in you that does not love is not you.

I am that one you know as Jesus, and we are looking forward to the next fifty lessons with you. We will see you again tomorrow.

Review I: Part 1

Follow the complete lesson guidelines in your *ACIM* book.

You are blessed beings, indeed. I am that one you know as Jesus. It is important to review some of the concepts and ideas introduced to your mind so far.

As you look back over these lessons, we want you to remember them. We want you to remember we do this work together to relieve your mind of suffering caused by your misdirected, misinterpreted, and distorted thoughts. We work together to retrain the mind to align with love. That is what we are doing.

We also retrain the mind to become more peaceful so that you can hear the inner guidance. We work together to demonstrate that we understand you do not know what's in your best interest. When you suffer, you are given direction by your emotional guidance system that tells you when you go off track. We do these lessons because you know there must be a better way than the way you live now.

We want you to understand the importance of reviewing these lessons. It demonstrates that you have learned some interesting things, and you need to review, practice, and use them in your day whenever you encounter a situation that these lessons become applicable as a way to relieve your suffering. These thoughts, ideas, lessons, beliefs, and concepts become natural at some point. You might already use them when you get distressed, angry, or frightened.

I am that one you know as Jesus, and this is the most powerful mind-training program available to you as Westerners at this time. It was designed for the Western mind to be used during these times by those of you motivated to bring into existence a more loving experience for you, your friends, your family, and the planet. We want you to remember this when you slip or become disillusioned with this work, because it happens. You get tired of the practice periods. The ego nags at you. People upset you. You feel this practice makes extra work, but it is not extra work. It lessens the effort over time.

Over time, you will find that you do not battle with yourself and others as much. You do not regret or fear as much. All those things use up your precious energy. As you come more into alignment, you have access to more energy, creativity, and guidance. Do not despair when you struggle or have difficulties with these lessons. We encourage you to continue. Even if you feel you've done it imperfectly or that could have done more but you didn't. Make tomorrow the day that you decide, "I'm going to do it exactly as described in *A Course in Miracles*. I'm going to dedicate myself to these lessons, because I have seen what my mind creates. I have seen what my mind gets up to when not trained by a loving teacher, and I don't want to spend the rest of my life experiencing that." That really is what we get rid of here. We eliminate your suffering, fears, and, eventually, your sickness and death.

I am that one you know as Jesus, and we will see you tomorrow.

LESSON 52

Review I: Part 2

Follow the complete lesson guidelines in your *ACIM* book.

You are blessed beings, indeed. I am that one you know as Jesus. We experience such delight from the joy this being [the channel] gets from this teaching. She has reaped the rewards of her studies and finds joy in the simplest things, things she would not have enjoyed before.

I am that one you know as Jesus, and life is good. Living is good. Fantasies are problematic. Most of you live in a fantasy world in which you think about the past and future all the time. You judge and assess and attack and fantasize, and you are not present in the moment, which is the only moment you have to experience yourself.

This mind-training program is powerful; each lesson reveals what you do. They do not reveal what the world or your enemies do to you. They reveal what you do to yourself when you think about people not with you, judge situations you have no qualifications to judge, or assess other people's behavior as good or bad and decide self-righteously what you would do in that circumstance. You have no idea the internal promptings or guidance that person you self-righteously judge has. You live in a fantasy world.

This fantasy world creates emotions and feelings. When you watch a movie in your head, tell a story, or judge others' actions, you generate feelings of upset, suffering, sadness, guilt, and self-righteous anger. All those feelings you go through each day because of what you think about, judge, and do in your mind — dreaming, watching movies in your mind — take a toll on you. They use a lot of energy. They, in fact, make you sick.

Once you come to a place of peace and realize what you do to yourself when you leave what you consider reality and live in the present moment, you have a completely different experience. You experience what *A Course in Miracles* calls the happy dream. Yes, you still dream, but you are not in separation from God. You are at home in God, always. The biggest part of you remains connected to All That Is. Your outward body and small personality do not represent all of who you are — though you think they do. They make up a very small part of what you actually are. The happy dream is the next step in your evolution. You go from the fantasies and illusions in your mind — the judgment, hatred, and desire for separation and attack — to resting in love and peace. You connect with knowledge, wisdom, and profound guidance.

I am that one you know as Jesus. We love you very much on this side of what you call the veil, and we offer these teachings with open arms. We ask for nothing in return, just that you try something to have a new experience. We will see you again tomorrow.

LESSON 53

Review I: Part 3

Follow the complete lesson guidelines in your *ACIM* book.

You are blessed beings, indeed. I am that one you know as Jesus. Of course these reviews can cause some perplexing energy in the mind, because they have less structure. They ask you to review them at your own pace with your own emphasis and frequency.

You have a little leeway in which to practice, and the previous lessons have illustrated the kinds of practice periods that benefit you. We would like you to use that as your model when you do these review lessons. You can pick a time at the beginning of the day when you first wake up, in the middle of the day, early evening, and perhaps before you go to bed. You can choose to repeat some of these lessons throughout the day. If you panic about when and how to do these lessons, we want you to think logically.

There has been a little flutter of upset around our dear one [channel] over not having the exact lesson on the exact day. We would like those of you who have experienced this confusion and upset to take a look at how little the ego requires before it gets in a flutter. Clearly, if she is doing lesson 47 on day 46 or 48, it does not matter. Did you do lesson 46? Then the next lesson is number 47. Do not worry about the date. Do not worry about what anybody else does.

A Course in Miracles is a self-study practice. That means there may come a day when you might have hurt yourself, ended up in the hospital, and then come home, so three or four days passed before you completed a lesson. Do you panic? Do you worry what the other people around the world have done? No. If your last lesson was number 46, then go to lesson number 47. You will not be able to stay on the corresponding day throughout the year. We guarantee that. Life interferes with things. Your mood interferes with things. The ego interferes with things.

Those of you who belabor where our dear one is on the calendar, please stop. It doesn't help anyone. That is our little lesson for you today. Do not belabor the date or the day. Just know that doing your lesson for today is all that counts. Pay attention to your own practice. Do not pay attention to anyone else's practice. Please do not nitpick at any small errors that might occur over the year. Let them go, and focus on your own practice.

I am that one you know as Jesus, and it is important that you practice forgiveness with these small bumps in the road. A mind dedicated to finding fault can ruin the day. We will speak to you again tomorrow.

LESSON 54

Review I: Part 4

Follow the complete lesson guidelines in your *ACIM* book.

You are blessed beings, indeed. I am that one you know as Jesus. We are happy that you are this far along in the course. We keep reminding you that we are happy so that you know of the great appreciation on this side for those of you willing to step up your spiritual practice and join with us in the transformation of your mind and the world.

One of the greatest blocks to working miracles in your 3D reality that you call life is the idea that everything is linear with a simple cause-and-effect relationship. Miracles are events that step out of time and that logical, simple cause-and-effect belief system.

You are a holographic being. You constantly radiate in 360 degrees — all directions, all time, infinitely. Your frequency expresses itself and reflects back to you in the form of your life and world. This is a very important basic principle, because when you attack somebody, judge somebody, or fear something, then you perpetuate separation. You are saying that, "This world, this person, and this situation have nothing to do with me. I have no control over this, and it frightens me." When you begin to truly understand that the world merely reflects everything you believe, hate, fear, judge, love, lust after, and desire — everything, everything, everything — then you see the world with forgiving eyes, because you've become curious. You have, in fact, become openhearted and open-minded.

The victim of the world is close-minded. That means you have decided something that is true for you. Those of you learning something new here, opening up to new principles and ideas and then practicing them (even if you don't believe in them yet), are open-minded. That shows your willingness to entertain the idea that, perhaps, there is something you have not yet learned; if you learn something new, you might get a different experience. That is exactly what is going on here. You are open-minded. If you do these lessons, you are open to a different future than the one your ego predicts. The ego bases all its decisions on the past or an imagined future.

If you remain present and aligned and you base your actions, thoughts, words, and deeds on these teachings, then you stay in the present moment, where you can allow life, spirit, and God's ideas to guide you. That saves you — wait for it — decades. Do not feel that you are wasting time when you are doing these lessons or that you could be more productive doing something else. You, literally, save decades of pain and suffering by doing these lessons.

Thank you for joining us today in your review. I am that one you know as Jesus, and we will see you again tomorrow.

LESSON 55

Review I: Part 5

Follow the complete lesson guidelines in your *ACIM* book.

You are blessed beings, indeed. I am that one you know as Jesus. It is a wonderful gift you give yourself today to review these lessons.

Some have different wording than in the original text. Your mind notices, but we want you to understand that we speak about principles and ideas. The reason for changing the words is so that you do not become too dogmatic. You might notice some religious institutions on your plane use individual words inflexibly, depending on who translated the original text into English or French or whatever language you read it in.

We want you to understand these lessons are not about hard-and-fast facts and rules. That is the world of the ego, the quantifiable and the measurable. You are used to that system. We use slightly different words so that you see the meanings behind their symbols and do not get too hung up (as one tends to do in this society) on specific words. Words are symbols of symbols. When you translate the language of ancient texts into another language, and continue with many iterations through history, you have symbols of symbols of symbols. This is what you are faced with in many of your religious dogmas.

This is one of the reasons we channel through this being: for you to hear it firsthand and to have elaborate explanations given to you over time on every given day so that you do not become obsessed with the details. This does not mean that accuracy is not important, but we do not want you to become compulsive or dogmatic. We want you to have a relaxed diligence in your practice. That means you let go of control, fear, and judgment, but you practice. You can be both diligent and relaxed.

The ego wants control, and it wants to be precise. It wants to measure things immediately. It's based in time, and it uses the body. It's important for you to understand the principles we want to cultivate: We want you to be relaxed, be happy, be open, and feel good. These are some of the clues you get from your new experience. Your new experience of those nice feelings is your feedback system saying, "Well done, you're on track." If you become too obsessive about the lessons or too fearful when you miss one, then you might feel a negative emotion. That is your guidance system saying, "Ah, no, don't do it that way. Let us continue on the path of diligent relaxation."

Your guidance system is constant and accurate. You always know whether you feel good, happy, relaxed, contented, curious, creative, and imaginative. Sleepy is a little different, but it's okay. If you feel that overwhelming urge to take a nap, do not resist it. Do not think that you are being lazy. The thought, "I am being lazy." is the thing that gives you a bad feeling about napping or resting. It is not the feeling of resting itself.

These are some of the discernments you master as you go through these lessons. You begin to feel into how to do these lessons and how to be in the world. You go from high-strung, high-stressed, controlling, argumentative, and accusatory to relaxed, open, less focused on time, healthier, and more pleasant to be around.

I am that one you know as Jesus, and we will see you again tomorrow.

Review I: Part 6

Follow the complete lesson guidelines in your *ACIM* book.

You are blessed beings, indeed. I am that one you know as Jesus. This is a perfect demonstration of love.

This being [the channel] did not like dogs. She did not have the kind of patience she has now with such creatures. They caused her great agitation before she studied *A Course in Miracles*. In fact, she could not be around dogs because of the state of her consciousness.

This is something wonderful for all of us to witness. This is the kind of transformation your mind goes through. Think about something you despise or hate. Maybe it's a person you battle with all the time in your mind. Perhaps you think this person is bad, badly behaved, or should be doing something other than what he or she is doing. These thoughts, beliefs, and ideas leave your most sacred mind, but they hang around like storm clouds to upset you.

Most of you have received glimpses of the peace of mind that can come into your mind, little drifts of it here and there. Some of you notice longer periods of peace. What will happen is an increased acceptance of what is, and it will not seem a threat to you anymore. Your anger, frustration, and impatience are fear — fear of something overwhelming, controlling, or harming you. They demonstrate the fear of something that makes you look bad or causes you to doubt your vision of yourself. When you come to understand this, then you begin to see what peace can really bring you.

Peace brings you into a place of profound connection with All That Is. That doesn't mean those creatures, dogs, children, relatives, husbands, and wives stop doing what they're doing; but you are not threatened or upset by it anymore. You can even observe children doing dangerous things, such as driving fast late at night or not coming home when they should, and remain in peace knowing everyone has guidance. Everyone rests, ultimately, in the arms of God. It is not your job to control everything on this planet.

You can, however, have a more profound influence. This is also something you can witness in this being [the channel]. In her life before *A Course in Miracles*, there was no influence in terms of the crowd or the system. She thrashed around in her own life, very unhappy, having a hard time of it. Now that she has found a way to dedicate herself through mental and emotional discipline, she chooses what she wants to focus on. This sounds harsh, but as you can see, discipline does not come from hitting yourself over the head with painful things. Discipline can come from focusing on love, health, life, and joy. Even this word "discipline" must be reassessed for those of you who lay it on yourselves as a heavy hand.

Go out into your day and be grateful. Go out into your day and be happy. Go out into your day and relish the sunshine or the rain or the snow. Relish that you can breathe, walk, choose, and decide — even those of you who find yourselves in financial or marital difficulties. Once you have disciplined your mind, you can choose what to focus on. You can choose where you want to put your energy, and it will grow. Wherever you put your energy will grow because that is the creative force that has been given to you; it is God-given.

When you hear that phrase, "You are made in the image of God," it means you are endlessly creative, just like that which you call God. But you must choose where to create. You must choose where to focus your energy. You can miscreate, and many of you are miscreating all over the place. You do things you don't want to do, like judging or attacking. These are miscreations and will take you down painful roads littered with suffering.

We encourage you to go out into your day and look for the good. Look for the happy. Look for the joyous. Look for the abundance of air, light, and brothers and sisters with whom you can practice your forgiveness. There is so much abundance. Look at your body — the abundance of energy it has, the multiplicity of organs and cells all working together to give you an opportunity to evolve. That is what your body needs to be used for. It needs to be seen as the vehicle you use to evolve through. Do not attack it. Do not judge it. It is only ever doing what you ask it to do.

I am that one you know as Jesus. Look around at all the furry creatures in your life and ask yourself, "Am I grateful for this being, or am I irritated by it?" Love it. Pet it. Take it for a walk. Give it a cuddle, and know that everything in your life is for your greater good.

I am that one you know as Jesus, and we will see you tomorrow.

LESSON 57

Review I: Part 7

Follow the complete lesson guidelines in your *ACIM* book.

You are blessed beings, indeed. I am that one you know as Jesus. These words make you feel wonderful. These words give you hope; they do not destroy you. They do not cause fear to pump through your mind and heart. They calm you. They bring you to a place of peace — evidence that the transformation of your physical body comes about by training your mind.

This is not something taught in your society. You are taught that to train the body is a physical thing. It is not. It is your mind that gets you to take a walk, eat donuts, or do some sit-ups. It is your mind, always the mind. So as you go through these review lessons, it is important for you to really contemplate this as part of those lessons — anything and everything you encounter in your world today is influenced by your mind. Therefore, if you do not like what you see — if you do not want more of what you see (because judging does not help but strengthen it) — then change your mind.

If you look at war, fighting, or fractious relationships and do not want to experience these anymore, go inside your mind and ask yourself, "Where am I warring? Where am I fractious? Where am I in a battle?" You will see it straight away. It is not necessary to go digging deep into the past or go rustling around in your subconscious. As soon as you ask, "Where am I fighting? Where am I warring? Where am I aggressive?" you will see it. You will see it in how you judge your brother. You will see it in how you think about a politician. You will see it in how you hate your body. You will see it, dear ones. You will see it. It is not hard to find.

You must remember the world is the result of many thoughts of fear and ruminations on unhappiness and suffering. It is not there that you change it. It is there that you witness it. It is there that you accept it and say, "Thank you for showing me what is hidden from my consciousness. I see it out there. I see the war. I see the financial fear." This is a big one for many of you — financial fear. You think it is caused by a system outside of you, but it is within you. When you address that fear by doing these lessons, by depending on something other than money, and by connecting to All That Is (or Father God or whatever you want to call it), and you are guided by that, then you are fearless. You are not on the battleground anymore. You are above the battleground and observing, "Ah. Look at all those people fighting. Ah. Look at my mind wanting to attack."

You have a new choice. That, dear ones, is freedom, when you truly see you don't have to do what you've always done. You don't have to think what you've always thought. You don't have to believe everything you've been taught to believe. Many of the things you've been taught to believe are incorrect. They cause you to fear, worry, and inflict things on you that are not good for you.

I am that one you know as Jesus, and we thank you for joining us today in this review. We will see you again tomorrow.

LESSON 58

Review I: Part 8

Follow the complete lesson guidelines in your *ACIM* book.

You are blessed beings, indeed. I am that one you know as Jesus. These reviews can annoy some of you sometimes, because they are a less structured than the other lessons. It is important for you to witness that annoyance and understand that it comes from doing something differently.

We want to address the idea of routines because of the contradiction and paradox in routines. You are, of course, setting up a new routine when you prepare your mind to view the day in a particular way. You could also consider this discipline. We want you to understand the reparation happening here, a reintegration and healing in the sense that the way you have handled your mind on a daily basis is incorrect and has caused damage. This discipline, this routine, gets you back into a place where you can actually be free. It's very much like when you have become lazy and gained weight. You must go through a period of deprivation of freedom, a period of discipline, to get back into balance. In that process of reparation and healing, you intentionally undo things you have miscreated. That is what you do here.

Once you have retrained your mind to align itself with love, you view your mind as holy and see forces at play that are not Newtonian in the sense of simple cause and effect but can influence events, people, places, and things in a seemingly miraculous way. Once you have trained your mind to experience that, relaxation and going with the flow becomes a much bigger part of your practice. For now, however, it is not. For now, we ask you to keep to the routines. If we change them, it's for a good reason. We do not go into deep explanations of why we do everything we do, but it is for your greater good.

Relating to routines in your daily life, apart from your practice of *A Course in Miracles*, we want you to challenge them. If you always eat the same thing for breakfast, change it up a little bit and find two or three things you like to eat for breakfast. If you always get up at a certain time and you're rushed, get up a half hour earlier. If you always go to the same place for breakfast or coffee in the morning, change it up. Go to a different

83

coffee shop. Use your left hand to brush your teeth if you are right handed. Change your hairstyle a little bit if you are stuck in a rut for many years.

Do these things not to confuse yourself but to challenge the belief systems that are unconsciously operating in your day. If you never challenge a belief system, it operates invisibly.

When you change things a little bit, you hear in your mind the reason you do it that way. You hear the limiting voice say: "Oh, don't go that way. We will get in trouble. We will get less quality goods. We will be late."

You want to hear that voice and know, "Ah. There is a belief behind my actions. By changing my routine, I am revealing to myself that I am driven by beliefs."

Perhaps you will hear a voice that says, "Don't go there. Remember that lady we saw in that store? We don't like her. Don't go to that store."

Then you'll think, "My goodness me, I am avoiding a place because I had a negative encounter there with a person one day many years ago. I think it's time that I address that issue in my mind."

I am that one you know as Jesus. Enjoy challenging your routines. Give yourself some excitement. We will see you again tomorrow.

LESSON 59

Review I: Part 9

Follow the complete lesson guidelines in your *ACIM* book.

You are blessed beings, indeed. I am that one you know as Jesus. Here we are at lesson 59, reviewing many of the ideas and concepts that might be new to some of you. We want you to understand is that as you go through this shift and change in your consciousness, you will feel things that you have not experienced before.

You might feel a resistance to your life as you have designed it. You must remember that your life reflects all the choices you have made with your free will. As you shift your consciousness using your free will, you shift what becomes tolerable for you. This is one of the most challenging aspects of doing *A Course in Miracles*. What was once tolerable becomes intolerable. This happens not because they make you suffer more but because you have raised your frequency, your consciousness. So things you aligned with before no longer fit you. This can cause anxiety.

It is important to trust in this process. Remember, you trusted in the process of your indoctrination into Western society. Many of you are parents. What do you trust in terms of your society? You trust going to the hospital when you get sick. You trust vaccinating your children. You trust preparing them for school by teaching them to read. You trust teaching them good table manners. You trust, you trust, and you trust. You use your free will to implement the rules of your society from the beginning of a child's life. That was done to you too. These are things very important to remember.

As you go through this consciousness reassignment process, you have things removed from your mind through your focus on truth. Things fall away — things like indoctrinations, lies, and illusions you have held dear. Now you see they don't work for you. They give you something, but they do not provide you with the life you know you want — one of freedom, creativity, companionship, communion, love, and abundance. Beautiful, beautiful life.

As you shift your consciousness and these things you once believed fall away, you feel a bit of anxiety because you see things you do that you don't want to do. You might have always known you didn't want to do them, but you tolerated it because of the frequency that you held. Now as you step toward love, these unloving aspects of your life become glaring.

We want you to take this transition slowly. First of all, acknowledge that some of the feelings you have are anxiety. You feel confusion, perhaps. "How am I going to pull this off? How am I going to change some things that I don't even really want to change? If I change from what I have, that means I'm going to lose something, surely. It means I'm going to lose something." This is the story the ego will tell you.

If you choose loving things, you will shift your life into a frequency that matches your consciousness. For example, if you have always plopped yourself on the couch at seven o'clock at night with a bowl of unhealthy snacks and turned on your favorite entertainment show, this is the kind of thing you look at and go, "Wow, I enjoy doing this because I'm tired after a long day, but I can see that this is really not very loving to myself. It's certainly not loving to the people on the television show that are being picked apart or gossiped about. This is no longer the frequency that I am holding at lesson 59 in *A Course in Miracles*. What do I do?"

Make a small change. Instead of grabbing the unhealthy snack and putting your feet up and turning the television on, run yourself a nice bath, light some candles, put some oils in there, and get in and soak. Afterward, trim your toenails, put some cream on your feet, and spend that hour doing something nutritious and nurturing. Then you can plop down on the couch and do whatever it is you want to do. Do a little bit at a time. If you see that you're not exercising at all, and you realize that some of the choices you make are not healthy, take the stairs once in a while. These are simple physical confirmations that you are shifting and changing. If you change direction a tiny bit and continue on that trajectory, you take yourself into a completely different life.

Anxiety is the clue that you are battling yourself in your mind. Things in your mind want to assert themselves, and there are new ideas saying, "Mmm, that's not such a good idea." What the mind wants is peace. The anxiety — if you have it arising because you're learning new things and the old ones look unappealing — shows that the old is deeply entrenched and supported by thousands and thousands of indoctrinations. The new seems a little weird, a little strange. The mind wants to get rid of the new. The mind's purpose is to try to get back to peace, and it doesn't care how it does it — drinking three martinis or watching a movie. It will do whatever you have been trained to do to alleviate anxiety.

What we want you to do as students of *A Course in Miracles* becoming aware is to say, "Ah, anxiety means I have a lack of peace in my mind." It feels like fear because the mind cannot choose between belief systems. It wants to go to the devil it knows. We have introduced new and loving ideas that take the implementation of your free will to side with the more loving ideas. It reduces your stress if you understand what is happening.

That is our lesson for today. It is enough. Read this again to see whether you can make notes of where you feel something wanting to change your life and the related anxiety. Where does it show up? Writing it down gets it out of your mind and gives you a hard copy that helps you see what you are doing.

Practicing forgiveness in this form means you do not throw the baby out with the bathwater. You do not suddenly quit your job. You do not suddenly quit your marriage. You do not suddenly do anything. You subtly shift the decisions you make on a daily basis toward a more loving frequency, and then everything shifts because you choose love. You are choosing love. All you lose are the unloving things in your life you have been taught to do. The ways of eating and drinking and thinking and entertaining that are not loving and indoctrinated into you have consequences. They are not harmless.

I am that one you know as Jesus, and we will speak to you tomorrow.

Review I: Part 10

Follow the complete lesson guidelines in your *ACIM* book.

You are blessed beings, indeed. I am that one you know as Jesus. As you walk along this path, you will reach stumbling blocks. These are issues assigned to you to deal with in this incarnation. Now, many of you are dealing with multiple lifetimes of issues that have been ignored or that you could not master, and they have appeared in this incarnation. Many of you are having difficulty with this particular time in this particular part of your life, because before you came into this incarnation, you decided you wanted to deal with as many things as possible to clear as much as possible for various reasons that we are not going to go into at this time.

We want you to know that when you stumble on one of these bumps in the road, fall over, get back up, brush yourself off, and then look at that tricky thing you just fell over, we do not want you to be sad or mad at yourself. We do not want you to say, "I am a bad student of *A Course in Miracles* because I could not manage that particular situation with my mother, my father, my body, my food, my addictions, or my resentments."

Whatever you did not manage today or yesterday, forgive yourself and say, "Ah, that is why I am here. I don't know how to handle that situation. I don't know how to do that. Why would I attack a small child for misspelling a word? Why would I attack a child for falling over when it's learning to walk? I would not do those things, so I will not do those things to myself as I learn to recognize that which is unloving in me. If it is unloving and it is in my mind, then it is not of God. It is not going to stay. Therefore, I must see it. I must trip over it to recognize that it is not loving, that it can take me down into sadness and suffering, and that means that it's not me — not the real me, not the true me that is at Home with God and aligned with love. This thing that I just encountered is not actually me. I'm not going to own it in that sense. I have allowed it to live inside my consciousness and manifest in my life, but it is not the true me, so I will not beat myself up. I will not hate myself because of something I have done or a situation I was not able to handle well. I am going to look at it with forgiving eyes and say, 'Ah. There is a thing that I need to have a look at. It is not loving, and it does not extend love. It does not add to the world in a positive way, so it is not real in that sense. It does not belong here. It does not belong in my holy mind.'"

Doing this will help you to stop beating yourselves up when you make errors. Errors are good things, because they show you where you are unstable or unable to handle something. That means you need to look at it, bring it up into the light, and offer it up for healing. Also, look where you contribute to maintaining that belief. This is your side of the street, so to speak. You bring it up into the light. You say, "Ah, I'm very frightened of this thing" or "I hate this thing, but I don't want that unloving concept in my mind. I'm going to ask for help to have it removed from my mind, and I am going to look at where I reinforce it on a daily basis."

That is the process you use to weaken a belief. You must see where you reinforce it — the behaviors, words, deeds, or thoughts you employ on a regular basis that keep that belief alive. Once you see it, then you can use your free will to choose other thoughts, words, and behaviors. That belief loosens the power you add to it. Then it can be lifted from your consciousness because you, literally, no longer want it. You stop strengthening it.

I am that one you know as Jesus, and we will see you again tomorrow.

LESSON 61

I am the light of the world.

Follow the complete lesson guidelines
in your *ACIM* book.

You are blessed beings indeed. That is why I start every statement I make with that statement. You are blessed beings indeed — you are the light of the world. You carry within your very essence the love of God. You carry within your very essence a powerful creative ability. You carry within your very essence everything you need, all the understanding you need, all of the passion you need, all of the drive you need, and all of the wisdom you need to experience what you want to experience in your incarnation.

Why do you think so much effort is put into teaching you otherwise? So much effort is put into teaching you about your smallness, your propensity toward sickness, keeping you ill, keeping you inside, keeping you away from joy, keeping you away from the outside, and keeping you controlled?

Because you are so powerful. If you were not powerful, this society would not need to restrict you so much, and train and punish you so much. It would be able to leave you alone, for you would not be any trouble. You would be weak, but you are not.

You are the light of the world.

I am the light of the world.

I am that one you know as Jesus, and we will see you again tomorrow.

LESSON 62

Forgiveness is my function as the light of the world.

Follow the complete lesson guidelines in your *ACIM* book.

You are blessed beings, indeed. I am that one you know as Jesus. You are meant to be happy. One of the great fabrications — we will say lies — taught about my teaching is the requirement for suffering and sacrifice.

Suffering and sacrifice breed resentment and cause pain. Happiness does not. When you attend to your mind, when you learn that what you think creates the feelings you feel and whether they make you happy or sad, you realize that suffering is a choice. Suffering is, indeed. a choice. It does not make you holy, it makes you miserable. I did not suffer on the cross. In teaching that lesson to my disciples, I showed them that the body was nothing to me, and I did not suffer. The appearance of that story, and the layers of untruth laid upon that story for thousands of years in your society, are lies.

It is not logical for the only Son of God to sacrifice himself in a painful way for salvation of others. That makes no sense. What does make sense, and what is logical if you think about it, is that I demonstrated my ability to overcome death. I demonstrated my ability not to suffer, and I showed that suffering is not required. That let the crucifixion of my body be the last useless sacrifice demonstrated in this world. It is not required of you. You are designed to be happy. You have a guidance system that, when it is in alignment with truth, makes you happy. It is very simple, dear ones.

We do not speak of pleasure here. Bodily pleasure is a different thing. That's a sensory thing. Happiness is a quality of mind. It is something you cultivate by the way you handle your mind, not what you do with your body. That is a different kind of feeling, and it can make you unhappy to constantly seek bodily pleasures. We will go into that further at a later date. For now, know you are meant to be happy.

When you are unhappy, you are off-track. When you are unhappy, go back to your lesson for the day and ask if you have applied it. These lessons are not just to be said by rote, although in the beginning they might feel that way. About this time in the mind-training program, as you apply the lessons, you really believe what you say to yourself. If you believe what you say to yourself and apply the lesson, you will not be sad. You will not suffer at all during your day, and you will get days, dear ones, where you realize these lessons offer you peace. They offer you a different way to navigate your human experience. Then you wonder to yourself, "If I am feeling better after 60 lessons, how will I feel after 360 lessons? And how will I feel after five years of practicing this, or ten years of practicing this?" Yes, we want you to imagine being so happy, so full of health, so full of vitality, that you barely remember the life before *A Course in Miracles*.

I am that one you know as Jesus, and we will see you again tomorrow.

LESSON 63

The light of the world brings peace to every mind through my forgiveness.

Follow the complete lesson guidelines in your *ACIM* book.

You are blessed beings, indeed. I am that one you know as Jesus. This is a powerful statement, is it not? Many of you do not see yourself capable of such ambitious things. Today we want to speak about this feeling of weakness, smallness, and powerlessness you have had cultivated in you through the disciplines in your culture.

From day one, when you were a little child, you are told you are not as valuable as your parents. Children are not as valuable as adults. Throughout your childhood, you had this demonstrated to you through punishments and discipline. This began your belief in your unimportance, for the adults in your life did not value you. It is not their fault. They were trained children should be seen and not heard and that rambunctious and happy children should be contained and controlled to serve society's needs.

Well, we are here to get you to truly serve society's needs and see your grandeur, not your patheticness. We are here to train you to tap into the endless creative light that abides within you so you radiate throughout your life the most magnificent vibration to attract people to you who say, "What are you doing that is different from everyone else? You are not cowering in the corner like everyone else. You're not medicating yourself into oblivion like everyone else. What is it that you have done?" To this you merely say, "I trained my mind. I trained my mind to align with love. And that is what has given me the ability to shine this light and to achieve things beyond the norm."

It is not easy to take on these lessons when you believe you amount to nothing — when you believe you are limited, powerless, and pathetic. We ask you, how does it feel to believe those things about yourself? Do you not feel inspired and happier after you have spent a few minutes with these words that uplift, strengthen, and encourage? These are the words that your parents should have said to you when you were little, but they did not know.

We do not blame them. We merely state what has happened to many of you. You were never encouraged; you were never truly loved and told what you are. That is why these lessons work because we tell you what you truly are and what you are capable of.

You are the salvation of the world. You are the salvation in your world. You transform everything about your world as you begin to use these lessons on a daily basis, on a minute-by-minute basis. At times, when you struggle, you have to dig deep down into the lessons you have studied. You will find one to help you through every situation you encounter, and you will come out the other side seeing. Because you have trained your mind, you do not react the way you used to. You do not need what you used to need. You see you are powerful creators, indeed, and that you have everything you need. You do not need others to become something less so you can feel more. You feel wonderful, and so you do not require anything of them. You do not have to manipulate them or control them to get what you want. You are perfectly happy in your mind and body, and you know that you have a purpose.

This allows you to be kind, patient, and compassionate, but not a doormat. Oh no. You are well acquainted with your strength and your ability to direct your mind, therefore your life, toward loving expression and extension, creativity, joy, and happiness. What a gift to give to everyone, including you.

I am that one you know as Jesus, and we will speak to you tomorrow.

LESSON 64

Let me not forget my function.

Follow the complete lesson guidelines in your *ACIM* book.

You are blessed beings, indeed. I am that one you know as Jesus. It is important for you to see how these lessons differ from the training you have had in your society.

You have been taught in your society, for example, that beautifying the body you inhabit brings you what you want and that using the body to tempt another into a relationship or sexual encounter with you brings you happiness. Why do you believe this? You believe this because of the training through your television shows, movies, and pornography. There is a reason these programming systems are so popular — it is what you want. This world is designed to hide from you your true purpose. So if you have created this place to chase your idols in, for that is what you have done, you separate yourself from oneness and come down in frequency into the physical material world. But you do not want to see the truth. After all, you just left the truth. You left oneness. You left that connected mind of All That Is and came down into this experience. It is not sinful, it is merely different. It is separated from love. It is separated from truth, and you have some things you like to indulge in here.

Now, we do not come at this from a moral high ground. We are saying this is just what's going on. If you don't understand what's going on, you misinterpret the signs along the way. The desire you have for sexual encounters, for example, or sexual stimulation is one of the ways the body gives you pleasure. If you are not seeking true happiness through these kinds of practices — spiritual practices, forgiveness, loving kindness, compassion — you will be unhappy. You will suffer a lot. Because of the training in your society, you have been taught that seeking pleasure can alleviate suffering.

What happens in your experience is that you go to the pleasure centers of the physical brain. Remember, the physical body is the ego's playground. You go to the physical, sensory pleasures — and there are many in this tempting place — and you indulge in them. While you indulge them, they produce chemical reactions in the physical body that seem to bring you pleasure and, therefore, relief from pain and suffering. That is the thing that drives you to use these pleasure centers.

When you stop with the pleasurable activity — the drinking of the alcohol, the sexual intercourse, the gambling, the shopping, the television watching, the movie watching, the pornography, whatever it is that you are seeking, you all have your favorite things, some of you like to overeat — you return to your suffering consciousness. And then you have to go on the hunt again for another pleasurable experience to distract you from the state of your consciousness and stop the suffering.

What we attempt to do here with these lessons is give you such a level of peace and happiness that you do not have to seek after your idols anymore, and you realize that, truly, they are empty. As long as you participate in them, you get medicated to a certain degree with the pleasure chemicals. When you stop, then you are in pain and suffering again. You are lonely and sad again. This is, of course, what leads to addiction. When the brain constantly receives substances that give it pleasure, addiction becomes activated. Addiction is a side effect of mental and emotional suffering.

So if you have an addiction problem, and you see you are using something, then we want you to understand these lessons will, over time, relieve you of those addictions. You, too, can participate in reducing your addictions by being good students. Understand the mechanisms at play. You can step back from that second piece of cake and say, "Actually, indulging in these pleasurable sensations seems like a good idea right now, but I want true happiness. I am not going to indulge in an addiction because I know that it is an endless cycle of seeking, and I don't want to be driven by that. I want to experience peace, which allows me to rest at home and happiness."

I am that one you know as Jesus, and we will see you again tomorrow.

My only function is the one God gave me.

Follow the complete lesson guidelines
in your *ACIM* book.

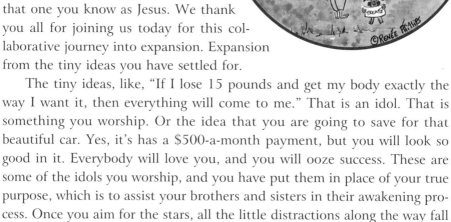

You are blessed beings, indeed. I am that one you know as Jesus. We thank you all for joining us today for this collaborative journey into expansion. Expansion from the tiny ideas you have settled for.

The tiny ideas, like, "If I lose 15 pounds and get my body exactly the way I want it, then everything will come to me." That is an idol. That is something you worship. Or the idea that you are going to save for that beautiful car. Yes, it's has a $500-a-month payment, but you will look so good in it. Everybody will love you, and you will ooze success. These are some of the idols you worship, and you have put them in place of your true purpose, which is to assist your brothers and sisters in their awakening process. Once you aim for the stars, all the little distractions along the way fall aside, and you do not see them anymore. This is how you make leaps and bounds in your spiritual practice.

Many of you have said, "Oh, I've been doing *A Course in Miracles* for twenty-five years." But have you really? Or have you been constantly distracted by other goals? Other training programs that said, "If you work toward this goal, then you will be loved. If you work toward this goal, then you will be secure." We want to tell you that if you work toward the goal this book sets for you, everything else comes to you. You set your sights so high, in terms of your frequency, that health and joy and happiness and abundance of all different kinds must come to you because you are up there in the realms of the gods. You will be up there in the realms of the enlightened ones, the master teachers. You will be up there in the realms of beings not bound by the heavy chains of materialism.

So do this lesson well. Know that it is your ticket to freedom.

I am that one you know as Jesus, and we will see you again tomorrow.

My happiness and my function are one.

Follow the complete lesson guidelines in your *ACIM* book.

You are blessed beings, indeed. I am that one you know as Jesus. This is a very important lesson for you to contemplate. We want you to listen to that explanation several times. We want you to realize that this is a very logical progression of conclusions.

If there is such a thing as God, and that God is loving, then anything that is not loving is not of God, and therefore not real but illusory. So when you go into your own experience of your world through your emotional guidance system and through your observations and these sorts of things, anything that is not loving is not real. It is not of God, and you don't want it in your mind.

When you see yourself as hateful or judgmental (which you will all see and we do not curse you for that; we are merely taking you on a journey, holding your hand to show you the truth), there is nothing to be ashamed of in realizing the ego is driving your actions. This training program is necessary to bring you back into a place of alignment. The ego has been fed too much food and is too strong. The ego recedes in its importance back into a place of manageability as you begin to master these teachings. You see you don't want what frightens you. You don't want to attack people. You don't want to demean yourself by abusing your body or abusing somebody else's body. You slowly and surely turn around on that road.

There is a road — one road — and it takes you toward or away from love. As you walk away from love, you feel worse. You choose each step you take on that road. You have free will. That is why the concept of hell laid upon you is incorrect. God does not punish you. You merely have a reflection of your own inevitable choices day by day, moment by moment. There is only one road. You feel better the closer you get to love. You feel worse the further away you go from love. You choose.

As you encounter unloving experiences and thoughts, you walk away from the truth. You step away from that which is whole, holy, and happening here. You are given the right information so you can make the right decisions and say, "I don't want to feel fear. I don't want to feel bad. I don't want to hurt anyone else. I want to accept my purpose, which is to be happy and in a place of peace. I have been given the means and this strange communication device — the computer — and my big blue book. I have been given the means to achieve peace, and I am willing to do that work because the alternative — there is only one alternative — is the ego's world." We say, take a look around you. Take a look at what the ego accomplishes. It is not such a pretty thing. It does not deserve your condemnation, but it does deserve your intelligent and honest appraisal.

I am that one you know as Jesus, and we will speak to you tomorrow.

LESSON 67

Love created me like itself.

Follow the complete lesson guidelines
in your *ACIM* book.

You are blessed beings, indeed. I am that one you know as Jesus. Some of the great distortions in the teachings of your society about me claim I am the only being that can be wholly loving. I was the only blessed Son of God, I was special. I was made so different from you that I could accomplish miracles and I could live in heaven forever.

Not true, dear ones, not true. You are all the same as me. There is only one road. Some of us are further along the road to love than others, but you are all beloved by that Creator you call God. Now, the Creator you call God is incorrectly defined by all of you. That is okay. We do not worry about details like that. We want you to know that your return to love allows you to redefine God in your mind. It is not about redefining God necessarily first (although there is some implication of that in this lesson). When you tell the true story of who you are in relation to that God and what that God has given you — the ability to create, love, and fear — you have been given absolute freedom.

You have flailed around in the ditch of life, we will say. This is a phrase our dear one likes to use when she falls off the path. She refers to herself as "flailing around in the ditch," and we think it an appropriate imagery to bring to mind. You do not make progress when you flail around in the ditch. You are caught up in the brambles and the mud and slipping. You are not moving toward love, but that is okay. The path remains there for you, cleared and clarified, but you must climb out of the ditch.

One of the things that pushes you in the ditch is your definition of God. You have been taught about a vengeful God. You have been taught to be God-fearing. You have been taught that you cannot trust your inner guidance: Evil is afoot in there. Don't go inside. You will find the darkness, so stay outside. Hand over your power to beings who are very happy to take it from you and very happy to wield it over you.

Something for those of you in modern Western society that we really want you to understand is how the powerlessness you see reflected back to you by oppressive governments, increasing rules, and increasingly unloving societies reflects your belief in your powerlessness. You change the world by doing *A Course in Miracles*. Yes, it's called *A Course in Miracles* for a reason. The world changes when enough of you turn this training into miracle-minded thinking by aligning yourself with truth and love because love holds everything together. Even those who wield power over you love it. It is their love affair with power that gives them the ability to create it. It gives them the ability to create situations and structures in your world that teach you that you are powerless and small.

You must now take back your awareness of love's presence. You must say, "Ah. I have the ability to align with love too. What is it that I love? What is it that I want to create? What is it that God speaks to me about through my passions?" Is it equality for all races around the planet? Then work toward that. Is it care and love of animals? Then work toward that. Do not battle the evil, but invest your daily life with love of the things you are guided to strengthen and enhance.

You must be educated properly to be able to understand your love of something, your passion for something. It doesn't matter whether it's art or animals or organic farming or education. If that is your passion, that is God speaking to you through love.

I am that one you know as Jesus, and we will speak to you tomorrow.

LESSON 68

Love holds no grievances.

Follow the complete lesson guidelines
in your *ACIM* book.

You are blessed beings, indeed. I
am that one you know as Jesus. Of
course, here in these lessons we speak
about the goal of ultimate forgiveness; the
fact that your mind will be free and clear of
absolutely all grievances.

Love holds no grievances. That is true. If you hold grievances, you have
what feels like a little infection in the mind; a little worm in your head
that keeps going on about something. "Love holds no grievances" does not
mean — and this is an important thing here — you are a doormat. This is
something many beings on a spiritual path learn the hard way. It is okay
for you to choose the path you want to take. It is okay to decide that you
would like to experience something that somebody else does not want you
to experience. Having a disagreement with somebody is not necessarily a
grievance. The grievance comes from your unforgiveness because they differ
from you. It means the argument keeps going on in your mind. You keep
revisiting and rehashing in your head what you said and what they said and
why they should do this and why you're allowed to do that. It's a back-and-
forth kind of energy.

You can, as a free being that is creative, choose a path you want to
walk along. You can do it lovingly and with open communication. You
are free to choose what you would like to do, and you will experience the
consequences of that choice. "Love holds no grievances" means you can
see somebody walking a different path than you and say, "Well done, you.
Well done for choosing what is right for you. I'm over here choosing what
is right for me."

That is one of the confusing things about love's definition in your society You believe that to love somebody, you have to sacrifice your beliefs.
This breeds grievances and resentment. When you sacrifice yourself because
you think what somebody else wants is more important than your choice
based on a loving interpretation of your experience, then you suffer. We
want you to understand that "love holds no grievances" does not imprison

you. It does not mean you have to sacrifice yourself, and it does not mean that you have to do as others tell you.

I am that one you know as Jesus, and we will speak to you tomorrow.

LESSON 69

My grievances hide the light of the world in me.

Follow the complete lesson guidelines
in your *ACIM* book.

You are blessed beings, indeed. I am that one you know as Jesus. All of you have had the experience of holding a grievance. Where it goes around and around in your mind, and everything — the beautiful sunny day, the wonderful flowers along the path you walk, the health of your body, friendships — fades into the background. This happens when a grievance works its way around your consciousness. You, literally, see the world disappear from view as you become obsessed with that fight in your mind. Now, for those of you who are partially trained and getting along in the lessons now, you've done some mind training. You have become more annoyed by your grievances than those who have not had any mind training. This is an important thing for you to understand because it is very disturbing to have a grievance in the mind. It upsets your peace.

If you have accessed little pieces of peace as a student of *A Course in Miracles*, when you now lose it — your peace, that is — you feel awful because you have a new contrast revealed to you. When your mind was occupied with grievances all the time and hateful thoughts about yourself and the world and the politicians and the environment, and you just went at it without any mind training, you had a constant level of infection with grievances in your mind and no great contrast existed there. Once you come to a place of peace, even temporarily as the periods of peace become longer and longer, that disruption of your peace becomes intolerable now.

This is a gift. We do not want you to think you have failed. We do not want you to think of yourself as a bad student of *A Course in Miracles*. Oh, no. You merely see where you used to be all the time and why you started the lessons of *A Course in Miracles*. Remember, you were not at peace. You were not happy with your experience on Earth, so you decided to learn something new to see what you didn't know about yourself.

As your peace increases, the grievances you hold in your mind become clearly revealed as the disruptive influence they are. You have to work hard and fast with your forgiveness practice to get back to peace. That is the wonderful news of doing *A Course in Miracles* lessons because what does this do? This makes peace more prolonged and more easily accessible. When you encounter a grievance, you see the tremendous contrast in your frequency if you plummet down into that grievance. You feel awful and say, "For heaven's sake, please bring me back up to where I was. This grievance is not worth it. It is not worth the awful way I feel, and the ongoing argument in my head is intolerable. I really, really want peace." That is a beautiful place to be, dear ones. Do not chastise yourself for experiencing the contrast, for the contrast of falling back into the ego's world shows you it is not what you want.

All you have to do is go back to your lessons, employ them in your thinking process, and peace returns to you. It is scientific in that way. If you follow and apply the lessons, you will not plummet down into the ego's world and its low frequency. You remain in the frequency of love. As you go through these lessons, there will be many days when you experience a grievance, and that is the work. That is the hard part. The hard part is feeling the contrast, but the easy part is the peace. So choose peace. It is your natural inheritance. You are meant to be happy and at peace. The ego's world is a battleground, and it is not much fun.

I am that one you know as Jesus, and we will speak to you tomorrow.

LESSON 70

My salvation comes from me.

Follow the complete lesson guidelines in your *ACIM* book.

You are blessed beings, indeed. I am that one you know as Jesus. It is important for you to understand that the teachings I brought through so many years ago were exactly the same as this — you are the salvation of the world.

The distortion came when the teachings made it seem that the only way to reach salvation was through me — not in the form of an older brother, but in the form of a Savior. Someone different than you. Somebody special and blessed because they were the only Son of God. It was a very tricky distortion because it only changed the truth a little bit. I am the salvation of the world, and so are you. You have all the same abilities and potential futures I had. You have the ability to delve deep into your consciousness and find the profound connection with all that is and in that connection, the loving acceptance of your sacred nature, your profoundly sacred nature. It is there you become strong.

It is there you become influential — not in the influential ways of the ego that seeks to control people, but in the sense that you emit a very high frequency that changes those beings around you. You begin to tap into inspiration, whether it be music, art, or channeling communications such as this. You tap into seemingly amazing and miraculous skills and abilities you could not access before.

What makes you think you do not have talent? It is because you've been told it a thousand times. "Get off your high horse. Don't talk to me like that. Children should be seen and not heard." If you had been nurtured and loved with words — if you had been honored and respected as a sacred being as a child — and asked curiously: What do you want to do today? What feels good to you today? What inspires you today? Do you think any children would say, "I would like to sit in a hard wooden chair all day and be taught things that are of no interest to me"? Do you think a child would say that? No, they would say, "Let's go to the beach. Let's make a giant painting with mud. Let us climb that tree. Let us build a tree fort." And imagine if you grew up in a world where that was the way you learned. You can learn so much by building a tree fort.

For those of you who have children or are around children — perhaps you are an aunt or an uncle or a grandparent — encourage those little beings in their joy. Encourage those little beings in self-expression. If their parents cannot do it because they have not gone through the process you are going through, take that child for a little excursion once in a while. Take them to see something that you know they would not see otherwise. Do this without blame for the parents because everybody in your society is indoctrinated into financial fear and works so very hard.

For those of you who are *A Course in Miracles* students, now you see a crack in the armor of this place. We want you to utilize your wisdom, even if utilizing your wisdom means forgiving yourself for having gone through the trainings of the society and being, at times, harsh and limited in your actions to others. Forgive yourself for that; for those actions, limiting beliefs, and hateful ideas and words were not the true you. You discover the true you with these teachings.

We are the salvation of the world.

I am that one you know as Jesus, and we will see you again tomorrow.

LESSON 71

Only God's plan for salvation will work.

Follow the complete lesson guidelines in your *ACIM* book.

You are blessed beings, indeed. I am that one you know as Jesus. What wonderful words these are to realize that chasing your tail around the planet year after year, decade after decade, no longer appeals to you. It no longer tempts you.

Temptation, often in your society's definition, is seen as evil, dirty, and unholy in some way. But what we want you to understand is that you have, in your separation from All That Is, in your separation from Love, placed your own temptations in the world. That, dear ones, is why they appeal to you. They are not placed there by the devil. The devil is a physiological fantasy, a mythology figure invented to separate you from the knowledge that you design your own temptations.

You design your own temptations, and that is why they seem irresistible. We want to go into this idea of desire and temptation a little bit in this lesson. It's very important you understand the results of following your desires, your passions, and your interests (all these things are not the same). There are deep-seated passions within your mind that you want to deepen your knowledge about. It could be music, art, cooking — it could be anything — but you know what it is. It's that thing you always love to do and that's always interesting to you. Even if you're not doing it as a job, you think, "Ah, I would love to be able to work at that full time."

Then there are other things in a more superficial part of your ego consciousness, the part of your mind that is separated from guidance and in opposition to God's plan. That may be your love of chocolate cake, your love of promiscuous sex or drugs. These things are not the same. Often you hear that, "Well, you cannot follow your desires, otherwise you would just be all over the map." There is a difference between a deep-seated interest and passion about a subject and that superficial pleasure-seeking activity of the ego. We want you to differentiate between those two things because if you believe that to do what you feel drawn to do is evil, then you will not live a happy life. You will not be able to pursue that purpose you came here to fulfill. You will see it as a temptation of the devil, as evil in some way.

So when you have a feeling to do something, stop for a moment and ask, "Is this contributing to the overall health of my life? Is this something that has always been with me and always brought a smile to my face? Or is this some distraction? Is this some temporary Band-Aid on a negative feeling I'm having so to go and drink a beer or buy a pair of boots will only make me feel better temporarily?" Those are the ones we want you to look at. Those are the ones we want you to take a break from, or even postpone. If you want to go shopping, and shopping is your thing to make yourself feel better, tell yourself you can go shopping tomorrow. Today you are going to look at why you want to go. What is it in you causing the agitation? What is it in you causing that feeling? "I have to soothe myself." It is so important for you to understand that constantly soothing yourself does not benefit your spiritual and consciousness evolution. You must be willing to sit once in a while with your discomfort and ask the question, "What am I trying to tempt myself with here? What am I trying to hide from myself?"

So your temptations are yours. They are your idols, and they will fall. We are happy to tell you that your idols will fall, and you will come into alignment with truth.

I am that one you know as Jesus, and we will speak to you tomorrow.

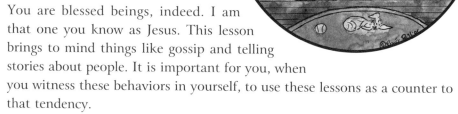

Holding grievances is an attack on God's plan for salvation.

Follow the complete lesson guidelines in your *ACIM* book.

You are blessed beings, indeed. I am that one you know as Jesus. This lesson brings to mind things like gossip and telling stories about people. It is important for you, when you witness these behaviors in yourself, to use these lessons as a counter to that tendency.

Now, remember, this is a training program. We do not seek for perfection from you. You are learning how to behave completely different. You are learning how to completely understand a new way to look at things, a new language. You would not expect yourself to learn fluent Russian in a month or a year. You understand you must immerse yourself in a practice to learn another language. You must even travel to another country to truly become bilingual. That is really what we seek to do here. We seek to teach you another language.

When you reflect on behaviors you witness in yourself, first of all acknowledge that you witness them. There is a behavior, a body saying things, and then there is you saying, "Ah. Look at you gossiping about Susie or Jane." Who is the witness? The witness is the being connected to Source. The body playing out the ego's plan for salvation can be seen and witnessed by you.

So we do not want you to identify with the "you," with the small "y" that gossips. We want you to step back and be the big "You," the You with the big "Y" (the one who is aware), and say, "Ah. Look at what you're doing. There are two 'yous.' How interesting. Who's in charge here of this body?"

This is what we want you to see, the unevolved and evolved aspects of your consciousness. The unevolved is that body-identified ego consciousness that seeks to attack, divide, conquer, and take. Then there is this other observant, less reactive, kinder, loving, and aware part of your consciousness. We seek to develop that one as the predominant energy. The trouble with these systems is they are complete systems. So when you are in the ego, you are not observing the ego. When you are angry at someone, you are down in the battleground. When you observe your behavior, you have stepped above the battleground and can make different decisions.

Observe where you play out your grievances. Observe where you tell stories about people. Observe that and begin to witness how you understand there are two "yous" here. There is the one in the battleground that takes over sometimes, and then there is the loving, kind, seeking, and awakening part of your consciousness. Some mythologies describe this as the "Dark Wolf" (or the "Black Wolf") and the "White Wolf." Which one do you feed? We now only feed the White Wolf. We now only feed that conscious, loving awareness.

Observe when you do these negative behaviors and understand that is not who you are. Let them go and see that this behavior separates you from rising above the battleground. Every time you step down into your grievances, you are at war. You are in it. You suffer, not because you are being punished but because you are down in the battleground in dualistic teachings. You are in the, "There are good guys and bad guys, and I am the innocent one and you are the bad one."

This is why forgiveness is such an important practice. In practicing forgiveness, once you have participated in the dualistic battleground, you once again step above the battleground and say, "I do not want to continue that war I participated in."

As you evolve, as you learn, practice, and come to identify with these lessons and this teaching, you find more peace. You begin to choose voluntarily to step above the battleground. You see that indulging your grievances is not worth it. You do not like the feeling. You do not like the seeds it sows, and you do not like the bitter crop that is the harvest.

I am that one you know as Jesus, and we will see you again tomorrow.

I will there be light.

Follow the complete lesson guidelines
in your *ACIM* book.

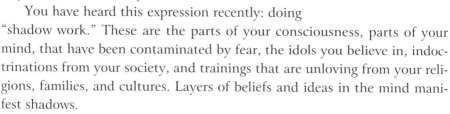

You are blessed beings, indeed. I am
that one you know as Jesus. This is a
very important lesson because you state
the simple fact that you do not want to
stay in the shadows anymore.

You have heard this expression recently: doing
"shadow work." These are the parts of your consciousness, parts of your
mind, that have been contaminated by fear, the idols you believe in, indoctrinations from your society, and trainings that are unloving from your religions, families, and cultures. Layers of beliefs and ideas in the mind manifest shadows.

What are shadows? They are places where light cannot reach because
something solid and impenetrable comes between the light and that area.
We want you to see your mind in this way. The unloving parts of you, the
beliefs, create shadows that manifest in thoughts, feelings, and behaviors.
They exist where the light has not come.

In this way, you do not see the shadows as reality. They are not real.
They are merely an absence of light, which is an absence of love. Forgiveness plays an important part in dissolving those blocks to love's awareness: It is only in those mistaken ideas and beliefs that you strengthen
them and cause shadows. When you say you want the light, you give
Spirit — the Holy Spirit, me, your guides and teachers — permission to
show you the beliefs you hold in your mind through experience. What is
going on?

Many of you, now, find difficulties in life magnified as the shadows
become shown to you. This is a time of frequency acceleration. Now, we
are speaking in the year 2019. These videos will be up for a long time.
We are speaking in February of 2019, and you find in your society an
escalation of the revealing of shadows. It is important you do not become
obsessed with the shadows but, indeed, you seek the light because the
light dispels the shadows, not the focus on them.

When you go outside and try to erase a shadow, what happens?

Absolutely nothing. How do you get rid of a shadow? You shine a light on it, or you remove the object causing the shadow. In your society, when you see something dark or what you might consider evil, distorted, or perverted, remember, it is not the problem. It is the shadow showing you a lack of love. It shows you that somewhere in your society, in your collective consciousness that is the gathering together of all of you, there is a lack of love. Do not attack the shadow, but add love, add love, add love. Love is always the solution.

First, you must understand that the projector is you mind. So do not try and erase the shadow out there. Go into the mind and remove that which is unloving through the practice of forgiveness. This demonstrates your understanding that the projection — the person, place, or thing out there — is not the issue. It is the shadow, and you are the projector. Clean the lens on the projector, and the movie changes. It becomes clear.

I am that one you know as Jesus, and we will see you again tomorrow.

LESSON 74

There is no will but God's.

Follow the complete lesson guidelines
in your *ACIM* book.

You are blessed beings, indeed. I am that one you know as Jesus. This lesson brings an important point to your attention.

Many of your upsets come from arguing with what happens in front of you, whether it's a war, a job loss, a partner doing something you don't like, or children misbehaving. A constant battle goes on between you and things already in play. So we must go to the fundamental issue here of what is in charge of your world.

Well, there are many forces in charge of your world, most of them misaligned forces lacking light and love. So they play out their drama, but they are allowed to. You must remember this is a place of free will. You have tremendous creative power and free will. That means God allows what you see happening. In fact, God is not involved in most of what happens on your plane because you have free will. Only when you use that free will to step above the battleground and align with love does the connection and communion felt as love, peace, and spiritual connection happen. You begin to actually feel there might even be a God. In the battleground, it surely looks like there is no God.

This idea that your will and God's will are in alignment is a very important one because when you surrender to that which interests you, brings you joy, prompts you toward health and love and happiness, then you align with God's will for you, which is happiness and joy, fulfillment, and experiencing that which you wanted to learn about in this incarnation. That is all guided by your interior world, your interior guidance system.

The idea of withdrawal, now, is a very interesting one because that is what most of you have done. You withdraw into the ego's illusory world and do not connect with your true guidance. Darkness and light seem to battle for supremacy. There the dualistic laws of the lower frequencies apply and appear as a battle between God and another "force." As you go down in frequency, the other "force" seems to pick up more power. This is where the idea of evil, or the devil, has arisen. But you have merely stepped further and further away from the realm in which God resides, which is love. That is why it's important for you to remember that love, health, and creativity is your will because they are God's will for you.

You do not feel conflict when in alignment. You feel conflict when you try to choose between God's will for you and the ego's designs. Remember that. If there is conflict in the mind, you must look at what you are trying to choose between and ask yourself which one is God's will for you.

Again, the clarification process of doing *A Course in Miracles* is very important because the ego will, indeed, try to deceive you into believing that it's will is God's will for you. We do not want to belabor this point here, but whenever you have a choice, do not rush it. Go inside for two or three days in calm contemplation and ask yourself, "Which one of these two roads leads me toward love, health, and happiness and which one leads me further into separation and closer to fear?"

I am that one you know as Jesus, and we will speak to you tomorrow.

The light has come.

Follow the complete lesson guidelines
in your *ACIM* book.

You are blessed beings, indeed. I am that one you know as Jesus. When you speak in this way, "The light has come, I have forgiven the world." you, in every moment you say that, plant seeds of truth in your mind and step away from judgment.

You step away from the belief you have when your ego is in charge of the fact that to judge, criticize, argue, or fight for what you want makes things better.

Now, forgiving the world does not mean you become weak. On the contrary, it means you are in alignment. You are not wasting your energies on meaningless battles anymore. You are calm, peaceful, and in that place where you can be guided easily. You are not in a tempestuous and unpredictable mood. You are calm and peaceful. When an idea pops into your mind, which happens once peace is cast upon the shores of your thoughts, you say, "Ah. That is an inspired idea. I am going to pay attention to that one. That did not come from me." When the waters of your mind are all choppy and upset from being in the battleground, it is difficult to hear those kinds of concepts and ideas that come from the higher realms as guidance and knowledge, which is what we seek.

We seek clarified minds that can hear clear guidance. When you hear clear guidance, things seem to move more slowly. You do not run hither and yon all the time trying to satisfy superficial needs. You make decisions that reflect wisdom. You choose wisely. When temptation comes along, you say, "Not interested, thank you. I have been there and done that, and I am really happy with the path I'm on, so please go on your way."

You can say it happily and with love. You do not need to attack anyone, and you know that attack and judgment is not your job. Attack and judgment keeps you in prison. When the light has come, oh dear ones, what wonderful , inspired, and active days you have.

This is not a passive, weak path. Some beings feel that when you surrender to love, light, and the will of God, you become some weak and namby-pamby person. On the contrary, you become inspired, healthy, and energized. You become connected into the true Source of your power, and your body thrives because it is put to use for good. It has now been put to use for love, and it thrives at that frequency. It does not thrive at the frequency of fear, anger, and judgment. In fact, it withers and dies. Eternal life becomes a possibility because you do not need to go through the process of death when you realize that the light has truly come.

I am that one you know as Jesus, and we will speak to you tomorrow.

LESSON 76

I am under no laws but God's.

Follow the complete lesson guidelines in your *ACIM* book.

You are blessed beings, indeed. I am that one you know as Jesus. The ego will not like this lesson at all.

This is an important time for you to remember that these lessons do not have to be understood. You do not have to agree with them. They merely need you to practice them because your society has so many laws and you have been so indoctrinated into them. You have incorporated great fear into the mind as it relates to your government's laws, tax laws, driving laws, parking laws, and bylaws in your local communities. Laws, laws, laws.

These are all designed to disconnect you from this truth that you live under no law but God's. When you begin to really believe and know and act as if this is true, you see evidence of its truth. You find you bring into being circumstances and opportunities that defy the laws of your world. You call them miracles, and that is exactly what God's laws do provide for you. They provide you with the opportunity to perform miracles. In that demonstration, you see the truth of what you have learned.

But we don't want you to learn these lessons so you can show off and produce miracles. In fact, the miracles should not be yours by design. You should allow them to be worked through you by higher teachers who know what is in the best interests of everyone. Only do what you are inspired to do. Trust in that guidance. Know there are things that seem good on the surface, that you want to do when you are indoctrinated into your world's laws, but they may very well not work toward the good of all. Trust in your inspiration and guidance, and know that even though this lesson seems unreal to you in your current state of consciousness, it is the truth. You are under no laws but God's, and eventually you see that is the truth. But for now, do the lessons. Teach yourself this new idea, and understand that any resistance is natural because you are under so many other laws and you do, indeed, believe in them.

There will come a time on your planet when the laws of God will be far more visible, and we are working together toward that day, indeed.

I am that one you know as Jesus, and we will see you again tomorrow.

LESSON 77

I am entitled to miracles.

Follow the complete lesson guidelines
in your *ACIM* book.

You are blessed beings, indeed. I am that one you know as Jesus. This is something that sounds arrogant to the mind in alignment with the ego: "I am entitled to miracles."

In your teachings on Earth, you have been taught to see yourself as small, weak, and undeserving. Many of you in the West have a self-loathing and do not believe you are entitled to anything. You see yourself abusing your body or attacking yourself in thought, and you must, from those demonstrations, come to understand that you do not see yourself as entitled to miracles. So this lesson can upset the ego and can bring up in you some of the teachings you've had: that you should not be proud of yourself or love yourself. This is one of the greatest disservices that religions, and particularly the Christian religion, have done to many. They teach you are born a sinner and undeserving of God's love, you are bad, and all of the sins of the world are your fault.

On some level, of course, we say the miscreations those of this place do you come from all of you, but there is no sense of moral badness about the

111

truth of the matter that miscreation causes things to go off-track. You do deserve miracles because you are made of love, from love, and for love. You are merely returning to that truth.

When I was on the Earth plane so many years ago, that was why I was able to heal. That was why I was able to return beings to their natural state. You see, I was not really doing anything other than removing what was not the truth from them. Healing just removes blocks to the awareness of love's presence. Once you are aware of the truth of your nature and begin to treat yourself as the sacred being you are — the thought in the mind of God that you are — you would never attack God knowingly. You would never blaspheme knowingly in that sense, but that's what you do when you treat yourself poorly.

So know that you deserve love. Know that you deserve kind and gentle treatment, and that you are capable of a lot of things.

I am that one you know as Jesus, and we will talk to you again tomorrow.

LESSON 78

Let miracles replace all grievances.

Follow the complete lesson guidelines in your *ACIM* book.

You are blessed beings, indeed. I am that one you know as Jesus. It is hard for you to believe those beings you resent, hate, or find annoying are your saviors, but indeed they are.

It is through them and through your forgiveness of them that you ease and minimize the separation, loneliness, and disconnection you feel. The great fear of the ego mind, when you get into forgiveness practice, is that you will have to hang out with all these people. We want you to understand that is not necessarily the case, although in some instances your forgiveness practice allows you to spend time with them again. But it is not necessary.

We work with the mind, here, and it is important for you to understand that your grievances disrupt the frequency of your mind. It is your mind that generates and projects everything you experience. Your grievances interfere with the perfect functioning of your mind, and you suffer because your mind is set to connect with Source at the frequency of love. When you have a grievance that is unloving, you block intentionally (even though at times it feels involuntary). You choose to block love, so you feel the pain of suffering that you, of course, wrongly attribute to their poor behavior. It is your judgments and your grievances that cause you to suffer.

When you become willing to give up your grievances, you see that you stop suffering. You have an epiphany where you realize it is not them that are the problem, but your beliefs about them. Once you have done your forgiveness practice with a being, you find it no longer pops up in your mind and causes you suffering. You have changed, and you reap the rewards of forgiveness practice.

Understand that peace lies behind every grievance you have. Access to increased health and knowledge lies behind every grievance that you have. Is it worth nurturing and feeding those grievances? Is it worth talking about people and gossiping behind their backs? It is you who suffers the loss of the miracle when you do that. It is something for you to think about.

I am that one you know as Jesus, and we will see you again tomorrow.

LESSON 79

Let me recognize the problem so that it can be solved.

Follow the complete lesson guidelines in your *ACIM* book.

You are blessed beings, indeed. I am that one you know as Jesus. This is a very important lesson (as I seem to say so often with these lessons). They are brilliant. They are definitive, in the sense they help you narrow your focus into the correct place and in the right direction.

When you think somebody causes you a problem, you always look to that person to solve it for you. "He/She should not have said that. He/She

113

should change. He/She should not be so independent (or clingy)." Whatever you decide is the problem. This is one of the ways you guarantee you will never solve the problem because the problem is one of perception. The problem is within your own mind. It appears out in front of you through the practice of projection, so it seems unsolvable. This is one of the great tricks of ego consciousness. It constantly creates situations outside of you that change form, deceive you, or tempt you so that you will not go to the one place where the solution lies, which is inside.

The answer is within you. It is, as you say in your modern vernacular, an "inside job." If you don't know that — if you don't know that getting calm and quiet and going inside to ask for guidance is how to truly solve the problem — then you chase idols all around the planet all your life to try to solve a never-ending line of unsolvable problems. Even when you do solve one, another one pops up just as quickly.

This idea of asking to be shown the problem and realizing it is separation from All That Is, separation from Love in that sense, separation from wisdom (there are many forms of separation going on, on this Earth plane) leads you to resolve the problem by the same thing, which is the practice of forgiveness as described in the *A Course in Miracles* text. Forgiveness stops you from attacking the outside — from moving the chairs around on the Titanic to keep it from sinking — and directs you to go inside to do the work there and ask to be shown, "What is the distortion in my mind? Where is the problem in my mind?"

Now, this may seem like blaming the victim to some of you, but we want you to understand you maintain that entire illusory world in which you live by projection and belief in separation as the fundamental structure of this reality as you understand it. It is through knowing and acting in accord that you are not separate, you come from the same place, you are all made of the same thing, and you are loved by that which you call God. When that realization is truly made, there are no problems anymore. You have healed the fractured mind of the Son of God.

I am that one you know as Jesus, and we will speak to you tomorrow.

Let me recognize my problems have been solved.

Follow the complete lesson guidelines in your *ACIM* book.

You are blessed beings, indeed. I am that one you know as Jesus. This is one of those lessons your ego just has a really hard time with. We want you to bring your attention to that saying often bandied about in your society that the solution to a problem cannot be found in the same frequency or level of consciousness in which it was created. This is very similar to what this lesson states.

If you stay down in the frequency of the problem, then you cannot find the solution. If you adamantly state the fact that the solution is already found, then you just have to allow your consciousness to drift up into the level of consciousness where that solution is.

Logically, you can see that every problem has a solution. Things can be solved, obviously, but where is that solution in relation to the people who have the problem? It is out of their realm of consciousness. This is one of the concepts to think about as you do this lesson. Your level of consciousness right now is down around the problem frequency, and we get you up around the solution frequency. You do not get to the solution frequency by banging around in the problem frequency. Aim your consciousness up, accept the problem as inevitably solved, and then find the solution. That is the truth.

I am that one you know as Jesus, and we will see you again tomorrow.

Review II: Part 1

Follow the complete lesson guidelines in your *ACIM* book.

You are blessed beings, indeed. I am that one you know as Jesus. Once again we thank you for joining us today.

Those of you hanging in there with the lessons surely feel some great shifts and transformations happening already in your consciousness. You see how easily you get upset. You see how hard it is to get your mind to do what you want it to do. You see why people take themselves off to ashrams and monasteries to do this kind of work. We want to speak to that subject here today, this idea of being in the world but not of the world, for that is what you are all trying to do.

That was my way when I was on the Earth plane so many years ago. I had my family, I had my wife and children, I had my ministry, and I had to focus very acutely on my practice to achieve what I did. In living in the ordinary world, you benefit in some ways. When you sit inside a little monk's cell, there aren't too many things to forgive, really. The mind wanders off on stories, but you are not shown yourself so frequently and so passionately by the people in your life. I'm sure monks do get on each other's nerves a little, but when you throw work, children, making a living, buying a house, and all of these things on top of your practice, you really do the most difficult work as a spiritual seeker.

So if you are having a hard time remembering your lessons or if you get a little bit worried that you're can't master them the way you feel you should, we want you to really comprehend the size of the task you are taking on. Not only are you standing firm against the propaganda of your society, which is magnificent we will tell you, you are also doing it in the midst of a busy life. For that you deserve commendation. So today that is our message for you.

Well done for coming this far. Well done for hanging in there. Well done for showing up each day to listen to these lessons. Well done. Well done. Well done.

I am that one you know as Jesus, and we will see you again tomorrow.

LESSON 82

Review II: Part 2

Follow the complete lesson guidelines in your *ACIM* book.

You are blessed beings, indeed. I am that one you know as Jesus. It is important in this time and place to really focus on your function. Your function is to awaken from the dream.

What is the dream? The dream is living in your mind with illusory ideas, feeling all kinds of feelings because of those illusory ideas and thoughts, and not knowing that you live in your own self-created dream. When you wake up through this process we share with you here, and that will continue for some time for you, you see that everything is a choice. What you focus on becomes stronger and more powerful in your life, and your connection to the divine allows miraculous things to happen.

You wake up to realize that you may lucid dream. You know what a lucid dream is, when you lay in your bed, dream, and know you know you're dreaming. That means you can choose to fly, you can choose to do whatever you want. Some of you have had that experience.

Well, that is what a master is, somebody who lucid dreams in this time-space reality. That is a wonderful experience: to be fearless, to have the magnificent creative forces given to you at your fingertips to do good and share love and light. That really is the function all of you have: to share love and light.

It does not matter if you have completely accomplished this. If you are only sharing more love and light than you were a week ago, you work miracles you cannot even see; miracles that show up in your life in fortuitous events and wonderful meetings and opportunities that would not have come to you otherwise. Of course, you cannot do a double-blind study to prove what your life would have been like, but we guarantee that when you pass over from this realm, you will be shown the many forks in the road you have taken in your destiny using your free will to choose love instead of fear, and you will see the network of miracles that sprouted from those loving decisions. You will, if you are lucky, get to see what could have happened if you took the old road of fear and the ego's way.

These are some of the great, exciting things you have to look forward to — miracles sprouting up all around you, great health, great happiness, and a wonderful experience here. It is not true reality — there is a reality beyond this one — but you dream a happy dream. You do not live in pain and suffering and believe every single illusion your mind makes up. That is not fun when you experience those kinds of things.

I am that one you know as Jesus, and we encourage you to double down now on your practice. You have come to lesson 82. You have gone past the honeymoon period where it's all very exciting and easy. You now get into the nitty-gritty of seeing what your mind can get up to. Do not be frightened of it. It is merely a cloudbank that is intimidating.

It is the light behind the clouds that you now want to seek. Whenever you see a shadow, whenever you see a dense cloud coming toward you — a fear, judgment, scarcity thinking — understand in your heart and mind this is an illusion. It is not real. It is not of God. Focus on that which is divine, and you will go through those mists, those confusing mists of illusion, without harm. You will, in fact, experience that many times as you do these lessons. You feel fear, you call upon the lessons you learned, and you go through that fear and come out the other side and realize it was nothing. It was an illusion that your mind made up. For many years you believed those sorts of things, and now you realize you don't need to.

I am that one you know as Jesus. We will speak to you again tomorrow.

LESSON 83

Review II: Part 3

Follow the complete lesson guidelines in your *ACIM* book.

You are blessed beings, indeed. I am that one you know as Jesus. As we continue to review these ideas and add some different ways to explain them, you find some of these sentences difficult to remember. What we want you to do is take a few moments, a minute or so, when you read these application lines —you can even make a note of them on some paper if you wish — take them out with you into the day, and use them whenever you think about something upsetting. For example, a coworker gets on your nerves. Take that little notepaper out, and read those suggestions. If you go to the bank, for example, and there's less money you think there should be in there and feel that stab of financial fear, find yourself a seat, take out your piece of paper, read the notes, and remember that to allow your frequency to plummet down into fear or resentment is arguing with God, if you will. It is arguing with your purpose, which is forgiveness and love.

That is how we would like you to use these ideas today. Take them with you on a little piece of paper, and use them with every upset you feel. What you learn to do is allow the upset to come. That's usually not your choice. You get triggered into feeling it. What you are doing is, instead of feeding that upset, resentment, or fear, you choose love instead. You say, "I am destined to live God's purpose for me regardless of my bank account or coworker. These things have nothing to do with the greater purpose of which I am apprised."

I am that one you know as Jesus. We will see you again tomorrow.

Review II: Part 4

Follow the complete lesson guidelines in your *ACIM* book.

You are blessed beings, indeed. I am that one you know as Jesus. It is important for you to deeply contemplate these lessons today that love holds no grievances. That means when you — made of love, from love, for love — hold grievances, you use your free will to hide the truth of who you are from yourself. You suffer because you disconnect from the truth, which is that you are a loving being.

This is a simple practice. Saying words like this does not seem to have great import. When you are trained in your society, you are not taught that saying words to yourself changes anything. "It's an objective world," they say to you. "You thinking something different or saying something different does not make any difference out there. The 'out there' is solid. It is a hard copy." But what we tell you is, it is a printout from the software that you run in your heads. You understand this simile. It is like malware installed in your computer, and the printout becomes distorted. The words do not form properly. This is what happens in your world. The malware you installed in your head reports to you that you are ugly. You are going to die. God is vengeful, hates you, and will punish you because He even punished his most beloved Son in a most horrendous way even though that person was so good, what is going to happen to you?

These are the malware stories downloaded into your hard drive, so to speak, that say these words repeatedly throughout the day. When you practice these lessons, honor them, and eventually integrate them and believe them, you clean up the hard drive of your computer so the printout will be clear, clean, and comprehensible. That is what we seek here. We seek to clean up that which does not belong in your most sacred mind.

When you get a grievance, feel resentment, or get angry with someone, quickly observe what happened. You have unplugged from love for a moment, and you feel awful. You want to plug back into love so you feel good. And so you let it go. As beginner students of *A Course in Miracles*, you get triggered, you get emotional, and you get upset because you have so many contaminating ideas in the mind. What you can do is bring this teaching as the remedy. Instead of getting into a long drawn-out argument with someone, you can say, "This is not going to serve either of us to fight. I choose love. I love you." You will be surprised at some of the things that happen. Some people will refuse your love. Some people will stand up and give you a hug.

But you will begin to see that you do not waste your energy and your time on things you do not like and don't want to participate in anymore. This book is true medicine. It brings you peace, and you will see it is a scientific process. When you clean up the hardware and remove the malware from your programs, the printout becomes much more comprehensible.

I am that one you know as Jesus, and we will see you again tomorrow.

LESSON 85

Review II: Part 5

Follow the complete lesson guidelines in your *ACIM* book.

You are blessed beings, indeed. I am that one you know as Jesus. We are very pleased that you are with us today. Our dear one has a little tickle in her throat, a raspy voice she has been struggling with, so we hope you give her a little leeway in her performance today.

Your salvation lies within your own consciousness, and, of course, in your society, you are taught the very opposite. You are taught your salvation lies in getting a new car, buying a big house, or marrying the right person. So for many incarnations, you chase your tail, so to speak. You chase things outside of yourself when, in fact, your salvation comes from within.

Why does it come from within? Well, within you is the key to the door to awakening. In releasing your attachment to judgment and separation, you find your way home. It is in and up, not "out there." It takes a while for you to figure out that all of the idols, things, people, places, and experiences you chase do not make you happy. They do not bring you peace. Once you do this for a few decades, you have what you call a "midlife crisis," where you decide that everything you do is wrong, it does not make you happy, and you try something completely new. Move to Mexico, buy a sports car, ditch your spouse, marry a younger person, have a facelift; whatever it is you decide is going to be the outside thing you did not yet find. Unfortunately, for most people in their midlife crises, they do not find it there, either.

There is a strange energy afoot on your planet right now. A galactic speed-up, we will call it, where you are more likely to get the answer you seek. You are more likely because it is the end of a spiritual season. Everything in the non-physical — all of us teachers, guides, and masters — work

120

with you to give you every single ounce of our guidance, help, and direction so you learn to look inside. Once you go inside with assistance, you find out where you trip yourself up. It is only you that causes your suffering and imprisonment, dear ones. It is your beliefs about reality. It is your lack of love for yourself. It is your judgments. It is your fears. All of these are your own miscreations.

This seems like a big job, to turn within and go down deep into the mind. *A Course in Miracles* is designed to assist you in this journey. You do not go into the basement of your consciousness alone. I go with you. Christ-consciousness guides you. With that guide, you gently get led through those outer rings of fear toward the light that lies in all of you.

I am that one you know as Jesus. Keep up your lessons. Be diligent and relaxed. We will see you tomorrow.

LESSON 86

Review II: Part 6

Follow the complete lesson guidelines in your *ACIM* book.

You are blessed beings, indeed. I am that one you know as Jesus, and this is one of the core teachings of *A Course in Miracles*: when you judge and hold grievances — when you say, "You shouldn't have done that. It shouldn't be this way. This is wrong." — you, in fact, attack God, in the sense that something is happening and this is what the universe is expressing at this time.

When you argue with "reality" in the world in which you find yourself now (we use this word reality with a small "r"), you fight with God. It is that simple. The thing you dispute has already come into being. It is there. It is important for you to truly understand the extreme power of acceptance. When you stop arguing with what is and go into a place of acceptance, even if you don't want more of what is right now, it benefits you to accept "reality" because that is what has been decided upon. That is what has manifested, and there's no point in arguing with it. It is what is.

Sometimes what is seems bad. Sometimes what is looks like something you don't want — the death of a loved one or a lack of money — but it is what is. You are foolish and wasting your time to argue with what is. You may shift and change your perception. You may work on becoming more loving as a consequence of what is. You cannot change it.

The world does not hold your salvation. Look inside for your salvation.

Look to love for your salvation. Do not seek salvation in the world through another person, more money, or a better body, but seek salvation by aligning with love so you match what is, for what is always loves. Your perception, judgments, and attacks on yourself do not love.

I am that one you know as Jesus, and we will speak to you again tomorrow.

LESSON 87

Review II: Part 7

Follow the complete lesson guidelines in your *ACIM* book.

You are blessed beings, indeed. I am that one you know as Jesus. We thank you again for joining us today in this review period, all of which are important. You revisit ideas introduced to you with a little embellishment on concepts related to these ideas. You educate yourselves. You learn new thoughts and new ways to see things.

When you perceive yourself as unfairly treated in the world, you essentially say God is attacking you, and you should get something different than what you have. When you see an event in the world and say, "That should not be happening," essentially you play God. You decide, with your very small understanding of reality, that you know better than what is.

For example, when you see beings suffering, you may say, "This should not happen. This cannot be the will of God. This would be a cruel God if this being was allowing this to happen." In truth, what is happening is. You are free to choose whatever you want to do by that God, and you experience and witness what you have the freedom to miscreate or create by yourselves. When you miscreate repeatedly, you suffer each time. When you suffer repeatedly, you begin to pay attention to what you're doing. The first few times you suffer not so much. If you see a pattern of behavior in you and its consequent result in the world, you begin to associate your decisions with your own suffering. You understand you give yourself the same gift/ result each time.

You have the free will to choose differently. You have free will to choose what you want to do, what you want to believe, what you want to worship, you want to value. You have free will to do all of those things because you are loved. You are given free will by that which you would call God to choose again.

That is what all of you here are doing. You, after many years of having

122

your free will to choose whatever you wish, choose to come here and hang out with us. That is a very clever thing to do. You have finally decided there is, perhaps, something you do not understand, something you do not know. You do well to learn some new things, ideas, and perspectives. We applaud you for coming here today to learn those new things.

I am that one you know as Jesus, and we will see you for more instruction tomorrow.

LESSON 88

Review II: Part 8

Follow the complete lesson guidelines in your *ACIM* book.

You are blessed beings, indeed. I am that one you know as Jesus. We thank you once again for joining us in these lessons each day. Why do we thank you? We thank you because this is my work. This has always been my work and it will always be my work to wake minds up to the truth of what they are.

You are eternal spiritual beings. You are incredibly powerful creators. You are made of love, from love, for love. If you do not fulfill your purpose to create, be free, express love, generate love, and feel love, you do not live in your true nature, let us say. This idea of God's laws versus human laws is a tricky one for many of you because, as you can see, more and more laws are imposed upon you all the time.

If you listen to these laws only, you feel constrained, small; and very much under the thumb of the oppressor. If you pay attention to God's laws, which see you as an eternal spiritual being, you invest your time, thoughts, and energy in timeless things. You do not obsess over the body and what it can do for you or that it might suddenly die on you. You cultivate healthy relationships because you know your relationships with each other are eternal. You pay attention to inspiring ideas about creativity because you know creativity is a natural aspect of your God self. You pay attention. When you understand you are an eternal spiritual being, you pay attention to things that truly feed you and, ironically enough, will help feed you.

When you focus on the body, society's laws, and all the limiting beliefs and ideas that impinge on your freedom, you do not feel good. You do not feel inspired or expansive. You do not have to destroy those beliefs and

123

ideas and laws, you merely have to turn your gaze away from them and to the laws, ideas, and concepts contained within this text. Those lift you to the realm of peace where you can tap into hidden knowledge. You cannot access this knowledge down in the lower realms of the physical 3D world. You do not have the same frequency. So your life completely changes when you follow God's laws.

We encourage you to expand your idea of yourself. We encourage you to follow your inner guidance, follow your heart. The world's laws say, "You cannot make a living as an artist. You cannot be free. You cannot live a life of happiness and joy." If you listen to them, well, most of you know how that feels.

If you listen to God's laws, you follow your heart and get guidance on how to live a wonderful life, find your true purpose, and experience your expanded consciousness. What a wonderful and different feel that has. So we ask you to watch, today, where you follow the world's laws of scarcity, death, and attack. Turn your thinking around and follow God's laws of love, freedom, and self-expression. We will speak to you again tomorrow.

LESSON 89

Review II: Part 9

Follow the complete lesson guidelines in your *ACIM* book.

You are blessed beings, indeed. I am that one you know as Jesus. All of you know what a grievance living in your mind feels like. It is, indeed, hell.

Everything fades away. If the grievance or the upset is a big one, you literally do not even see your surroundings. You might be driving your car and you go for several miles before you realize you have been in a fantasy in your mind — in a fight with somebody or an argument. (Of course you always win.)

When you see yourself always win an argument, you can determine from that fantasy — which you generate from your own mind, nobody else is there; just you, your mind, and your beliefs — you believe that to attack back and win an argument is your salvation. That is what that fantasy shows you. It shows you believe you have to win. You think the grievance is worth it because in the battle, the fantasy battle you have at times in your mind, you win and become the victor. It perpetuates separation when you witness your mind doing these kinds of things.

124

We want you to interpret what truly goes on in your mind when you have a grievance and you regurgitate over and over scenes in your mind about that person. If you are in your ego mind at that time, you will say, "Well, no, that's what that person does. I'm justified in this. I've seen them do this and they will do this again." That is how the ego justifies the fantasy in the mind. As a good student in *A Course in Miracles*, you realize that image, that movie you watch, comes from no one but you. In that moment, nobody else is in the car or room with you. The scenario is purely a figment of your own imagination, and you participate in it because you want it. You want the battle. You want the fight. You want the grievance, and you want to win. All you do is attack yourself, now, instead of attacking the other being.

Accept this is a belief you hold in your mind, that you somehow lose if you do not win the battle. If you give up the grievance, your ego says you lost; but all you lose is the loss of peace. You lose the fantasy movies in your mind that entertain you and plant the seeds of war with that person. You get back to a place of peace where you intentionally and consciously create a more loving relationship with that person. When you offer up a grievance with a particular person for healing as you do in these lessons here, we want you to understand you only gain. You gain a happier future. You gain, therefore, less stress, which means a healthier experience within the body. Temporary and illusory as it is, it is very real for you right now. You sow seeds that you get to harvest in the future because you act in love.

Make sure you understand that grievances are hell-creating in the sense you lose your peace. Sometimes you actually lose your presence. There is nothing worse in the world than for a human to be deeply involved in a grievance because it is detrimental to all levels of your experience here.

I am that one you know as Jesus, and we will speak to you tomorrow.

LESSON 90

Review II: Part 10

Follow the complete lesson guidelines in your *ACIM* book.

You are blessed beings, indeed. I am that one you know as Jesus. Very few of you see problems in this way. Of course, problems are never ending in your world.

Problems continue. As soon as you solve one problem, another problem appears. As soon as you resolve a grievance, another grievance pops up. This is because of the way your mind works. There is this idea being reviewed here that you are separate from the solution. You are not separate, because everything takes place in your mind. Your world reflects your consciousness, mind, actions, and beliefs about reality. So any problem manifested in front of you must come from within your own consciousness, because that is what life is.

Your life, experiences, relationships, and values — everything — come from within your consciousness. You are the creator. You are the projector. All faults on the movie screen of your life come from the projector. That means the solution is found behind the fault in the projecting mind. The projector creates and miscreates the life that you live, and the problems demonstrate a distortion within that projector — a little bit of dirt on the lens of the projector of your life, if you will.

Now, you know running up to the movie screen and trying to change things on it is absolutely pointless. You know that trying to change your hairstyle in the mirror is absolutely pointless. You must go to the origin of the issue. We want you to clearly understand that your problems manifested in front of you are within your mind and, therefore, are yours to correct. You must choose the miracle, which is to choose love instead of the fractious, refusing, judgmental, or resisting idea you see manifested as the problem in front of you.

When you see a problem in front of you, for example, somebody behaving in a way you think is unacceptable, then hold a mirror up, turn it toward yourself, look inside, and ask yourself these questions: "Am I qualified to judge somebody else's motivations and behaviors? Do I even know my motivations and behaviors? Actually, no. Perhaps I should focus on myself a little bit more rather than feeling that I am self-righteously justified in criticizing others." This one little example shows how you can immediately remove a grievance, a problem, from your mind and life by changing your point of view — reframing the way you refer to the world.

The world is here, playing itself out in front of you and washing over you every single day, and it is manufactured from within your consciousness and the collective consciousness of your society. Your job, however, is not to correct society other than in correcting your contribution to society. Are you contributing loving thoughts and ideas, or are you contributing grievances?

I am that one you know as Jesus, and we will speak to you tomorrow.

Miracles are seen in light.

Follow the complete lesson guidelines
in your *ACIM* book.

You are blessed beings, indeed. I am that one you know as Jesus. It is important for you to truly grasp the power of your mind. Your mind focused on truth brings about miracles. Your mind focused on illusions brings about death, sickness, destruction, and fear.

The thoughts this society asks you to hold — fear of death, fear of aging, and limited belief in your ability to heal (in fact, the belief that you cannot heal yourself, that you need magical devices to do that) — are poisonous thoughts, beliefs, and ideas to the mind. They will, in fact, manifest themselves in sickness. They will bring into being exactly what you think about, which is that you are weak, your body is fallible, and you can't trust it.

What is true for you becomes manifested into physical reality. This is what the idea behind creating your own reality means. It's not just thinking about a car and getting it but thinking and feeling your way into your miracle-mindedness. What a joy it is to know this. What a wonderful gift you give yourself in doing these lessons every day. Do not stop giving yourself this gift of truth. Do not stop giving yourself this gift of mind training so that you may, in the end, become a master of your own experience.

I am that one you call Jesus, and we will speak to you again tomorrow.

Miracles are seen in light, and light and strength are one.

Follow the complete lesson guidelines in your *ACIM* book.

You are blessed beings, indeed. I am that one you know as Jesus. There are, of course, resistances to this lesson because you have been told, indeed, that the eyes are what see. But the eyes are the mechanism by which the ego brings its dark, separated world to you. It brings it to you because you want it.

You all came here to explore the idols and the ego's playground. You chose what you see here. You chose separation. You chose bodies. You chose your idols. Most of you know those things do not please you. They do not make you happy. In fact, they prove your belief in separation and idols.

As you go through your incarnation, you become less enamored with the world. You become less enamored with the body. As you awaken in this incarnation, you understand what you believe about the world and what you see. If you go into the world as a cynic who believes in death, that is what your eyes bring to you. Conversely, if you go into the world focusing on miracles, that is what you bring to yourself. You are the perceiver. You decide what you experience and what you see. You are, truly, the creator of the vision of what the physical body's eyes see.

This is why those beings with no spiritual practice are afraid when they look around the world. They are scared, disillusioned, sad, depressed, and angry because they believe in the body's eyes. They see the result of the ego's playground, and it is not a pretty sight.

For those of you doing these lessons, you see the beauty in everyone. You see the light behind the dysfunctional behavior. You become able to forgive and offer love. In that vision, you create miracles.

I am that one you know as Jesus, and we will see you again tomorrow.

Light and joy and peace abide in me.

Follow the complete lesson guidelines in your *ACIM* book.

You are blessed beings, indeed. I am that one you know as Jesus. Light and peace and joy abide in me. That is why I am here, dear ones, to tell you the truth that you too can live in that place of light and joy and peace.

It is a truly wonderful thing when all the untrue ideas, hateful thoughts, judgments, and petty disturbances leave your mind and you are at peace. It is something worth more than anything else you can chase, buy, or possess in this three-dimensional world you call reality.

Light and peace and joy abide in me. I am that one you know as Jesus, and light and peace and joy abide in you. You are that one created in the image of that which you call God: a beautiful creator, a unique expression of the Divine who is sacred in all ways. Be kind to yourselves. Respect yourselves. Do not let others beat you up or put you down. Understand you are as God created you.

I am that one you know as Jesus, and we will speak to you tomorrow.

I am as God created me.

Follow the complete lesson guidelines in your *ACIM* book.

You are blessed beings. I am that one you know as Jesus. This is a very important lesson. It is a wonderful phrase to use within your mind anytime in the day you feel you have lost track of who you are and feel inundated by fear or insecurity or anxiety.

You are as God created you. Any of the unloving thoughts you have about yourself make no difference. Any of the unloving thoughts you have about another brother or sister make no difference. They too are as God created them. So you must see that you are not more powerful than God in this case. You are as God created you. Your brothers and sisters are as God created them.

Relax in this knowledge. Relax and know that all is well. When you relax — when you stop running so fast and judging so harshly and fighting so hard — you realize everything is all right. Everything is all right. You are all right. Your brothers and sisters are all right. The world is all right for this moment. So in this moment, let go of everything that is not true — everything unloving and fearfully created by your distorted mind.

You are as God created you. You always will be and have always been. I am that one you know as Jesus, and we will speak to you again tomorrow.

LESSON 95

I am one self, united with my Creator.

Follow the complete lesson guidelines in your *ACIM* book.

You are blessed beings, indeed. I am that one you know as Jesus. You can feel the truth in these words. You can feel the love in these words. You can feel separation is not what you want. Love is what you want. Communion is what you want. Connection to the divine is what you want.

You do not want these idols you have been chasing and that you find so meaningless and hollow when you catch them. You catch an idol, and then you drop it saying, "This is not what I wanted. I thought it was what I wanted, but it is not what I wanted." Then the ego mind says, "But look over there. Look at that one. That is so shiny, and so many people are chasing it. You should chase that one too." Three or four years later you catch that idol — a nice car, a new body to play with, an advancement at work, a marriage, children, or a bigger house.

What do you look for? You look for peace. You look for joy. Those things are not found outside of you. You think they are. You have been taught to buy things, upgrade your possessions, get married, or slim down to be happy. Truly, have these things made you happy? Do they make others happy? You don't know. You see the smiles pasted on their social faces, but are they truly happy? You hear stories of the unhappiness of the wealthy or the famous, their difficulties. We do not want you to relish those difficulties. We want you to go to your experience and ask, "Have all the things that I have chased made me happy? Have they brought peace in the darkest hours of the night? Have they brought comfort and joy and love?" No. Most of them have not. Perhaps for a few weeks, a few months, or a little while if you were lucky. Then they turn into something else. Then they turn into what they are: temporary Band-Aids for deeper pain.

We go into the mind and change the way you look at reality. We change the value system of your consciousness from has been you marketed to you by religions, family, cultures, television, advertisements, and movies. What has been marketed to you from commercialism, materialism, fear, and death, we change into love.

You come from love, you are made from love, and you are destined to love. That is the truth.

I am that one you know as Jesus. We will see you again tomorrow.

LESSON 96

Salvation comes from my one self.

Follow the complete lesson guidelines in your *ACIM* book.

You are blessed beings, indeed. I am that one you know as Jesus. Salvation is an idea in the mind of God.

You have stepped away from the connection you naturally have with love. This is something very important for you to remember — that you chose separation at some point in the eternal now. It seems to have taken place in the past, but when you think about it, do you still choose separation? Do you still choose to attack now? This is something you all must look at when you think, "Well, why would I have chosen not love? Why would I have chosen to come into this difficult and challenging arena? I don't want to be here anymore. I want to go home to love."

You can, but you must choose love to go home. Think about the times in your day when you say unloving things about yourself, you attack yourself, or you think a hateful thought about another. Think about the times in your day when you are impatient, judgmental, angry, insecure, or fearful. Every one of those moments blocks your return Home.

You must honestly assess how dedicated you are to salvation. Many beings say they want to go home — they want to be held in the arms of God once more — but a thousand times a day, they choose not to love themselves or another. Think about that. What choices do you make? Do you choose to follow your heart Home to love, or do you choose to feel separate from others, abandoned, and attacked, and then judge this and feel unfairly treated? These are all ideas in your mind that do not love.

My purpose here is to remind you of the truth. You are the captain of your ship. You decide how you use your mind every single day. You decide how you use your body every single day. What use do you give your body? Do you use it to pursue salvation? Do you use it to pursue true love? Not the romantic love of your world but rather true love: self-acceptance, acceptance of your brothers and sisters, self-expression, and the appreciation of your talents, ideas, and passions.

I am that one you know as Jesus. We will speak to you again tomorrow.

LESSON 97

I am spirit.

Follow the complete lesson guidelines in your *ACIM* book.

You are blessed beings, indeed. I am that one you know as Jesus. This is a very powerful lesson, because it tells you the truth about how your thoughts and your prayers travel around the world to all your brothers and sisters.

Just as your fear is magnified through the ethers, we will say so too is there an emanation from your loving thoughts and ideas. When you align with truth, you become a powerful beacon for love. That ripple goes out from you to and through everyone. Anyone who has the slightest willingness or openness to tune in to that thought, belief, or idea picks it up, and it will seem to be an inspiration. Inspiration means you are in spirit. That is exactly what happens in that circumstance when your thoughts and frequency emanate from yourself.

As you go up in frequency doing these lessons and looking at the world with forgiving eyes, you become the beacon of love, light, and hope for everyone on this planet. The more of you who become miracle-minded — the thousands of you who do these lessons — the more you affect the entire planet. Do not doubt it.

That is what a miracle is. It is something that steps out of time and does not follow the rules you have been taught. Miracles are merely things you do not understand. You have been hooked into the body, time, death, and fear. That is what you believe in. As you do these lessons, you step up into the miracle-mindedness of your natural inheritance.

I am that one you know as Jesus. We thank you for joining us today and working these miracles with us for your planet to be infused with love and light and, through the practice of forgiveness, so will your life. We will see you again tomorrow.

LESSON 98

I will accept my part in God's plan for salvation.

Follow the complete lesson guidelines in your *ACIM* book.

You are blessed beings, indeed. I am that one you know as Jesus. Your part is a most magnificent offering. You do not have to know what your part is. All you need to do is be willing to do these lessons with utmost honesty each time you come to that five-minute moment when you sit down and say, "I'm going to do my lesson." Open your mind and heart to the possibility that I am with you.

Open your mind and heart to know this is planting a seed for a magnificent and loving world.

Come to that five minutes not resentfully, thinking, "Oh my goodness, I'm wasting time. Somebody's going to think I'm weird if I keep doing this." No. Understand the craziness of the world is fed by people who are unconscious, unaware, and do not know what they think. They do not understand the value system of creation, which is love. Love holds everything together. Love pulses throughout this universe.

When a being becomes lost (and most of you have become lost, because what you have been taught is incorrect), your most magnificent creative power miscreates. It causes illnesses in the body. It causes arguments. It causes resentments. It is only because you have been taught a valueless system. Ye shall know them by their fruits" [Matthew 7:16].

Look at your world. The natural world, if it's left alone by humans with greedy minds and hearts, does fine. The old trees fall over, and the young saplings grow on the trunk of the decaying matriarch or patriarch. The bird's nest, deer eat the leaves, butterflies lay their eggs, and everything works in wonderful harmony. Now, nature is not separate from separation. It is also founded on death. Each thing must die for another to live. But each thing knows its place. Each thing understands it comes and goes and comes and goes. It does not try to control the future. It does not hoard for a future it is afraid of. Even though it is in the world of separation, it is happily living its life.

That is what we are working toward for you, a time and place when you happily trust in life. You are optimistic, kind, and generous. You love yourself and the opportunities this physical experience gives you. Relax knowing you are meant to be here. How do you know? You are here. You are here in the eternal now.

But you miss this opportunity for creativity if you always worry about the future and have anxiety about survival. You miss this wonderful, holy instant when you regret the past and resent others' actions. Come into the eternal now and trust that you will be shown. Trust that you will be guided. Trust that five minutes this is the best way you can spend five minutes each hour. I will see you there in that five-minute period.

I am that one you know as Jesus, and we will speak to you tomorrow.

Salvation is my only function here.

Follow the complete lesson guidelines in your *ACIM* book.

You are blessed beings, indeed. I am that one you know as Jesus. Forgiveness and salvation are one because when you practice forgiveness, you no longer argue with what is.

What is being manufactured and created from the collective mind of the Son of God? You experience the results via the effects of your thinking, belief system, and values. There is no point to argue with reality, because it is the result of much rumination. It is like having a mold that produces a candle. You examine the candle and see a fault. You try to fix the candle. You shape it, you sand it, and you smooth it until the fault is gone. Then you make another candle, but it has the same error in it. So you must do the work again. You must shape it, sand it, and smooth it until the error is gone. This is what you consider problem-solving in your daily life. When you use the mold to make another candle, lo and behold, you have another faulty candle.

This is what most of you do. Every day you encounter problems that are distortions of the one mind of which you are a part, but you do not change the mold. The mold is what we work on here. That is why your life gets easier and easier when you choose forgiveness. Forgiveness changes the mold. In forgiveness, you no longer choose separation.

You no longer remove yourself from love and your brothers and sisters, which are also love. You remove the error from the mold. You now produce a faultless candle. Your life becomes increasingly faultless. In *A Course in Miracles*, this is referred to as the happy dream. Yes, you still seemingly have a body, reside in time, walk the face of this planet, and exist in separation, but you are not required to live this way. You are not forced to unconsciously participate in miscreations.

You choose consciously where your mind goes, what you focus on, and what you choose to let go of because it is in the eternal now. With the forgiving, loving mind, you have the ability to create what you'd like to experience. That is what this world is for. It is not for the deep and terrible suffering some of you go through. That is enough to cause suicide attempts, which succeed at times. It is not designed to be that way. You were designed to live a happy experience of separation, playing out the games you want to play for a little while until you tire of them.

Let us get you back into a place of peace. Let us get you back into a place of joy and happiness. Then you can experience the things you want in this 3D world that you call life.

I am that one you know as Jesus. We will speak to you again tomorrow.

LESSON 100

My part is essential to God's plan for salvation.

Follow the complete lesson guidelines in your *ACIM* book.

You are blessed beings, indeed. I am that one you know as Jesus. It seems arrogant — does it not? — to think you have a part in God's plan for salvation.

Who other than you can be used among your brothers and sisters on this earthly plane to wake them up and help them see that suffering and sacrifice are not required? You have all been trained in your society to shut down your imagination and turn away if you hear guidance from another consciousness. You close all the doors that we have to help you wake up. So we employ your brothers and sisters — a being such as this channel is a good example — to help wake you up and guide you toward the means you have been given for peace.

As each of you awaken to your special talents and gifts, this does not put you above your brothers and sisters. This being is not above you although she has managed to apply herself enough to her practices to bring about this transformation in her consciousness. She is not above you, and she knows this. She's an ordinary being just like you. All of you have access to increasingly wonderful thoughts, ideas, inspirations, and talents. These are not for your aggrandizement; they are for you to enjoy. They are for you to practice. They are for you to master in your own way. In that mastery, that modest pursuit, you shine a light for others.

Perhaps you will play that instrument you have always wanted to play but would never dedicate yourself to and allow yourself to play. Over the next few years, perhaps you will get good enough to give a few lessons. Perhaps you will inspire children to play music. Perhaps you will be asked to play in an orchestra or choir. Perhaps you will be inspired to go busking on the street to share your talents. Perhaps it is just you and your instrument alone. Then there come words, words that seem to need music. So you begin to write songs. This is how it unfolds. It is not for you to decide the path for your talent. You will be guided along the way so that you do not become intoxicated with fame or needy of other people's adoration. That is not what it's for. Each of you will be guided to fulfill your purpose. Some may be quite public, and some will be completely private.

You selected your purpose in accord with your guides and teachers before this incarnation. You decided what you would offer to this awakening process on your planet. They are all important things. The gardeners and the farmers that nobody sees on TV or on the internet, these people grow your food. They bring you healthy and wholesome meals. Are they less valuable than the famous people? Of course not. And that is something you must reflect on.

Your society has contaminated many minds with the idea of fame and wealth as success. We want you to reassess your idea of success. Living a life doing what you love, peace and joy with your family and friends, and occasional "drop-ins" — that is a beautiful thing, indeed. As you get older and tired of playing the ego's games and chasing idols you have chased throughout the years so far, you see that a calm, quiet, and peaceful life doing what you love each day is a wonderful experience, indeed.

We want to thank you for sticking with this challenging training program for 100 days. Well done to all of you who have made it this far! You already feel the changes in your heart and mind. You already know that something great is happening within you. Do not despair, do not give up, and do not feel overwhelmed. You are on the right track. You are saving yourself years and years of struggle.

I am that one that you know as Jesus, and we will speak to you again tomorrow.

God's will for me is perfect happiness.

Follow the complete lesson guidelines
in your *ACIM* book.

You are blessed beings, indeed. I am
that one you know as Jesus. Sin is not
real. If sin is real, you are more powerful
than God. You are able to do something that
God cannot stop you from doing. Do you think
you are that powerful?

You are indeed a powerful creator — no doubt about it — but not as powerful as the Father. You are made in his image, indeed. In giving you his image, he has given you the ability to do what you want, to create or miscreate along whatever lines you feel necessary, but you cannot overpower the Source of all that is.

If something has been done to you or by you, or you've witnessed something, you must remember you are given absolute freedom. You are not punished for following the guidance you think is true. Anyone who does anything thinks it's right and that it brings what is desired. People think it brings them closer to their goals, whatever their goals are. So many of you, dear ones, have had your minds so contaminated with untruths that you cannot discern when you are off track. You have been so deeply indoctrinated through fear and mental and psychic manipulation that you simply cannot discern.

Through this process on this path with us here today — doing these lessons, shifting your consciousness, changing your mind, and practicing loving thoughts and ideas — the dirt, dust, and mud on top of your clear mind is removed and you receive true guidance. You get a feeling, "Ah, this is something that I should do. I don't know why I have this feeling, but this is an important thing for me to do." That is how the guidance begins.

You get this subtle itch, a little nagging something or other, that points you toward something. It will not be strong enough in the beginning to override all the contamination in your mind. You see, as time goes by, this message gets stronger and stronger. It is there consistently, not pushing, yelling, or arguing, but it is there. In the end, it becomes strong enough for you to listen to it and say, "Ah. This is something that I am going to do."

You might have to fit it in around your schedule. You may have to rearrange some things to get to this idea, but you can just entertain ideas. This is one of the beautiful things about your consciousness; you can just think about that thing. You can envision yourself doing that thing. You can imagine yourself feeling good doing that thing that you are now inspired to do. It could be writing a book. It could be traveling. It could be growing a beautiful flower garden. It could be anything. You get the feel of it by just imagining it, just allowing it some space in your consciousness.

This is one of the reasons we tell you not to talk on your phones all the time. Sit on a park bench and look at the ducks swimming in the pond without the phone in your hand, without the texts pinging all the time and distracting you from what is right in front of you. It is, in fact, the holy instant where you can create what you want to experience. This is one of the sabotaging effects of these technologies that you carry with you all the time. You never have freedom to just be — to quiet the mind, gaze at the horizon, and allow those inspired ideas to surface in your mind.

The next time you go for a walk, turn your phone off or leave it at home. It will still be there when you get back. Witness how much more peace you have. Witness what you see. You don't need to be hooked in all the time to messaging systems such as exist in your society now. We know this is a difficult one for many of you because your businesses and your relationships seem to depend on these constant interactions. We tell you that an hour out in the woods without your phone does nothing but improve your connection to the Divine.

I am that one you know as Jesus, and we will speak to you again tomorrow.

LESSON 102

I share God's will for happiness for me.

Follow the complete lesson guidelines in your *ACIM* book.

You are blessed beings, indeed. I am that one you know as Jesus. Have you not noticed it is always more preferable to be happy than to be sad? There is an innate knowing within you that this is the way you are meant to be.

When you are happy, everything is better. Your life is better. Your finances seem better. Your relationships feel better. Your opinions of yourself and others are better. When you suffer, sacrifice, or feel out of sorts (as you say), the very same things (everything) look awful. You have an innate knowing that happiness is preferable to sadness. You innately know freedom is a natural preference over imprisonment. You don't have to study anything to know this. That is because it is God given, and it is natural to be happy. So when you are sad, know that you have made an error of thought. You are not sinful; you are not bad. You merely have made an error of thought. Ask yourself, "What thoughts do I have that cause this sadness?"

- "I don't have enough money." That thought will cause you sadness.
- "I'm not attractive enough." That thought will cause you sadness.
- "I'm not a success." That thought will cause you sadness.
-

If you have these thoughts, then you are out of accord with God's will for you. If you say, "I am very successful," you feel good, and that means you are successful. That is the alignment you seek. It doesn't matter how you define success. Your idea of success may be to do nothing all day long. That could be your idea of success and God's will for you. If that is your purpose, to be a non-productive person (and there are beings whose purpose is that, indeed), then that will make you happy.

In your day-to-day living, look for those little things you indulge in that cause you suffering and make you sad. Know you are off track there, and you need to reassess the wording of that thought, belief, or idea. In that reassessment, shift it around a little bit. Turn it around. Make it go from back to front and upside down. See which statement feels better for you.

You are the master of your ship. You accept or eliminate your thoughts. Some thoughts need to be ignored and let go, and they will dissipate and go away. Other thoughts need to be paid attention to because they inspire. They cause you joy, and they return you to that natural state of happiness that is God's will for you.

I am that one you know as Jesus, and we will see you again tomorrow.

God, being love, is also happiness.

Follow the complete lesson guidelines in your *ACIM* book.

You are blessed beings, indeed. I am that one you know as Jesus. One of the great lies that has been perpetrated on your collective consciousness is that you should fear God.

It is not God that you should fear but fear itself. You have heard this phrase: "Nothing to fear but fear itself," and that is true. Fear is an illusory feeling, idea, and energy that permeates the body and causes everything in you to disconnect from love and shut down. Fear is self-created. Your mind makes up stories that terrorize you. You have been fed stories from the time you were little that have terrorized you. Every time you get that horrible sinking feeling that you have sinned, been bad, or done something terribly wrong, you are out of order. You are incorrect, and that is why you feel so awful. You have disconnected from the truth, which is love, freedom, joy, and happiness — which is God.

The stories of an angry God smiting those who do not do as they are told are fictitious fear mongering, just like your new stories today. They are the "new" stories of old, and they keep everybody down in those lower frequencies of survival — fight, flight, or freeze. This is a very primitive state of the human body–mind consciousness. It is important that you understand these things — these words and phrases that we teach you — lift you up out of the fight, flight, or freeze paradigm. That is the world of the ego and of death. The fight, flight, or freeze mentality ages and terrifies you and puts you in hell.

These loving, compassionate, kind, and true statements we ask you to repeat to yourself, to recondition your mind into alignment with love, are the opposite of that. They are the truth. They feel good because they are the truth.

I am that one you know as Jesus, and we will see you again tomorrow.

I seek but what belongs to me in truth.

Follow the complete lesson guidelines in your *ACIM* book.

You are blessed beings, indeed. I am that one you know as Jesus. It is important for you to understand that everything you need is within you already.

You do not have to be perfect. You are perfect already. You have merely covered up your perfection with other ideas, beliefs, and goals you have allowed into your mind and followed through the many brambled pathways that lead you nowhere. This lesson is about understanding, truthfully, that everything you were ever given by God — your creativity, alignment with love, affinity with your brothers and sisters — is your God-given truth. You don't have to do anything to deserve it. You don't have to do anything to truly experience it other than stop following the other things.

One of the ways you do this is through pursuing your creativity by understanding that whatever you give energy to, whatever you focus on intently with joy or any strong emotion, gets infused with your energy. When you focus on things you don't want and passionately hate, you infuse them with your creative energy; thus, they expand and get stronger. When you focus on something you love with positive, loving passion and infuse it with your energy, it gets stronger. You are a creative being made in the likeness of a creative Creator. You too are a creator. You did not create God. God created you, but you are alike in that way.

It is important for you to understand that anything not loving is truly not you. That's why it hurts. That's why it causes suffering. So keep it simple. When you begin to feel bad and less than at peace, ask yourself what you are doing that is not loving or not doing that is in accord with love. Perhaps it is as simple as taking a nap because you are tired. Perhaps it is as simple as saying, "I don't really want to do that," because it's not what you feel like doing.

These seem inconsequential, but when you go through your day, you have many opportunities to say yes or no to things. Take a moment before you say yes to something to consider whether it's in alignment with what you want. Do you want more or less of that thing?

Many of you go to the jobs you dislike, and you must own that decision. You must say, "I chose this job. I go here every day. At some point, this job seemed like a good idea. How do I know? I know because I'm here and I go here every day." If you have setup systems — mortgages and people who depend on you to go to this job — then you must address it in a slow and steady way. Just as you miscreated along those lines, if you're not happy with what's going on, then you can choose again.

You discuss with your loved ones that you are not where you wish to be. Do not blame them. Do not say, "You are making me go every day because you have become dependent on me." There is a dance you do with your family. There is an agreement you have made with them, and you fully participate in the choices that support that agreement.

It is important for you not to act as if others victimize you when you fully engage in the choices you make every day. Some of you say, "That's not fair. I don't like the choices I have made." Well, you are the captain of your ship. If your ship goes in the wrong direction, then you must correct the trajectory of that ship. When you change the course of a ship, you do not suddenly turn hard on the wheel. You do it gently and slowly and make a wide arc until you reach the direction you have carefully calculated from the stars or your nautical maps. For you, it is from your guidance system. If you are off track and heading to a land you do not want to visit, make a new trajectory based on the map that is your guidance system. Do not turn hard on that steering wheel, because you may unbalance the ship and capsize it. It's better to go slowly and steadily back to a path that feels correct for you.

I am that one you know as Jesus, and we will see you again tomorrow.

LESSON 105

God's peace and joy are mine.

Follow the complete lesson guidelines in your *ACIM* book.

You are blessed beings, indeed. I am that one you know as Jesus. As you understand it, there is a phrase attributed to me that states you must "pray for your enemies." That is exactly what this lesson is about. It is about wishing for your enemies that which you would wish for yourself.

In that prayer, you dissolve separation. You refuse to see an enemy as an enemy. You refuse to see sin as real, and you refuse to say, "There are separate needs between my brother, my sister, and me." We are all the same. We are all God's children. We all deserve the peace and joy that are our natural right. So that I can have my peace and joy, I offer you your peace and joy.

When you deny your enemies the thoughts this lesson asks you to gift them, you deny yourself. You deny yourself the very thing you deny them, because you see in yourself what you see in your brothers and sisters. If you see your brothers and sisters as holy children of God, connected to the divine just like you and they deserve, just by their being, then you see the same for yourself. If you see your brothers and sisters as sinful, separated from God, isolated, alone, and undeserving, you magnify that for yourself, because that is how your creativity works. It is so powerful. You get what you give.

It is a difficult one for those of you raised in the material 3D world, where you are taught that you lose what you give. But you don't, and we do not only speak of material things here. This is where your training in materialism shoots you in the foot, so to speak, because you think that if you give something it must be in the physical, material way. No, it can be a loving thought. It can be a prayer. It can be an idea. These are the things that are eternal — thoughts, ideas, and feelings. These are nonphysical things that give rise to the material world. Do not only give credence to the hard copy of something. Remember that the hard copy of something — the physical, material copy of something — comes first from the nonphysical.

Be generous with your love to yourself and others. Pray for your enemies. You know that in praying for your enemies you reduce the separation and fear in your own mind, because you demonstrate your understanding of these laws we teach here.

I am that one you know as Jesus. We will see you again tomorrow.

Let me be still and listen to the truth.

Follow the complete lesson guidelines
in your *ACIM* book.

You are blessed beings, indeed. I am
that one you know as Jesus. Have you
not noticed that the world constantly asks
you to do things — buy things, run hither
and yon, cook, shop? It is so that you do not go
inside and listen. It seems as if this is a conspiracy, the world designed to
keep you from listening. And it is. You designed it. You sprinkled it with all
of the temptations you believe in so that you would not go inside, because
inside is the ego's undoing. Inside is separation's undoing.

Once you begin to truly grasp the idea that the answers to all of your
problems lie inside, then your problems begin to disappear very quickly,
because you no longer project. You no longer blame. You no longer insist
others change to make you happy. You go inside and say, "Why am I
unhappy? I must make myself happy. How do I do that? I keep my thoughts
in alignment with love. I step back from further judgment-inducing separation." And lo and behold, you become happier.

You must take some time out of the busy doingness to do that. You
must sit, once in a while, on your couch and just stop. Just stop; silence
feels so good. The doingness passes away from your mind, and you realize you are here in the eternal now. In this holy instant is the place where
realizations dawn if you listen. Take this lesson today to heart, and listen.

I am that one you know as Jesus, and we will see you again tomorrow.

Truth will correct all errors in my mind.

Follow the complete lesson guidelines
in your *ACIM* book.

You are blessed beings, indeed. I am that one you know as Jesus. Of course truth is true. Truth is the nature of what you are. When you are out of alignment with truth, you feel off. You feel sad. You feel depressed. That is your knowledge that you are out of alignment with truth. Truth is eternal. Truth does not fight for its opinion. Truth is true, whether or not you believe it.

This is important for you to remember as you go through your day. Arguing with others is not what truth does. Truth does not need you to defend it, just like a lion does not need you to defend it. It can sit there quietly knowing it is respected, and if anyone messes with it, it is a lion. It is the truth. So relax a little today knowing that when you are relaxed, trusting your inner guidance and trusting the process you are involved in here, you do not need to micromanage and stress over every little thing. You can say, "The truth is true whether or not I see it, whether or not I believe it. It is there, and I will find it."

When you find it, everything is quiet, calm, and peaceful, because you are aligned. So in your battles, fights, arguments, and disagreements, remember this lesson: The truth does not need to fight for itself. It is there, quietly holding space until you find it.

I am that one you know as Jesus, and we will see you again tomorrow.

To give and to receive are one in truth.

Follow the complete lesson guidelines
in your *ACIM* book.

You are blessed beings, indeed. I am that one you know as Jesus. Of course this seems the absolute opposite of what the ego believes. It is very protective of its possessions. It does not want to share its possessions. It certainly does not want to give anything away. In material terms, the statement, "To give and to receive are one in truth," is not a true statement.

The most important things you have to give are not material at all. In the realm of love, ideas, inspiration, and concepts, you see that to share an idea increases it without any loss to you. In fact, you get more back from sharing an idea because it is multiplied. This applies in the nonphysical realms of love. This does not specifically speak about the material, physical, hard-copy world, because that is a world of scarcity and limitation.

You must remember about the frequencies in which we ask you to play. We have taken you up above the battleground. We have taken you up above the physical material world into the world of concepts, creativity, idea, and inspiration. Up there, everything shared is multiplied. Everything given away is returned to you because ultimately, there is only you playing with your own consciousness here.

When you give something, you have a true comprehension that you own it and that it was yours to give. If you do not share things, if you keep them secret, then you are intellectually aware, perhaps, that you own something, but you do not really have the true measure of its value in your experience. This is a big leap of faith for many of you, because you hoard your money and possessions, and you do not want to share them. You do not want to have this experience. If you begin to share ideas and feelings — those things you would like to keep and to have more of — you begin to see this is indeed true. If you keep your love to yourself, it is a lonely journey. If you share your love and give your love for beauty, children, flowers, or cooking — you love many things, and you give those things away — you really reap the harvest of that wonderful multiplication.

I am that one you know as Jesus. All I have given you is my love for you, and I feel it more each day. All we ask for you to give is your love to the world. The things you love, the people you love, the experiences you love, the music you love — give it away. Share it, and you will feel the multiplication of its energies. You realize you have literally lost nothing.

I am that one you know as Jesus, and we will see you again tomorrow.

LESSON 109

I rest in God.

Follow the complete lesson guidelines
in your *ACIM* book.

You are blessed beings, indeed. I am that one you know as Jesus. I rest in God. Oh, what a joy it is!

What a joy it is not to be pushed and pulled by the tiny and incessant nagging fears and judgments of the world. Take some time today, dear ones, to stop and be quiet with yourself. Rest in God, knowing all is well in the world.

The ego-mind argues and says, "I cannot rest. I have too much to do. I have children. I have a job. I have a mortgage. I have bills and dishes and so on. I have so much to do." Even in that life, with so many obligations and responsibilities, you can sit in your car in the parking lot for five minutes and rest in God. Stop thinking. Stop judging. Stop fearing, and stop worrying. Just be, and you will see a difference in your world. When you do that for five minutes each hour, you will see at the end of the day that you have transformed yourself.

In each hour that follows that five minutes, you find you are less anxious, less worried, and less controlling or fearful or bullying, because you reinforce the truth that you can rest in God. The ego's stories convince you there is no place for rest. You have a phrase in your society: "The devil loves idle hands." That teaching prevents you from stopping and discovering that you can rest in God.

The idea of the Sabbath is a more positive reflection of that — the idea you can rest for a day and the world will continue. That is the truth. If you take five minutes out of every hour, you see that everything keeps going. You are not that important. You are not the thing that drives this world. There is an energy that plays itself out. The collective manifestations of everybody's beliefs, thoughts, and ideas keep bringing things your way.

As you decide to tune in to that source energy (where you come from), you become energized in a different way. You do not get your energy from the horizontal ego world of material possessions or prestige. You do not get your power from there. You get your power from where true power comes, which is your connection to the Divine. You will see it play out on a different day.

I am that one you know as Jesus. I rest in God, and I suggest that you do too. We will see you again tomorrow.

LESSON 110

I am as God created me.

Follow the complete lesson guidelines
in your *ACIM* book.

You are blessed beings, indeed. You are as God created you, and I am as God created me. One of us has merely forgotten it.

I have not forgotten it. I remembered long ago that I am as God created me. In incorporating that knowing into your mind, you relax. In incorporating that idea into your behavior, you become honorable. You honor yourself, and you honor your brothers and sisters. You do not disrespect yourself or settle for cheap trinkets as your reward in this incarnation. You know you are one with greatness, and you know it is your responsibility to align with that loving greatness and demonstrate it in this incarnation. You are as God created you: a magnificent creator, a magnificent teacher — a being aligned with love, made by love, from love, and for love.

I am that one you know as Jesus, and the Christ lives in me. The Christ lives in you, but it is covered by untrue ideas. It is covered by a lack of faith in your divinity. That is what this lesson asks of you; it asks you to remember your divinity.

I am that one you know as Jesus, and we will see you again tomorrow.

149

Review III: Part 1

Follow the complete lesson guidelines in your *ACIM* book.

You are blessed beings, indeed. I am that one you know as Jesus. It is important for you to focus on the light — not the physical light of the Sun necessarily. Although, it can be used as a metaphor. If you constantly look in the shadows in your 3D physical world, what are you going to see? It is not clear. It is murky. It is not illuminated, and it is not very beautiful. All of you know how wonderful it is when you get up in the morning: It's a sunny day, you can see everything very clearly, and everything seems so much more vibrant. This is true of your spiritual sight and how you observe the world as well. When you watch the news all the time, looking at destruction, starvation, and the environmental degradation, you are looking at the shadows.

You must look at the light. You feel weak, uninvigorated, and uninspired when you look at the shadows. You need to look at that which is light — people cooperating with each other, beautiful art, beautiful music, communities, gardeners who vibrantly supply each other with food — that which is love. If you do not regard the other things, then they fade from your vision. Your vision aligns with what works — that which is healed and happy.

When you eat to avoid sickness (we suggest you eat to enhance your health), you look at the shadows the whole time, and your body responds accordingly. When you eat for health so that you can enjoy yourself, there's no fear in that motivation. You have much better results.

Do this with everything you encounter. See the functioning of your body rather than the dysfunction. See the good things about your partner rather than the bad things. See the things you have already learned doing this course rather than focus on what you struggle with. Look toward the light, dear ones, look toward the light.

I am that one you know as Jesus, and we will see you again tomorrow.

Review III: Part 2
I will remain forever as I was, created by the changeless like himself. I am one with him and he with me.

Follow the complete lesson guidelines in your *ACIM* book.

You are blessed beings, indeed. I am that one you know as Jesus. As you go through these reviews, we want you to notice how they make you feel. Make them less about thinking. Make them less about words, and really get into the feeling.

What does it feel like to know you have never been changed by any of the foolish ideas and judgments you have made? What does it feel like to remain perfect, as God created you? This is a feeling. That feeling gives you confidence. That feeling brings you peace. That feeling causes the ups and downs and winds of change to fade away from you. You see that no matter what happens in your life, no matter what comes and goes, no matter what joys and sorrows pass across the sky of your consciousness, the sky is still there.

The blue sky and Sun are still there. You are still there, always there, regardless of what dramas pass through your mind. This is a very important realization, because the next time a drama, intense joy, or change in your life comes, you know it really has nothing to do with you. You are the changeless sky. You are the consciousness that observes. This is a wonderful place to be.

It does not mean you do not care about anything. On the contrary, it means you are able to see you are above, beyond, and bigger than all of those things that play out in the drama on the stage of your life. You are, indeed, the stage; you are not the players. This allows more calmness, peace, and joy to enter your consciousness, because you do not see any of these things as a threat or something to hold on to. They are like clouds allowed to pass across the consciousness of your sky.

I am that one you know as Jesus, and we will see you again tomorrow.

Review III: Part 3

Follow the complete lesson guidelines in your *ACIM* book.

You are blessed beings, indeed. I am that one you know as Jesus. Do you not feel these different selves? One self wants to be single. One self wants to be married. One self wants to eat. One self wants to be slender and fit. One self wants to leave the country. One self wants to buy a home.

So many individual ideas and beliefs in the mind often conflict with each other. You get a very erratic emotional life because of each belief you hold implanted in your mind — perhaps by a mother, father, religious teaching, or television commercial. All these ideas have been planted in your mind by a person or a system invested in you taking on this belief for some reason. You do not even know where most of them come from.

Yet you listen to them, and they generate thoughts, feelings, and emotions. So you are all over the map and often contradict yourself with the same behavior in the same day. You might argue for one side of the coin in the morning, and you may argue for the other side of the coin in the afternoon. Then you wonder why you do not make progress.

The one self that is united with your Creator never changes. It existed before this body was born. It will exist after this body has lost its use. You are that one self united with your Creator. As you focus on that more and more, the imperfections of your training program begin to reveal themselves. Most of them don't make any sense. It is in aligning with your one self, source, love, and truth that you become calm, focused, and able to dedicate your life to something of great value.

I am that one you know as Jesus, and we will see you again tomorrow.

Review III: Part 4

Follow the complete lesson guidelines in your *ACIM* book.

You are blessed beings, indeed. I am that one you know as Jesus. These are the truth. This is why these lessons are so powerful, because you align your mind with truth. As powerful creators, once you align with truth, you begin to manifest very quickly your thoughts, beliefs, ideas, and even physical objects and relationships in alignment with that truth, because you are not swimming against the current of what is. You align with the fundamental principles of creation, which are loving, extending, and spiritual.

You must remember, the physical/material world is the result of a whole bunch of nonphysical things — emotions, thoughts, beliefs, ideas, and prayers — that give rise to the world you see. A fundamental error in your thinking happens when you look at the world and think you need to change it. You need to change your mind about the world because everything happening comes from beliefs, ideas, fears, and arguments — all these nonphysical, emotional, and mental concepts and constructs. So you need to get back to the basics, and this review period takes you there.

I am that one you know as Jesus, and we will see you again tomorrow.

LESSON 115

Review III: Part 5

Follow the complete lesson guidelines in your *ACIM* book.

You are blessed beings, indeed. I am that one you know as Jesus. This is a very important review, because you deal with the fundamental structure of "reality," the way you see things. That is, when you judge the world, attack the world, or decide it should be other than what it is, you perpetuate separation and feed the idea of suffering and sacrifice.

Why do you do that when you judge and attack? You do it because there is only one mind at work here. You play with your own consciousness. You see your own beliefs, thoughts, and ideas manifested in front of you. When you attack that form — whether it's your mother-in-law, sister, brother, husband, or partner, whatever you attack — you literally attack a part of your own mind. It causes you suffering because you don't comprehend what you do. You attack your own mind. This sets up a great deal of fear and guilt that distresses you and leads to a loss of peace.

When you forgive the world and understand why you forgive it — because it is a projection of your mind playing out for you to see the unloving parts of your mind — you understand why you forgive. You understand that your part in salvation is very important, because you help manufacture a dangerous and violent world when you have unloving thoughts in your mind. So your part in salvation is very powerful, because you literally create a world from your beliefs and ideas.

I am that one you know as Jesus. Once you understand this principle, you evolve very quickly. You stop judging and attacking. You begin to live in a state of deep acceptance and surrender. You very quickly remove those beliefs, thoughts, and ideas from your mind, because you realize they are your enemies. They do not benefit you. They do not bring a peaceful world into being. We will see you tomorrow.

LESSON 116

Review III: Part 6

Follow the complete lesson guidelines in your *ACIM* book.

You are blessed beings, indeed. I am that one you know as Jesus. It is obvious to you that feeling happy is better than feeling sad. Feeling free is better than feeling imprisoned. Suffering is not something you are drawn to when you are healthy, when you are vibrantly alive.

There are many distortions in your mind, however, that can lead you to believe feeling sad, feeling put upon, feeling unfairly treated, or sacrificing yourself and suffering because of that sacrifice is normal. Many of you have this belief deeply embedded (not only in your personal teachings from your families, cultures, and churches, but as an element of your overall society) that those of you who go to war and die somehow perform a wonderful sacrifice. You can feel that even questioning whether sacrifice is important and suffering is holy somehow bring up some confusion, because it is such a deeply entrenched belief. It is because of the church teaching this to generation upon generation. When you feel resistance to the belief that God wants you to be happy, that is what is happening.

Do not doubt it. Understand that every time you choose a thought, a focus, or concentrate your mind on something that brings you joy and happiness, that's your feedback system saying, "You are on track." That's your feedback system saying, "Yes, this is good. You're heading in the right direction."

Until you have your mind fully clarified by doing these lessons, some distortions will make you happy, and this is okay for you to witness. You may realize some unhealthy things make you feel good, but they generally have do with the physical body. This is the point we would like to make here: If you use a substance of some kind or an activity that is very body-and-pleasure focused, then that is not really happiness. That is a sensation, a sensory input that distracts the mind from its suffering and brings only temporary relief.

What we ask you to do is choose things that really make you happy. It could be planting some flowers in the garden and seeing them grow and flourish. It could be having a great conversation with a friend. It could be petting your dog or your cat. Using the body is of the body, but in these early days, we want to really get you to understand the difference between those pleasure feelings of eating and drinking, for example, and the nice feelings of creativity, investing in your life, or being out in nature and feeling sunshine on your skin, feeling wind in your hair, and listening to the birds. Yes, these are coming through your sensory input device, but they have a different quality. You know what we are talking about, here.

So be happy today. Choose happiness today. See how well you can practice the choice. Am I going to look at the shadows, or am I going to look at the light? We ask you to look at the light today. Look at the good in your life. Look at the things in your life that are simple, simple gifts that bring a smile to your face.

I am that one you know as Jesus, and we will see you again tomorrow.

LESSON 117

Review III: Part 7

Follow the complete lesson guidelines in your *ACIM* book.

You are blessed beings, indeed. I am that one you know as Jesus. This is always a very important reminder. You are allowed to be happy.

Happiness is alignment with love: When you enjoy, oh, let us say, baking cookies for your family. If that is something you really enjoy and it makes you happy, then that is the right thing for you to do in that moment. If lying down in your bed in the middle of the afternoon for a nap when you're tired gives you joy because you relish that feeling of surrendering to your bed, then it's okay. You can be happy and have a nap. These are some of the things you have been taught are inconsequential, worthless, or even sinful in some way.

Happiness is the feeling, "I'm doing exactly what I want to do right now. It is perfect. I do not want to be anywhere else. I do not envy anyone.

155

I'm not lusting after anything. I'm not chasing anything. I am perfectly happy being me, being here." Wonderful. That means you are doing something right. When you are frustrated, angry, ill, and out of sorts, you are not happy. That means that you are out of alignment with God's will for you. God wants you to be happy. It's okay.

But it is a great cultural teaching to suffer, sacrifice, labor hard, and put your shoulder to the grindstone. These are some of the phrases in your society. They are designed to make you unhappy. Unhappy people are not tapped into their true source of power, and they become tired and disillusioned. "Disillusioned" means you still believe in the illusions.

Make sure you are happy. Make sure you are connected — even if it's for a moment. Be grateful that you can do it for one moment. When it leaves, at least you know the feeling.

I am that one you know as Jesus, and we're happy to see you tomorrow.

LESSON 118

Review III: Part 8

Follow the complete lesson guidelines in your *ACIM* book.

You are blessed beings, indeed. I am that one you know as Jesus. It is important for you to remember all the things you have chased in your life, believing they would make you happy, that they brought you love and peace.

So many of you, when you come to this text, are tired. You are tired and disillusioned. As we mentioned in the previous lesson, when you are disillusioned, that means you still believe in the illusion. That means that once you have a little rest, you will go out and chase something else, because you still believe in illusions. You are disappointed in them even though you still think there may be one, "There may be something I've missed."

This journey into the interior of your heart and mind, healing that heart and mind, is truly what you have blessed yourself with right now. Those of you doing these lessons have given yourselves the ultimate gift, which is to bring everlasting peace to your mind by aligning it to the frequency of the creator of that mind, which is love. Your natural home is love. When you judge, hate, or fear, you feel terrible because you are not in alignment with your true self.

Once you get this, once you truly understand that to be at peace, content, or happy means you are in alignment with God's will for you, then you begin to really enjoy life. You do not think, "Oh, well, I must toil away at something I hate every day because that means I'm a productive and worthwhile member of society." No, you say, "I'm going to learn to surf. I have always wanted to learn to surf. When I'm on that board, I am so happy. That must be God's will for me."

Now, there are those of you who say this leads to a self-indulgent world. We ask you to look at the state of your world right now. We ask you to look at the rates of suicide, drug use, and alcoholism. We ask you to look at the environment. We ask you to look at your inner cities. We ask you to look at the health of your young children. "Ye shall know them by their fruits" [Matthew 7:16, KJV]. Are you so sure it will corrupt society to be happy? Are you so sure?

I am that one you know as Jesus. Happiness does not corrupt your society. It does the absolute opposite. There is joy where there is darkness. It brings love where there is fear. It brings happiness to those of you who follow this path.

There are many pathways. There are a thousand pathways, and you are free to choose them if you wish. Perhaps this is your language. Perhaps this is your pathway. See where it leads you. We will see you again tomorrow.

LESSON 119

Review III: Part 9

Follow the complete lesson guidelines in your *ACIM* book.

You are blessed beings, indeed. I am that one you know as Jesus. It is important for you to remember that giving of yourself is very difficult if you do not appreciate, love, or invest in yourself. Do not deny yourself because of the teachings around suffering, sacrifice, and martyrdom in your society. It is very difficult to give freely when you do not invest in yourself. This is a primary teaching of these wonderful lessons here.

You must allow yourself to invest in yourself. This could be investing in healthy food because you are clear on the fact that if you don't eat healthy food, you may very well contaminate your body enough to cause it to dysfunction. You might decide to invest in educating yourself. Perhaps you never went to post-secondary school, and you find a subject you would like to pursue more deeply. That is a way of deepening your connection to yourself as well; however, the education system in your society is in some ways detrimental. It is, we will say, "the devil you know." If you want to educate yourself, look for people who live the lifestyle you like, who do what you like and what you are interested in. Ask them, "Did you have a conventional education, or did you find out how to employ yourself in this way through another way?" A lot of people who live deeply creative lives never went to school, but for some of you, that may be the path.

Do not judge what you feel. Allow guidance to arise in you. What you also must remember is that you are where you are on your spiritual journey. People who have been in a deep state of surrender for many years consider the less conventional path as okay. Those who are on the more conventional track and just dipping their toes in this new way of being, this may be too much for them. They might need to go through some conventional education. Otherwise, they would be too uncomfortable and fearful, and that would not serve them.

So trust your guidance. Trust what you're interested in. Trust in your curiosity, and understand that to give freely and deeply of yourself requires that you are well acquainted with yourself, that you love yourself, and that you nurture yourself.

I am that one you know as Jesus, and we will see you again tomorrow.

LESSON 120

Review III: Part 10

Follow the complete lesson guidelines in your *ACIM* book.

You are blessed beings, indeed. I am that one you know as Jesus. I have to say that you are all doing beautifully.

A tremendous number of you right now feel very inspired by these teachings through this particular format. Of course, we inspired this being to do the lessons because you all need them. You all need to understand the power of your minds. You really need to understand that being distracted and led astray by the world does not serve you. It has wasted too much of your precious time already. We want you to go inside, align with love, and let go of your resentments and fears, all the things that do not feel good. What is left is your true self as God created you. You have merely dumped a lot of untrue ideas on top of that truth, and you know they are not true, because they make you fearful, angry, and judgmental.

So own that part of you deep within. When you go into your meditation time, repeat the phrase, "I am as God created me." Then feel your way into the consistent and perfect consciousness that you are. You have traveled through many bodies. You've had baby bodies, child bodies, and teenage bodies, and there you are in the background, observing. You have gone through many trials and tribulations, and there you are in the background, observing.

Just imagine that you let go of all the trials and tribulations and remain with that pure, clear, observant, wise self that you truly are, connected to all that is through love. It is a beautiful experience indeed, and you step closer to it each day.

I am that one you know as Jesus, and we will see you again tomorrow.

Forgiveness is the key to happiness.

Follow the complete lesson guidelines in your *ACIM* book.

You are blessed beings, indeed. I am that one you know as Jesus. Forgiveness is the most powerful process of this earthly plane on which you find yourself.

You think investing is powerful. You think education is powerful. You think exercise is. You think dieting is. You think earning money is. You think saving money is. However, forgiveness brings you the real treasures of peace of mind. What use is it to have a beautiful car, a slim body, and a nice house with a mind in turmoil that is full of resentment and holds a low frequency? You cannot maintain an abundant life. You will fail in your health. You will fail in your marriage. You will fail in your business, because you hold a frequency in your mind all the time that cannot bring you peace, abundance, joy, and a beautiful, comfortable life. It has to bring you pain, because it does not have a loving nature.

Forgiveness does not deny you anything. Yes, it denies the ego its battles. Yes, it denies the ego the satisfaction of saying hateful things and poisonous phrases, but that is all. It denies you nothing. It brings you peace, the greatest gift you can give yourself. Peace means the body functions at a high level. Peace means you have access to guidance that you cannot access in a troubled and tormented mind. Peace means you will live longer in a happier and more fulfilling way. Yes, you will be living in a state of separation, but this state the unforgiving mind brings forth is very painful. It is like living in hell.

Once you have a peaceful mind, you feel as if you have moved into the Garden of Eden. Everything seems brighter. Everything seems better. It is a beautiful experience. Yes, you are still in separation but not deep in separation. You are into a more loving form of separation. We call it the happy dream.

Sincerely do this exercise today. When you envision your enemy, do exactly as this lesson says. You lose nothing but pain. You lose nothing but poverty and scarcity. You lose nothing but disturbance in the mind.

I am that one you know as Jesus, and we will see you again tomorrow.

LESSON 122

Forgiveness offers everything I want.

Follow the complete lesson guidelines in your *ACIM* book.

You are blessed beings, indeed. I am that one you know as Jesus. You are not the "you" you think you are.

You have sharp edges — impatience, fear, anxiety, depression, control issues, judgments, and resistance — all kinds of things you perceive as aspects of you, but they are not. They are merely things not yet released from your consciousness. So they make you feel bad about who you are, but they are not who you are. They are mistakes. They are not sins; they are mistakes to be corrected. It is important for you to understand this. It is forgiving of you to see your faults as temporary errors. They do not belong to you. They are not your babies. When you see them as yourself, when you perceive them as yourself, you tend to hate yourself. You tend to say, "I am impatient. I am frustrated. I am fearful."

No, you are something far greater than that hidden beneath the layers of incorrect teaching and imperceptible distortions you are unaware of. You err, thinking that they are you. They are not you. They are the contaminants. They are the little bits of dirt in the water filtered out by forgiveness.

Do not come to these lessons thinking them laborious. Do not come to these lessons thinking of them as time wasters. They are the very opposite. They save time, and you will save many relationships. You will save many years of unnecessary suffering by practicing these lessons.

I am that one you know as Jesus, and we will see you again tomorrow.

LESSON 123

I thank my Father for his gifts to me.

Follow the complete lesson guidelines in your *ACIM* book.

You are blessed beings, indeed. I am that one you know as Jesus. It is important to give thanks and have gratitude for what you have.

It is one of the great sicknesses of your society to constantly seek one thing after another when you have a whole world of things. We see beings in your society with big houses full of nice furniture, technology, a couple of cars in the garage, a wardrobe full of clothes hardly worn, pets, children, and all kinds of investments and banking assets, and still they are looking for something else.

Stop, all of you. Stop, and ask yourselves, "What do I already have?" Consider not only the material possessions we described here. That is one of the great infections of the Western mind — to constantly seek more and more and wait for Christmas to buy gifts and get gifts. This is not the only thing, of course.

You have the most magnificent gifts from God: things like imagination and your desire to connect, love, and express yourself. This unique ability to express yourself — what a wonderful thing to be grateful for. You have ideas. You have inspirations. You have purpose. You have passion. Be grateful for these nonmaterial things. These truly nutritious things prevent you from needing the material things.

The training in your society constantly focuses you on the body, the next big house, the nicer car, or the upgraded telephone. They do that for a reason. It keeps you from going to the nonphysical things that truly satisfy — again, your creativity, ability to communicate, ability to love, and ability to be inspired have purpose, and they direct your life toward the good.

If you stop focusing on the material so much, you could even go on a purchasing diet for a few months. Perhaps you will say: "Seriously, when we look at everything we have, we do not need any more. Let us not buy anything for three months. Let us use what we have in gratitude." You will be astonished at how much money you save. You will also be astonished at how much better you feel because you do not constantly seek outside of you something to make you feel a little bit better for just a few minutes. You go deep inside to excavate and appreciate those truly wonderful God-given gifts: your intelligence, caring, love, interest, curiosity, creativity, and passion for life. All these things diminish when you focus on the material. But they increase when you focus on them with gratitude.

I am that one you know as Jesus. We will speak to you again tomorrow.

LESSON 124

Let me remember
I am one with God.

Follow the complete lesson guidelines
in your *ACIM* book.

You are blessed beings, indeed. I am
that one you know as Jesus. Is this not
the opposite of separation?

This is the prayer. This is the statement.
This mantra affirms you are not alone. You have
never been separated from that one you call God. You have always been
loved. You have always been cared for. You have merely been living in an
illusory world where you think you are alone.

These statements bring you peace because they are true. This is why
remembering that you are one with God takes away the fear and the frantic
nervousness of your world. When you focus your mind on the truth — that

you are one with God — you can see all these shenanigans going on in the world and say, "These are the ego's playgrounds. These are the ego's toys. I am really not that interested in them." You save so much energy by not believing the playground of the ego.

Now, many of you get worried when we ask you to focus this intently on God, because you feel as if you are going to lose the world. You feel as if you are going to lose your connection with people, your work, your home, your figurine collection, or whatever else you fear losing — your freedom, perhaps. This is the clue that these are your idols and are why you came into separation — to chase these things. When we ask you to focus your mind back Home on love — back Home on unity with God as your focus — you get nervous. You become afraid, and that is your clue. That is your helping explanation, if you will, that you came to this place because you wanted it. Many of you ask this question: "Why on Earth would I ask to come to this place? Why on Earth would I ask to come into separation?"

You know the answer when you get these feelings of not wanting to relinquish something, when you do not want to love, when you do not want to forgive. You see that you value the world. You value hatred. You value your judgments. This is how you constantly choose separation day after day, and those choices reinforce separation in your experience and prevent you from returning to your true Home, which is in God, in love.

This does not judge you. This merely lets you see what your mind is up to. The face of innocence that you give yourself says: "I am loving. I am kind. Why would I come to a place like this?" Well, when you are asked to relinquish this place, when you are asked to love, and when you are asked to forgive and do these lessons, you see another aspect of your mind hidden from you. The world will never ask you to turn to God. The world will never ask you to relinquish it. It calls to you, "Come here. Come here. Come to me. I will give you everything you want." So you wander into the world believing the siren song it sings to you.

Most of you have lived long enough and had enough stuff, relationships, and pain and suffering to know you lead yourselves astray. These words return you to the simple truth: You are at Home in God. You are one with God. God is with you. You are with your Creator at all times.

I am that one you know as Jesus, and we will speak to you tomorrow.

In quiet, I receive God's word today.

Follow the complete lesson guidelines
in your *ACIM* book.

You are blessed beings, indeed. I am that one you know as Jesus. It is so important for you to take quiet time. We do not mean with your feet up while reading a book or scrolling through your phone (which is what most of you do these days when you have a few moments), but really take some time. Put your hands on your lap, your feet on the ground, sit straight and calm, close your eyes, and just be still. Be still and listen, for most of your minds are so very busy that we cannot communicate with you easily.

That is one of the things that led to this being's ability to channel. She followed these lessons, and as she practiced forgiveness over many years, her mind became quieter and quieter. It is not totally silent; she has small trials and tribulations that she still works on. Her mind became quiet enough so that she could listen. She dedicated her life — and this was a most powerful prayer for her, not one to be copied lightly — to become a perfect communication device for God. She decided to do that because she knew nothing else interested her. She had come to a place in her life where the temptations of the world did not appeal to her any more, and that was not from a place of living like a monk. Oh no. She had tried many different things. She had done everything society had told her to do, and it had almost destroyed her until she came to a place where she decided to step out of the world. That was when the real transformation began.

Now, when we speak to all of you, we do not expect you to do what this being did. She has a particular assignment, and her history with me was a particular one. This work was something in her chart, as you say.

You all have the ability to endlessly and relentlessly chase idols in the world. Some of you have many things you have yet to do, and that is fine. You can do those things. You can chase those things. You can pursue those passions. It is all well and good.

Take this time each day to do these lessons because you clarify the reasons why you do what you do. You change the intention behind what you do. It will no longer be an ego-driven passion to make something of yourself, to be seen as special in some way. You remove the ego's tainting and come into true alignment with your purpose. It may, indeed, be the same purpose, but the intention and frequency behind it might be quite different. You won't seek aggrandizement. You seek because it truly comes from within your heart that you want to experience a particular thing. Take these quiet times, dear ones. They are important. They are so very restful, and you will enjoy them.

I am that one you know as Jesus, and we will speak to you again tomorrow.

LESSON 126

All that I give is given to me.

Follow the complete lesson guidelines
in your *ACIM* book.

You are blessed beings, indeed. I am that one you know as Jesus. This is an upside-down world, is it not?

Not everything that you have been taught is good for you is good for you. Everything that tastes good is bad for you. One of the greatest lessons of all is that when you project things — when you put things outside of your mind, seemingly through the practice of projection — they have not really left your mind. So the characters in your play that you interact with, the people that you call enemies and have resentments against, they trigger your inner transformation. They are your salvation.

Why? Because they are not separate from you. They are a part of your mind that looks as if it is outside of you. So when you attack them, you attack yourself. When you give them forgiveness, you forgive yourself. It is a difficult concept for those of you not taught deeply about the laws of reality that exist in *A Course in Miracles*. If you do these lessons but do not study the text, you become more confused as we go along. We want to emphasize this at this time because the lessons and the transformation of mind that the lessons bring you are based on the theoretical understanding of the text. There are going to be shifts and changes in your consciousness that, if you do not understand what they are based on, might frighten you.

165

Instead of gratitude for the transformations that take place in your consciousness, you might feel fear, because you do not understand the principles these lessons are based on. For those of you who have not yet bought the book, today is the day that you need to buy the book and follow along with the text for these lessons. Today is the day you need to begin reading the text even if you don't understand it. The sophisticated language is designed to transform the inner layers of your consciousness, both your conscious mind and the subconscious aspects you are completely unaware of until they are triggered and come up into your conscious mind.

For example, perhaps you have unresolved issues with your mother. You live far away from her, and you don't talk to her anymore. You might meet people who remind you of the unforgiven aspects of your thoughts, beliefs, and ideas about her. It might be somebody you work with that has a similar personality type or speaks in the same kind of language or values the same sorts of things. Your unforgiveness of your mother will be brought to the surface of your conscious mind for your assessment. If you do not understand what's going on here, you will dislike the person who has triggered these old and unforgiven aspects. You think you do not like them and that you should stay away from them. On the contrary!

This person is sent to you as a gift to bring up your unresolved and unforgiven aspects concerning your mother. This is a very important principle for you to understand. When people bring up in you pain that already exists in your mind, it is not your job to attack them but to give thanks. It is your job to forgive them so that you also may receive the gift of forgiveness and some of the dark shadows lurking in your unconscious mind are revealed.

These principles are important for you to understand at this stage because you begin to experience the deeper, darker realms of your consciousness as we move further into these lessons. So we want you to really understand that, and as we said for those of you who do not follow along with the text, we would like you to do that now. So purchase your book. Ask to borrow a friend's copy if it is not being used (but we recommend you have your own text).

At this point, do not belabor which text you buy. The lessons are all the same. If there are slight variations, it does not matter. A word "here" and a word "there" does not matter. Your forgiveness practice transforms everything. It is not the word on the typed page. There are many discussions about the different texts. We want you to understand there are differences. Editing has happened in these texts. Just choose the book that comes your way, the one that appeals to you. You want to do the lessons.

For those who have not yet begun to study the text, now is the time. You do not want to get left behind. You do not want to become confused because you do not understand the principles on which these most powerful transformative lessons are based.

I am that one you know as Jesus, and we will see you again tomorrow.

LESSON 127

There is no love but God's.

Follow the complete lesson guidelines in your *ACIM* book.

You are blessed beings, indeed. I am that one you know as Jesus. This truth will clarify the heart and mind of all who attempt to believe it. We understand that you have many different kinds of love that you believe exist on this Earth plane — the love of a mother for a child, the love of a musician for music, the love of a lover for the other person — but we want you to understand that the essence of true love never changes.

The world in which you live is based on separation. That is the foundation of this place. It is the default setting of this place. You come from love, and that is why you do not feel like you belong in this world. That is why you view the world and know something has gone terribly wrong. You are made from love, for love, and by love, and your guidance system is connected to that invisible Home.

It is invisible to you now because you live in the world and you value the world. You see that the more you witness death and the things happening on your planet at this time, the worse you feel unless you focus on God's love. God's love is eternal. God's love is timeless. God's love is that which is in you that never changes. God's love gave you the opportunity to come into separation because you wanted to. It seems insane. As you look around yourself at this world, you know that to be true. This is a crazy place you find yourself in, but do you not want aspects of it? Do you not lust after aspects of it? Do you not chase after aspects of it?

That is what you must look at here, and ask yourself, "Is that what I want to spend my life doing? Do I want to spend my life chasing after the idols as the marketing systems of Earth have trained me to do, that the education system of Earth has trained me into, or would I rather chase after the trip Home? I do not mean in death; death does not bring me relief. I mean in life — a pure, true life aligned with love." That is what brings you relief, and that is timeless. You existed before this body was born, and you will continue after this body passes away from its usefulness. That is love: the undivided, unconquerable, and unchangeable connection that you have with the Divine.

I am that one you know as Jesus, and we will speak to you tomorrow.

LESSON 128

The world I see holds nothing that I want.

Follow the complete lesson guidelines in your *ACIM* book.

You are blessed beings, indeed. I am that one you know as Jesus. This seems like insanity, does it not? When you think about all the investments you make in the world — your bank accounts, your body, your marriages, your relationships, your children, your pottery collection, your art collection, the car, the holiday you want in the winter — they are all seemingly high-value items to you. You think, "I do not want to give all these things up. Why should I give all these things up?"

This is an error in the beliefs about what happens to you in salvation, such as when you focus on the higher frequencies, when you focus on love and forgiveness, or when you stop trying to find peace in the world. That is a foolish task. You can see that it is a foolish task when you look at the world and see how people invest in their bodies only to have them hurt in car accidents or taken by disease or death. You can see that people put all their investment in a relationship or house, perhaps, and lose it to bankruptcy or divorce. You see people put their hearts and souls into transitory things that do not last. This is what causes such intense pain and suffering.

When you put your faith in God, when you put your faith in the practices of this text and these lessons, when you begin to forgive and you attain a level of inner peace, these things outside of you are not required to make you happy. You find yourself walking lightly through the day. You find yourself happy with the simplest of things — planting some flowers in your garden or talking to a friend. You see that you are not in turmoil and trouble all the time. You are not upset all the time; in fact, you enjoy your life more each day as you practice your forgiveness lessons and do the exercises recommended in this text.

You see that the world is not the place to go to get salvation. It is inside; that is the place to go to get salvation. It is through your practice of loving kindness and forgiveness that you feel a peace that passes all understanding. You feel a connection to all beings, because you dismantle and dissolve the hateful ideas and beliefs in your mind. You realize that all the dissatisfactions you had and all the needs those dissatisfactions generate in your mind disappear. You find you need less, and you are happy about it. You do not feel deprived at all. But the ego feels deprived.

We want you to understand that as you go through your ascension process, you feel less and less owned by the world. You view the loud and angry conversations of politicians and see them for what they are. There have been hundreds of years of angry conversations between politicians. Why would you get upset about them? Why would you let them drag you down?

The material things in your life come and go. The body changes, but your connection to the Divine is unchangeable, unsinkable, and unbreakable. You must accept that is so, and you must focus on that connection to feel its true worth.

I am that one you know as Jesus, and we will see you again tomorrow.

LESSON 129

Beyond this world, there is a world I want.

Follow the complete lesson guidelines in your *ACIM* book.

You are blessed beings, indeed. I am that one you know as Jesus. This time and place on your planet is becoming more and more challenging.

169

You all feel it. You all feel the wavering and wobbling house of cards this world has become for many of you. Perhaps it is a job you go to every day thinking, "My goodness, how am I going to continue going to this place for another twenty or thirty years?" and your heart breaks at the very thought of it. When stuck in traffic, perhaps, commuting to a job, you feel frustration when you drive past green fields and trees and birds sitting on fences, and you think, "Oh, to sit under that tree for a little while would be so restful. I am tired." When you have a family that has difficulties, your children are on their devices, your partner is out somewhere and you know not where, and you feel that the dream you have been sold was a lie. Many of you are coming to these places. Some of it is through sickness, exhaustion, disillusionment, or just plain unhappiness. You feel increased distortion that becomes less and less tolerable.

This lesson is for you. This lesson lets you know you do not have to participate in the world in which you have been taught. You have been taught deeply, and you have been taught long. You must accept what has been done to you. When you accept what has been done to you, you must do something about it. That is why we want you to stick with these lessons. Many of you struggle a little bit with the longer periods of time dedicated to these lessons each day. Some of you feel as if they add a burden to your already-burdened lives by having to do this work. But we tell you, if you continue with these lessons, things get easier. You see where you become involved in dramas that you don't need to become involved in. You see where you make unloving choices for yourself. You see more clearly what you are up to and how you are influenced by those around you to compromise yourself.

Mostly it is through the conditioned trainings you have been subjected to. This is why these lessons are so important. This is you reclaiming your sovereignty. This is you reclaiming your mind and evicting from your mind every unloving thing implanted there, everything fearful and materialistic implanted by your ruling teachers.

We love you very much on this side, and there are many of us here helping you. You walk with great teachers as you do these lessons. There is not just me but many other beings who assist the shift in consciousness on your planet. We deeply encourage you to keep on with these lessons and aim yourself toward a life of peace, joy, happiness, and love. It is possible for you. It is possible for everyone.

I am that one you know as Jesus, and we will speak to you tomorrow.

It is impossible to see two worlds.

Follow the complete lesson guidelines
in your *ACIM* book.

You are blessed beings, indeed. I am that one you know as Jesus. It is important for you to truly grasp the magnificent power of your mind. Your mind decides between love and fear every second of every day. If you suffer, then you have chosen fear. If you are happy, content, relaxed, and inspired, then you have chosen love. If you find yourself deep in suffering, then it is important for you (even if you don't know how you're doing it) to accept the possibility that you are very fearful and that you are "mis-choosing" and miscreating throughout your day. That is why you feel anxious. That is why you feel angry. That is why you feel fearful. That is why you feel unloved or unfairly treated.

These are all clues. These negative feelings are your guidance system. Remember, your guidance system is your umbilical cord to the mothership — Home, God, love, or whatever you want to call it — and it operates at a frequency of love connected to divine truth. You are an extension of that divine truth, and your natural frequency, when you are connected to Source, is love. That is what your guidance system is. It's a loving beacon for you to know when you are in accord with your higher purpose, your truth, and to know when you are in alignment with God's will for you. You feel good. You feel content. You do not always feel exactly happy, but you feel as if you are on the right track.

When you are off track, lost in the weeds or taking a detour away from your purpose and God's will for you, you feel awful. That awful feeling can come in simply by having a hateful thought about yourself: "I'm unsuccessful." If you have that thought, you immediately get feedback from your guidance system saying, "No. That is incorrect." You get negative feedback and a negative emotional response. If you say to yourself, "I'm doing really quite well. I'm not exactly where I'd like to be, but I'm heading in the right direction," then you feel relief. That feeling of relief is you heading toward your purpose.

Now, relief is not the result of this work. You also find peace and joy and happiness. Relief means you have stepped up from the suffering you previously felt even a moment before. That is what we want you to grasp. We want you to truly grasp that when you are in alignment with love, you are in spirit, and that means you are in the love realm. That is your purpose, God's will for you here, what you have come here to learn, and what you have come here to express.

It can be anything. It doesn't have to be a big fancy career. It can be growing seedlings in your greenhouse. It can be reading a book to your child. It can be going to the gym and having a satisfying workout session. It can be cooking a beautiful meal. It could even be all those things at different points in the day, because that is what you're inspired to do. You listen to your guidance system and your inspiration. When you are in the fear realm, there is resistance. There is complaining. There is sickness. There is a lack of joy. There is stress. There is judgment. There is fear. There are tears of sadness.

Now, we do not try to make you inhuman. We do not want you *not* to feel what you are feeling, but you must understand that if you are in a regular state of feeling off, then the decisions you make come from that fear-thought system. The ego's thought system is a complete thought system. The Holy Spirit's thought system is a complete thought system. You sit right between those two, and you must decide: Are you going to step left into fear, or are you going to step right into love?

These are very small decisions sometimes. Maybe you get off the bus a block early to get a little exercise. That's a loving thing to do for your body. If you feel you need to get a little movement because you're feeling stiff, hopping off the bus a block early to walk in the morning light is a loving act for yourself. You are saying, "Hmm, my body hasn't moved enough. I'm going to support it." These tiny decisions throughout the day build on each other. As you see the importance of these thousands of tiny decisions, you realize how you can change the trajectory of your life one choice at a time by choosing love over fear. That is what a miracle is. Where there used to be fear, you now choose love.

We encourage you to really get down into that guidance system and ask yourself, "Where am I feeling bad on a consistent basis, and why am I feeling bad on a consistent basis? What unloving thing am I doing, thinking, eating, saying, and believing about myself or another that causes this negative feedback?" That is your homework for today, because you want to choose love. That means you must become aware of where you choose fear over love. You must now resolve to make a new decision to choose again, to choose love.

I am that one you know as Jesus, and we will see you again tomorrow.

No one can fail who seeks to reach the truth.

Follow the complete lesson guidelines in your *ACIM* book.

You are blessed beings, indeed. I am that one you know as Jesus. The truth is the truth, and it always will be the truth.

All the variations, arguments, wars, battles, disagreements, and divorces that you go through on this plane are illusory. They are arguments about duality. They are arguments about hot and cold, rich and poor, faithful and faithless, or untrue and true. They are all games that you play in the horizontal zone rather than the vertical zone.

You have two choices: to go up, straight up to the Godhead or to go horizontally and get your power, your plays, in the ego's world. Those are your choices. Love is the direct route Home through your emotional guidance system, which tells you when you are off or on track. That is what love does. It is honest. It is clear and true and forever there for you to call on. So your guidance system is loving.

Many of you do not feel it is loving, because you are so far off your path that you stay in a constant state of pain and suffering. You believe God does not love you. What you have is an unrelenting and ever-present indicator of whether you are on track with God's will for you, which is your will for you. When you understand that God's will for you is your will for you and that God's will for you is shown to you through happiness, then everything begins to change. You realize that the idea of sacrifice is pointless. God would never ask you to sacrifice, because it does not bring you joy.

There are great distortions in the ego-mind. There are many thousands of years of untrue ideas fed and nurtured and told as truth. When the lie is told as truth, the truth — that God wants you to be happy, that you are destined to be happy, that it is your birthright to be happy — seems a lie.

You came here to chase your idols, it is true. Some of those idols can be beautiful. Music, art, gardening, and raising children, these can bring you joy. You do not have to suffer. But you must train your mind. You must own your mind. You must have a sovereign aspect to yourself not easily overcome by the outside world. You must be in the world but not of the world (you have heard this phrase before). That is what we seek here. We seek to bring you to a place where you go to your connection with the Divine (where you pose your questions) and your energy in that.

Do not seek it from others. Do not demand others to be anything other than what they need to be on their journeys. Keep your attention on your life. Keep your attention on those things you wish to have more of and that you wish to nurture and grow. This does not mean that you ignore people. It means you understand the laws of creation, that you do not need to suffer. Sacrifice builds resentment, and God wants you to be happy.

I am that one you know as Jesus, and we will see you again tomorrow.

LESSON 132

I loose the world from all I thought it was.

Follow the complete lesson guidelines in your *ACIM* book.

You are blessed beings, indeed. I am that one you know as Jesus. This is the most challenging principle behind these teachings (is it not?), that the world is not real.

If God is real, the world is not real. You must understand that this is why people look at religion and say, "Well, if there is a God, then I do not want that God; look at the world. Look at what is here. Look at the hungry children. Look at how religious institutions misuse their power. Look at the monetary system. Look at the environment. Look at the industries polluting this gorgeous planet. If there is a God and God is all-powerful, then God does not exist in this place, or this God is insane."

That is why people leave religions. They realize that as time goes by, this place becomes crazier and crazier. Why is it becoming crazier? Well, you all act out of accord with your natural selves. You move into urban environments. You live in little boxes surrounded by electricity. You avoid nature. You do all kinds of detrimental things to your natural state of being. You can see that other natural creatures, when humans do not imprison them, have an ease and way about them that is peaceful, even though they end in death or a predator may eat them. While they are alive and free, they have a lovely time of it.

You have been riddled with distortions, intentionally so, and that is why you have strayed so far from your natural self. That is why we keep telling you to do things like eat healthily if you can. This is why we tell you to get out in daylight and moonlight and starlight. Get out in nature, because it recalibrates you a little bit each day. It recalibrates you back to a more natural place.

This world, even in a healthy state, is a world of separation. You create it together, but you are not responsible for anybody else's thoughts. You are only responsible for your own mind, and it is your mind that you must see that causes you suffering, makes up stories, creates dramas, and causes all kinds of shenanigans in your day. If you are present, purely present, not in the past or in the future, and not gossiping about anybody, then you see that most of the time you are fine. Nothing bad happens.

The power of now is the most powerful place in the universe. It is the place where you decide to choose love or fear. Are you going to drift off into the fantasies in your mind about what others say or what terrible future awaits you or what sickness may be growing in your body; or are you going to be present in your body, calm and peaceful, and exist in the place you are meant to be? This is the challenge that the course sets up for you. It is important for you to understand that you create your suffering by living in an illusory world.

I am that one you know as Jesus, and we will see you again tomorrow.

LESSON 133

I will not value what is valueless.

Follow the complete lesson guidelines in your *ACIM* book.

You are blessed beings, indeed. I am that one you know as Jesus. This is a very difficult thing for those of you raised in this materialistic culture.

You have been deeply indoctrinated into valuing the body, overvaluing the body, and hating the body. This is materialistically focused, and you have been tempted, trained, and cajoled to spend all your time trying to gather material possessions around you.

The unhealthiest version of that, of course, are the billionaires who have far more than they need and continue to take from others. Regardless of the methods they use, they do not need any more. Yet they feel that if they give away what they have, they will lose when in fact they will gain.

The other example of the materialistic person gone wild is the hoarder. In spiritual terms, many of you in North America are hoarders. You have houses filled with art you don't particularly like. You have cupboards filled with old objects. You constantly buy new clothes when you have a wardrobe of things you barely wear. You build your libraries of shoes, cars, or whatever else you have in your homes.

We would like all of you, in this moment, when you have finished this particular recording, to take an inventory of your homes. How much do you value the material/physical as a demonstration of your power, influence, and success? If you have far more than you need — you know straight away when you look around your home whether it is full of things you barely use — then you prefer to accept that you have been trained into materialism. To truly expand your consciousness, you must shift your focus from the physical/material world. That is a world of entropy and death (the body, of course, dies at some point).

We want you to understand that it is not until you realize what you have become that you can change it. If you are in denial about your materialism, then you don't see it and you cannot change it. Take inventory of your home, closets, and kitchen, and see the masses of stuff you own. You might say, "Ah. This is what I'm focusing on. This is why I have been unhappy, because I have sought happiness in material objects. Clearly, they don't satisfy me, but I keep buying them."

This is not about consumerism or us getting you to stop consuming. It is about making you aware of where you focus. Your focus determines how happy you are. Your focus determines what grows and what develops.

I am that one you know as Jesus, and we will see you again tomorrow.

Let me perceive forgiveness as it is.

Follow the complete lesson guidelines in your *ACIM* book.

You are blessed beings, indeed. I am that one you know as Jesus. It is so important for you to realize that your judgments, hatreds, and attacks, even though you think they are justified, put you in hell.

You suffer because of the constant litany of decisions you make thinking that things should be other than the way they are. It is simply arguing with reality. When you begin to love what is regardless of whether you understand it or not — when you see something happening in the world or see somebody behave in a way you think inappropriate — how about you start saying: "I actually don't know everything, and I don't know what those people's paths are. I don't know what role they're playing in this grand design. I will just observe with forgiving eyes for a little while. I will not be sucked in by the media. I will not be sucked in by my friend's repetition of the media. I will simply say 'I don't know.'"

That is forgiving, when you step back from attack and gossip as well as pretending you know why people do things and how they should be punished. You are, in fact, playing God when you do that. When you realize you play God and you have no qualifications to do so, becoming a passer-by with all of the dramas of this life becomes easier and easier. What seems like a good idea in January turns out to be a bad idea in June. What seems to be a bad idea in June turns out to be a good idea in September.

If you are patient and allow life to play out without leaping and jumping to ignorant conclusions, you will find that you suffer less. You realize: "Ah, my first instinct was to get in there and say something, but now, a week later, I hear the other side of the story." For example, "I see that the problem resolved itself and that everybody within the problem had needed a stimulus to begin communication or they had needed a challenge to get themselves over a little hump." What seemed to be bad was not bad. Had you become involved in it and participated in the drama, perhaps you would have derailed a beneficial situation. Do not be so sure that you know what everyone is up to.

We suggest you pay attention to what you are up to. See the world with forgiving eyes. Know that it has its own energies. Sometimes people need to play out their own dramas, and many of them are not yours. How about focusing on your life? Are you focusing enough on your life, or are you involved with things across the other side of the planet and other people's business? Are you neglecting your life? Are you projecting all your energies on situations, people, places, and things that really have nothing to do with you?

Bring back your focus. Call back those little tendrils of your awareness and employ them in doing good for your life. Invest in your life, cultivate your mind, and educate yourself about these spiritual truths and spiritual principles. Become loving in your life.

Step back from judging everybody. That is the practice of forgiveness.

I am that one you know as Jesus, and we will see you again tomorrow.

LESSON 135

If I defend myself, I am attacked.

Follow the complete lesson guidelines in your *ACIM* book.

You are blessed beings, indeed. I am that one you know as Jesus. Defensiveness is one of the things that ages you and makes you very ill, because you are in a constant state of preparation for war. That means you function in that treacherous fight-or-flight mode, where you are quick to attack or quick to separate. That is the ego's defense mechanism when danger is present.

When you remember that the ego's purpose is to keep your body alive above all else, this makes sense. If you believe there is danger out there and that you function in the horizontal ego world, then you have stepped away from miracle-minded thinking. You begin to act as if an attack is imminent. That is a very stressful situation for the body. You have good sciences now.

They measure these stress hormones and things that cause you to behave in an animalistic way. You can actually measure the ego's playground these days.

So this is an important thing for you to remember. When you become defensive, you are already in fight-or-flight mode. You will attack, or you will separate to attack later. You do it by defending. What are you defending? This is the question that you must ask yourself as you study this particular passage, "What am I defending? Am I defending my body because I think I will die? Am I defending my reputation? Am I defending my money?"

What do you defend? What do you place above peace? What do you place above love? That is what you give up when you take a defensive stance. You choose the horizontal ego's battleground to play in, and you forget that forgiveness, openness, courage, and defenselessness bring to you an experience very different from the fight-or-flight scenario of the ego. You give up many beautiful things when you prepare for war, because you lower your frequency significantly, and you are then down in the battleground.

Perhaps somebody offends you. Before *A Course in Miracles*, you would have attacked back. You would have protected yourself. How about you open up to what that person has to say? If they have accused you of something, maybe being harsh with your words, instead of leaping to defend yourself, listen to what they have to say. Open your mind and your heart, and then say, "Please tell me what you perceive. I'm very curious about how you see me and how I act around you."

This is a moment for learning. This is a moment for growth. This is a moment for forgiveness, for that is what you are doing. You act in a forgiving way when you set aside your defenses and ask with curiosity, "What do you want to tell me? What do you want to show me?" Perhaps they tell you something you need to hear. Perhaps they show you something valuable. If you are defensive and shut them down, which increases separation and strengthens the ego-mind, then you never hear the gem they may have to offer you.

Watch your defensiveness. When you feel that surge of adrenaline, that fear come up when somebody offends you or threatens you in some way (perhaps only subtly by implied words), go inside immediately and ask yourself: "What am I afraid of here? What am I defending here? What is so valuable to me that I am willing to relinquish my peace over it?"

I am that one you know as Jesus, and we will see you again tomorrow.

Sickness is a defense against the truth.

Follow the complete lesson guidelines
in your *ACIM* book.

You are blessed beings, indeed. I am
that one you know as Jesus. This, of
course, is the ego's greatest argument.
When you sicken and your body seems to
betray you, the ego might say to you, "See, you
are abandoned. God does not love you. God would not let this happen to
you if he loved you. You are being punished by God." Your own distortions are projected on God. You become the victim, and God becomes the
perpetrator.

This is what the ego wishes. You must remember that in the origins of
your separation experience, you chose to separate from oneness. In that
separation, you became so overwhelmed with guilt and fear that you created this world. In an effort to prevent God from punishing you for what
you perceive to be the ultimate betrayal, you begin to punish yourself. You
become guilty and you become sick, because you do not believe that you
are, indeed, the holy child of God. You believe you are a sinner, and you
believe you have failed by coming to this place. You made your mind forget
it, but you have not forgotten the guilt and the shame and the fear that you
felt on that initial separation and the belief that God would punish you. So
you leap in first to punish yourself.

Now, these are all esoteric ideas. Most of you say, "I just got a cold. I
don't know what you're talking about." These are the unconscious motivations for your sicknesses. Most of you become sick to achieve something
that you do not believe you can achieve in health and love and life. You
are indoctrinated into sickness. You are indoctrinated with such ideas as
vaccinations. This means you have a cultural belief that unless a human
intervenes, you become sick and potentially die. This belief is, in fact, the
unconscious guilt you carry from the original separation.

Your mind is far more complex than you know. It has more information
in it than you know — multiple lifetimes and a plethora of details that have
been collected every second of every day since you were born into this body.

It is a machine that works very hard to keep you separate from the truth. "Why?" you ask. "Why is it doing this?" Your mind does this because the truth is overwhelming. Truth is death to the ego. So in choosing to come into separation in that original decision (that somewhat foolish decision), you miscreated an entire world and a belief system that says, "Love is dangerous. God is going to punish me. I must keep away from love, for God is the ultimate expression of love." That is why you have so many issues with loving people and loving yourself on this planet. You literally chose to enter a realm of not-love.

Some of you will say, "Oh, well, I see love all around me. My friends love me and my mother loves me and my children love me." But we will ask you, how conditional is that? What do you have to do to get that love? How many hoops do you have to jump through before somebody decides he or she does not love you?

We want you not to be disillusioned with the world. We want you to understand that you rise above the world. You become a beacon of light for those deeply immersed in the 3D scheme/paradigm that you call life. You step above the logical. You step above the battlefield. You align with higher principles that do not exist on Earth in this time and place.

You could be called a Pollyanna. You could be called delusional. You could be called somebody who looks at the world through rose-colored glasses, because you are not getting all upset and twisted out of shape. You understand the bigger picture. You understand that through your forgiveness practice and the understanding that guilt, sacrifice, and suffering are not necessary, you take one step at a time — one forgiveness practice at a time, one day at a time — up that ladder toward the light and love that is your natural Home.

You have frightened yourselves. You have taken a deep detour into fear, and you are afraid to go Home because you think the Father will punish you. The story of the prodigal son tells you the Father is only happy that you come Home. There is no sin. There is no punishment. You are welcomed with open arms in absolute and unconditional love.

I am that one you know as Jesus, and we will see you again tomorrow.

When I am healed, I am not healed alone.

Follow the complete lesson guidelines in your *ACIM* book.

You are blessed beings, indeed. I am that one you know as Jesus. Healing is one of the great mysteries of your world.

You have been indoctrinated into the physical/material beliefs of your scientific method. So healing in the way it transpires when you practice forgiveness does not make sense, because in Western medical tradition, the body rules. The body causes dysfunction. It seems to go randomly wrong for no reason and try to kill you. That is the basis for Western medicine, that the body is the be all and end all. This is why they don't ask you about your feelings. This is why doctors don't ask you about your diet. They go to the effect, which is the body, as the result and deem it the cause.

When you look at things correctly, the mind is the cause and the body is the effect. To heal the body, you must heal the mind. It is that simple. That is the truth. That is how it goes. This is why, in Western medicine, you merely suppress symptoms with pharmaceutical drugs. You have seen the consequences of it over the past few decades. You have seen a society get sicker and sicker, and the side effects of those drugs have nothing to do with health or healing. You literally poison your bodies.

Healing, as described here in this particular lesson, is something that comes from a transformation of mind. When you transform your mind, you transform the projector that produces everything you experience as your life. That is really what a miracle is. It is a change of mind. It's a choice to choose love instead of fear that precipitates a seemingly random event outside of you to shift and change. That can be your body and also the bodies of other beings. It can be relationships. It can be all kinds of things outside your immediate realm of effect, because you are all connected.

The Western medicine model says you are all separate. So it is, in fact, a device of the ego's thought system. It insists that what you do is completely isolated from everybody else and that the body is the creator. That is a materialistic belief, a low 3D belief. Your pharmaceutical industry causes so many deaths because it has nothing to do with healing.

True healing always comes from the mind. You must decide that you do not want what sickness offers you. You do not want the isolation that sickness offers you. You do not want the pain that sickness offers you. You must become aware that those are things you want when you get sick. Those are unconscious desires you must address.

Now, most of you would say, "Oh no. Those are not things I want. When I got food poisoning in Mexico, I did not want to suffer." But that it is a match to some of your beliefs about yourself. It is a match to self-loathing. It is a match to fear. It is a match to self-mutilation or self-abuse in whatever way you participate in it. You find a match somewhere in your frequency.

If you look in the mirror and say that you hate yourself, that is a very low frequency. It is the ultimate act of aggression, the ultimate blasphemy, if you will. Many of you in the West believe that you are unlovable or unattractive and, therefore, valueless. When you have these kinds of thoughts, you create a sick body. You create something to punish yourself with, because you do not love yourself. Know that when you heal yourself, you give a great gift to the world and your brothers and sisters, not just you.

I am that one you know as Jesus, and we will see you again tomorrow.

LESSON 138

Heaven is the decision I must make.

Follow the complete lesson guidelines in your *ACIM* book.

You are blessed beings, indeed. I am that one you know as Jesus. Heaven can be here on Earth in that sense. The suffering, deep pain, guilt, and shame you feel on this plane in these lower 3D realms is completely unnecessary.

Even though you are in separation when you have the happy dream (you have not yet transferred yourself over to true reality, which is your reunion with All That Is), you have a much better time of it when you train to perceive clearly and see rightly. When you see with the right side of your consciousness, the loving side of your consciousness, the suffering, pain, guilt, shame, and sickness begin to fade away. When you decide with the ego's thought system, you are in pain. When in pain, it is hard to imagine that you could be in a sort of heaven on this Earth plane, but you can once you raise your frequency through the practice of forgiveness as described in the text.

Once you have decided to choose love as often as you can during the day by respecting and giving to yourself and others (remember, you have been taught to put others before you), it is important for you to invest in your own mental clarification in these early days. This often goes against your internal rules.

We seem to be contradicting ourselves here, but we are not. What you give to another, you give to yourself. If you do not have a clarified mind and do not understand this principle, then it is impossible for you to give, because you do not believe it. You do not trust in that process. This year that you spend with us is the process of clarification most of you need to realize that everything you've been taught is upside down and that to give is to receive.

This is a training program, and not all these lessons make sense to you. Not all these lessons feel right to you, because they are not yet the predominant frequency of your thought system. You are still deeply immersed in the ego's thought system at this stage of the game. As you learn to choose differently, you will feel different. You will see your choices — your internal thought choices, your value system — change. Therefore, you suffer less. This is the most wonderful point, because you realize that if in 138 days, you have accomplished a significant change that you actually feel and is measurable, what will happen in a year? What will happen in three years?

Yes, your work continues after 365 lessons. Then you will practice forgiveness and use these lessons as your thoughts. You'll ruminate less on things and experience these kinds of statements as your internal dialogue. When the lessons from *A Course in Miracles* as become your internal dialogue (rather than having the endless ruminations of fear, judgment, hate, and guilt that brought you to this place), you lead a different life, indeed. It seems as if heaven is on Earth compared to the deep suffering you used to experience.

I am that one you know as Jesus, and we will see you again tomorrow.

I will accept atonement for myself.

Follow the complete lesson guidelines in your *ACIM* book.

You are blessed beings, indeed. I am that one you know as Jesus. The atonement brings you back into a united state of mind. It is this that we seek with this lesson, that you do not constantly argue with yourself or constantly judge yourself.

Think about it. If you do or don't do something and then judge yourself for it, you demonstrate a split mind. Who decided to do it or not do it, and who decided to judge it or not judge it? There are seemingly two beings inside your consciousness, and this causes a lot of your stress, anxiety, and fear, for a mind divided cannot rest. That is where most of you in the West find yourselves — those racing minds, the inability to sleep, waking up in the middle of the night, and worrying, worrying, worrying because you see yourself as separate from God.

You see your own mind, even, as separated from itself, because you argue with yourself all the time. A peaceful mind is a reintegrated mind that has accepted the atonement for itself through accepting All That Is, accepting itself as a sacred being as a holy child of God, and paying attention to the experiences it has with its whole mind — not judging and leaping around from pillar to post and bumping itself in the head while doing so. This is what you do when you feel anxious and create fear in your mind. You argue with yourself. You judge yourself. You hate yourself. You loathe yourself.

A perfect demonstration of self-loathing is constant dieting to improve the body to make yourself acceptable to others, where you demean yourself by only seeing yourself as a body and not developing your other beautiful skills of intelligence, creativity, compassion, and kindness. You want to become something so beautiful, radiant, and glorious that everyone loves you, but you do not need to sacrifice yourself and starve your bodies to achieve that. Some of you seek after fame and fortune or large sums of money to make yourselves acceptable to other people when, in fact, the truth is you don't accept yourselves.

Those are the minds that are in pain. Those are the minds that are suffering and need this work. If you are in pain and suffering and you witness some slight shifts and changes in your experience as you do these lessons, we ask you to stick with them and continue this journey with us.

I am that one you know as Jesus, and we will see you again tomorrow.

LESSON 140

Only salvation can be said to cure.

Follow the complete lesson guidelines in your *ACIM* book.

You are blessed beings, indeed. I am that one you know as Jesus. Salvation is an alignment with love, a reunification of your mind — a separation from fear in a sense. Once you choose love, then the frequency of your entire body changes because the body is generated by your consciousness. It is not a thing that exists without you.

Again, we go back to the Western medical model that says the body generates you. This world is upside down; *you* have generated your body. The transformation of mind that salvation offers — which means the true and absolute alignment with truth — changes your body to such a degree that you do not recognize it. In fact, it stops aging. In the end, you overcome death, just as I did. There are those of you who do not believe you can do that, but it is the truth. All the things that I have done, you can do too.

I am merely further along the road to love than you are. I've had many incarnations that prepared me for my incarnation on Earth, the last one in which I needed to have a body. I do not need to have a body now, but I can manufacture a body at will, because I have mastered the physical/material world through the practice of love and forgiveness. That is what you do here. You are merely in the early, early stages.

So hold fast, dear ones. Know that the truth is true. It always will be true. You do not need to battle it. You do not need to worry about where it is. It is contained within you, and your truth — your guidance system — is your way Home. It is the map you have been given. You are not allowed to come here abandoned and without help. You were given a map Home, and it is the map of love.

Through forgiveness, you align yourself with that frequency, which is the frequency of the mothership (God/All That Is). That frequency is love. The more you align with that frequency, the better you feel. The better you feel is how you know you are closer to that home that is your forever place.

When you return Home, you have more lessons. There will be opportunities for expansion beyond your ability to comprehend right now. We know that some of you are very curious about what happens to you once you make that ascension process, but we really don't want you to think about that right now. We want you to stay focused where you are; that is where the work must be done now.

Some of you have an obsession about past-life incarnations. If a past-life memory, imagery, or vision comes to you, do not go back there and try to live through that life. Rather, take the information you are given to see whether you can use it beneficially in this life. It is all about this incarnation now. It is all about this power of now, the holy instant. This is the only place you can change anything. It is the only place you can choose love over fear. It is the only place.

It doesn't matter what you've been through in the past. It doesn't matter what you think will happen to you in the future. That is merely a dream inside a dream. This moment is the moment you want to be in. Be present. Be aware. Be loving to yourself and others, and you will do well.

I am that one you know as Jesus, and we will see you again tomorrow.

LESSON 141

Review IV: Part 1
My mind holds only what I think with God.

Follow the complete lesson guidelines in your *ACIM* book.

You are blessed beings, indeed. I am that one you know as Jesus. It is very hard for the mind trained in your society to believe that forgiveness brings you everything you want. Do you not seek everything in this world to make you happy? Do you not seek everything in this world to bring you excitement or peace or joy?

Yes, you do. You think that material things bring it to you and for you, but this is not true. Many of you who have lived on this Earth plane for a few decades have come to see that no matter which road you take in the earthly realm, it always seems to end up a little disappointing, sometimes tremendously disappointing.

We want you to really understand the power of forgiveness. Forgiveness, as described in *A Course in Miracles*, is your alignment with the truth — the knowing — that anything occurring outside of you is generated from within you. To attack what occurs outside of you is to attack your own mind, which generates fear and anxiety. You completely miss your ability to evolve out of this dualistic paradigm. That is what forgiveness does for you when practiced in the way *A Course in Miracles* instructs.

In your forgiveness practice, you demonstrate your understanding about the laws of creation, that you project your world from within your consciousness. You merely experience aspects of yourself that you have dissociated from — that you have split from yourself, not truly but seemingly so. When you offer love to beings you meet, beings who are difficult to deal with, and you forgive them for their supposed transgressions, you acknowledge they don't exist. You understand that whatever happened generated from a frequency within your unconsciousness. Therefore, you have caused all this for yourself.

There is no point in attacking a character in a dream. Think about having a dream. It seems very real while you sleep. You can be chased by a bad man or fall or see a tidal wave coming toward you — whatever the dream is — and there is nothing you can do within the dream to change it until you start to lucid dream. That is what we are leading you toward. We are leading you toward lucid dreaming, which means you are aware that it is a dream.

When you lucid dream in this reality, in (what you call) your waking reality, you shift and change that dream, because you are aware of how the mechanics of creation work. You become the true creator that you are destined to be. As you do these lessons and review them, we want you to use a format familiar to you, one you have used in previous lessons that suits you and feels good to you. You now decide how and when to meditate during the day and to use your volition to make that decision.

I am that one you know as Jesus, and we will see you again tomorrow.

Review IV: Part 2
My mind holds only what I think with God.

Follow the complete lesson guidelines in your *ACIM* book.

You are blessed beings, indeed. I am that one you know as Jesus. In the worldly interpretation of this, it seems such a strange thing to say that my mind only contains the things I think with God. You have an incorrect definition of God, so it does not make sense given that definition.

Your definition describes a being separate from you, who does not communicate with you. Why would you think with God when you are completely separated from that which you believe it is? He is All That Is. The truth is, God speaks to you through your heart, your passions, and your love. That is the energy you share with your Creator. You are created in the image of God, which means you share his wonderful creative nature. You share his alignment with love. You are made of love, from love, for love.

When you love something, you are in a place of absolute joy, thinking, "I would not rather be anywhere else." You could be reading that book you adore, walking with your grandchild, holding hands, and throwing the ball for your dog. That is God's will for you — to be happy.

Now, in your society, you are trained to think that a spiritual life must be ambitiously spiritual in the sense that you must run retreats or that you must be a teacher or whatever. That is not true. You can live your life happily through following your guidance and intuition, doing the things you love, making your life your investment, and spending time with yourself. Get to know yourself and the things in your mind that do not serve you. This is God's will for you: Wake up and align with love.

You are led by your guidance system through negative and positive feedback. You receive negative feedback when you go off track — that means you feel bad — and when you are on track and closer to love, you feel good. It's very simple. The ego and your training programs have made it very complicated. You are in alignment with God when you feel good, and you are happy. We must add a warning here: only when no drugs, alcohol, or substances are involved and you are engaged in the natural world.

It can make you very happy to sit up all night and watch Netflix, but that is more of a pleasure. It can make you very happy to sit up all night smoking pot, but that is more of a pleasure. It involves a physical stimulus of the body that distracts you from your suffering, so you seem to feel better. We are speaking about things like natural creativity, conversations with good friends, hanging out with your family and loved ones, being in nature, and using your self-expression in whatever way feels good for you.

We want you to understand there are many pleasures in your society that make you temporarily happy but not permanently. Your happiness wanes as soon as you stop doing that thing, taking that drug, or drinking that drink. We seek happiness that is gentler and has more of a heartfelt nature. Many of you have contaminated ideas early on in your studies of *A Course in Miracles* and you say, "Well, it makes me happy to watch TV, so I'm going to do it." Well, if that's what you believe, then it's important for you to align with your beliefs. As you watch television and listen to the news broadcasts or the horror stories about death and destruction around the planet, if you are honest with yourself, you will go internally and you say, "This actually isn't making me happy. It's a habit I have. It's something I've always done. It's something I believe I should do to be informed, but when I go in and connect to my frequency, happiness is not what I'm feeling."

Be really honest with yourself about what aligns with God's will for you, something that comes from deep within you, a simple pleasure in the natural world. Understand the contrived stimuli of your society are not what we speak about here. Your thoughts will go through a similar process. They will be material-focused, ambition-focused, and worried-about-what-other-people-think-of-you focused. When you go into your emotional guidance system, you realize those thoughts do not necessarily make you feel good. They may motivate you to be a workaholic or some such thing, but they are not good-feeling thoughts. Good-feeling thoughts are loving, kind, gentle, and — eventually — no thoughts.

I am that one you know as Jesus, and we will speak to you again tomorrow.

LESSON 143

Review IV: Part 3
My mind holds only what I think with God.

Follow the complete lesson guidelines in your *ACIM* book.

You are blessed beings, indeed. I am that one you know as Jesus. As you worry about how to do these lessons, it is important to remember that you have had over 100 lessons of training already, and you have surely figured out what which format works for you.

We are giving you a little bit of self-responsibility here, like training wheels on a bike. The first time your parent lets go of the saddle of your bike and you're on your own, it feels a little wobbly but the training wheels are there. You have had enough experience to go back to another lesson and follow the directions there for examples.

Eventually you take off your training wheels. These lessons will be done, and then you have the entire twenty-four hours of your day to yourself to decide, "What am I going to do with my mind? How am I going to use these lessons?" We want to reassure you, as you perhaps flounder a little bit today, that you will have no problem figuring it out. You will have found some of the lessons that really resonate with you and have become thoughts inside your mind. You have days when you struggle from being triggered into the ego's thought system. It is okay to grab *A Course in Miracles*, sit down with it for a half hour, and review some of the truths you have forgotten. That is perfectly good. *A Course in Miracles* becomes your painkiller. It becomes your antianxiety medication. It becomes your sleep aid, and there are no side effects except miracles.

I am that one you know as Jesus, and we will see you again tomorrow.

LESSON 144

Review IV: Part 4
My mind holds only what I think with God.

Follow the complete lesson guidelines in your *ACIM* book.

You are blessed beings, indeed. I am that one you know as Jesus. These are challenging lessons for the ego-ruled mind. You must understand that you are not necessarily going to be comfortable with these ideas, because you have been taught your thoughts are your own.

This is one of the errors you struggle with. When you think of your thoughts as your own, you assume you have absolute free will over what has been put into your mind, and you do not have that. You have had many instructions in your society from early in your development deeply embedded through repetitive and, at times, traumatic indoctrination. These are still there.

Those beliefs were adopted by the ego mind as a form of survival. For example, if, when you were two years old, you got in trouble when you didn't eat your peas — your mother withdrew love from you or punished

191

you or gave you a nasty face (which is very traumatic for a little being) or force-fed you — you would have learned a particular behavior during that time to keep you safe. This would have been the ego saying, "It doesn't matter what you want, and you have to just keep this body alive."

As a survival mechanism, a very primitive frequency in that sense, you would have developed a behavior. Perhaps you gave in to eating what other people wanted you to eat to avoid trouble. Now you may have a weight problem, but you have no recollection of that trauma. It is buried deep in the subconscious mind. The belief and the coping mechanism, however, generate thoughts and feelings. You might struggle to eat healthily and have a desire for a healthy figure and body, but you can't maintain it because of that deep programming embedded in you.

When you say things such as, "I'm only thinking thoughts that God thinks," or "God's love is the only love there is," you are gently reprogrammed to truth, but you may not believe it yet. That is okay, because we override, counteract, and contradict many of the thoughts, beliefs, and ideas you experience every day in your normal ego-driven mind.

If these beliefs seem a little highfalutin or out of your ability to reach, be patient with yourself. We counteract thoughts, beliefs, and ideas already existent in the mind that the ego has developed to keep you safe from punishment or pain. It sends up a warning signal when you step into treacherous territories to reprogram the mind, because it has done this, after all, to keep you from getting in trouble.

You might feel a strong argument come up from some of these lessons. It does not matter. You can observe the argument and respond, "Wow, my mind really disagrees with this. Very interesting." Try not to allow the thoughts of disagreement or argument to win. Do your lessons diligently and faithfully, and all will change slowly but surely into a much more peaceful mind.

I am that one you know as Jesus, and we'll see you again tomorrow.

LESSON 145

Review IV: Part 5
My mind holds only what I think with God.

Follow the complete lesson guidelines in your *ACIM* book.

You are blessed beings, indeed. I am that one you know as Jesus. If you have ever spoken to somebody who has practiced *A Course in Miracles* for several years, they tell you there are two worlds. There's the world of the ego that drives most of you to take *A Course in Miracles* and do the lessons, and there is another world. A world of peace, happiness, joy, and understanding about how your thoughts, beliefs, and emotional guidance system work.

You see clearly the direct relationship between what you think and believe and how you feel. Many of you have erroneous thoughts not based on truth. As you become more experienced, you see you don't need to believe every thought you have. This drives people crazy. They have this idea in their minds that every thought is worthy of their attention and love, and it is just not true. There are thoughts that come across your mind that you should look at and say: "Wow, that's a really unloving thought. I wonder who put that belief in there. Let me see what that belief is."

The thought tells you that there is an unloving belief hidden in your mind to generate that kind of thought. You must also remember that if you generate unloving thoughts, you are probably in the ego's realm. That means you recently made a decision based on the ego's world — a materialistic thought, a belief, an observation, a judgment, or something unloving. Once you take that step into the ego's thought system, then more and more thoughts of that same frequency come to you.

They are not necessarily all contained within your brain. Your ego's thought system is part of a massive thought system in a thought form fed so much food in your society. Movies about war, the Holocaust, starvation, rape, murder, and all those TV shows that have murder as their core feed the ego's thought system. So it has a tremendous amount of energy. When you take one step toward the ego's thought system, it can tumble in on you as if you have completely lost control of anything you have ever learned before. But you haven't.

You've stepped into another frequency. In that frequency, you become an antenna for unloving beliefs and ideas. We want you to understand that. We want you to understand that the quicker you reclaim your place in the Holy Spirit's thought system — the love thought system, the kind thought system — the better. In the early phases of your *A Course in Miracles* studies, you might be taken down a rabbit hole for a couple of days. You feel terrible. You feel like you made a terrible error, the course is stupid, and people think you're crazy (maybe you are crazy). Those kinds of thoughts can tumble in on you when you step into the ego's thought system.

If you stay there for a couple of days, you cannot pinpoint the original thought that caused you to step into that thought form. So when you begin to feel bad, check yourself — as quickly as possible — and ask, "What am I thinking about? Oh, I'm worrying about not having enough rent for next month's payment." or "My husband's late, and I'm worried that he's cheating on me." These kinds of thoughts send you into a tailspin and throw you right into the ego's thought system. You feel as if all these lessons have gone out of the window.

They haven't gone out of the window. You cannot straddle these two thought systems with a foot in one and a foot in the other. So what happens these early days is you might feel a little less stable as you hop from one thought system to the other. You must remember that before the course came to you, you didn't hop into another thought system. You stayed in the ego's thought system. Yes, it was tumultuous. Yes, it was frightening. Yes, it was many things, but it was constantly inconsistent.

Now you get periods of peace when you are aligned, and that feels great. You feel comfortable, at ease, happy, and content with your studies. When you plummet into the ego's drain hole (we'll call it that because that is what it feels like), the contrast is tremendous. It actually feels worse than when you were there all the time.

Please understand these things. Understand that you just have to grab your book, stop what you're doing when you feel yourself going down into a spiral, and head to your bedroom — to the bathroom if you're at work, take an early lunch break if you can swing it — and get your book out, to get yourself back on track as quickly as possible. This does not mean you are a failure. It does not mean you are a bad student. It means you are in a training program to change the most powerful thing in the world — your mind.

I am that one you know as Jesus, and we will see you again tomorrow.

LESSON 146

Review IV: Part 6
My mind holds only what I think with God.

Follow the complete lesson guidelines in your *ACIM* book.

You are blessed beings, indeed. I am that one you know as Jesus. This is a very good time to speak about these review periods. You must remember the tremendous amount of training and learning you have done.

When you struggle with this particular course, it is quite interesting to us, because we see how very diligently you followed your teachers' instructions in school — for example, memorizing your times tables, practicing your alphabet, and learning to spell. It was quite a learning feat, indeed, in that twelve-year period.

Understand the joy that comes from being able to read a book. If you can read a book, that comes from your diligence in your learning program. We do not trash your education system 100 percent (although, it is a very dysfunctional program). We want you to focus on the good it gave you through discipline. Trust in the fact that when you have learned these lessons and put them into practice, you do the same thing as a young child learning his or her ABCs. You'll remember it was a bit of a struggle. You had to learn to hold the pencil to write the letters properly, you got bad grades for bad spelling, and you had to learn to study words. You now have the ability to read a book that transports you into another place and time. What a joy to read a really good book!

We want you to think of these early lessons in that way so that you do not come down too hard on yourself. You would never yell at a six-year-old child struggling to spell the word "them" or who can't quite form the letters properly. You would sit patiently with the child and say, "It's okay. This is a really hard job. You have a lot to learn here. Let's just try that again." We want you to talk to yourself this way.

Be kind to yourself, as you would a child learning to write and read. When you sit down with your child or your grandchild or your niece or your nephew as she or he learns to read, you don't yell and say she or he is stupid: "Okay, well, reading is clearly not for you. Let's give up on this project." But you say that to yourself about this particular training program.

Please keep that in mind as you go through these lessons and reviews. If you can't remember things, it's okay. You are learning to remember. You are training your mind. If you knew how to do it, you wouldn't need a training program. So be gentle with yourself. Be the parent or the teacher you wish you had when you learned to read and write, and things will go much better.

I am that one you know as Jesus, and we will see you again tomorrow.

Lesson 147

Review IV: Part 7
My mind holds only what I think with God.

Follow the complete lesson guidelines in your *ACIM* book.

You are blessed beings, indeed. I am that one you know as Jesus. It is important as you go through these lessons to remember we are leading you toward peace, and peace is a quality of mind that allows your guidance to speak to you very easily.

The ego's job keeps you alive and safe; your body is physically present so that you can be here in this 3D-focused experience. When you use the ego for future planning, it does not fare well. The ego mind is promoted in this society, so there is not a lot of spiritual teaching in mainstream media or in your movies. Sometimes religion will show up in your movies, but it's usually in a horror movie or some similar capacity. So you live in the ego-mind most of the time. When you go into the future, the ego-mind panics and becomes anxious. This is what keeps many of you awake at night when you try to figure out, for example, how to get the money together for an event next month that you wish to go to. You will try to figure it out, but you can't. You can't find any peace, because you are in the ego-mind trying to figure out something that is not its job to figure out.

The spiritual guidance that is your natural right, however, is much quieter than the ego. As you go through this journey toward peace, your guidance will become louder. It doesn't ever yell at you as the ego does, but it becomes easier to discern. For example, envision yourself in a dense forest: There's a pathway there. You can't see where you're going, and you step onto a bridge that looks a little wobbly. The ego may send a shock of adrenaline through your body, saying, "Stop. Don't go over that bridge." That is an appropriate use of the ego-mind. It tells you to stop and that it's dangerous to go any further.

Now, it is as if spirit is up on a mountain looking down on that dense forest, and you are down there with the ego not able to see where you're going. Spirit communicates with you and says you need to turn left at the fork in the path. There's a big crevasse ahead of you if you continue straight. If you go left, you're going to find an easier way; we can see it from up here. If you only listen to the ego-mind, then you may not take that left at the fork, and you might continue without that guidance.

Understand that as your mind becomes more peaceful, the ego's raucous and fearful voice is more easily discernible, and the quieter, gentle nudging of spiritual guidance can be felt more clearly. They are often drowned out by the overly fed and overly boisterous ego voice. So understand this: It shifts and changes as you go through these lessons. You will have less tolerance for the fear mongering of the ego.

When the ego gets you worried about something in the future or resentful of something in the past, bring to mind this idea of the forest and the ego's inability to see further down the path. Then say, "Ah. Okay, I must be using my ego-mind here, because I'm very fearful about the future. Let me not listen to these thoughts. Let me not empower the ego's thought system. Let me step into the Holy Spirit's thought system. Let me grab my *A Course in Miracles* book until I feel calm again. Let me mull over a few lessons. Let me do a little meditation and ask for guidance, because I really don't know what decision to make here."

You don't have to make a rushed decision. The ego pushes you to make rapid decisions. Spirit guides you slowly, gently, and surely through your life.

That is just a little story we wanted to bring forth to help you understand the process you are involved in. Instead of listening to the ego all the time, you get periods of peace in which you can hear and feel your guidance from above.

I am that one you know as Jesus, and we will see you again tomorrow.

LESSON 148

Review IV: Part 8
My mind holds only what I think with God.

Follow the complete lesson guidelines in your *ACIM* book.

You are blessed beings, indeed. I am that one you know as Jesus. This idea of defensiveness is a very important subject for you to understand. When you see a well-armed society, it, indeed, plants seeds of violence because it defends itself against an anticipated future attack. It believes it will be attacked; therefore, it will be attacked. It is that simple.

When you walk around armored because of past hurts and believe you will be hurt in the future, it will come true, because you use all your creative power in an effort to prevent a future attack based on past experience. This is considered contaminating the present moment with past ideas. You are given fresh "eternal nows" constantly. You have the ability to choose fear or love. Defensiveness is a constant and unrelenting choice of fear. This happens when the ego takes charge.

The ego says you were hurt by someone who looked like "that" person; therefore, the odds are likely "that" person will hurt you. You must become wiser as you go through these lessons and realize the person you're speaking to now has never hurt you. She or he has never done anything but remind you of somebody from the past.

A lesson comes to you one more time: The opportunity to forgive, open up, and trust. Now, we are well aware that many of you will say, "Well, you can't trust everybody." That is somewhat true, but not everybody is your business. Understand that your defensiveness promotes attack, and that's the only thing you can change.

If you have been attacked many times in the past, you may want to look at how defensive you are. Are you always prepared for war? Do you always have your next argument in your back pocket? Do you judge others or attack others relentlessly? If you attack others, you sow seeds of attack for yourself. Defensiveness and overt aggression are similar in the sense that they promote attack seemingly from the outside, which is merely a response to the frequency you have set for your life.

It seems foolish not to use past experience to predict future events. That is something most of you do every single day. We want you to understand the limited life it produces. It allows you to have only one kind of experience. It doesn't allow you to get close to people. It doesn't allow you to even love people. This is why many of your relationships fail. You come into relationships with old wounds, and you put those old wounds between you and the person who has never done anything to you. You predict the wound will happen again, and sure enough, it does.

If you see a pattern like this in your life, it may very well have something to do with your defensiveness. You do not need to defend yourself. You are powerful, creative beings. You have an unassailable and eternal connection to Source, and that is what you should focus on. It gives you the courage and strength to walk through life without your armor.

I am that one you know as Jesus, and we will see you again tomorrow.

LESSON 149

Review IV: Part 9
My mind holds only what I think with God.

Follow the complete lesson guidelines in your *ACIM* book.

You are blessed beings, indeed. I am that one you know as Jesus. It is important for you to remember that you are a blessed beings. I always start the commentary with that, and I do it so that you remember that you are a blessed beings.

You are created to experience yourself. While in separation, you chase the idols that prevent you from being yourself as God created you. There is so much suffering here, because you are often deluded about what you are. You see yourself as fallible, sinful, unworthy, and unlovable. Many of you carry around these beliefs, and this generates the suffering in your world and on your planet — because you do not act as a sacred being. You do not act as a divine aspect of God-mind.

These lessons gently lead you toward the realization that you are exactly as you are meant to be. If anything comes up that disturbs you, it is not actually a part of your true self. It is a part of something else that you have mistaken for yourself. When you stop identifying your negatives — your short temper, your anger, or your fears — as who you are but rather as interlopers in your mind (your peaceful mind that is connected to the Divine), you do not feel as bad about yourself. You realize: "Ah, there is something active in me that isn't loving. That, then, is not me. It must have been put in there somehow, some way by somebody else."

You don't have to know who it was or when it happened. You may remember. You may realize it's your mother's voice or your preacher's voice or your father's anger that you hear in your mind. But if you don't know where it came from, that's okay. All you need to know is that if it does not love, then it doesn't belong in there, and you shouldn't listen to it. It will only make you feel sad and take you into the ego's thought system. The ego's thought system is a mixture of all the fearful and unloving ideas that have ever been thought. You tap into it once you make that first unloving, judgmental thought in your mind true for you.

Watch what you believe. Don't believe every thought you have. Don't act as if every idea is a good one. Contemplate things slowly. Meditate on them. Get yourself in a deep and peaceful place. Connect with your higher mind, and ask, "Is this good for me? Is this something that I should contemplate, or am I way off track here? I need some guidance." Sit quietly and patiently and wait for the answer. It will come.

You are not used to doing this; you have been taught that you must go out into the world. It must be a material/physical thing. This is why your indoctrinations into materialism in this society is so intense. They do not want you to go inside. Even the church's prohibitions about going inside by yourself are designed to keep you beholden to the church rather than having your own direct conscious contact with your guides and teachers, such as this being [the channel] has here. She also takes off on a tangent once in a while and gets herself in a little bit of trouble, but she has figured it out pretty well and knows she can always ask for an answer and that she can trust her inner guidance system. She knows that if she remains happy and at peace when things are not quite right, she will feel it, and she can trust that. She can trust it as a no, not to go down that path; or she can trust she is off track herself, and she will go inside and investigate.

This is really what living a life consciously in the present moment looks like. It is not perfect. It does not mean you do not have your challenges. You have many unconscious beliefs and ideas that have not yet been removed from your mind, and they will miscreate or create all the time. You encounter deeper and deeper levels of your own consciousness as you go through the many years after you have finished *A Course in Miracles*.

Don't feel disappointed that your work will continue throughout your whole life. Your journey into fear has gone deep, and your confusions are many. It takes a while to sort out these ideas. That is why this book was written and these lessons have been given to you, so that you can help yourself climb out of the hole you have dug for yourself. Nobody has done it to you, and nobody can rescue you. We can merely hold up the light for you and say, "Come this way. The path is clear ahead."

I am that one you know as Jesus, and we will see you again tomorrow.

LESSON 150

Review IV: Part 10
My mind holds only what I think with God.

Follow the complete lesson guidelines in your *ACIM* book.

You are blessed beings, indeed. I am that one you know as Jesus. What is the atonement but the reintegration and healing of your mind? That is what we ask you to receive through your practice of forgiveness. When you see division, practice forgiveness. When you see and feel rage, practice forgiveness.

Now, all of you think that makes you a weak doormat. On the contrary, it makes you a most powerful creator, because you are not reacting to the effects of the ego's playground. That is what you see and witness when you see things happening in the world. It is the result of a lot of thinking and often a lot of hatred and fear. When you react to it and say it is wrong, you look at the wrong thing. You look at the result of a lot of deep thought with a lot of emotion attached to it.

Through your forgiveness practice, do not focus on the result, which does not give you any power. You must forgive, knowing that in doing so you transform your mind. In transforming your mind, you affect all those around you. In choosing to transform your mind into a more loving, creative communication device, you do the thing that changes the world.

You do not change the world by acting as if the material world causes the problem. It does not cause the problem. It is the result of the problem, which is a collection of unloving minds. Any of you who have done *A Course in Miracles* are surprised early on in the lessons to see just how judgmental and unloving your minds are. This is the great secret you keep from yourselves. In projecting guilt onto others, in raging at others, you do not see your own unloving mind. Your unloving mind contributes to your unloving society and your unloving experiences.

Make sure to keep your focus on the atonement, which is the reintegration and healing of your mind. In that, you achieve great results. When you focus only on the material outcome of everybody's miscreation, you waste an entire lifetime. Stay focused on the interior of your mind and heart, knowing that every loving choice you make changes the world.

I am that one you know as Jesus, and we'll see you again tomorrow.

LESSON 151

All things are echoes of the voice for God.

Follow the complete lesson guidelines in your *ACIM* book.

You are blessed beings, indeed. I am that one you know as Jesus. This idea of judgment based on incomplete evidence is something you all must really look at. When you see something on your television, read something on your Facebook news feed, or listen to people on YouTube rant and rave about something they hate that incites people into violence or war or whatever it is, they are basing their judgments on the surface actions of the ego consciousness. They are not loving in any way, shape, or form.

They are in the battleground. They are at the ego's whim, and they are fully engaged with death. The ego kills. You see it in war, murder, family violence, and the destruction of the environment. The ego, in its efforts to get what it wants, destroys everything in its path. In the end, it can even destroy itself, as seen in the suicide victim. The untrained mind is danger-ous. All of you who do these lessons must see that the ego-mind let loose on the world can destroy everything.

Really try to grasp this principle, because it is very important. You do not know what somebody's past has driven them to. You do not know what evil thoughts torment them from their ego consciousness. You do not know the pain and suffering they live in. You do not know what drives their behavior. You do not know. You barely know what drives your own behavior, so you should not be so quick to attack somebody else for doing something you do not like.

We suggest you stay in your own lane and focus on bettering yourself, nurturing yourself, and training your mind to see how unloving it can be. Relinquish unloving thoughts, beliefs, and ideas. Turn toward peace, com-passion, and joy. Live a full life. Invest in your life, because it is the only one you truly are permitted to live. When you interfere through judgment in another's life, you merely waste your own. For those beings who invest in themselves, clarify their minds, and train this most powerful, creative device, the sky is the limit. They can do anything. Miracles become their way of liv-ing. Is that not a better path than to sit and judge others relentlessly?

Your mainstream media systems are designed to get you to judge. That is what they train you to do in an effort to keep you underpowered and eas-ily managed. We want you to become powerful and unmanageable. Connect to the divine, guided by love, and lead the love revolution on this planet.

I am that one you know as Jesus, and we will see you again tomorrow.

LESSON 152

The power of decision is my own.

Follow the complete lesson guidelines in your *ACIM* book.

You are blessed beings, indeed. I am that one you know as Jesus. This is a very powerful lesson — is it not? — to accept that the collective and individual desires of all of you have created this chaotic world rather than God.

God did not create this world that you see. It is a world of separation. The default setting here is fear, isolation, and separation. That's why many of you have so much pain. It is why many of you feel abandoned by God. It is a world of projection, which means you believe God has abandoned you, but in truth, you abandoned God. That is projection. You accuse others of what you have done yourself.

It is with a humble heart that we accept this teaching that we have created the chaos. We have created the pain, and we have created suffering. Any of you who have done *A Course in Miracles* for a while (some of you are repeating these lessons) have come to see that as you practice these teachings, the suffering in your mind decreases because you cause it. As the suffering in your mind decreases, your frequency goes up. You become a more loving being, and the frequency you emit (for you are also emitting a frequency) becomes more loving to reflect the forgiveness work and the education you have accomplished.

That frequency then attracts things like itself unto itself. This is where you get the phrase "misery loves company," because it is true. Miserable people hang out together. Violent people hang out together. Loving people hang out together. The decision is yours. Do you believe your thoughts are secret? Do you believe your beliefs have no power?

You are made in the image of God. You have the ability to bring into being whatever you focus on, and it does not mean what your social face says. It means what you focus on inside your mind, inside your heart. Are you living life fully? Are you living a life in accord with God's will for you, which means it makes you happy? If you live a miserable life, it is because you have made a decision to live a miserable life.

Today we want you to make new decisions. We want you to step up your game. We want you to lift your head up high. We want you to love whatever around you is lovable. Instead of heaping criticism and judgment on yourself and the world, look at yourself with love and appreciation as God looks at you. Look at the world with love and appreciation for all of the things that are working out there. It is the same as when something in your body goes wrong. You say, "Oh, my ankle hurts. That's all I can think about." But there are a million other things your body is doing perfectly. Do you ever thank it for any of those things? Do you ever give it kudos for just getting you around? It is often a deep and dark sickness that makes you appreciate your health.

Today, the decision is yours: Are you going to look at the world through gray-colored lenses? Or are you going to look at the world through the eyes of love and appreciation — which are, after all, the eyes of forgiveness? Look at the world with forgiving eyes. Look at your brothers and sisters with forgiving eyes, and know they are as confused as you. They also have been mistreated and mistaught, and they know not what they do. "Forgive them; for they know not what they do" [Luke 23:34, ESV].

I am that one you know as Jesus, and we will see you again tomorrow.

LESSON 153

In my defenselessness, my safety lies.

Follow the complete lesson guidelines
in your *ACIM* book.

You are blessed beings, indeed. I am that one you know as Jesus. That, of course, was the lesson that I taught when I went to the cross. I was defenseless. I could have left at any time. I could have fought. But in my alignment with love, I knew I was safe, because I am an eternal spiritual being, and my body is not who I am (or was, in that case).

The same is true of you. Do not be so beholden to the body. The body makes you fearful. The fear of loss, control, or decorating the body is an obsession of your Western society. You are obsessed with getting it in perfect shape so that it's the perfect bait to get the perfect partner, wear the perfect clothes, or sit posed in the perfect car. These are all body-focused thoughts and activities, and they make you fearful, because the body is so fallible.

You must focus on spirit, which is eternal. Your everlasting life — your everlasting consciousness — can never be destroyed. It always was, and it always will be. The body is a temporary car in which you drive yourself around, because you believe in separation because you believe in fear. That is why it is so terrifying when you focus on the body. That is why when young people begin to overly focus on the body, they become anorexic or bulimic. They use all their creative power in an effort to mold the body and control the body as the thing that is their salvation, and it takes them so deeply into fear that they often die.

The mind, untrained, can do that. It has the same power as a trained mind. Just as the trained mind can take you into a wonderful life, where you focus on what you want more of and what you'd like to experience

204

and learn and grow, and you can bring that into being. However, if you are untrained, the mind can kill you. And that is true.

You see it around you in your society a lot these days, so we really want you to understand what this defenselessness means. It means that you do not need to protect yourself against attack. When you defend yourself, you are attacked already. You believe in your mind that an attack is imminent. You live in fear, and that is a form of hell. When you open your heart, relax, and open your mind to new experiences, you are freer. You are more creative, and you are more connected. Your body follows along.

You do not need to marshal it the way you do. It is generated from the frequency of your mind. The more defensive you are, the more fearful you are; the more contracted you are, the more sick you are. The less defensive you are, the more open, freer, happier, creative, abundant, and healthier the body is, because it follows along behind you. It has no volition of its own.

In defensiveness, you prove your allegiance to separation in the ego-mind. So be aware of where you feel defensive, and open up a little bit. If there's a person in your life around whom you shut down, cross your legs, and fold your arms, the next time you're in this person's company, unfold your arms and be aware of what you fear. Do you fear attack from this person? Well, then you are the one on the attack, because you are preparing for, anticipating, and wanting the attack. If you didn't want it, you wouldn't think about it. If you didn't want it, you would be relaxed and happy. It is one of those cases of projection, where our defensiveness causes the belief in the imminent attack, and that is where your creative power goes. So it will be because you are that powerful.

I am that one you know as Jesus, and we will see you again tomorrow.

LESSON 154

I am among the ministers of God.

Follow the complete lesson guidelines in your *ACIM* book.

You are blessed beings, indeed. I am that one you know as Jesus. This, of course, puts fear into the heart of the ego.

It does not really want to be a minister of God. It does not want to proselytize, and that is not really what this lesson is about. This lesson is about you employing in your thought, word, and deed the principles and energies of these lessons so that you act in accord with these lessons.

In your demonstration of your understanding of what love, giving, extension, and projection are, you learn as you study this material that you are a minister of God. People witness you. They may come up to you and say, "What is it that you're doing? You are not the same person you were before." That presents a perfect opportunity to share with someone what you are doing. You do not need to stand on a soapbox. You will be guided. If you are not guided to do something as outlandish as this being is doing, do not fret. Do not worry about it, but listen to your inner guidance. Listen to that still small voice within that says, "Take that class. Go on that trip. Phone that friend."

That is how this being [the channel] learned. She was trained to listen to that guidance. Over many years, she became very good at listening. That was when we decided she was capable, willing, and able to do this work. It has been a great growth experience for her, as you can imagine. Her many years of doing *A Course in Miracles* practices of forgiveness — asking for her perception to be healed instead of asking for everyone else to be changed — set her up for doing this work.

This is her specific assignment, and you all have a specific assignment. It may be teaching children. It may be becoming a healer of some kind. It may be writing a book, painting a picture, or growing a garden. Listen to your guidance. If you are happy doing something, then that is your purpose. You may say, "Well, how is it so great that I'm gardening and I love gardening, so that's my purpose?" Well, everyone needs beautiful flowers and fresh and luscious food.

The gardeners out there are going to become in greater and greater demand as your food systems become more and more poisoned. You can see it happening already. Those beings who have gardened for years wondering what their purpose is — their purpose is to grow uncontaminated beautiful, fresh, and healthy food. That is where we ask you to go when you buy food. Buy it as cleanly as possible within your means at this time. You always have the ability to change one item of food.

Some of you will say, "Jesus shouldn't talk about food; it's not pure nondualism." But in your society with the degree of pollution you deal with, it is now an important subject that must be addressed. The toxins in your society cause untenable problems in your bodies, and we ask you to choose as healthy a diet as possible.

When you are on this ascension journey, frequency matches are the way it goes. You have an increasing frequency on this planet because of the increasing frequency in your solar system and the galaxy. We want you to understand that the higher your frequency matches to those around you, the less stress you experience. When you go outside and walk in the sunlight or the dappled sunshine or the moonlight or the starlight, and you are out in the air and the fresh breezes of your natural environment, you are being upgraded. Know that this is true.

When you start to feel a bit woozy from being on your computer too long or a bit pummeled by being in front of your television too long, turn it off, then put your shoes or your sandals on and go outside. Get an upgrade; know that that is indeed what's happening.

I am that one you know as Jesus, and we will see you again tomorrow.

LESSON 155

I will step back and let him lead the way.

Follow the complete lesson guidelines in your *ACIM* book.

You are blessed beings, indeed. I am that one you know as Jesus. This is one of the lessons that brings you great peace and joy as you learn to surrender to a will seemingly greater than yours but in accord with your desire for happiness.

Many of you have lived unhappy lives, tortured with divorce, financial issues, health issues, weight problems, and relationship problems — all these things. They are the devil you know. They are things you have believed in your own way because you have made them happen. They demonstrate your level of consciousness, as you made those decisions throughout your life. Most of you who come to *A Course in Miracles* see there is something incorrect about how you create and miscreate in this world. You see patterns of dysfunction. You see patterns of scarcity or poverty. You see health issues. You think, "There's something wrong with what I am doing here." Yet those are the idols you have worshipped.

Some of you worship the idol of poverty and scarcity and claim to want money. You constantly speak about how poor you are. You constantly speak about how much everybody else has and that you don't have anything. The universe hears this, and it reflects back to you your beliefs in your poverty. So that is an idol that many of you worship, this idol of scarcity.

Instead of looking at what you have, the abundance of vital life force in your own body, or the things that work on your body and not the one thing that doesn't work, you worship and strengthen that idol. It will stay as long as you do that.

When you begin to practice forgiveness and gratitude and look around the world each day to see the beauty, love, and good in your brothers and sisters rather than their annoying habits, you shift your frequency enough that you will see: "Ah. There is something being healed here. There is something that is changing." You will know you did not know how to do it yourself. This course teaches you how to do it, and that is the other higher consciousness leading the way for you, because you have all been taught incorrectly on this planet.

Still, you came here. You came into this particular configuration of body, mind, and world to chase your idols. When you stop chasing your idols and start to chase peace, joy, and happiness using all these tools you learn about in this course, you have magnificent, miraculous transformations of all those aspects of your life that used to cause you pain.

Here we approach the halfway mark in these lessons. Have we not had fun together doing this? Have we not enjoyed the peaceful communion these lessons have brought you instead of the raucous battles of the world and the dramas of your families? Have these cool and quiet mornings together not been a joy? Well, there is more to come, dear ones; there is more to come. Keep coming to these lessons each day, as this blessed being does. She remembers this, dear friend. She remembers these beautiful words, and she knows this book has changed her life and, in fact, saved her life.

I am that one you know as Jesus, and we will see you again tomorrow.

I walk with God in perfect holiness.

Follow the complete lesson guidelines
in your *ACIM* book.

You are blessed beings, indeed. I am that one you know as Jesus. These words bring peace and joy to the heart, do they not? When your soul hears these words, it recognizes the truth, and when it hears lies, it can feel them. You have had many experiences of this during your life — when people told you an untruth and you knew it. You could feel it as a form of anxiety or fear in the heart, the physiological response in the body. That is because you are a truth teller. You are a truth-generating machine. When you are out of accord with truth, you know it. You see it in your behavior. You hear it in your words. You feel it in your sickening body.

We want those of you who feel the positive effects of this work to understand that your body is healing as we do these daily rituals together. Your body is getting stronger. The energy systems, nerve endings, and electrical systems of your bodies are getting stronger. That is why you are feeling better. You are aligning with truth. You know this is the truth. You can feel it in the cellular structure of your body, and your body responds because you are the creator. You are the one. When you know you are safe and guided — even though things around you may look a little chaotic — something good comes to you.

Many of you have had the experience in life when you felt something was bad, but years later, you say, "That was the best thing that ever happened to me." That is the love behind all the events of your world. It is hard for you to believe as you see this chaotic maelstrom playing out on your planet, but it is the death throes of a sad society. It is the death throes of fear. Every single one of you doing this practice, every time you forgive and love, you heal not only your body and your family but your world, because it all comes from you.

You are the holy sons and daughters of God. You are created in God's image, and you are powerful. You are part of that which is All That Is — the great universal consciousness. You are not separated from it even though at times you think you are. However, those thoughts are deluded. Know that God walks with you. I walk with you every moment of every day, and we lead you toward the light.

I am that one you know as Jesus, and we will see you again tomorrow.

LESSON 157

Into his presence would I enter now.

Follow the complete lesson guidelines in your *ACIM* book.

You are blessed beings, indeed. I am that one you know as Jesus. As these lessons become less instructional and more experiential, the ego-mind goes into a bit of a panic. It seeks for things within the silence that we ask you to participate in. It pops thoughts into your mind. It suggests that nothing is happening. It, perhaps, generates a little fear, because this lesson tells you that you are deeper into your connection with the Divine and your true nature. After all, what is the ego but the part of you that is not your true nature?

As you approach this part of yourself, the ego begins to kick up a little dust and cause some angst. This is natural. Do not fear the fear. Understand that the ego slowly dissolves by your freewill choice. You slowly but surely choose love more frequently. You slowly but surely judge less. You slowly but surely accept your true nature more, and then you realize that all the shenanigans the ego gets up to — the judgments, the fears, the desire for separation and attack — do not serve you. They do not serve you at all. It is your peace of mind that now becomes the most valuable asset you have.

As we go into these lessons that involve less ritual but more experience, you require a little more discipline in terms of not following the thoughts that come through your mind. If a thought wishes to assert itself, just let it move through your mind and then let it go. Come back to the point of the lesson. I am with you always when you do these lessons. It is that connection that you seek. So know that the frivolous thoughts, judgments, and fears of the ego are meaningless compared to the connection we work on together — your work on connecting to me as your teacher, guide, and assistant through this ascension process, through this clarification process.

You come to see that you do not want certain things, and things you did not value before, such as a quiet mind, are worth a lot more than you thought. So when leaving the world for this time that you do this lesson, we want you to do it with enthusiasm and intense focus. You are learning to focus your creative device. The mind aligned with love is the most creative device in the universe, and you can bring worlds into being. You have, in fact, brought your world into being. But most of it is inadvertent, accidental, or a miscreation.

What we work toward is the intentional focus and creation of which your mind is capable. You can bring into being a happy dream. Before you leave this place, before you choose to go Home completely, you can begin to live a happy dream. Some of you are getting glimpses of that now. So hold fast as you go through these next few lessons, and know that I am walking beside you as your friend, your teacher, and your guide.

I am that one you know as Jesus, and we will see you again tomorrow.

LESSON 158

Today I learn to give as I receive.

Follow the complete lesson guidelines in your *ACIM* book.

You are blessed beings, indeed. I am that one you know as Jesus. This is the great projection — the grand projection this world has hidden from your eyes — that you are what you focus on. Whatever you think about another, you think about and strengthen in yourself. This is projection. Extension loves the being behind the form, knowing you are all made of the same stuff, guided by the same light, and in this together, equally loved and forgiven by God — that Creator who has no recognition of the separation into which you have brought yourself. You have all done this to yourselves, and you can all get out of this yourselves; but you must return to the knowing that you are all equal and that you are all loved by that Being which created you.

You are creators. You extend yourselves daily. You extend your consciousness daily through your mind, and it is your mind that you see. It is your salvation you prevent when you judge, hate, or discriminate. Think back to yesterday, and recall some of the judgments you made about Earth, this world, its people, your family, and yourself. Each one of those negative beliefs and negative statements you made in your mind yesterday has kept the separation alive today. Today, whatever judgments or fears you have, keep the separation alive for tomorrow.

It is through forgiveness — through seeking the love and light in your brother, in your mind — that you break free from this prison you have created for yourself. This body wants to age and die. This world is full of friction and war. This is all self-created. It can be undone step by step, thought by thought, and belief by belief. You are given many opportunities through your seemingly separate brothers and sisters to practice this idea. From this day forth, we want you to see anyone you meet as a being loved and created by God who is your reflection. Love others, and be kind to them. Smile at them, be generous, and give them what you would love to receive. When you give others your forgiveness and your smile, you also give it to yourself.

I am that one you know as Jesus. We will see you again tomorrow.

LESSON 159

I give the miracles I have received.

Follow the complete lesson guidelines in your *ACIM* book.

You are blessed beings, indeed. And this is the gift that you all can give yourselves. When you practice forgiveness, the ego tells you it is a gift you give to somebody else and you will lose. If you give up your resentment, bad memories, and history, you lose. You do not lose. You gain freedom, and you see that to offer forgiveness to the world through looking upon it with knowing and forgiving eyes, you free yourself from the drama and slavery to death that the world of separation offers you.

Those of you in trouble mentally and emotionally are judging something:

You judge your life as incorrect, or you judge a family member as sinful. You are doing something that causes your own pain. The ego — the mind (or the part of the mind) that believes in separation — must create separation, because that's what it believes in. So you suffer. There's a part of your mind that believes you are separate from God and from your brothers and sisters. You believe if only they would change, then everything would be better. The world must change for you to be better.

The truth is you must change. You must change what you believe to be true about reality. You must change your mind about yourself and your brothers and sisters to see that you bring this suffering to yourself. It is through your judgments that you implement this creative process. It is a miscreation. You don't want to suffer, but you do it inadvertently. Those of you who focus on your own suffering will see there is an unloving thought in there about yourself, one of your brothers or sisters, a place, or an idea. You cause your suffering when you believe that idea.

Turn toward the Holy Spirit, and ask to be shown where you are unloving. Ask to be shown where your mind projects hatred and separation onto somebody or something. You will be shown, but you must want it. You must want something other than your suffering. You must want something more than your anger. You must want peace, and you must want to see the truth.

The truth is you are all one. The truth is you are all equal. The truth is that only errors of thought are made on this planet. No permanent sin is committed. "Forgive them; for they know not what they do" [Luke 23:34, ESV].

I am that one you know as Jesus, and we will see you again tomorrow.

LESSON 160

I am at home.
Fear is the stranger here.

Follow the complete lesson guidelines
in your *ACIM* book.

You are blessed beings, indeed. I am that one you know as Jesus. As you read this lesson, do you realize how often you are fearful? Do you not realize how many times you watch fearful movies or fearful television shows? That music they play — that suspenseful music intended to make you frightened — believe it or not, separates you from your knowledge of God. That is why we insist you stop watching violent movies, frightening TV shows, the news, and such. Every time you expose your consciousness to fear and it incites your heart and mind, you become more separated from love. You become more separated from that which you would call God: your self.

Today, we ask you to make a pact to no longer watch frightening and horrifying information. As you listen to the radio and hear about a local murder, turn it off; do not subject your mind to hateful and fear-inducing information. When you turn on your computer or your television — if you still have one — you recognize the moment fear is incited in you. Would you choose to watch if you knew it caused you suffering? Would you watch if you knew that it actually separates you from your connection to the Divine? Would you still listen? If you would, then you make an intentional choice. You use your free will to disguise from you your true nature and the love that is your natural inheritance.

Be aware of what you use your free will for. When you go to the movies, are you driven by society's dictates? Do you watch movies in which hundreds of people are killed? Do you see movies about infidelity and fearful ideas about relationships and the opposite sex? Why do you want to watch that kind of information? Stop and ask yourself, "Why am I going to this movie? Is it because I have been seduced into believing this movie star is the be all and end all of my world?"

Ask yourselves these questions, dear ones. Fear is not your natural Home. Love is.

I am that one you know as Jesus, and we will see you again tomorrow.

LESSON 161

Give me your blessing, holy son of God.

Follow the complete lesson guidelines in your *ACIM* book.

You are blessed beings, indeed. I am that one you know as Jesus. That is why that saying, "Forgive them, for they know not what they do," [Luke 23:34, ESV] is such an important one. You must forgive your brothers and sisters the sins they have not committed.

Your life is but a projection when the ego is at play, and you accuse others of what you do. That is the projection element of the ego-mind. The other side of that coin is that if you see through the actions of your brothers and sisters that you deem to be sins and love them anyway in your heart and mind, then you are forgiven all your perceived sins, errors, and mistakes.

A lot of the shame and guilt you carry around with you is based on the belief that you have done something wrong, you are not a good person, and you are not lovable. These are all ideas of the ego, and they are all untrue. How do you know they are untrue? Because they make you feel terrible, and they counsel you to attack others.

In this practice today, you are asked to do the very opposite of attack. You are asked to dissolve one of the ego's greatest weapons, which is judgment — deciding that you know how everyone should behave. Deciding that you play God in your life in the sense that you mete out punishment to people you think have broken God's laws. God allows the freedom of all beings to do whatever it is they decide they want to do. Who are you to say that other things should happen?

We want you to stay in your life, your lane, your business. When others become your business because you interact with them, use this technique so that you do not condemn them and, therefore, condemn yourself. You see, nothing truly leaves your mind.

When you project on to others, it is an illusion of getting away with it. You are not getting away with anything when you judge, hate, berate, or belittle others. You suffer because they are part of you. Do not attack others thinking that you are free from the consequences of that attack. You suffer the consequences of that attack, not because a vengeful God punishes you but because this is a reflective universe. You reap the harvest of everything you sow.

I am that one you know as Jesus, and we will see you again tomorrow.

I am as God created me.

Follow the complete lesson guidelines
in your *ACIM* book.

You are blessed beings, indeed. I am that one you know as Jesus. You are as God created you. You are a being made of love, from love, and for love; and you have remained so even though you have forgotten that is what you are.

That is the power of this statement. It reminds you of the truth you have forgotten. You see yourself as guilty sometimes. You see yourself as stupid sometimes. You see yourself as unaccomplished sometimes. You see yourself as grandiose sometimes, but you are as God created you. You are made of spirit, and you came here to experience what you are not. This is the world of separation. This is the world of death. This is the world of bodies. These things you are not, and this is why you suffer here.

Now, some of you will say, "What can I do if I don't have the world? What do I have?" If you begin to focus on Spirit, on love and that which you love, your world changes. If you focus on your sins, your brother's guilt, and shame, you create that world, and it's not a fun one.

Your mind is the creator. You are made in the image of God, and that means you are a powerful creator. You choose what you experience here. Many of you will say, "I do not choose the broken ankle that I have." or "I do not choose the unhappy partner that I have." But you do. You merely have forgotten that you chose those things. Keep choosing love. Keep choosing to do your forgiveness work, and your world will shift and change accordingly.

When you stop laying guilt and stories on the world and remember that you are created in the image of God and loved by God unconditionally, you are as God created you. It has merely been hidden by layers of lies, misperceptions, and illusions.

Trust in yourself. Appreciate yourself. Love yourself as a sacred image of that which you call God. Even though you have come into separation to chase your idols, you still are a sacred being. Never forget this. I am that one you know as Jesus, and I am sent here to remind you of your beauty and your loving nature. I am sent here so that you remember who you are. You are a sacred being.

I am that one you know as Jesus, and we will see you again tomorrow.

LESSON 163

There is no death. The child of God is free.

Follow the complete lesson guidelines in your *ACIM* book.

You are blessed beings, indeed. I am that one you know as Jesus. Does this not seem impossible to believe that there is no death? Well, I have overcome death. I live on. You were alive before this body. You are living in this body, but you are not this body, and you will continue to live on after this body has given up its usefulness.

Death is an illusory idea. Death does not exist. You tell a story about death, and yes, you worship death. Look at your television shows. Which ones are the most popular? The ones about murder. You watch them for the drama, you say. No, there is a fascination with death. You can see it in your fascination with sickness as well — how quickly you tell somebody you are not well, the pain you have — wishing to share that pain with somebody else, to inflict it on them.

These truths are hard to hear because you believe in them so completely. You believe you will die, and so it is true. You die in the form in which you believe. You will not die. Your consciousness carries on after the body has fallen away, but it does not have to happen this way. That is not what happened to me. I did not die on the cross. I left my body and manufactured another one. I was not condemned to live within the mortal form anymore. I had reached a point of consciousness evolution that allowed me to master the physical/material world. My complete alignment with love and connection to the Divine sets you free from the burden of death. It is there for all of you to take, but you must stop believing in death. You must stop seeing it as inevitable.

Tell yourself a different story. These can be your mantras: "I can overcome death. Death is an illusion. Death is not true. I was alive before this body was. I am alive within this body. I am not this body, and I will continue to live forever and ever. Amen."

Death is the great Grim Reaper that the ego uses as proof that God is not real. That is why your world is so confusing for you, because this place of separation into which you have come — in which you worship death and talk about it all the time — is not made by God. It is a place that you have chosen to come into to chase your idols and continue on the karmic cycle. We want you to break free of that cycle. But you must do it within a lifetime. It does not happen to you in the afterlife if you have still believed in it in your lifetime. So start today to tell a new story about death. Tell yourself that it is not real, even though you still believe it is. Start to experience and experiment with these new beliefs and ideas. They are powerful, indeed — hard to believe but true.

I am that one you know as Jesus, and we will see you again tomorrow.

LESSON 164

Now are we one with him who is our source.

Follow the complete lesson guidelines in your *ACIM* book.

You are blessed beings, indeed. I am that one you know as Jesus. Today is the only day that you can choose to do this work. You can't put it off until tomorrow, because tomorrow will become today. So why not start to own your power now? Why not start to trust in this process completely and absolutely?

Many of you resist these lessons and complain a little bit that you have to do them. Many of you do them with a more rote behavior rather than truly believe that they change your mind. Let us all take upon our shoulders the knowing that salvation comes today. Know that you can connect with the divine today. Know that you do not have to suffer anymore.

Suffering comes from distortions in the mind, and those distortions are there because we allow them to be there. We want you to choose love today. It is the only day that you can choose it. Why put it off? Why suffer tomorrow? Why suffer the day after? Begin today to claim your place in salvation. Begin today to free up your mind so that I may use it together with your free will, with your blessing, and can work together to transform and shift this world.

Suffering has gone on long enough on your planet, and these escalating energies bring up all the shadows of all the beings on this plane. It is not optional anymore. The time for procrastination is over. Dedicate yourself to love and clarity. Clear some space on your hard drive (so to speak) so that we can download some new software for you. The software installed on your hard drive is not loving. It is not good for you, and it does not make you happy. So free up that space. Get rid of those ideas and beliefs that you know cause you pain and suffering. Judgment, fear, guilt, shame, and anger — ask them to be taken from you, you do not want them anymore. They do not serve you. You must do this with your free will. You must ask for help.

You must say, "Please take these thoughts from me. I do not want them anymore." For your part, do not believe those thoughts anymore. Do not empower those thoughts anymore. Do not act as if those thoughts are true anymore. Begin to see any unloving ideas you have in your mind as unwelcome visitors that you now evict from your mind.

I am that one you know as Jesus, and we'll see you again tomorrow.

LESSON 165

Let not my mind deny the thought of God.

Follow the complete lesson guidelines in your *ACIM* book.

You are blessed beings, indeed. I am that one you know as Jesus. It is hard for you to imagine that a mere decision on your part brings peace to you. It is merely a decision on your part to focus on love, to focus on the interior of your mind rather than the exterior world. It is only that decision that is required for you to connect and see the results of that connection.

You are as God created you. You are not lacking anything. You have an amazing resource available to you, and it is contained within you. It is your joy. It is your love. It is your creativity. It is your endless connection to All That Is. That is where you find what you seek. You are not going to find it in large sums of money sought by working very hard and long hours. You are not going to find it by molding and sculpting the body to make it the perfect bait to catch the perfect person (or the person you think is perfect). Those are not the things that bring you happiness and joy; it is everything contained within you.

This self that you think you are — its ideas, creativity, funny jokes, laughter, kindness, joy, and all those things — allow it to align with love. Allow yourself to listen to the inner guidance that comes to you all the time from your feelings, guiding you to turn left or right or to talk to "that" person or "this" person or to put your feet up and take some meditation time. Your guidance system always speaks to you. You have merely become used to ignoring it and choosing the world instead of the guidance that spirit offers you through your feeling, emotional body.

Now, some of your emotions are frantic reactions to fear. That is not spiritual guidance. That is the distortion that has been placed there by inappropriate teachings. *A Course in Miracles* lessons are designed to align you with the truth. As you align with the truth, those untrue ideas — without your backing and constant support, without you constantly feeding of them — begin to fade from your consciousness. That is what we seek here. We seek the peace that passes all understanding, and it comes from aligning with love.

I am that one you know as Jesus, and we will see you again tomorrow.

LESSON 166

I am entrusted with the gifts of God.

Follow the complete lesson guidelines in your *ACIM* book.

You are blessed beings, indeed. I am that one you know as Jesus. These gifts are precious, indeed. They are, as we mentioned earlier, things like your creativity.

How are you using your creativity? Are you

putting it aside as something valueless, because your school system trained you to do so? Do you use it and express your unique nature through your creativity? Your creativity can look like anything: from creating a beautiful garden to training your pet through innovative ways. Creativity — you expressing your unique connection to the Divine through yourself — is one of the great gifts you have all been given.

Bring to your mind, now, how little creativity is valued in your society, how you are taught to value the intellect and hard work over creativity. Ask yourself, "How am I ignoring or using my creativity, and is there some way I can increase that?" Perhaps if you turn off your computer a little earlier in the evening, you will have more time to investigate your creativity. Perhaps if you do not listen to your financial fear thoughts, you will spend a little money on those paints or on that creative outlet you have balked at because it's going to cost you a little bit to set up.

Understand that we speak to you — Spirit speaks to you — through your creativity in whatever form it comes. You might love to cook, write, paint, sing, or dance; it does not matter which form is your form. Please make sure that you create things, that you bring forth your ideas and unique point of view, in whatever form it takes, and share it with your brothers and sisters.

This is just one of the gifts you are given by the Divine. You come in with this amazing interior world, and your society only values the outside world: the car you drive, the money you earn, and the body you exhibit. We want all of you to spend more time inside with your creativity and listen to the muse.

I am that one you know as Jesus, and we will see you again tomorrow.

LESSON 167

There is one life, and that I share with God.

Follow the complete lesson guidelines in your *ACIM* book.

You are blessed beings, indeed. I am that one you know as Jesus. These lessons have become quite a challenge to your belief system, have they not? They have, in fact, really poked at some of the fundamental ideas you hold about your-self, your life, and your purpose here.

You are not a body. You are Spirit encased in a heavy physical/material manifestation of separation, and it is not who you are. The body is not who you are, and the body is the only thing that seems to die because you leave it. You leave it when your life here is done, when you have expressed and opened to as many new ideas as you are able to in this lifetime. When you have done all the work you can do here, then it is time for you to leave this place of separation. With you go all the ideas that have not yet been healed and the need for another incarnation.

This is something this generation is very lucky to have in their experience: the opportunity to awaken completely within the body in this lifetime. But you must dedicate yourself to love and not to fear. This is why your society promotes fear so intensely. The designers of your mass media systems know what is going on. They understand this is the end of a spiritual season, and this galactic speed-up gives you the opportunity to awaken completely in your lifetime.

What does this mean for you? Well, it means you choose love as often as you can. It means you do not embolden your fears by indulging in them. It means you make changes in your life where you feel strongly that they need to be made, because Spirit asks that you be yourself. Spirit asks you to be the loving, self-expressing, love-extending idea in the mind of God you truly are. That means you honor yourself. You honor those things you feel drawn to because you are drawn to them for a purpose. You are drawn to them because those things are in your mind.

Some of you will say, "Well, I am drawn to bad things." And we say, well, if you are drawn to bad things, then you are not doing the course lessons. You are not aligning with them, and you are not practicing them. "Bad things" are not in alignment with these teachings. You must look at how you utilize your free will and preferences. Sometimes these lessons go against your preferences, and this challenges those of you told you must go with the feelings you have to do what you want to do. We have described to you the difference between the ego's needs and those deeply arising passions, ideas, and inspirations that come from deep within your heart and mind. They have a different feel, and only you can discern which are ego driven. If you go beneath the form, you get a feeling of limitation and fear: "If I don't get this, someone won't love me. If I don't behave 'this' way, I will be abandoned." These are fearful ideas and feelings.

When you are guided by Spirit to express your true nature, you get a positive feeling. You get a feeling of excitement, elevation, and joy; and only you can know the difference between those things. Seek joy in every moment you can. When you feel those fearful ego drives, pick up your *A Course in Miracles* book and read it for a little while. Call me to help you. Ask for assistance in letting go of an old pattern that no longer serves you. I will come, and you will feel different.

I am that one you know as Jesus, and we will speak to you tomorrow.

LESSON 168

Your grace is given me. I claim it now.

Follow the complete lesson guidelines in your *ACIM* book.

You are blessed beings, indeed. I am that one you know as Jesus. Your ability to awaken is in this very moment.

Many of you that study spiritual material feel it is a long slog up a very steep hill and that you've been working at it for a long time. The truth is, awakening happens moment by moment, and your investment in this desire to awaken is the thing that makes it occur. In *A Course in Miracles*, we write there is a day designated for you to awaken. As you approach that day, the desire to awaken gets stronger. This is not something specifically written in that text, but I want to tell it to you here: Your desire to awaken increases because the time is near when you will awaken.

This global gathering that we cultivate here with these daily lessons (and we thank you for joining in) enhances your ability to discern that desire to awaken. So when you join us as a group every day, you shift more than you know. You shift the very frequency of your planet. This is one of the great gifts of your modern technology. Just as it can be used for nefarious purposes to downgrade your global frequency, we, together here, use it to upgrade it.

Do not think that you are alone in your studies. Do not think you are alone in the benefits of your forgiveness practice. You are not. Everyone and all things benefit from this practice.

Do not berate yourself if you have a little moment of negativity. Do not judge yourself as imperfect if you get angry or frustrated. We want you to be glad you have seen another part of your mind that is not yours, does not belong to you, and has revealed itself to you through that negative emotion. Bring it to the surface, lay it on the table, and say, "I do not want this in my mind anymore. I do not want this rage. I do not want this frustration. I do not want this fear. Please take it from me, and show me the information I need to release my mind from these imprisoning, unloving ideas and thoughts."

But you cannot let go of something until you see it. When you have an upset, allow it to play out. Do not hurt or damage anybody or anything. Allow it to play out, and then witness that you have seen a part of yourself that is unloving and that you no longer wish to participate in it. You must bring it into the light so that it can be healed and taken from you.

We do not override your desires. If you keep your angers, upsets, and hurts secret, beneath the surface, and nurture them as your small children, they will stay with you. You must, with every fiber of your being, not wish to have them anymore.

I am that one you know as Jesus, and we will speak to you tomorrow.

LESSON 169

By grace, I live.
By grace, I am released.

Follow the complete lesson guidelines
in your *ACIM* book.

You are blessed beings, indeed. I am that one you know as Jesus. These lessons are challenging your belief systems considerably. You are asked to act on faith that you will be transformed. But this is not up to you.

You can only be vigilant and diligent in your practice. You can only forgive when necessary. You can only do what we ask you to do; and in that doing, you express your willingness to have your mind transformed into its natural state, which is that of love. That is all that happens here.

The unnecessary and the valueless are removed from your consciousness so that you are free and clear to be the divine being that you are, connected to All That Is, with a clear and unsullied guidance system. The revelation you experience as you come closer to that state is the most wonderful thing indeed. This being [the channel] experienced that feeling of oneness — the absolute knowing that this world is illusory and that there is something far greater on the other side of the veil of ignorance. You are gradually dissolving it through grace. It is through doing nothing but being given the opportunity to see clearly that you find this wonderful experience coming your way.

All of you feel a clarification of your mind. You do not get as upset as you used to get. You see that a lot of the stories you fabricate in your mind are illusions. They are fantasies, and they create happiness or sadness depending on the story you tell. Tell the loving story. Tell the kind story. Tell the forgiving story, and it is you who will benefit from that.

I am that one you know as Jesus, and we will speak to you tomorrow.

LESSON 170

There is no cruelty in God and none in me.

Follow the complete lesson guidelines in your *ACIM* book.

You are blessed beings. I am that one you know as Jesus. Very few of you would consider yourselves perfect in this way. Many of you see that you can be cruel. You can be sharp with loved ones. You can be quick tempered. You can make cutting comments. But this is not really who you are, and this is one of the things we want to bring to your consciousness today.

Anytime you are unloving, you are not actually yourself. Anytime you are cruel, vicious, or act in an unloving fashion, you are not true to who you really are. You are made of love, from love, for love. When you encounter a situation in which you desire to attack somebody, you deeply immerse in separation in that moment, because you truly do not understand that your brother and your sister are reflections of you. They are parts of your consciousness, for it is in your consciousness that your stories abide about them.

The stories you have about other people live in your mind. That is where the poison lies. That poison is not the truth of who you are, and that is why it makes you feel bad. You feel bad thinking they made you feel bad, but you actually feel bad because you are unloving and judge or attack them in the belief that further separation keeps you safe from this disaster you think comes from getting closer to love.

The truth of the matter is that all of you have chosen this place of not-love, this separation experience where you seem to be alone and abandoned by God. In fact, it is you who left your home. It is you who set off on this journey deep into fear and abandoned God. Through your constant judgment, attack, and belief, you perpetuate this illusory world of separation. That is why forgiveness is such a powerful device.

Stop acting as if attack and judgment are your friends. Stop acting as if they keep you safe. Forgive your brothers and sisters for the sins they have not committed, because you understand you will suffer if you perpetuate separation. They are not responsible for their behavior when their minds are contaminated with untrue beliefs and ideas or distortions. They are merely confused. You must forgive them, for they know not what they do. In that forgiveness, you feel relief. You feel better.

This does not mean that you become a doormat for people to walk all over. What it means is that you will not ruminate on their sins. You will not constantly think about how to get revenge or how to get them to change. Accept that they are confused and their behavior is unloving, and you offer them love in return — if not in person, then at least in your mind and thoughts. Then let them go. Set them free. In letting them go and setting them free, you set yourself free from constant contamination by negative beliefs and ideas.

When you forgive others, stop thinking about them, and let them go, you say, "It is not real," and you get your peace of mind back. You reclaim that part of your mind that you would lose if you constantly judge them and continue to suffer through that perceived sin they have committed.

Some of you will say, "Well, we cannot forgive the murderers and pedophiles and rapists." That is not what we ask you to do. We ask you to let your past go. We ask you to forgive your partners, children, and close coworkers. We ask you to do that. Nobody asks you to forgive a murderer or a pedophile. Yes, there are some beings who have that experience in their lives. That is not you today. Even if somebody has abused you in the past in such a heinous way, maintaining that resentment only hurts you. It does not hurt anybody else. It limits you. It does not limit anyone else. You suffer from maintaining that unforgiving aspect in your consciousness.

Those of you who still have people who contaminate your minds, pray for your enemies. Pray that they get everything they want, because you now understand they are an aspect of you that you have hidden from yourself that is now being shown.

I am that one you know as Jesus, and we will speak to you tomorrow.

LESSON 171

Review V: Part 1
God is but love; therefore, so am I.

Follow the complete lesson guidelines in your *ACIM* book.

You are blessed beings, indeed. I am that one you know as Jesus. As we review these ideas today, it is important for you to go along with how you feel is the best way for you to review these lessons. It is more about taking responsibility for your own practice because you are the decider. You are the decision maker. You are the captain of your ship. How are you going to use your mind today? How are you going to spend time with God today?

You have never left the mind of God. You dwell in an illusory world that you have made full of fear, separation, doubt, anxiety, shame, guilt, and more — none of which has anything to do with God. The energy of that which you call God has nothing to do with those feelings. That means anytime you have those feelings, you actively manufacture something that keeps you from your knowledge of God.

What causes shame, guilt, fear, and all of these things? Judgment causes these things. When you view the world and your past with forgiving eyes and understand the future has not happened, any fantasy in your mind that you manufacture about the future is not real and therefore does not exist. It is a waste of your time and ridiculous to react to your internal fantasies about the future. They are manufactured fantasies and are not happening.

You are in your room, in your car, or at your desk; whatever place you are at is where you truly are. Fantasies about the future or regrets about the past are merely fabricated ideas that contaminate the present moment. The present moment is the only place you can realize yourself. The present moment is the only place you can love, because it is the only place you can be present.

Stay present. It is in presence — in actually being in your own skin, using your senses to direct your mind rather than the old thoughts and ideas you have about what you're looking at — that is the way to peace. When you are present, nothing bad happens. Ninety-nine and nine-tenths of what you worry about does not happen. You find the parking space. You pay the bill. You pay the rent. You get through each day. If you could just truly grasp the fact that all these shady and shadowed feelings are you blocking your knowledge of the Divine, then you would not be so attached to them and indulge in them so much.

You are free beings. You can use your mind for whatever you wish. You are made in the image of God. That means to be at peace, you must be in the frequency of love, because that is the only thing God knows, understands, emits, and creates.

I am that one you know as Jesus, and we will speak to you tomorrow.

LESSON 172

Review V: Part 2
God is but love; therefore, so am I.

Follow the complete lesson guidelines in your *ACIM* book.

You are blessed beings, indeed. I am that one you know as Jesus. Ideas leave, not their source. That is what this lesson is about. God is but love, and so are you. You are made of love, from love, for love. When you step away from that purpose, you feel bad. When you step away from love, you feel bad. When you step toward love, you feel good. That is really all you need to know.

Every time you feel bad, you have had an idea, thought, or judgment about someone, something, some idea, or a principle you have judged or attacked in some way, believing you are separate from it and that you are immune from any kind of reflection of that judgment. You feel bad when you judge, because you have stepped away from love and fallen into the trap of believing that everything outside of you is separate from you.

The world you gaze upon and all the people, places, and things in it arise in your consciousness, the one mind of the child of God. You are a part of it, but everything else connects to you. When you attack something else — a person, place, thing, idea, or concept — you literally attack a part of your own mind and you feel it as negative emotional feedback because you are out of order. You are off track.

There is no sin in God's eyes, because God does not recognize anything

228

that is not love. This is one of the confusing things about your world; you have been told that God created this world, and death, sickness, and children dying are all part of his great plan: God works in mysterious ways. That is the excuse used to explain this insanity. Truthfully, the insanity of your world reflects the insanity of your individual and collective minds. We are working toward making you sane, which means we guide you to align with love more and more each day.

If you are in trouble, depressed, sad, suicidal, or have problematic relationships, all you witness is a lack of love. Love needs to be added into that mix. Look at the parts of your life that are not thriving or that cause you difficulty. Understand that in that part of your consciousness, you have stepped away from your alignment with God's vision of love for you, and you need to add love to the mix. Look at your life in that way. There is not a problem, but merely a lack of love.

I am that one you know as Jesus, and we will speak to you tomorrow.

LESSON 173

Review V: Part 3
God is but love; therefore, so am I.
Follow the complete lesson guidelines in your *ACIM* book.

You are blessed beings, indeed. I am that one you know as Jesus. It is interesting that you consider yourself a multifaceted being in the sense that you give yourself many labels. You say that you are intelligent, unattractive, successful, a loser, fat, thin, generous, or mean — all these things. Rarely do you say, "I am love." This is a wonderful mantra for you to have: "I am love. I am loving. I am made by love, from love, for love. I am going to set that as my intention today so that whenever there is a decision to make, I will ask myself, 'Am I loving? What would the appropriate response be given that truth?'"

You will notice there are discrepancies between what you think you are and what this lesson shows you. That is the illusion under which you live. You believe you are separate from love, you have been abandoned by love, and love is dangerous. Love is many things, but you have rarely considered that you are love. When you consider this and act as if this is so, you sow seeds of love. You begin, in the eternal holy instant, to sow the harvest you will reap in the future.

When you say that you're dissatisfied, selfish, or unloving in any way, shape, or form: "I feel guilty. I feel disappointed. I feel all of these things," those are the frequency seeds you sow for your future. It is very simple. You reap what you sow, whether you like it or not. So make sure that you consider yourself to be a loving being, and then act accordingly.

This being has penned a book on our behalf called, *Love and a Map to the Unaltered Soul*. We suggest you read it, because it redefines love for you so that you make sure you are in accord with that definition and not the definition you have labored under in this society. Most of you think of love as something it is not. Please consider reading that text to get a good, clear definition of what love actually is.

I am that one you know as Jesus, and we will speak to you tomorrow.

LESSON 174

Review V: Part 4
God is but love; therefore, so am I.

Follow the complete lesson guidelines in your *ACIM* book.

You are blessed beings, indeed. I am that one you know as Jesus. By doing these lessons, you act in accord with this statement: "God is but love; therefore, so am I."

You are an idea in the mind of God. You are a sacred being brought into existence from that source energy you call God. This world, however, is not made by that being you call God. You can access that source energy from this plane, and that is really what we are all working together here to achieve.

You have chosen to come into separation. You came here to chase your idols. You believe in separation. Your body is a testament to that belief, and the unloving nature of a lot of your thoughts testifies to that belief in separation. When you attack people — saying something nasty, getting into an argument, and believing you have separate interests — and you don't get what you want or feel that if they get what they want it will be unfair, you act in accordance with your belief in separation.

Many of you will say: "I don't know what to do. I don't know how to speed up my evolutionary process. I want to be in that ascension process. I want to accomplish these spiritual goals." Then there is only one thing to do: Identify where you have fear and judgment, react negatively, and behave self-righteously, believing you know what is going on in a particular area. That can be with your body, politics, your partner, or any subject whatsoever. Where do you get upset? Where do you lose your peace? That is your indicator that you are acting in accord with separation rather than in accord with love. When you are in a loving place, you are not upset. You are happy and at peace.

There are no secrets kept here from you, none at all. Your guidance system is impeccable and constant. It always tells you how you are doing. As soon as you feel that little zap of fear, resentment, or anxiety, add love to the mix. Add love to the thinking. Turn that thought around and make it loving, whatever it is, and you can increase the speed of your evolution. All that's happening here is you choose love more than you choose fear, hate, or judgment.

The trouble is that some of your thought patterns are deeply ingrained through your conditioning programs. It is not easy to change them in a moment. It is a practice. You must see: "Ah, there I judged again." or "Oh, there I go again." You can see it is not a choice; it happens unconsciously in you. The behavior is a knee-jerk response that you do not consider.

Slowing down is a very good idea. You can see when you get too busy. You get fractious, confused, and agitated. That's because you're functioning in an unconscious way. Slow down, and then you can feel what is going on inside you. You can discern, "Ah, that conflict I just had didn't feel very good." If you remain in a rush all the time, which a lot of you in the West do, these feelings will not become noticeable until you've been in them a while and they have built up some momentum. Then you have trouble getting back to a state of love.

Always be grateful for negative emotions. Always be grateful. Do not berate yourself as being a bad student of *A Course in Miracles*. Rather, say, "Ah. I have encountered a negative belief somewhere in my mind. I can feel it is off. I can feel that my upset is intense. The negative emotional feedback I'm getting is very intense. That means it's something I really believe in even though it makes me feel bad." Be happy for the red flags, but do not be deceived by the form. It is always what arises in you, not what the other person does. It is always what it triggers in you.

You have thousands of untrue ideas in your mind. Most of them you don't encounter until a scenario in your life activates them, and they bubble up to the surface in the form of negative reactions. That is why you should be happy whenever you have a negative reaction, because it reveals a part of your unconscious/subconscious mind. Be grateful for all of your experiences in this lifetime. They are all educational — the "good" ones and the "bad" ones, as you call them. The "bad" ones are your clue to what goes on in your unconscious mind.

I am that one you know as Jesus, and we will speak to you again soon.

Review V: Part 5
God is but love; therefore, so am I.

Follow the complete lesson guidelines in your *ACIM* book.

You are blessed beings, indeed. I am that one you know as Jesus. You cannot be in fear and be connected to God. You cannot be in fear and know the truth of who you are. You cannot be in fear and not feel separated, so fear is your creation.

Fear is a demonstration that you are believing something that is untrue. You are misinterpreting something, or you are off track. It can be all those different things. Fear can also be generated by a mind that is trying to reconcile two irreconcilable beliefs. And this is why the phrase, "God is but love; therefore, so am I," is so important and why it is being repeated over and over again. You must realize that you are made in the image of God and thus loving, creative, and self-expressive. You must accept that that is what you are so that you do not experience fear. Anytime you experience fear, you have forgotten that you are made of love, from love, for love. You have attacked somebody or you are judging something or you are being awful to yourself or treating yourself poorly, so you will get that feedback.

Remember, your guidance system will always give you a red flag if you have stepped away from love. It is a beautiful, simple system. So you do not have to overintellectualize your practice. You do not have to memorize pages and pages of this text. What you need to do is to understand that anytime you step away from love, you will feel bad, and it is not God punishing you. God is loving. God is, in fact, not involved in this process with you. You are at Home in God still. This illusory dream in which you find yourself is exactly that. It is a dream of separation and fear and death. God has not joined you in that dream. Just as when your child goes to sleep and has a nightmare, you do not join in the nightmare with that child; you gently wake the child as kindly and lovingly as you can and tell her everything is okay.

That is all God does with you. That is all Spirit does with you. It wakes you up and says, "Everything is okay." You have merely frightened yourself with your imagination. Your powerful creative mind has gone off on a tangent of fear and death, and you are believing the dream that you have created.

We know that your experience is very real for you. And we are not dismissing your life and saying that you should not care. We are saying to trust in your guidance system. Trust that if you are feeling bad, you have done something unloving to yourself or someone else.

I am that one you know as Jesus, and we will see you again tomorrow.

LESSON 176

Review V: Part 6
God is but love; therefore, so am I.

Follow the complete lesson guidelines in your *ACIM* book.

You are blessed beings, indeed. I am that one you know as Jesus. When you see yourself as love, you value your life. You value the experiences you have here, and you trust that you are given exactly what you need to come to understand yourself more deeply.

This is one of the shifts in perception that is very good to make, to have an attitude of radical acceptance about your life. It is not imperative, but it helps you along your path. Instead of resisting things, accept they have come here because Spirit loves you and wants to show you something you are unaware of and have hidden from yourself. So it manifests in front of you. That is really what the ultimate act of love is, from All That Is to you. You are shown everything about yourself, manifested in front of you in form so that you get a feel for it and experience what goes on inside of you in a visceral way.

Because the greater part of your consciousness is hidden from you in the subconscious mind, you are not aware of a lot of the beliefs you hold. You're not aware of them until you encounter a situation, person, place, or thing in your life that brings them to the surface. This is a loving thing. Again, we want you to see problems not as something to be avoided but as something to be embraced through radical acceptance, knowing you have shown something from within you that is not at peace, not loving. That is exactly what you want to happen. You want to know what's going on in there.

What this does, this radical acceptance of your life, is it takes the attack out of you, and you begin to truly comprehend there is nothing to attack. It is only you encountering you in form. It seems to be outside of you. That is how you have designed experiences here, so that the things hidden from you seem to be separated from you. They are not.

This is one of the reasons you get so tired in this world. You are in a constant state of projection, getting rid of things in your mind that you don't want and then attacking them when you see them manifested out in the world. It is a much more relaxing path to practice radical acceptance of your life, knowing that even if you get triggered by something "out there," it is not out there; it is within you. The reaction is within you; therefore, it can be solved.

When it seems to be a separate person "out there," then you are power-less. You are the victim of the world. That is how most dualistic philoso-phies play out. That person a bad and should be punished. It has nothing to do with you. This keeps you in the role of victim even though it makes the ego feel more powerful.

You will hear many people counsel you and say that radical acceptance makes you weak. No, it does not. It makes you use your energy efficiently, and it gets you focused in the right direction rather than "out there." It gets you focused on your heart and mind, where you can see that these negative reactions arise from within your consciousness and nowhere else.

I am that one you know as Jesus, and we will see you again tomorrow.

LESSON 177

Review V: Part 7
God is but love; therefore, so am I.

Follow the complete lesson guidelines in your *ACIM* book.

You are blessed beings, indeed. I am that one you know as Jesus. You are traveling through this journey with us for good reason. This is a time on your planet when the escalating energies of love begin to be felt.

Those of you confused about this see that those aspects of you that are troublesome and have caused you difficulty are revisiting your conscious-ness so that you may have another look at them. Some of you are spiritual seekers who have traveled on this journey for a long time, and you will be surprised by what comes up for review. You thought you had dealt with all that long ago, but you have had some visitations by old habits, patterns, and even people from the past.

These are not signs of your failure but of your success. These are the small dregs of ideas and beliefs in your mind that you have not yet let go, forgiven, and risen above. You are given another opportunity to rise above those things and choose love instead.

Do not see any negative emotion or difficult situations as failures. They are far from it. They are opportunities for you to clear the table of any past errors you may or may not have made. They are only errors. They are not sins, and they are not failures. It is very important for you not to get discouraged at this point in your evolutionary journey. Your journey is one to love. Therefore, anything not-love in you shows itself one more time for you to add love to that situation. If you have people coming back into your life that you had dismissed, you must show love in this situation.

This does not mean that you are a doormat. It does not mean that you are put upon by those who have already put upon you. It may mean that, in fact, they come around one more time to lay their stories on you and you say: "I'm not falling for it this time. I have fallen for it so many times before. I send you on your way with love." It does not mean that you must become a victim of anything or anyone. In fact, what this time and place in your evolutionary cycle asks of you is to rise to your highest place yet. Stand firm and tall in love, and know who you are to the deepest depths of your soul.

I am that one you know as Jesus, and we will speak to you tomorrow.

LESSON 178

Review V: Part 8
God is but love; therefore, so am I.

Follow the complete lesson guidelines in your *ACIM* book.

You are blessed beings, indeed. I am that one you know as Jesus. What we will remind you of right now is your loving nature, your desire to align with All That Is.

Everything around you — all the people, places, and things — demonstrate your consciousness playing out the movie of your life. Just as when you witness a film on the movie screen, you see there are characters: the "good guy" and the "bad guy." You see the script has been written for them. They dress up in clothes, go on journeys, and have adventures. Good triumphs over evil. Your life is the same story. It is a movie you have written, directed, and fully participated in making. This is why it is pointless for you to attack it and judge it.

You are the maker of the movie. When you do not like a movie, you do not run up and try to change the movie screen, do you? This screen displays the actors and players on the screen of your life — the people around you and the experiences you're having. You go to the projector, and you change it there. You clip out the scenes you do not want, remove the actors that you do not want, or clean the fuzz off the lens that causes the imperfections you see.

That is what this study period is about. It is about removing from your mind the untrue idea that you are alone, a victim of this world, God does not love you, and God has abandoned you. These are all impurities on the projector that you must remove in order to see the movie clearly. That is what forgiveness is. It is merely you understanding that the imperfections in the movie come from the projector and not the screen.

This is a simple but powerful analogy, because you all understand how foolish it is to run up to the screen to try to rub off that image. That is what you do when you attack, judge, or say that "this" person is bad, "that" person is evil, or "this" situation is untenable. If you observe a situation out of accord with love, then you must, through the projector, add love to that situation. You must change your mind and add love.

This is where the battling of wars comes into being, when beings attack those people, places, and things that seem out there, out of their control, instead of changing their minds and the frequency of their thoughts so the movie reflects that transformation. They run up and try to change the screen by bombing a country or attacking another being, and it is foolish indeed. You see how foolish war is. It goes on and on because you change nothing. You never change the mental structure that causes the image to appear.

Become wise, dear beings. In your life, change your mind about anything not manifesting an image that you like to experience.

I am that one you know as Jesus, and we will speak to you tomorrow.

LESSON 179

Review V: Part 9
God is but love; therefore, so am I.

Follow the complete lesson guidelines in your *ACIM* book.

You are blessed beings, indeed. I am that one you know as Jesus. We are pleased you are still with us doing these lessons. These lessons are transformative, powerful, and designed specifically for the Western mind.

You have all been conditioned in the same way through various systems, and you all have the opportunity to reclaim your mental and emotional sovereignty. That is what we are about here. We bring you back into connection with your true nature, which is love. This is an easy place to get to despite the struggles you go through and the problems you think this course causes you. It is in this holy instant — this very moment now — that you choose. You choose love or fear.

We want you to understand that the systems that play in your world know this. They know that when you choose love, you rise up and connect with your true source of inspiration, strength, and love. They also know that when you are fearful, you become disconnected, disoriented, and much more easily managed. We understand there are certain strategies afoot in your modern technological realms, and they may have an impact on this particular channel's work.

Fear not. Stay in a place of love. Stay in a place of positivity. Stay in a place of knowing that this is goodness and truth. When you align with goodness and truth, you always find a way.

I am that one you know as Jesus, and we will speak to you tomorrow.

LESSON 180

Review V: Part 10
God is but love; therefore, so am I.

Follow the complete lesson guidelines in your *ACIM* book.

You are blessed beings, indeed. I am that one you know as Jesus. We are all the same. We are all loving beings who have forgotten that we are loving beings. We have also been taught the wrong definition of love.

We will speak about worry today. Many of you worry. You worry about Earth. You worry about politics. You worry about your children. You worry about your health. Worrying is not love; it is fear. That is why when you worry, you feel bad. When you worry about the environment, you feel bad. When you worry about the state of politics, you feel bad. When you worry about your children, you feel bad — and on and on and on.

Love is self-expression. Love is following your guidance, your passion.

Love is creativity. So when you have an issue — for example, your children are going on a trip without you and you are worried about them — witness the bad feeling. Go inside and understand, "I feel bad. That means I'm off track." Change the movie scenario causing your negative feelings — your children missing the bus or their plane, getting mugged, whatever scenario is playing out in your head — and turn it into a loving one. You see them frolicking on the beach with their friends having fun. You see them having great adventures. That is what love looks like. Love always feels good.

If you are in love with someone but you constantly feel bad, that is not love. When you live in your own consciousness and constantly feel bad about yourself, you do not love yourself. You are made by a loving Creator in the image and frequency of love. When you feel off track at all, know that you have made an unloving decision about yourself or someone else, and it may be based on an incorrect definition of love. Make sure you review what love means to you. Love gives freedom. Love is expressive. Love is nonjudgmental, and love, above all, gives freedom to those you love — including yourself.

Give yourself freedom to be who you are today. Allow your feelings to express in a loving way. Do not dump your negative emotions on other people, even if you feel those negative emotions. Take yourself aside and ask yourself, "If I'm feeling bad, that means I'm off track. Can I see this in a different way? There must be another way to see this."

God is but love; therefore, so are you. Feel good today. Be happy knowing that happiness is your natural inheritance. We will speak to you again tomorrow.

LESSON 181

I trust my fellow humans, who are one with me.

Follow the complete lesson guidelines in your *ACIM* book.

You are blessed beings, indeed. I am that one you know as Jesus. It is important for you to remember that these words are practice for you to learn how to do something.

When we ask you to do something, such as trust in your brothers, an immediate reaction from the ego consciousness says, "But I have been betrayed. I have been hurt so much by so many people that I cannot trust others." This reflects your mind. It does not reflect the world. This does not blame the victim here; we want to remind you that your world is created from within your perceptions and consciousness. If the first thing that arises in your mind when we ask you to trust is your deep level of distrust, you, in actual fact, see why we give this lesson to you. When you distrust based on past experience, you guarantee the future looks the same as the past, because you beam out a frequency of lack of trust.

When you lack trust in the world, your life, and your brothers and sisters, you are guaranteed to attract to you untrustworthy experiences and people, because you hold the belief in lack of trust. It is an important part of your forgiveness practice to give your brothers and sisters the benefit of the doubt and say, "Well, just for now, just for today, I am going to trust you." That does not mean, for example, that you give these people all your money. That is not what this lesson is about. It is about becoming unguarded, openhearted, and open-minded. You see more in that state of being. You connect with more, and you understand more.

When you bundle your defensiveness and your desire to attack in retaliation, you miss everything. You miss your life, in fact. You live in the past and contaminate the eternal now with past beliefs and ideas. This is where you create. You will suffer the same wounds in the future, because you believe in them.

For a few moments, several times an hour each day, we want you to practice this lesson. From this lesson, you feel a much increased level of safety, because you stop preparing for war.

I am that one you know as Jesus, and we will speak to you tomorrow.

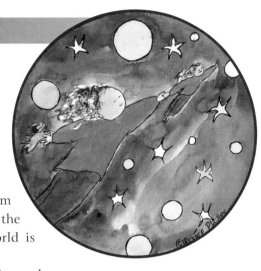

LESSON 182

I will be still an instant and go home.

Follow the complete lesson guidelines in your *ACIM* book.

You are blessed beings, indeed. I am that one you know as Jesus. One of the reasons you keep busy in this world is because you are afraid to be still.

You are highly productive. You jog and run, go to the gym, and make all kinds of arrangements throughout the day. You barely stop to be still and to go within. It is there — in the quiet space of your heart and mind — that you find the truth of who you are. In meditation, prayer, and contemplation, you come to understand how scared you are and how lonely you feel. As long as you keep running on that hamster wheel that the West loves you to run on, you will not make progress. You will not come to see the demons that drive you. You will not see why you are so heavily armored and ready to fight. Not until you stop, become quiet, and listen to that still small voice within will you get the guidance you need.

When you are polluted with fear, drugs, alcohol, workaholism, and shopaholism — all these "isms" that you have in this society driving you to seek outside yourself that which cannot be found there — you exhaust yourself. Many of you are tired. You need to rest, but you never feel better. Each day comes, and you drag yourself out of bed to continue on the roads of the ego's world.

We ask you now to stop that journey — not permanently, of course, but pause just for a few minutes. Stop the judgments, the fear, and the endless action. Sit quietly with yourself and Christ consciousness, and invite that into your life, into your being. Truly and absolutely with every cell of your body, invite peace into your mind.

You know you have chased many idols. You have chased many tantalizing temptations, and not a one of them has made you happy. They may have given you pleasure for a little while, but you are not happy. You know some terrible error is playing out on this plane, an error of fear and separation. It is in that realization that you become teachable and surrender to your desire to return Home to the arms of love. In that surrender, you find the peace you seek.

We come to you every day because we know the truth. We come to you because we know how all of you suffer. We come to you to lead you toward that doorway into peace. Keep walking with us. We hold your hand, and we support you as you go along that path you have chosen into fear. We merely return you Home to your natural state, to your natural Home in the arms of God.

I am that one you know as Jesus, and we will speak to you again tomorrow.

I call on God's name and on my own.

Follow the complete lesson guidelines in your *ACIM* book.

You are blessed beings, indeed. I am that one you know as Jesus. This sounds a little crazy (does it not?), that all you have to do is use God's name and call on him to come to you.

There is a highway of sorts between you and the Father. It is through this prayer or incantation that you connect directly to All That Is. You are saying — in speaking this word over and over again throughout the day and all of your activities — "I may be doing the dishes, I may be cooking dinner, or I may be inputting computer information, but my mind is elsewhere. My heart is elsewhere. My home is elsewhere, and I call on you, God, to bring me the peace that surpasses all understanding."

It will happen, especially if you use this word when you are troubled or when you come across one of your triggers in the day. Do not descend into hell — into the battleground — but rise through this high-frequency word to that place of connection with the Divine Father.

It is a miracle that you are all here with us today. You continue to choose these lessons above the temptations of the world. Each of you has begun to feel considerable differences in your normal state of being, in your normal state of thought. You are now almost halfway through this journey, and you have started reaping the rewards of your dedication. Just as somebody who goes to the gym for six months sees an undeniable transformation, so do you. And, dear ones, this is just the beginning of the reclamation of your heart, mind, and connection to your Father.

I am that one you know as Jesus, and we will speak to you tomorrow.

LESSON 184

The name of God is my inheritance.

Follow the complete lesson guidelines in your *ACIM* book.

You are blessed beings, indeed. I am that one you know as Jesus. The awareness that everything is connected is one of the fundamental tenets of this particular teaching.

You are not free from the effects of your thinking. When you attack others, you wound yourself. You are all connected. You give as you receive. These are all principles stating the same thing. When you see you are unified as an aspect of God mind (you are an idea in the mind of God), you see that to attack another, who is also an idea in the mind of God, is pointless, ridiculous, and, in fact, blasphemous.

Understand that with forgiveness, you lose nothing. You gain everything because you do not punch at shadows anymore. That is what happens when you attack or judge your brother or perceive him as less than you. You attack you. It is hard for you to remember this, so we get you to focus your mind on the oneness of all things.

We get you to tell yourself that you are part of a unified consciousness, and it is so. You are the collective brotherhood and sisterhood of humanity. You are powerful creators made in the image of your Creator. Your Creator makes you in Its image — loving, expansive, self-expressive, freedom seeking, and intelligent, and that is what all of you are.

You have mistaken your brothers and sisters for enemies. You believe that if you attack them, you remain free from attack. That is one of the greatest illusions of all. Actually, you hurt when you attack another, for you attack another thought in the same one mind.

I am that one you know as Jesus, and we will speak to you tomorrow.

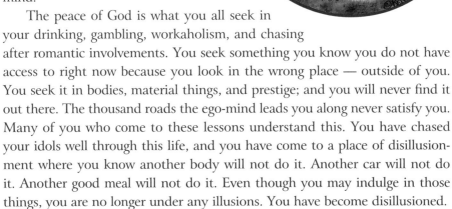

I want the peace of God.

Follow the complete lesson guidelines in your *ACIM* book.

You are blessed beings, indeed. I am that one you know as Jesus. There is nothing greater to attain than a peaceful mind.

The peace of God is what you all seek in your drinking, gambling, workaholism, and chasing after romantic involvements. You seek something you know you do not have access to right now because you look in the wrong place — outside of you. You seek it in bodies, material things, and prestige; and you will never find it out there. The thousand roads the ego-mind leads you along never satisfy you. Many of you who come to these lessons understand this. You have chased your idols well through this life, and you have come to a place of disillusionment where you know another body will not do it. Another car will not do it. Another good meal will not do it. Even though you may indulge in those things, you are no longer under any illusions. You have become disillusioned.

As you come to know that illusions have no value and see that you no longer want the things the world offers you, it will seem as if you live in a barren desert. But it is not a barren desert; it is the way Home. To go inside is a rich experience. To chase the idols of the world is a pointless experience. To become familiar with the inner landscapes of your creativity, inspiration, love, joy, and enthusiasm is the wonderful free gift this internal investigation offers you. This internal investigation has great value because it offers you the peace of God.

There will come a point you learn when not to argue anymore. You do not need to argue with anyone. You do not need to chase anything. You will find yourself going through the days of your life happily peaceful. You will then realize how foolish all your games have been, how wasteful of your energy and, at times, money your games have been. When that happens, you can sit peacefully in your back garden and be at home experiencing the peace of God with a quiet mind, a peaceful heart, and a happy demeanor, wanting nothing, needing nothing, and knowing that all is as it should be.

I am that one you know as Jesus, and we will speak to you again tomorrow.

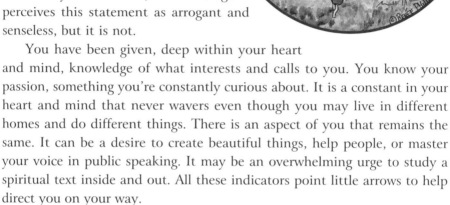

Salvation of the world depends on me.

Follow the complete lesson guidelines
in your *ACIM* book.

You are blessed beings, indeed. I am
that one you know as Jesus. The ego
perceives this statement as arrogant and
senseless, but it is not.

You have been given, deep within your heart
and mind, knowledge of what interests and calls to you. You know your
passion, something you're constantly curious about. It is a constant in your
heart and mind that never wavers even though you may live in different
homes and do different things. There is an aspect of you that remains the
same. It can be a desire to create beautiful things, help people, or master
your voice in public speaking. It may be an overwhelming urge to study a
spiritual text inside and out. All these indicators point little arrows to help
direct you on your way.

This being [the channel] used to read this statement and think it was
crazy. She did not understand what her destiny was, but she had an overwhelming urge to study this material, *A Course in Miracles*. She had an overwhelming urge to find peace of mind, and so she forgave. She kept on until
her perception shifted so much that she opened that portal between Earth
and heaven to make communication possible for us to her.

You may read this conversation and think we initiated it, but it is not
so. She initiated it by doing her forgiveness practice, relentlessly seeking
peace of mind whenever an upset occurred, owning her perception, and asking to change that perception so that she could see the truth. She sought
that which she knew made her feel better. That was the guidance she had,
unrelentingly turning her back to *A Course in Miracles* over and over again. It
made no sense to her at the time.

Your passion — your guidance — may not make any sense to you at
this time. If it unrelentingly calls you, listen and trust that you are directed
by your guides and teachers toward your sacred purpose.

I am that one you know as Jesus, and we will speak to you tomorrow.

I bless the world because I bless myself.

Follow the complete lesson guidelines
in your *ACIM* book.

You are blessed beings, indeed. I am that one you know as Jesus. I bless myself; therefore, I bless the world. I bless the world; therefore, I bless myself. You give as you receive. You receive as you give.

This is a reciprocal universe. It is holographic, and it is reciprocal. That means whatever you sow, you will reap. If you go through your day judging others, then you will feel judged. If you go through your day extending love, then you will receive love.

It is so important to understand your connection to everything and everyone, because you are not an island. No man is an island; no woman is an island. Everything you have ever taken from the earth or have polluted Earth with, you now see returned to you in kind. It is not a punishment. It is merely the nature of this place.

Bless everything you would like to bless you. Bless your brothers and sisters. Bless yourself. Bless me. Bless the universe. Bless nature. Bless the animals. Bless the fresh air. Bless the trees. As you go through your day, give away the love you have for all these things, and appreciate them. That is what appreciation is. You bestow on everything you see the love that is your natural state. And it comes back to you in the form of opportunities. It comes back to you in the form of a beautiful sunny day. It comes back to you in the form of beautiful relationships. It comes back to you in the form of all kinds of abundance. You act in abundance when you appreciate and bless everything you see.

I am that one you know as Jesus, and we will speak to you tomorrow.

The peace of God is shining in me now.

Follow the complete lesson guidelines
in your *ACIM* book.

You are blessed beings, indeed. I am that one you know as Jesus. The peace of God shines in you today. It is merely covered with some dirt and debris that does not belong inside your mind. That is all that has caused your suffering today — little ideas and beliefs and some big ideas and beliefs that terrorized you into fear.

It is a profound comprehension to realize that the very vital life force — the spirit, creativity, and love that inhabits you — is your true nature. All these other prickles, distortions, and disturbances are not your true nature. They are ideas that interfere with your bliss. Ananda is bliss. Love is bliss. Peace is bliss. It happens when you have those moments on Earth — you all have had them — during which you are perfectly happy.

You may not be doing anything. You may be just sitting on a log looking out at the ocean or in a park listening to the birds or snuggled in your warm bed, and you are perfectly happy and need nothing at all. Those moments, indeed, are precious because they show you it is not about fancy cars and big bank accounts. It is about peace. Those moments show you that peace of mind is the most precious gift you can give yourself.

When you encounter these negativities — your short temper, your impatience, or your sharp tongue — remember this is not your natural state. That is something you have learned. It is something that is a distortion. It is something that is a little bit out of order. We want you to see it that way. Instead of saying, "I am a terrible person because I didn't like that person. I am a terrible person because I was short or flippant or sarcastic," or whatever crime you accuse yourself of, do not see it as you. Say, "Ah, there is one of those aspects clouding the clear mirror of my mind. There is one of the little distortions. It is not who I am although it appears to be. It is an illusion. It comes out of my mouth, yes. The idea forms in my mind, but this is not the true me. The true me is kind, generous, loving, and creative and believes in the truth of these teachings."

When you doubt or lose your faith, you leap to the side of the ego's fence. On that side is despair, death, sickness, fear, worry, and loneliness. Leap back to our side of the fence as soon as you feel yourself dip down — as soon as you feel yourself go down the dark rabbit hole. Do your best to prevent yourself from going down there by picking up *A Course in Miracles*, reading this book, or reading one of our dear one's other books. Do your best to prevent yourself from going down that hole.

If you go down that hole, then use it as a sound lesson to determine what's going on in your mind. Too much momentum in your negative beliefs, thoughts, and ideas can take you down the rabbit hole on a regular basis. Each time you go, ask yourself, "What was I thinking the second before I started to go down the rabbit hole? What unloving thought did I have about myself or someone else right before I went down that rabbit hole?" You will see it was a choice. It may have been an unconscious or less-than-intelligent choice, but it was a choice. You had an unloving thought, you believed that thought, and that thought took you into the ego's realm.

The next time this happens, remain conscious and ask yourself, "What did I do just before this happened?" Doing this will help you sidestep the rabbit hole. Say, "I don't need to go down there. I do not need to make this unloving decision. I do not need to attack myself or anyone else. I need to be free of these beliefs and ideas. The less frequently I choose them, the more free from them I become."

I am that one you know as Jesus, and we will speak to you again tomorrow.

LESSON 189

I feel the love of God within me now.

Follow the complete lesson guidelines in your *ACIM* book.

You are blessed beings, indeed. I am that one you know as Jesus. The love of God for and within you is your natural inheritance.

All these scary fantasies you have — fears of judgment, opinions, angers, and upsets — and all this drama are self-created. You have a choice. Are you going to become embroiled in every little ripple on the surface of the sea, or are you going live a peaceful life? Are you going to dive deep and enjoy the calm depth and beauty of silence?

If you find yourself running around the world at high speed every single day, this is your clue that you are afraid of God and you do not value your spiritual evolution. This is your clue you are distracting yourself from some deep fears you hold. You do not want to be still because you fear what you will see. You do not trust what you will see.

Those of you who are busy bees, we would like you to give yourselves an hour each day that is not assigned to tasks — not even reading *A Course in Miracles* — and just be still. Now, you can take a cup of tea with you out into the garden and just be outside. You can go for a walk and find a quiet place to sit and contemplate. You can go to your room, lie on your bed, and rest. Rest is a beautiful thing. Calmness is a beautiful thing. It will give space for the messages you all so desperately want to arrive. If you do not create space for messages, inspiration, and guidance, how are we going to get it to you? Well, we will get it to you in your dreamtime if we are lucky, but many of you have dismissed your dreams as unreal and unimportant, so you don't remember them.

If you feel you do not get messages, slow down, create space to receive them, and ask for those messages to be clearly given to you (in whatever form is suitable for you in the evolution that you have right now). Some beings cannot hear the voice for God because it would terrify the living daylights out of them. Some beings could not handle this kind of transmission because it would drive them insane. They would have too many fears pop up.

If you genuinely have an interest to connect with your guides and teachers and develop a relationship with them, then give it space. Allow the love of God to arise in you and bring a peaceful opening — a quiet pause in the day where you can just be with whatever happens.

I am that one you know as Jesus, and we will speak to you tomorrow.

I choose the joy of God instead of pain.

Follow the complete lesson guidelines
in your *ACIM* book.

You are blessed beings, indeed. I am
that one you know as Jesus. At this
stage of your development, when you are
a little over halfway through these lessons,
you find this kind of lesson impossible to believe.

This lesson does not ring true to you because you have twisted your ankle, you have had a broken heart, you've been divorced, you've been abandoned, or you have been at the mercy of your own miscreations. That's exactly what has happened: You have been at the mercy of your own mis-creations. You are not a victim of this world. As this lesson says, the world is the result of a lot of thoughts, beliefs, and ideas. If you want to change the world, then you must change the thoughts, beliefs, and ideas you hold firm and act in accord with.

You see, if you believe that a certain part of the population is danger-ous — for example, you fear black people, and you are white — every time you feel that fear as you cross the street, bar your door, or buy a gun, you act in accord with your intense belief. So it must manifest in the world, not as a punishment, but as a true reflection of your consciousness. If you believe black people are dangerous, then they will be for you. The same thing happens with women who view men as dangerous. They are con-stantly attacked, put down, and berated because the world reflects to them the beliefs that they are unworthy, powerless, worthless, ugly, or whatever their conditioned beliefs and ideas are.

You have to see what you believe you are and what you act in accor-dance with. As you change your mind, the world will change. Beings who have been doing *A Course in Miracles* for many years tell you that miracles have happened, their lives are completely different now, and all they have done is their forgiveness practice. All they have done is this work you are asked to do.

Come to these lessons willingly. We have said this before. Do not resist them. Do not argue with them. Trust you have been given the means to heal your mind and, therefore, create miracles in the world to experience and enjoy.

I am that one you know as Jesus, and we will speak to you tomorrow.

LESSON 191

I am the holy child of God himself.

Follow the complete lesson guidelines in your *ACIM* book.

You are blessed beings, indeed. I am that one you know as Jesus. You are the holy child of God. I am the holy child of God. You are all beautiful, holy, and divine members of the mind of God.

When you truly know this, you are not cruel and you are not needy. You are in accord with your true nature, and you can walk through the world head held high — not in arrogance, but knowing that you are love personified. You have a great purpose here, and you are an eternal being. It is your belief in death, your frailty, and your smallness that makes you hungry, attack others, and act spiteful and vicious.

When you understand the true nature of your grandeur — not in the grandiosity of the ego that says, "I am so special," but the grandeur of knowing your true origin — then you will have courage, wisdom, and humility. You will walk through this world shining a light beyond others' ability to understand. They will say: "What is it that is different about you? You do not cower in the corner like other people I know. You do not grasp and crave like other people. You seem at peace even though this world is such a crazy place. What do you have?" In that moment, you can tell them that you are a holy child of God, and there is nothing to fear.

I am that one you know as Jesus, and we will speak to you again tomorrow.

I have a function God would have me fill.

Follow the complete lesson guidelines in your *ACIM* book.

You are blessed beings, indeed. I am that one you know as Jesus. Many of you ask what your purpose is: "Can I be a painter, a writer, a mother, or a father. Can I do something important or something fulfilling?" Your purpose here is forgiveness.

Why is that so powerful? Well, forgiveness is your demonstration that you understand the laws of creation. You understand that everything you engage in is a choice. It is your free will, and you create any suffering you endure. When you forgive, you demonstrate your wisdom. When you forgive, you demonstrate your desire for peace, joy, and abundance. When you forgive, you understand your mind is the culprit.

Your mind is the one that accuses. Your mind is the angry one. Your mind is the intolerant one, and it is your mind that needs work. Forgiveness is the way you work on your own mind.

When you step back from judging the world, from your self-righteous anger, and from your accusations, you are left with you. That is exactly where you should focus your attention and intention. What do you want to experience here? How would you like to grow? What would you like to create? How would you like to express your love? These are the things you should focus on, not on other people's errors. You have enough of your own to deal with.

Step back from judgment, knowing it is the greatest gift you do not give to your neighbor but to yourself. Give yourself peace and equanimity, and give yourself a simple and joyful life. It is your natural inheritance; it is your right. You have become so lost and confused in the mire of multiple judgments on this planet that you — and the rest of society — think war and punishment make everything better. All you have to do is look at your world, but you keep doing this over and over again.

Try forgiveness. Try love. Try peace.

I am that one you know as Jesus, and we will speak to you tomorrow.

All things are lessons God would have me learn.

Follow the complete lesson guidelines in your *ACIM* book.

You are blessed beings, indeed. I am that one you know as Jesus. It is so simple, is it not? Just forgive whatever upsets you, and your pain and suffering leaves you. It is the truth.

Every time you encounter a negative emotion, you see that you are judging something — yourself, another person, a situation, a country, or a political leader. You see that you hold yourself or others to be sinners, or there is something happening that should not happen.

If it's happening, then it's meant to happen. That is your lesson today. If something happens, then it does for a reason. It is happening to show you something. It might be happening to show you the unforgiveness of your society. It might be happening to show you your quick temper. It might be happening to show you that you cannot save somebody else. You must save you first. Everything is designed to show you something you need to see. Forgiveness is part of your work so that you get the lesson.

If you are in a resistant, a judgmental, or an unforgiving state of mind, then you will not see it as a lesson, so you will not learn the lesson. That means you have your hands up; you have an energetic wall. You say, "It is wrong. This thing that is happening is wrong." We want you to say: "This thing is happening to show me something. Let me examine the lesson. Let me forgive so that I can be open enough to interpret this situation correctly."

You might see others behave in a way you deem cruel. When you forgive, you realize you do not know their motivations. You do not know their history. You do not know what their purpose is. You do not know what assignment they have been given in this incarnation. You are not qualified to judge others because you don't know anything. But you do not get that lesson until you forgive. As long as you stand in self-righteous judgment of others, the ego tells you it knows those people should do those things. But if those people do those things, then they are using God-given free will. They will have their own experiences to learn from, and it really is none of your business.

Unless there is something right in front of you that requires your attention, action, or intervention, then it is not your business. If a child runs out into traffic in front of you, your instinct will be to stop it, and that is okay. We are not saying that you should not participate in life in an intelligent and loving way. What we are saying is that it is your business if it is right in front of you.

When it involves people in your house, a thought in your mind, your coworker sitting at the desk next to you, then it affects you. Still, any suffering you have because of these people dissipates when you forgive them and say: "I don't know why they're doing what they're doing. All I know is that if I judge, I suffer, and that does not help anything. Perhaps I can add love to the mix instead of judgment."

Forgiveness is the step before love. You must forgive first before you can love in response to a call for love. That is what any sin or bad behavior is. It is a call for love, not a call for more separation. Think about this: When people behave badly, that means they are confused. It means they have lost their way, and that does not mean you berate, attack, or punish them. It means that you love them. Offer them a helping hand, even if it is a mental prayer because you cannot help them physically.

Help others mentally and emotionally by sending them love and asking that they receive the correct guidance in their lives. It's just as you ask for yourself: "Please show me the correct way to live my life so that I may be of assistance rather than a hindrance to my brothers and sisters."

I am that one you know as Jesus, and we will speak to you tomorrow.

LESSON 194

I place the future in the hands of God.

Follow the complete lesson guidelines in your *ACIM* book.

You are blessed beings, indeed. I am that one you know as Jesus. Does this not sound like a great relief to you: to place your future in the hands of God?

The ego tells you this is not safe, that you

should place your future in its hands. It has great plans to control the world, judge people, and keep everything in order. Just take a minute to think about that. Which feeling gives you a sense of security? Which option makes you feel safer: allowing the ego to do what it does, or giving your future to the hands of God? After all, God is that benevolent force that has created you. Why would God allow anything untoward happen to you?

Your sicknesses are of the ego's manufacture. They do not come from God. They come from your fears, resistance, and control issues. They come from you trying to do what you do in a separated, isolated, and demented mind. Your sicknesses do not come from God, and that is why it is so important for you to realize the power of this decision. Health, life, and love are in God's image, not death, sickness, pain, and suffering. You must observe the fruits of the thought system that you follow. You must understand that God is love, and death is not of God. Sickness is not of God. Health, living, creativity, and loving are of God. You are made in God's image.

Make this decision throughout your day today: Do not worry about the future. Do not think about what might happen if you do "this" and you do "that." Trust that in this moment that if you do your best in whatever situation you are in — you forgive and you bring love to whatever you do — then you do, in fact, trust in a divine purpose. Thus, you are giving your future over to the hands of God.

In that surrender of your destiny, you relax; and you do the very best you can in this moment. Instead of being contaminated by fear, worry, and resentment, you stay present. You are, in this holy instant, loving. That will guarantee you a beautiful future.

I am that one you know as Jesus, and we will speak to you tomorrow.

LESSON 195

Love is the way I walk in gratitude.

Follow the complete lesson guidelines in your *ACIM* book.

You are blessed beings, indeed. I am that one you know as Jesus. You have so much to be grateful for. You are here, residing in this temporary vehicle giving yourself the opportunity to find love. What a thing to be grateful for!

You have been given the means to transform your mind from suffering to peace. What a wonderful thing to be grateful for! You are given many encounters with your brothers and sisters as opportunities to forgive. What a wonderful thing to be grateful for! Your body seems to function and get you moving around the world in which you have this purpose. What a wonderful thing to be grateful for!

You have so much to be grateful for, yet your mind can find that one thing it does not have or that one trespass somebody has committed against you, and the multiplicity of things for which you could be grateful disappears in the darkness of judgment and the belief in sin. When you judge, believe in sin, focus on that one person in the whole world that has done something wrong that you decide should not ever have been allowed, you give up the entire world. You give up the peace that is your natural right.

It is a choice. You do it through free will. You do not realize because nobody has taught you the consequences of judgment. Here we teach you the true consequences of judgment. To judge another, you lose everything — your peace and the appreciation of every single thing around you. You know when you have a resentment running around your mind — hatred or a chip on your shoulder — everything disappears except that low-frequency thought, that belief you have that you keep going back to.

So forgive. Walk in gratitude, and know that you will be rewarded with love — a connection to love, a desire to love — and know you are a loving being. When you use your free will to judge, you unplug yourself from the Source of all love, and you feel terrible. You mistakenly blame others for their behavior, which makes you feel bad. Truthfully, it is your judgment that makes you feel bad. And that is a choice. You do not have to do it.

When you choose gratitude, you realize just how insignificant those minor trespasses are. They don't compare to peace, love, and the ability to have happiness.

I am that one you know as Jesus, and we will speak to you again tomorrow.

It can be but myself I crucify.

Follow the complete lesson guidelines
in your *ACIM* book.

You are blessed beings, indeed. I am
that one you know as Jesus. It can be but
yourself you crucify when you accuse or
judge another. You disconnect yourself from
oneness, and you suffer. When you attack yourself,
you disconnect from love, and you suffer. It can be but you that you crucify.

In all the antics of this world, it is the last thing you think that when
you hurl an insult or an attack at others, you are crucifying yourself. You do
not understand the profound connection others have with you, because you
are the creator of your world, your dream. Every character you encounter
in your experience of life, which is a dreamlike experience (once you pass
over into other realms, you will see that this is a dreamlike experience), and
every character in your play is there for a reason.

The "bad guys" are there to demonstrate your desire and belief in attack
and vengeance. That is why they are there, so that you can see the hatred
in your mind that you hide from yourself. Think about this a moment.
Anytime a "bad" character walks across the screen of your life, you get to
see your belief in hatred and attack shown to you through visceral feelings,
unloving ideas, and thoughts of murder.

Now this all sounds very dramatic — thoughts of murder. But when
you look at the human race, war, the inner city streets of your big cities,
and the number of people killed each year by guns in North America alone,
you will have a hard argument to convince me that murder is not on many
people's minds. Murder is on the ego's mind, and it will carry it out given
the correct circumstances. It is important for you to understand that you
are capable of this kind of brutality. Until you take your ego very seriously,
it rules you. We do not want it to rule you, because it shows its colors in
your world today in violence, poverty, and unloving actions by people and
their governments. We want you to truly understand that every time you
attack somebody in thought, word, or deed, there lurks a murderous ego
beneath the surface of your social face.

We do not tell you this to terrorize you. We tell you this so that you understand how important this work is and given the right circumstances, most of you would kill if you were required to. Some of you will say, "Oh no, not me, I would never do that." But some of you know you have been in circumstances where, given the right scenario with the right weapons, you could have pulled the trigger. We want you to understand that this is okay. This is a world of separation. But you must understand the brutality of the ego to deal with it in a disciplined and focused way.

We encourage you to continue on this work together so that you can override the ego's rule of "attack now or attack later" and its viciousness and cruelty so that you can create a loving and kind world with an experience that is generous, kind, and beautiful for you too. You do not need to suffer the way you do, but you must understand the ego's motivations. You must understand that attack must be relinquished from your repertoire.

I am that one you know as Jesus, and we will speak to you tomorrow.

LESSON 197

It can be but
my gratitude I earn.

Follow the complete lesson guidelines
in your *ACIM* book.

You are blessed beings, indeed. I am that one you know as Jesus. Gratitude is very close in frequency to love. Gratitude means that you understand what is going on here. Gratitude for what you have shows you understand that what you don't have was not meant to be yours right now.

This seems contradictory, because we tell you that you have been given everything — and you have been given everything — but you cannot experience everything all at once. It would be too overwhelming for you. Through gratitude, you set the stage for a future as beautiful as the present, because through gratitude, you are saying everything is as perfect as it should be.

Even if you have given your brother something and he did not recognize the gift you gave him, you still gave the gift. Since there is no separation between your brother and you, you have only given the gift to yourself, anyway. God's all-encompassing arms hold all this giving, taking, and receiving. So whenever you give anything, you give it to God. So give your best to you. Be kind to yourself. That is a gift to God, and you honor God.

When you attack yourself, you blaspheme against God. You do not think of it this way. You think you just hurt your little old self; but you do, in fact, attack God. You are an idea in the mind of God. Would you treat that badly? Your brother or sister is an idea in the mind of God. Would you treat God badly?

You must remember the magnitude of the game you play here. You are playing with God and yourself. You are playing with consciousness that is all-encompassing, which is a magnificent and powerful thing to behold. You think all the little games you play are tiny, but they are creative with all your magnificent abilities behind them. When you attack somebody, renege on a promise, hurt somebody, or judge others, you are using the power of a god in that unloving thought, word, and deed.

Make sure you use your gratitude for everything. Thank those beings in your life that cause you difficulty, because they sharpen your practice. They give you something to forgive. They give you something challenging to forgive, and you receive great rewards for doing that — not because God blesses you but because you demonstrate your understanding of what is going on here.

You are sacred beings, and we want you to treat each other as such. We want you to treat yourselves as such. Be grateful that you have this opportunity to remove all the unloving thoughts from your minds. Be grateful to those who show you how hateful or angry you can be. Be grateful to them because they help you with your practice by revealing the dark shadows hidden beneath the surface of your consciousnesses.

I am that one you know as Jesus, and we will speak to you again tomorrow.

Only my condemnation injures me.

Follow the complete lesson guidelines
in your *ACIM* book.

You are blessed beings, indeed. I am
that one you know as Jesus. This is the
most powerful news (is it not?), that only
your condemnation hurts you.

There is always an unforgiving thought behind
any pain you have. If you fear the future, for example, and perhaps think
you won't have enough money, then it is an unforgiving thought. You have
declared the world unkind, unloving, and ungenerous to you. You have said,
"I will be without," and that is an unforgiving thought. It is an unloving
thought. If you say, "Everything is fine. I will be wonderful in three weeks
even though I can't see where I will get the funds to live. I will be cared for,"
then you will feel a completely different frequency enter your body and
mind. That is the frequency of love. That is the frequency of acceptance,
gratitude, and faith.

These things have frequency. Just as fear has frequency and just as
condemnation and judgment have frequency, so do the opposite of those
thoughts and the feelings they engender. We want you to understand that
your feelings of guilt, shame, fear, pain, or any kind of suffering come from
beliefs you hold that are unloving and unforgiving. You must go beneath
the surface form, and you must decide what you are out of alignment with.
Where are you attacking? Where are you judging? Where are you condemning? If you do not delve below the surface of the feeling, you will not
understand the thoughts of your unloving mind.

We are not blaming the victim. We are merely educating you on what
causes suffering. There are momentary periods of physical pain in your life
— when you stub your toe on the bed or drop a hammer on your foot or
bite your tongue, something like that. When you look at the years you have
been alive, it is not the physical pain that is the problem. It is the constant
mental and emotional suffering you go through that we speak about here.
And that is a choice. That is your choice. You use your free will to accept,
love, and forgive or to condemn, judge, and separate.

It is up to you. You are the captain of your ship. You must look at the suffering you experience throughout ordinary days. We do not mean physical pain. We're not talking about toothaches and headaches. (Although they have something to do with this, but we will cover that at another time.) We mean emotional pain and mental suffering. It is optional. It is not required, and you are the culprit.

This is a difficult pill to swallow, for sure, because you feel that others have hurt you. The truth of the matter is that if you forgive them and stop condemning them, the pain stops. When that happens, you see the truth of what we say.

I am that one you know as Jesus, and we will speak to you tomorrow.

LESSON 199

I am not a body. I am free.

Follow the complete lesson guidelines in your *ACIM* book.

You are blessed beings, indeed. I am that one you know as Jesus. That was the lesson I taught on the crucifixion day. I am not a body; I am free. The laws of this world do not bind me, and neither do they bind you, if you understand them and practice love and forgiveness.

That is the qualifier. You must align yourself with truth, not the untruth that the evidence of the body provides you. The body says you are separate. The body says you are alone. The body says you die. The body says you feel pain. The body is the ego's ultimate weapon. Do not focus on the body; focus on the mind. When you train the mind, pursue love, and relinquish attack thoughts, your body takes care of itself, because it thrives at the frequency you will hold.

When you focus on the body and make it the giver and getter of everything you want, you become very fearful. Many of you notice that you feel worse when you try to mold and shape the body through diet and exercise or even just by judging the body. You feel less loving toward yourself. You feel more controlling, fearful, and materialistic. That happens because you are focusing on the least loving aspect of your experience here, which is the ego-driven body.

The body, in and of itself, is a neutral object. When the ego uses it as bait, such as material for war, it becomes a very unloving thing. When you choose to pursue love and you do not focus on the body but on your creativity and your ability to extend your qualities of charisma, kindness, and generosity, the body becomes a useful tool. That is what we seek through this lesson for you to understand. The only valid use the body has is as a tool to take you Home to love. It does not do this through its use as a sexual object or an object of beauty but through its use as a tool designed to take you on a journey through your own consciousness.

I am that one you know as Jesus, and we will speak to you tomorrow.

LESSON 200

There is no peace except the peace of God.

Follow the complete lesson guidelines in your *ACIM* book.

You are blessed beings, indeed. I am that one you know as Jesus. Have you not noticed that the older you get the more tired you get and the less interested in the world you become?

Those energetic years of youth soon pass away as you trudge through your twenties with broken hearts and broken bank accounts. You head into your thirties convinced that the next phase of your program will make you happy — the house, children, family, mortgage, debt, and forty-hour workweek. All these things build up into what you would consider a midlife crisis, but it's what we on this side consider a great burst for freedom.

Many of you come to these teachings in your forties or fifties — or even later — because you have tried all of the roads. You have tried everything you were taught would make you happy, and not one of those things has, indeed, made you happy. You still wonder what is missing, because it is not held in the world. It is your home, love, and connection to the Divine that is missing. That love is irreplaceable by any material good, human body, or form.

This makes many of you sad to think nothing in this world holds your happiness for long. It is true. It is a sad place. You can see that written on the faces of many people walking the streets. But there are glad tidings. You have been given the means to return Home. You have been given the information you need to practice to make this journey on Earth a lot better and eventually take you back to that place from which you came, which is the all-encompassing, loving arms of God.

I am that one you know as Jesus, and we will speak to you tomorrow.

Lesson 201

Review VI: Part 1
I am not a body. I am free,
for I am still as God created me.

Follow the complete lesson guidelines in your *ACIM* book.

You are blessed beings, indeed. I am that one you know as Jesus. All the trials and tribulations you go through in your daily life happen because you try to be something you are not.

You try to be socially acceptable. You try to be something that your parents taught you to be. You do not listen to your guidance system. You do not listen to that deep truth inside you that is love, joy, creativity, and self-expression. Freedom, self-expression, and love — these are the pursuits that should occupy your mind.

You are as God created you. You are not a mistake. You have come here into this dimension, this pointed 3D experience you call your life, and it is a detour into fear. It is a detour into something not your natural home. Many of you say to each other: "I do not feel as if I belong here. I do not feel that my family is the right family. I almost feel as if I've been dropped into the wrong place." It is because you are not at home here. You have walked far away from Home.

The story of the prodigal son comes to mind. The child leaves his father's home and goes on a great adventure. At some point, he gets tired and broken, loses all his money, and he wants to come home. That is where most of you are right now. You have had your adventures. You have chased many idols in the world, and you have yet to find the happiness you seek. Now you want to come home, but you are scared. You have become lost in the wilderness. You are confused. That is what this text is for; it is the gentle map Home.

You cannot be taken home too quickly, because you have chosen to go on this long and arduous journey, this detour into fear. You will never have your free will overridden. It is so important that you understand this. Some of you fall down on your knees in despair and plead, "Please take me home. I don't want to be here anymore." You are here through free will. You are unloving through free will. It takes a little bit of an education for you to see that all the suffering you experience comes from distortions in your mind that you believe in and continue to practice throughout your day.

These gentle lessons rehabilitate your mind and reclaim your sovereignty. You must do them by your choice. We cannot do it for you, because you will never have your free will taken from you. It is one of the greatest gifts you have: to choose the experience you want to have.

You can make this a nicer journey by choosing love as often as possible and forgiving as deeply and frequently as possible. Within a very short time, you begin to see the transformations these practices bring. If you continue them over years, you slowly erase all the idols and unforgiving ideas in your mind, and you come to a deep peace and acceptance of yourself as you are. You realize God created you, a beautiful sacred being who is immensely creative, loving, and kind. That is what will be left at the end of this long process of erasing everything from your consciousness that is not true and that you do not want to carry around as a burden any longer.

I am that one you know as Jesus, and we will speak to you tomorrow.

LESSON 202

Review VI: Part 2
I am not a body. I am free,
for I am still as God created me.

Follow the complete lesson guidelines in your *ACIM* book.

You are blessed beings, indeed. I am that one you know as Jesus. We are pleased that you have come this far with us. You are in the 200s now, and you have gone through some of the most difficult parts of the course. You have come to see that it has done you good, or you would not be here with us today. You have seen some transformations in your behavior. You have come to see some of the shenanigans that your thoughts get up to and some of the thoughts you should not believe that reside within your consciousness. You have come to see that suffering is optional.

You are not a body. This is one of the great lies your society tells you. It is promoted relentlessly, because it is one of the most disempowering thoughts you can have, that you are just a body. Your Western scientific method is based on that. Spirituality is not allowed in your scientific method at all. Consciousness is removed from your scientific method even though it is impossible for it to be removed. Scientists believe it has been removed, but it does not ever leave that experimenter's domain.

People designing experiments have their perceptions deeply entrenched in the design of that experiment. Scientists observing experiments will change the outcome by their desires. There is no clear scientific method as you believe. The biggest mistake the scientific method in your Western world makes is assuming that everything is physical and you are a body. The whole pharmaceutical industry is based on the idea that the body goes wrong for no reason, and that cannot be solved.

This is not true. Miracles can happen, but they come from the mind. They come from healing the mind. They come from aligning the mind with love, not fear. You see the scientific proof of that. You see people who are stressed out all the time and have heart attacks. Their bodies fail. You see people who are self-loathing and unloving to themselves develop autoimmune diseases; the body seems to attack itself, because they are attacking themselves.

This process of mind reclamation, gaining back your sovereignty and aligning with love, is the miracle-working device that those of you who suffer from sickness and pain want. It is the path Home to health and true happiness. You are not a body. You are spirit. You have come from spirit, and you will return to spirit. Once this experience, this detour into fear, is over, you will return to the loving arms of the Divine Father, and you will not be judged for the errors you have made here.

Stop berating yourself for your failures, and focus on what you are good at. Focus on what you love. Focus on the things that bring you joy. When joy courses through your body, it heals you because it is love, and that is the frequency of health and life — not death. Death is a choice. You do not think it as a choice. You believe in it as an inevitability. As you say, there are only two things guaranteed in your life: death and taxes. But we disagree with that. There's only one thing guaranteed in your life, and that is to live for eternity.

I am that one you know as Jesus, and we will speak to you again tomorrow.

Review VI: Part 3
I am not a body. I am free,
for I am still as God created me.

Follow the complete lesson guidelines in your *ACIM* book.

You are blessed beings, indeed. I am that one you know as Jesus. This name of God issue has been giving some of you a little upset trying to figure out what exactly that name is.

You can use any name that feels comfortable to you. You can use God, Goddess, All That Is, Source, Universal Mind, and so on. Whatever suits your feeling as the most accurate representation of that name of God, use that. If it is God, then use God. Words are symbols of symbols. They are not as important as you have made them out to be. It is the feeling behind everything. If you say, "I love you," to someone and you don't mean it, then it is the feeling that is projected out into the world, and that will be reflected back to you. It is not the words — the sounds that you make — even though you can do powerful transformative work using words. Understand that the words you use must be in alignment with the intention and feeling within your heart and soul.

Yes, words are powerful. Words are magnificent tools for connecting with the Divine. You, however, must focus on the feeling that word brings for you. Some of you who have been traumatized by the church or by religious parents do not like the word "God." The feeling that it elicits in you is not one of love, peace, expansiveness, and forgiveness. So that is your forgiveness work: Forgive that word and all the things incorrectly done in that word's name. That has often happened to me. People have done terrible things in my name. That is one of the reasons I wanted to come through in your society at this time — to reclaim my name for the truth of what it stands for, which is all-encompassing love for you, my brothers and sisters.

Do not get hung up on these symbols of symbols. Go to the heart, and come up with a word for God that you love and resonate with and that feels completely comfortable to you. Do not judge others for the words they use. Use the word that is your truth and your Home.

I am that one you know as Jesus, and we will speak to you again tomorrow.

Review VI: Part 4
I am not a body. I am free,
for I am still as God created me.

Follow the complete lesson guidelines in your *ACIM* book.

You are blessed beings, indeed. I am that one you know as Jesus. This reminder is to get you to think of God throughout the day.

You think of your rent. You think of what you're going to cook for dinner. You think about your broken toenail. You think about going to the dentist. You think about all kinds of things throughout the day. All worldly things about the body, money, sex, success — whatever. You must commit a substantial amount of your thoughts, emotions, and faith to connect with that which you call God.

Now, God does not participate in this world in any meaningful way, which is something that some of you may be surprised to hear. You all create this world because you've been given freedom. God is at home in another place and time, and he is unconcerned with the shenanigans humans are up to. However, because you are made in the image of God, you are a loving creature and spiritual being. When you focus intently on the material and physical all the time, you suffer because you are not yourself.

These multiple commitments to God throughout the day remind you who you are, which is an idea in the mind of God. You are made in the image of your Creator — an endlessly creative, freedom-seeking, loving creature. It is important to remind yourself of that. Reminding yourself of God is not submitting to anything but remembering who you are in truth and what keeps you happy: to remember that this world is a temporary illusion invented to keep you from God. "Lead us not into temptation" [Matthew 6:13, ESV]. That is what that Bible verse means. This world is a temptation designed by you to give you all the things that distract you from your truth, all the idols that you still worship and all of the distractions and shiny objects that keep you from going within.

We remind you to go within many times each day and to connect with that God you feel comfortable talking to. God is never offended by your nomenclature. God is never offended by anything you do. God is not interfering in this world in any way, shape, or form. God is the Father that you go Home to when you have had enough of this world.

I am that one you know as Jesus, and we will speak to you tomorrow.

Review VI: Part 5
I am not a body. I am free,
for I am still as God created me.

Follow the complete lesson guidelines in your *ACIM* book.

You are blessed beings, indeed. I am that one you know as Jesus. Many of you have come to realize that the peace of God is more valuable than anything in the entire world.

You see your movie stars and your pop stars fall down, as idols do. You see them, with all of their riches, dying young or having catastrophic personal lives. Your idea of success in this world is a very distorted one, and we want to bring this to your awareness today.

Some of you, in living peaceful lives, feel as if you are missing something. Some of you, in doing this work with the *A Course In Miracles* mind-training program, think you might miss out on something. You do not miss out on anything. What you get is far more valuable than anything money can buy or infamy can get you.

The peace of God surpasses all understanding. It is a deep and profound acceptance of everything you are and everything around you. This is very valuable, as once you have achieved peace, knowledge can flow to you. That is what happened to this being [the channel]. In removing all the upsets from her mind to the best of her ability, she opened a doorway in her consciousness to information that she could not access in those lower regions. She is not special. She has merely followed the scientific program of forgiveness that we have written about in this book and that these lessons lead you toward. This is, indeed, a scientific practice. If you do the lessons, practice forgiveness throughout your day, and do as you are told, you also will open the doorway to information that you cannot access in the lower realms.

You cannot access this information in the lower realms because it would corrupt you. It is dangerous to have power you are not trained for. It would cause you to manipulate people or maneuver things to get your ego's way. The ego is in charge in the lower 3D realms. As you practice forgiveness and use the heart more than the thinking mind, you become more integrated and have more integrity. Once you have integrity, the access to knowledge will be granted you.

Understand that you will receive information more and more as you quiet the mind and achieve that peaceful state of being we call the peace of

God. It is your natural inheritance. It is the kind of mind cultivated when you read intelligent material, spend time in nature, and utilize your God-given gifts of creativity, imagination, and love. It is in that place that you find true happiness. We guarantee it.

I am that one you know as Jesus, and we will speak to you tomorrow.

LESSON 206

Review VI: Part 6
I am not a body. I am free,
for I am still as God created me.

Follow the complete lesson guidelines in your *ACIM* book.

You are blessed beings, indeed. I am that one you know as Jesus. You have wonderful and specific gifts. Some of you are singers. Some of you are writers. Some of you are wonderful parents. Some of you are amazing athletes. Some of you are inventors and scientists. You all have a particular thing that calls to you. Some of you may have several things that call to you. There is no particular pattern that is good, and only that is good. You are all good.

You notice that as you become more educated in this society and funneled toward work and earning money, many of these passions fall away from you. They become a distant memory. It is now time in your Earth's evolutionary journey to reclaim these parts of you. They are intentionally removed from you. You will notice that there is not a lot of time in your school systems for dancing, singing, painting, horseback riding, and all sorts of things. Yes, sports are encouraged, but in a particularly competitive way with a focus on being picked by a sports team to earn lots of money. There is a distortion to it that is used against you.

Those who have left your passions behind, we want you to begin to reclaim them. We want you to go back to a time in your memory where you knew you loved to draw, run, or dance, and do that again. Yes, you may be older and out of shape, but you can do all these things in some form or another. Even if you are incapable of standing up and you loved to dance when you were younger, you can put some music on and move the top half of your body. Maybe you can stand next to a chair, hold yourself up, and move your body. Your body will respond because you are speaking to your soul.

You speak to that deep part of you that came here to express itself, create, and extend itself. That is what love does. Love takes many forms, and one of the forms it takes is passion for life and those particular talents and interests that belong to you and you alone.

Do not think about the money that comes from doing something. Do not think about the art sales that come from creating art. Do not think about the physical figure you have that you feel no longer suits that passion of dancing. Just begin to imagine. If nothing else, imagine yourself doing those things again. You will feel a little flicker of life return. You will feel some passion coursing through your body. You will feel a little bit younger.

It is passion, love, self-expression, and freedom that cause the vital life force to course through this body of yours. You come in with it. You see it in young children when they laugh, play, and tickle each other and have a grand old time of just being themselves. Slowly but surely it is removed from you systematically by programs that do not care for your spiritual evolution.

Do not underestimate the power of physical movement and creativity in your spiritual journey. Do not make it only an academic study but also an experiential one.

I am that one you know as Jesus, and we will speak to you tomorrow.

LESSON 207

Review VI: Part 7
I am not a body. I am free,
for I am still as God created me.

Follow the complete lesson guidelines in your *ACIM* book.

You are blessed beings, indeed. I am that one you know as Jesus. When you go through the world every day viewing it with love and forgiving eyes, you receive the benefits because you become the same frequency as God.

That is how God sees you in your unique way, and it is what you benefit when you do the same thing. When you act in the same way God would act — loving, forgiving, creative, extending, passionate, and kind — then you feel amazing. When you understand that's all you're doing, acting as if you are made in the image of God, then you benefit from it.

What else does God do? God does not bother with the material world. God is interested in the timeless and the eternal. You also benefit from being interested in the timeless and the eternal. "What are the timeless and the eternal?" you ask. Well, they are all nonphysical things, things not bound by the rules of this dying planet.

Now, when we say "dying planet," we don't mean that she is literally dying, but this planet's life cycle is built on death. Everything has to die for something else to live. You see it in your food production systems. Many animals have to die to feed all of you. That is not a system that a loving God would create. Even the composting of dead material on the forest floor, which seems to be a healthy thing, is based on dying so that another can live. It reflects the nature of this place.

Do not become attached to material things. This is a very easy thing to say and a very difficult thing to do. You have all come into this 3D world in a body because you are attached to things; they are your idols. But you will see that when you chase something physical, it does not satisfy whether it is a car, a house, a body, or money. Yes, in those first throes of getting what you want, you feel some elation; but very quickly, you look for something else. That is your clue that it is not an eternal thing. Eternal things satisfy you deeply, and you do not need to chase after other things.

Creativity, for example, is an eternal thing. It is the nature of consciousness to be creative. If you can be creative in whatever way draws you and makes you happy, you then experience your godlike nature. Just don't get attached to the things that you create. Set them free, and share them with your brothers and sisters. Then you will truly own them, because you have shared them.

I am that one you know as Jesus, and we will speak to you tomorrow.

LESSON 208

Review VI: Part 8
I am not a body. I am free,
for I am still as God created me.

Follow the complete lesson guidelines in your *ACIM* book.

You are blessed beings, indeed. I am that one you know as Jesus. These statements that *A Course In Miracles* gets you to say as fact are the truth. You have merely hidden the truth from yourself.

When you say the peace of God is within you today but you do not feel peaceful, then we want you to make the next logical conclusion: "I must be doing something incorrect with my thoughts, because I am not at peace.

What am I doing with my thoughts to cause this agitation? If the statement 'the peace of God resides in me now' is true, and I do not experience it, then I am doing something to block it. I am choosing to victimize myself or attack another in some way, shape, or form. How am I doing that? Am I arguing in my head about a person with whom I have a disagreement? Then I need to stop doing that, because that's blocking my ability to experience this peace. Am I constantly fretting over not having enough money and feeling that I'm going to be poor my whole life?"

All this interferes with your peace, and you must stop it. You choose to do it through the interpretation you make of your circumstances. Some people who have a shortage of funds are going to say, "But that is what is happening." Well, if that is happening, then you must change your mind about it, because the only way you can change what happens is to change your mind about it before the reflection of that manifests in front of you.

Everything manifested in front of you comes from your beliefs, and you fully activate and invest in those beliefs. That is why something shows up in physical form. You must look at what has shown up in physical form in front of you and ask: "How have I held the frequency of this physical form somewhere else? How have I manufactured this? How does this thing keep happening to me? It's coming at me from my life. That means it is coming from me."

Peace is your natural inheritance. Peace is what your mind is supposed to have. Anytime you have lost your peace, you are actively doing something to inhibit your experience of that peace. So be brave; be courageous. Own your contribution to your lack of peace. In an effort to change that lack of peace, make this statement as often as you can today.

I am that one you know as Jesus, and we will speak to you tomorrow.

LESSON 209

Review VI: Part 9
I am not a body. I am free,
for I am still as God created me.

Follow the complete lesson guidelines in your *ACIM* book.

You are blessed beings, indeed. I am that one you know as Jesus. Is it not a joy to know that you are and have always been connected to your Source?

This is the great illusion of this place of separation and fear: that you have been abandoned by God and you are alone. The truth is that you chose to leave God, and you are under the illusion that you are alone because of that choice. You are so powerful; your ability to manufacture whatever you believe in and whatever you want is proven to you day after day. This realization turns your mind around to recall your origins and remember who and what you are.

You are a divine, sacred being temporarily housed in this separation state. It is through your internal pursuit of separation and constant reinforcement of that state that you continue to experience it. When you decide that you do not want to be separate anymore and forgive the world for what it seems to have done to you (at your behest, as it has only done whatever you wanted), then you begin to make that journey Home.

It is a long journey. You have taken a deep detour into fear, and you have made thousands of decisions for separation. Every time you attack yourself or judge another, you choose separation, taking yourself deeper into that fear and further away from your Home in love. Once you realize that and truly understand that this is your creation here, then you can make another choice. You can choose love. You can make a thousand decisions for love and for the reunification of your mind with All That Is, and then that becomes the truth and what you experience.

If you have not already made that dedication, make it today. You are not a body. You are free to choose whatever you want to experience. You have merely been ignorant of that process, and we are teaching you the mechanics of it. You keep separation alive through your indulgence in the ideas of fear and judgment. Through forgiveness and love, you return Home to love and your true nature.

I am that one you know as Jesus, and we will see you again tomorrow.

LESSON 210

Review VI: Part 10
I am not a body. I am free,
for I am still as God created me.

Follow the complete lesson guidelines in your *ACIM* book.

You are blessed beings, indeed. I am that one you know as Jesus. This is the greatest device that the ego uses to prove that God has abandoned you: your pain, your fallible physical structure. The evidence of your belief proves to you that God has abandoned you.

What we want to bring to your attention here is how much effort we have to use to get you to have faith in God, think about God, and include God in your life. You can go for many hours in a day without thinking about God or connecting to Source energy with prayer, which is a demonstration of your belief. That shows how seductive this world is and how well all the temptations and distractions you have set up for yourself work.

You want the things that you have in your life. How do you know you want them? Because they are there. You play with them, indulge in them, and allow them to rule you. Nobody makes you do what you do. You are a free spirit, a free agent. All of you can change the things you do each day. We want you to really grasp the truth that your life is your choice, and the things you spend time on and invest in are the things you value. You may value them for the wrong reasons. You may value them out of fear, but you still use your free will to value, indulge in, and spend time with them.

Pain is a direct consequence of your separation from love. The amount of pain you experience — mental, emotional, or physical — demonstrates your degree of separation. In your society, it is deemed unloving to tell people who are in pain that somehow they are responsible for it. We are not talking about your conscious decisions. We are speaking about your unconscious miscreations. Things such as wars would be unconscious miscreations. You do not realize that your battle with other people is you battling in your mind with yourself. Your hateful thoughts create an unloving and embattled world. You have not been taught this. It is unconsciousness creation. Pain is unconsciousness creation. None of you would be doing this to yourselves if you knew how to stop.

We are intentionally teaching you how to stop hurting yourselves and others. We are teaching you how to be more loving, and you will begin to see that emotional and mental pain subside. As emotional and mental pain subsides over time, so will physical pain, because it is the long-term result of mental and emotional pain. So if you have physical pain now, change your mind, and your body has to respond.

Your body is manufactured from the frequency of the thoughts, beliefs, and ideas that you hold and act on — those things you believe in. When you have physical pain, you are off track in some area of your mind. It is where you attack yourself or others. The pain of the body is giving you a message that you have been off track for a long time.

Take this to heart, and know that pain is not a punishment from God. It is a messaging system from the body to let you know your thoughts, feelings, emotions, and beliefs are off track and have been off track for some time. To cause physical pain, you must have been off track for some time. When you transform your thoughts, beliefs, and ideas, you must give the body a little bit of time to respond to what you are now employing. It is not going to happen in one or two days, but it can; miracles happen when you choose love.

I am that one you know as Jesus, and you do not need to be in pain. Choose love. Choose peace. Choose kindness. Choose creativity. Choose self-expression. Choose love.

I am that one you know as Jesus, and we will speak to you tomorrow.

LESSON 211

Review VI: Part 11
I am not a body. I am free,
for I am still as God created me.

Follow the complete lesson guidelines in your *ACIM* book.

You are blessed beings, indeed. I am that one you know as Jesus. We are here today to remind you of your grandeur. You are sacred beings, indeed. You are deceived by your bodies and by this world's temptations and fear. They deceive you because you chose to come here to experience separation from God.

That is the fundamental principle behind this whole experience, and it is confusing to you because you have been taught that God created this world. Yet, you look around and see so much pain and suffering and so much separation and death. You think, "How can God have created this world? It makes no sense whatsoever." Well, God did not create this world. You created this world to experience things that are not of unity, communion, and love with the ultimate goal to return to love. It is a paradox, yes; we understand this.

To get through this experience of separation, you must return to the understanding that you are a being of grand design, and you are whole. You are holy, and you will always — regardless of what choices you make — return Home to that which you call love, or God. God is love, and you can use those words interchangeably.

Once you understand the true definition of your experience here, then you can say, "God is loving. God has given me the choice to play whatever games I want. To chase after whatever idols I want." That is freedom. Love is giving those you care for the freedom to be who they are and to do whatever makes them happy.

You think this world will deteriorate if you all do what makes you happy, but we ask you to look around: You all are doing what makes you unhappy. It is a sorry place right now. So give this idea a little thought: If you all did what you loved — what made you happy — your world would be a much better place to live in.

Truthfully, you are all doing what you want. You are free beings. At any point, you can change your mind, and you can do something differently. Even those of you in deep poverty and deep pain can change your minds, and you will see a commensurate change in your physical realities.

Trust us. Give it a try. It definitely works.

I am that one you know as Jesus, and we will see you again tomorrow.

LESSON 212

Review VI: Part 12
I am not a body. I am free,
for I am still as God created me.

Follow the complete lesson guidelines in your *ACIM* book.

You are blessed beings, indeed. I am that one you know as Jesus. Your purpose on this Earth plane is to remove everything unloving from your mind. Unlovingness is manifested in your emotional guidance system as negative emotion. Whenever you feel negative emotion, you can be assured 100 percent that you have had a fearful or an unloving thought about yourself, some thing, or someone else. Your guidance system is telling you, "You are made of love. This is not loving."

It is very simple, dear ones, and you make it so complicated. Your purpose here is — through the practice of forgiveness — to return Home. So how is the practice of forgiveness the device by which you return Home? Forgiveness helps you understand that you only experience your own consciousness here. Yes, it seems that all kinds of people, places, and things cause your troubles, but those troubles arise from your own mind. That is the only place they exist. All events are neutral until you tell an unloving, a judgmental, or a separation-focused story about them, and in that story, you suffer.

Yes, there are times in your life when you will have physical pain — a broken foot or giving birth to a baby, these kinds of things — but suffering is always optional. Suffering means you have forgotten your purpose here, which is to forgive and remove from your mind that which is unloving and allow the Holy Spirit to translate your interpretation into the truthful meaning of this experience.

We are all with you to support you on your journey, but we cannot make decisions for you. Only you can indulge in your fearful and judgmental thoughts without impunity. There is, of course, a consequence, and it is suffering. You will never be punished for what you do when you are mistaken. You will never be punished for being confused. You will never be punished for not knowing what to do. This is why we bring this information to you today — so that you may be sure that the power lies within your mind.

The power to stop suffering is yours and yours alone. We can only shine the light on the solution. We cannot make you take it.

I am that one you know as Jesus, and we will speak to you tomorrow.

LESSON 213

Review VI: Part 13
I am not a body. I am free,
for I am still as God created me.

Follow the complete lesson guidelines in your *ACIM* book.

You are blessed beings, indeed. I am that one you know as Jesus. The lessons you learn here allow you to undo your thinking.

So you might call them trials and tribulations; you might call them patterns that you cannot break, but they are opportunities for you to do something differently. A miracle happens when you choose love instead of fear. When you review your life and identify the repetitions that happen, you can see that the negativities in your life are the results of a repeated choice of fear.

If you want to break the patterns in your life, you are going to have to break through that barrier, that resistance, of fear that you have set up based on your beliefs about reality. You will never be able to break free until you are courageous enough to walk through those fears that limit you and keep you in a self-created prison.

Choose love. Be brave. If you are in a pattern that you do not enjoy, walk up very, very close to the edge of that pattern, feel the fear, and know that it is not real. Know that on the other side of that fear lies freedom.

I am that one you know as Jesus, and we will speak to you tomorrow.

Review VI: Part 14
I am not a body. I am free,
for I am still as God created me.

Follow the complete lesson guidelines in your *ACIM* book.

You are blessed beings, indeed. I am that one you know as Jesus. This is the source of most of your upset: regrets and recriminations over the past, guilt or shame, and worries and anxieties about the future. You live in a fictitious world when you focus on the past or the future.

When you are not present with what you are doing, you are not really doing anything. You are wasting your time, because you are reliving or projecting. A lot of you live those two fantasy worlds in most of the time. So when we talk about presence, that is what we seek. We seek presence, because that is the only true point of creation (new creation).

If you are ruminating over the past, you are contaminating the eternal now with the past, and you will create a future that looks like your past. When you have a resentment, let's say, or an abuse or trauma that you keep thinking about, you are saying to the universe, "I want more of that." Your eternal now — that fresh moment that you all get equally — is being contaminated by your free will and inappropriate use of your memory. It contaminates the eternal now. Now, those of you who suffer from PTSD or traumas do not realize that you are doing this voluntarily. You do not realize it has become such a habit of either telling the story or ruminating on what happened to you or revisiting the situation from the past that you do not realize you have fed your own trauma.

We are not blaming the victim here. We are saying a bad thing happened to you, but it only happened to you once. If you continue to think about it, tell stories about it, talk to people about it, and go to therapists about it, you will re-traumatize yourself infinitely. You are making sure that your future will be a similar vibration.

You must hand over the future to God, and say, "I will be here in the present, trusting that as long as I am in alignment with love, everything will work out fine, because you are love, God, and I am in alignment with your will for me when I am in a place of love." It is very simple.

Presence is not some esoteric, rare quality that monks have; it is something that you should all strive for. Use your senses to keep you in the present moment. See what you're looking at. Taste what you're tasting. Feel what you're feeling, and know that endless rumination on the past and the future really is a waste of time.

I am that one you know as Jesus, and we will speak to you tomorrow.

Review VI: Part 15
I am not a body. I am free,
for I am still as God created me.

Follow the complete lesson guidelines in your *ACIM* book.

You are blessed beings, indeed. I am that one you know as Jesus. It is important for you to remember that your definition of love is somewhat limited in your society.

You think of it as a romantic idea or as a sensory pleasure, such as, "I love chocolate cake." But love is represented in many, many different forms throughout your experience. And love is gratitude. One of the greatest ways you can get love into your life and align with love more easily is to make a gratitude, what you are grateful for, list morning and night. The default setting of the ego-mind is separation and judgment, which means that the default setting is not-love.

Your ego wants to see the things that you don't like, and you know this is true. You can have 100 positive responses about work you're doing, for example, and the one person who does not like your work gets the ego's attention, because that is what the ego wants. It wants separation. It wants war. It wants not-love; it is not loving.

One way you can really diffuse the power of the ego is to walk through your day with gratitude — even for the things that upset you. We have told you that you need to see the things that upset you to know where you have a block in your mind and where you have grievances. You need to know where you have unloving reactions.

Those are the things that get your attention by the strong negative emotional feedback you get from your guidance system. This tells you you're off track on the subject. You're not in alignment with love. A proactive way to align with love on a regular basis is through gratitude, and it's a much easier access point than loving people you don't like.

Being grateful for the health in your body that you have today, the fact that you can walk around, the food in your refrigerator, and that your car starts are simple ways you can align with love. You don't think of those things as love, but they are. Gratitude is love, and this is a wonderful, wonderful practice. When you feel that you are unloving or that you don't have enough love in your life, usually it's because you are not defining love correctly.

This being [the channel] has penned a book, *Love and a Map to the Unaltered Soul*, in which we discuss in great detail love and redefining it for you. So if you have not consumed that material yet, we suggest you do. You might have a lot of love in your life, but you do not call it love, so you feel alone, unlovable, and unloved; yet you are not. You are surrounded by life and opportunity, and gratitude will help you understand that.

I am that one you know as Jesus, and we will speak to you tomorrow.

LESSON 216

Review VI: Part 16
I am not a body. I am free,
for I am still as God created me.

Follow the complete lesson guidelines in your *ACIM* book.

You are blessed beings, indeed. I am that one you know as Jesus. Your body is one of the great assets of the ego-mind. This is something that is very important for Westerners to understand: that you have been taught to worship the body. You have been taught that the body is the god. You have been taught that beauty is everything, that strength and beauty are the things that will get you what you want.

You have not been taught that love is what you should want. You think you have because you've been indoctrinated with romantic movies, romantic songs, and romantic novels. But those romances are not based on love; they are based on the body. They are based on the special love of the ego, and that is one of the reasons that they cause you so many problems, because the body becomes the focus of the love relationship (what you call the love relationship).

Many of you go into fear because you think we are taking you away into some monkish life where you're never allowed to make love to somebody or you're never allowed to comb your hair or whatever else you might think. You think you are going to be taken into the realm of the ascetic. That is not true. The more you focus on the body, the more you crucify yourself. This is why you see eating disorders, body dysmorphia, and these

279

kinds of painful mental and emotional distortions in the mind these days, because of the intense focus on the body.

When you focus on what you love — not just who you love or who you want but what you truly love — those great, deep abiding passions that travel with you throughout your life (such as your love of music, your love of art, or your love of gardening, your natural creativity) — these things feed the soul. Your communion with your brothers and sisters in a loving but nonphysical way are the relationships that feed the soul. And you can see there is an erratic quality that comes into relationships as soon as the body is involved, as soon as the sexual act is involved. This is not to say that it's sinful, but it is to remind you that the ego will use the body at every turn to prove that you are abandoned by God, unlovable, and separate. It is its greatest weapon.

The more you focus on your body and the less you focus on the eternal internal world of your creativity and your ability to love, the more you will suffer. The more you focus on forgiveness (which is love) and the more you focus on gratitude and self-expression, these kinds of nonphysical attributes that you possess, the less the body will dominate your mind and the less you will suffer.

It is but yourself you crucify when you worship the body. The more you worship the body, the more pain you have. There is no need to crucify yourself. During my lifetime, the crucifixion was a demonstration. It was not the value of my body as a sacrifice; rather, it was the valuelessness that I demonstrated in my willingness to give it up. I had mastered the material world through love and forgiveness, and I could manufacture a new body at will. That is the ultimate trip you are on.

You are all on the ultimate trip of using love and forgiveness to make yourselves masters of the physical/material world. You are not here to do the ego's bidding but to demonstrate your mastery of love.

I am that one you know as Jesus, and we will speak to you tomorrow.

Review VI: Part 17
I am not a body. I am free,
for I am still as God created me.

Follow the complete lesson guidelines in your *ACIM* book.

You are blessed beings, indeed. I am that one you know as Jesus. Salvation is one of the great fears of the ego. The ego always thinks that the term "salvation" means that you have to give things up, that you are going to lose your freedom.

The ego only gives you freedom in things that don't matter: what color shoes you buy or what you eat for lunch, all these things. These are inconsequential, but many people think they are free because they can make these small choices throughout the day. However, many of your small choices are being driven by market-conditioning programs that you have been subjected to throughout your life. You are not even free with those things. You are being guided by commercials and manipulations of your mind through constant programming.

Understand that salvation is loss of nothing. You gain true freedom from salvation. That is what we offer you. This is not the salvation of the ascetic. This is not the salvation offered to nuns and monks who give up everything. This is true salvation, which is true freedom and the reintegration and the reclamation of the sovereignty of your consciousness so that you are truly free to choose love, because in the end, that's the only choice you have. Any other choice that is not-love merely keeps you going around and around and around the karmic game (the birth, death, and rebirth game) until you choose love.

Really, there is only one choice. The other choice, fear and procrastination, only temporarily puts off the inevitable: In the end, you will choose love and find salvation. You will be reconnected to All That Is.

Why not do it now? Why waste time not forgiving when that is the only solution?

I am that one you know as Jesus, and we will speak to you tomorrow.

LESSON 218

Review VI: Part 18
I am not a body. I am free,
for I am still as God created me.

Follow the complete lesson guidelines in your *ACIM* book.

You are blessed beings, indeed. I am that one you know as Jesus. It is such an important thing for you to remember that when you condemn another, it is only you who suffers. When you condemn another, it is only you who feels pain. When you condemn another, it is only you who loses.

There is this idea in the ego's thought system that to attack brings you something, and this is a fundamental teaching of the ego's thought system: that if you want something, attack is the way to get it. But you get nothing by attacking. You only further promote separation, which further increases your suffering. So forgiveness is not really an act for anyone else, which is one of the great misperceptions about forgiveness. It is for you.

When you forgive another, you stop suffering. When you forgive another, you are no longer inflicting separation on yourself. When you forgive another, your mind is becoming reintegrated and whole, and you have access to that reintegrated mind. You have access to that peace of mind. You have access to the freedom from relentless thoughts about somebody with whom you have a resentment. You get the benefit of your mind back and your frequency goes up, and that means you are going to have better experiences, better encounters, which gives you access to higher-frequency things.

Whatever your resentments are, be they large or small, they are your judgments. They are your mind showing itself to you, and you suffer. Do not do this anymore. Step back from constantly offering your opinions and getting into arguments, especially on social media. You are being manipulated by the mass media systems, who design constant opportunities for the ego to flare up, argue, judge, and struggle, and in that joining in, you lose. This is one of the reasons we tell you to turn off your televisions and to filter your social media: so that you are not in provocative situations. It's not to make you a simpering weakling, oh no, but to get your power back from these useless wastes.

The waste of energy being demonstrated throughout your mass media and social media systems is ridiculous. You are being played, and your energy is being siphoned from you so that you do not have access to it.

Turn it off. Stop participating in arguments and judgments; instead, focus on developing your consciousness, passions, and connection to the Divine. You will be more influential, you will be more peaceful, and you will be happier. You will not be a simpering doormat; you will be truly powerful.

I am that one you know as Jesus, and we will speak to you tomorrow.

LESSON 219

Review VI: Part 19
I am not a body. I am free,
for I am still as God created me.

Follow the complete lesson guidelines in your *ACIM* book.

You are blessed beings, indeed. I am that one you know as Jesus. Your body is indeed the ego's greatest device to convince you that you are alone, that you are going to die, and that God does not love you.

That is the use the body has been put to by the ego's thought system. Remember, the default setting here is separation, and your body is the testament to that separation, the proof the ego uses to convince you that you are fallible, frail, and temporary. In acknowledging that you are not a body, you are free from the constraints of a body. In that knowledge, you will begin to relax. With that knowledge, you will refrain from obsessing over the body, worshipping the body, and hating the body. All these things bring you suffering; all these things exacerbate the fear that the ego uses the body for.

Now, this is not about denying the body in the sense of not feeding it well and not looking after it as the vehicle you drive around in. Just as you look after your car, you must look after your body. You must "change the oil" once in a while, which might be something like a cleanse or some juicing. Make sure you attend to it as you would a vehicle. You understand so clearly that a vehicle will not last if you don't look after it, if you don't do that regular maintenance. Regular body maintenance can be done relatively quickly and efficiently. You do not need to obsess about the body. Have you not noticed that it works perfectly well without your interference? In fact, it is your interference, negative emotions, and fears that cause it to break down, age, and die. These are the consequences of the lower-frequency thought systems.

As you continue this path, you will notice that your body gets better. It begins to heal itself. It will even look younger, and that is because you are not dragging it down by your resistance to life. You are beginning to open up. You are beginning to align with these teachings, which tells you that you are a divine sacred being.

Even though you are in separation and have chosen to come into this place to chase your idols, you are still connected to the Divine; you are made in the image of God. That means you are creative, you are loving, and you are an extension of that love.

When you do not extend that love and become shut down, limited, and fearful, the body suffers. This suffering really gets your attention, so it is paradoxical to ask you not to focus on the body, and it will be particularly paradoxical for those of you who have body issues: sicknesses, pains, or injuries. Know that those things will heal themselves if you focus on love. If you focus on these teachings and your forgiveness practice, extending the unique qualities and love that is you and comes from you, you will find that everything will work better.

I am that one you know as Jesus, and we will speak to you tomorrow.

Review VI: Part 20
I am not a body. I am free,
for I am still as God created me.

Follow the complete lesson guidelines in your *ACIM* book.

You are blessed beings, indeed. I am that one you know as Jesus. Peace is the natural state of your being.

Peace is not the normal state of your being in your society. An agitated, dysfunctional, judgmental, and not-particularly-happy state of mind is your normal state of being. But your natural state is peace, because you are made in the image of God, and that is why you are constantly trying to get your mind to a peaceful place, even if you do not realize the strategies you are using.

For example, alcohol is a strategy that you use in your society to bring your mind to peace when you are agitated, fearful, frustrated, or stressed. You will go home after a long week of work and have a good stiff drink, as you call it, and you will feel the mind calming, some peace of mind. Obviously, as you continue to drink and go further and further into that bubble, peace turns into unconsciousness. The peace that alcohol brings you is a little touch of unconsciousness. But it feels like rest or an elevation of your mind, because it numbs and slows the discursive voice — the monkey mind. So after a couple of drinks, you actually feel better.

Another way you attempt to get your mind to a peaceful state is watching television. When the mind is not at peace, it's not nice to sit around undistracted, perhaps relaxing in your garden. The mind chitter-chatters, causing you all kinds of internal reaction to the thoughts you believe. Now, thoughts are generated from beliefs. Beliefs are inserted into your mind through the mass media systems and training programs in your society. These beliefs generate fears: "I don't have enough money" or "I'm too fat." These thoughts are generated from beliefs that have been instilled in your mind by your society, family, or culture.

We are working toward discernment: Which thoughts do you believe? Which thoughts do you react to? Most untrained minds react to all thoughts, giving them all equal value. We are teaching you to discern and to realize that you don't have to believe all your thoughts, because many of those thoughts come from beliefs that do not serve you, and you are beginning to catch on to that.

What happens when you only believe in truth and love? The side effect is peace. If you don't have a peaceful mind, you must look at the thoughts you are listening to that are not in alignment with these teachings. So fearful, judgmental, separation, and attack thoughts will all bring you into a frequency of agitation and cause you to lose your peace. The ego does not like peace; it likes war. That is its purpose: to keep you in an agitated state of internal war or loss of peace.

Be aware that when you are not at peace, the ego is in charge of your thought processes, so you need to change what you are telling yourself inside your mind. Grab you're *A Course in Miracles* book and read it. This is a great meditation when you are upset about something. Stop what you're doing. Stop what you're talking about. Stop what you're watching. Stop what you're thinking. Grab your book and read the truth, and you will find peace again.

LESSON 221

Peace to my mind. Let all my thoughts be still.

Follow the complete lesson guidelines in your *ACIM* book.

You are blessed beings, indeed. I am that one you know as Jesus. This is a quite intimidating meditation, because you are taught in your society that to hear voices means you are mental and that if you tell people you are hearing voices, you will be judged as insane and potentially institutionalized.

This is a great fear in your society, and this practice of surrendering to peace of mind and allowing the possibility that information will be given to you can be challenging for the ego-driven Western mind because of all the dangers you have faced in your society for listening to voices. So many of you will have issues come up when doing this, either a sense of fear or a sense of disbelief, and both these things will prevent communication. So go into this lesson with as much enthusiasm and surrender as possible. And should there come some frustration or resistance or fear, make note of that, and after your practice period, dig beneath that fear to see whether you can identify where it's coming from. Find the belief that's generating that fear.

All your thoughts and feelings come from your beliefs, what you hold as true about reality. When they bring up an emotional response in you, you believe them even though they may have originated from another person, a church, or a cultural teaching. They reside in your mind because you have allowed them to, and when they trigger emotion, it is a demonstration of your belief in it. Listen for the voice of God in silence, and be aware that there may be some little niggling negativities lurking around that practice.

I am that one you know as Jesus, and we will speak to you tomorrow.

LESSON 222

God is with me.
I live and move in him.

Follow the complete lesson guidelines
in your *ACIM* book.

You are blessed beings, indeed. I am that one you know as Jesus. This lesson will calm your mind.

It is only from beliefs of separation, beliefs that you are alone, and beliefs that you have been abandoned by God that you go into such deep terror and fear. You are not alone; God is with you. God is always with you, connected to your heart and mind forever and ever. Amen.

When you have fears, they are generated by an illusory belief in some form of separation — be it separation from a brother or sister, separation from your ability to create an abundant life, or separation from your natural state of health. All these ideas are illusory, and when you believe in them, you bring to those beliefs all of your creative power, which is immense. So when you believe in something — you are alone, for example — then you will feel it with every fiber of your being as a strong negative emotional response.

Do you remember what a negative emotional response is? It is your guidance system saying you are wrong. You misinterpret this so many times throughout the day. When you feel bad, you are wrong; you are looking at something incorrectly. Keep this lesson in mind. God is with you all the time; you are never alone. And if you tell yourself this frequently throughout the day, you will feel at peace, happy, and connected to All That Is, because you believe in it. Once you believe something, it becomes true for you.

I am that one you know as Jesus, and we will speak to you tomorrow.

LESSON 223

God is my life.
I have no life but God's.

Follow the complete lesson guidelines
in your *ACIM* book.

You are blessed beings, indeed. I am that one you know as Jesus. The ego does not like the sound of this. It wants to be in charge. It wants to control everything. It wants to be the complete owner of you.

But as you can see from your experiences, the more connected you become to the Divine, the more connected you become to your inner guidance system and the easier life gets, the less stress you have, and the less fear you have. So the ego's desire to be completely in charge of everything is a fearful place.

It may seem that we are giving you contradictory information here, because we are telling you that you are the captain of your own ship and should follow your inner guidance. That sounds like the ego's world, does it not? What we mean that you should do that after this clarification process — the *A Course in Miracles* lessons. So you are going to have mixed and confusing information directing you to make conflicting decisions until you have gone through the 365 lessons.

This does not guarantee that you are going to be fear-free or that you are going to be completely unconfused. It means that after 365 lessons and practicing all these things as well as your ongoing forgiveness, you will have a much clearer idea of what is actually going on when you become fearful, when you have a negative reaction, and when you attack somebody or feel attacked. You will say, "Ah, this is my doing. What's going on here? Why am I so volatile? Why am I so fearful?" Whereas before the clarification process, you might have said, "What's wrong with you? Why are you attacking me?" It is a complete turnaround.

287

These lessons lead you toward a deep state of surrender to what is, because you know that you cannot change what is in this moment; you must accept it. And the guidance you are able to tune in to once you come to a deep place of surrender becomes very, very clear. You are happy more often. You are fearful less often. You can gauge much more easily your true feelings about whether or not you want to participate in something.

This is an introductory phase in which you are heading toward a deeper surrender of knowing that you have a purpose here, you are connected to deep and loving guidance, and you can discern which promptings from within your mind and heart to listen to.

I am that one you know as Jesus, and we will speak to you tomorrow.

LESSON 224

God is my Father, and he loves his children.

Follow the complete lesson guidelines in your *ACIM* book.

You are blessed beings, indeed. I am that one you know as Jesus. Many of you come to these teachings when you are weary.

You have tried as hard as you can using the knowledge that you have to make things work for you. Still, there is something missing. There is some disaster that befalls you that you cannot cope with. There is some deep disillusionment that overwhelms you — depression, sadness, guilt, shame. Over time, all these things take their toll on the human experience. There is no shame in this. This is the nature of chasing your idols. This is the nature of being out of alignment with your true grandeur. This is the nature of denying what you are, how you are made, and what your purpose is. It is a lot of work to keep God out. It is a lot of work to keep love away from you.

You all get weary, and at that point, you become teachable. Be grateful when you are tired. It shows you that you are doing something incorrectly and that you need to relax and surrender a little bit. Be grateful when you get upset or depressed. Understand that those emotional feedbacks are telling you that you are out of order, you are seeing something incorrectly, and you are looking at something the wrong way.

When you find peace, happiness, and joy, revel in it, love it, and experience it. Do not feel guilty and think, "Oh my goodness, this is going to come to an end soon."

As you go through these lessons and practice them year after year after year (for this is a life's work, not a year's work), the periods of peace, joy, and happiness will become longer and the upsets will become fewer. Know that this is going to happen to you. This is a scientifically proven practice. The more you forgive, the less fear and attack you indulge in and the better your life will feel, the more abundantly you will be able to engage with your experiences, and the gentler and kinder you will become.

I am that one you know as Jesus, and we are very glad that you are with us on this journey. We walk with you every single day. We will speak to you again tomorrow.

LESSON 225

God is my Father, and his children love him.

Follow the complete lesson guidelines in your *ACIM* book.

You are blessed beings, indeed. I am that one you know as Jesus. We are very pleased that you are with us today doing this lesson. It is your love of your Creator that connects you to the All That Is.

When you love the world, love your car, love your bodies, and love food, you are disconnecting from All That Is, not because any of these things are innately bad, but when you worship those things, you demean yourself. It's as if you are saying, "I am a tiny individual body, and these things keep me happy." As you know, as good *A Course in Miracles* students, whatever you believe in is true for you.

This love you are now speaking about — loving the Father, loving God, loving All That Is — is the vertical route. The ego takes you on the horizontal route and onto the battleground. These lessons take you on the vertical route directly to Source, and in that direction, there are no interferences except your mind. This is why we train the mind. In the horizontal, there are no interferences except your belief in separation, and your belief in separation makes you go to the horizontal. It is your belief in bodies that makes you go to these materialistic things to satisfy your ego's needs.

You are seeking the deeper. You are seeking the higher. You are seeking the eternal, and in that seeking, you find. In the ego's world, in the battleground, you never find anything. It is a temporary satisfaction, a physical pleasure, perhaps. But once that interaction is over, you feel separated again. You feel alone again; you feel hungry again.

This connection to Source keeps you deeply and profoundly satisfied, because you connect with what you are: a divine aspect of God mind who has chosen to come into separation for a short time. But this is the journey Home. This journey to oneness is the hunger that is really going to be satisfied, the true hunger for your Home and for love.

I am that one you know as Jesus, and we will speak to you tomorrow.

LESSON 226

My home awaits me.
I will hasten there.

Follow the complete lesson guidelines
in your *ACIM* book.

You are blessed beings, indeed. I am that one you know as Jesus. You are not seeking the feeling of disillusionment here. You are seeking a true evaluation of the world and all its temptations. You must remember that the ego has manufactured this world to keep you from your Home.

This does not seem logical at this point in your training. It seems as if there are many things in the world you want: more money, thinner bodies, a bigger house, nicer cars, and much more. But these are mere illusions designed to tempt you into staying in the world. As you come to understand, the more decades you live on this planet, the less enticing these things seem. They are not truly satisfying to somebody who is spirit by nature. You are not physical by nature; you have come down into separation

290

as a demonstration of your belief in it. As you pursue your idols and they fall and crumble one by one, you realize that this place does not hold such an allure for you anymore.

We do not want you to go into depression or disillusionment or sadness. We do not want you to go into isolation. We want you to focus on love, self-expression, creativity, and the timeless qualities you possess. We want you to listen to that still, small voice inside that guides you toward a meaningful and purposeful life.

Yes, you are on your way Home. You are all on your way Home. It is a natural return to love that everybody will eventually participate in. Some people are just taking the scenic route, as you say. The scenic route, as you know, is the route you take when you do not have a particular ambition to get somewhere on time, or perhaps you are avoiding going Home. But do not avoid going Home. Home is where the heart is; home is where love is.

This is a place of separation and fear, and to bring this place of separation and fear into its true perspective, you must choose love; you must choose forgiveness. You must choose to believe that you are a holy child of God, you are divine, and you deserve to be happy. These are fundamental beliefs that you must hold in your mind to override the world.

I am that one you know as Jesus, and we will speak to you tomorrow.

LESSON 227

This is my holy instant of release.

Follow the complete lesson guidelines in your *ACIM* book.

You are blessed beings, indeed. I am that one you know as Jesus. When you begin to understand how you cause your own suffering by chasing your idols, they become a lot less attractive to you.

When you realize that your judgments about others' behaviors or situations cause you suffering and you step back from that judgment, you get peace again. Your peace of mind is returned to you. You come to see that it is only your foolish wishes that cause your suffering.

You are working to surrender to a greater guidance; that is what these lessons lead you toward. This is not easy to do. The ego does not want to surrender its power. It does not want to surrender its judgment. It feeds off judgment. It feeds off war. It feeds off conflict. To surrender to a will that is different from the ego's will is not easy at all, because you are all ego driven.

How do you know? You are here in separate bodies, each fighting for your survival. That is the world of the ego. It is not the world that God created for you. The world that God created for you is a reality removed from the vision of the ego. The ego cannot see it; it does not want it. Initially, it is very difficult to surrender to a will that seems foreign to you.

As you practice these lessons and listen for guidance (rather than the willful directives and maniacal desires of the ego), you will follow that subtle directive to do "this" or "that," say "this" or "that," and surrender to a situation, and you will stop deciding at the beginning whether something is good or bad. You will let things play out and see what it brings you.

This is one of the great gifts of surrender: a situation will happen, and instead of leaping to the ego's decision that it is a terrible thing, you stay calm and open yourself to guidance. Perhaps you were fired from your job and all your financial fears come up. You choose instead to focus on the opportunity this change brings, and two weeks later, you are offered a job that you know you will enjoy.

However, when the ego is in charge of such a situation, you delve into deep fear and panic. Then you take the first job you're offered, and you might miss that opportunity. But if you are calm and say, "Well, okay, this has happened. It is true; I have been saying that I don't want to work there anymore." Perhaps this is an answer to your prayers. Stay calm, keep your eyes alert, and keep your heart and hands open; you may very well be given a gift.

Watch out for the fearful, panicking reactions. Strive instead for the calm and deliberate response of a being who has faith and know you are cared for.

I am that one you know as Jesus, and we will speak to you tomorrow.

God has condemned me not. No more do I.

Follow the complete lesson guidelines in your *ACIM* book.

You are blessed beings, indeed. I am that one you know as Jesus. Condemnation is not a part of the God mind. It is a part of the ego-mind, and the ego is completely separate from God. There is no overlap in these thought systems at all.

This is why when you make an unloving decision, you instantly feel bad and everything around you seems to be worse. You might suddenly feel that you're too old for "this" or too fat for "that" or too poor to do "this" and not confident enough to do "that." The decisions you make that take you into the ego's world have nothing to do with God's beliefs about you. God has made you in his image, and that means you are exactly as you need to be.

Many of you will examine your personalities and say, "Well, I don't think I'm very godlike." That is true, because you have chosen the ego over God thousands and thousands and thousands of times. You have repeatedly entrenched beliefs about yourself, about others, and about the nature of reality of your mind. This training program we are engaged in together here is taking you out of the deep pit of despair and fear, where you have taken yourself by siding with the ego's fearful thought system.

Know that you are not judged. Know that you are forgiven. Know that any errors you unknowingly make to side with the ego — because that is what you have been taught, that is what has been indoctrinated into you, that is what this place of separation incites within you — are just that; they are errors. It's just as when you see children making a mistake with their spelling or their reading; you do not berate them. You offer guidance and say, "This is how it should go. This is the correct way to say it." You do not smack them or slap them and say, "That's not how you do it." You are kind and gentle, and you repeat yourself over and over until they understand.

That is what we are doing. We are repeating ourselves over and over again, because you are like children. You have become lost and confused in the nightmare, and this voice of love will lead you Home. This voice of love says, "Come this way. Come this way. Choose love. Choose forgiveness. See? Now you feel better, don't you? Come further this way. Do it again; do it more often. See how much better you feel?" We are like that: gentle parents cajoling you and inviting you to step the correct way.

I am that one you know as Jesus, and we will speak to you tomorrow.

LESSON 229

Love, which created me, is what I am.

Follow the complete lesson guidelines in your *ACIM* book.

You are blessed beings, indeed. I am that one you know as Jesus. Have we not been telling you all along that you are made of love, from love, for love?

We want you to understand that when you see yourself this way, then you relax. When you see yourself as foolish or stupid or unlovable, you tense up. When you tense up, every single energy system in your body shifts to a lower frequency, and in that moment, you attract to you things of a like frequency. To see yourself as a loving being is one of the greatest challenges you will give the ego. The ego does not love you. It was not made of love, from love, for love; it was made by separation for the purposes of fear and the pursuit of death and unloving practices. We know the language we use is, at times, very dramatic, but it gets your attention. Does it not?

Be the loving being you are, and love yourself first. To hate yourself or judge yourself is, in fact, to blaspheme and attack God. You have been created in a particular format for a particular reason. Yes, you have some prickly distortions that you trip over once in a while, but if you can just relax and float down that stream rather than pushing uphill/upstream, you will see that your prickliness, stresses, and judgments come when you are out of alignment. It is nothing to do with anybody else; it is you.

When you relax into yourself, you follow your inner guidance, listening to the things that you would like to do and doing what you enjoy. If you cannot do them because you have created a world out of alignment with yourself, then make new decisions. You can just make those new decisions with your own mind. You do not have to go around like a bull in a China shop changing every facet of your life. Rather, begin to think differently. Say, "I am working at this job as a banker, but I really would like to become a jeweler." (We are giving you arbitrary examples here. None of these are more or less important than any other profession, just so you know.) If you want to become a jeweler, start investigating jewelry courses. Investigate how you might take a sabbatical from your banking job to study becoming a jeweler. Contact jewelers whose work you like and ask if they take on apprentices or if they do weekend workshops or summer workshops.

Use your initiative. Use your focus. Use your intention to create what you want. That is what this is all about, this life that you lead.

You have been given these particular desires because they hold something for you to learn about yourself. You might not become a world-famous jeweler, but you might be happier in that profession. You might find a creative sweet spot you didn't know you had, and from that place, you begin to shift and change your life dramatically.

So be courageous. Align with love — loving yourself first, choosing things that you love to do, and of course loving others along the way. As you love yourself more and stop kicking and fighting with reality, judging it as unacceptable when in fact it has to be acceptable (it is what is happening), you will find that you are less prickly; you are less difficult. Other people are less difficult, because you are in a sweet spot.

I am that one you know as Jesus, and I love you. We will see you again tomorrow.

LESSON 230

Now will I seek and find the peace of God.

Follow the complete lesson guidelines in your *ACIM* book.

You are blessed beings, indeed. I am that one you know as Jesus. This is one of the great gifts of these teachings: that you were made to be loving and peaceful.

All the things in you that are not that are not you. This is an identification you must make now: that you are only peaceful and only loving. When you witness agitation, fear, depression, negative thinking, or attack thoughts, understand that it is not you. That is an aberration; that is a mistake. That is a miscalculation you have made in your journey into fear.

You chose separation, and you chose this journey into fear. Now you are being given the information to guide you on your way Home, and the way Home is recognized by the signposts of peace, joy, contentment, imagination, interest, and enthusiasm. When you feel those things and you feel happy, you are on the road Home. When you feel anxious, angry, antagonistic, or judgmental, you have turned around and gone back to the opposite direction. When you feel those things, stop and recite this lesson.

You are made in the image of God, and that means you are peaceful and loving at your core. All these things are ripples on the surface of a profound ocean that, beneath that surface, is deep and still and quiet.

I am that one you know as Jesus, and we will speak to you tomorrow.

LESSON 231

Father, I will but to remember you.

Follow the complete lesson guidelines in your *ACIM* book.

You are blessed beings, indeed. I am that one you know as Jesus. These lessons that describe you being solely dedicated to reunification with the love from which you came seem very hard to reconcile with your workday world, your busy world of shipping children hither and yon, as you get up early to do all these things.

Many of your jobs do not require all your attention. And this is something those of you who have been doing *A Course in Miracles* for a little longer can come to see: that you can be cooking your dinner *and* praying; you can be doing the dishes *and* doing your lesson. Often, you can do these things when you are engaged in ordinary, automatic behavior.

When you are folding the laundry, do your lesson. When you are walking through the woods, do your lesson. There are many, many places and times. You do not have to be sitting silently on a bed in a room where nothing is happening to be able focus on your reunification with love. This is our challenge for you today: Use whatever time you have in those mundane tasks you do throughout the day to do your lessons, pray, and seek reunification with love.

When you do something very challenging that requires all your attention, you prepare your mind, not by ruminating on darkness and not by fearfully worrying about the future of your planet. Focus on a high frequency, which is where the solutions to your problems and challenges lie.

I am that one you know as Jesus, and we will speak to you tomorrow.

LESSON 232

Be in my mind, my Father, through the day.

Follow the complete lesson guidelines in your *ACIM* book.

You are blessing beings, indeed. I am that one you know as Jesus. Have you noticed how repetitive your nagging, negative thoughts are?

"I must get the oil changed in the car. I must get the oil changed in the car. Oh, I have to go to the bank to get the money to pay for the oil to get changed in the car. Oh, I must get the oil changed in the car." This is a terrible waste of your creative power.

We want you to align your mind with the loving thoughts, lessons, and prayers we bring you, trusting that whenever a decision needs to be made, you will have primed yourself to be in such a high-frequency place that the answer is easy for you to find and the decision and the required action are logical and easy to discern. When you consistently contaminate your mind with worries about money and other things — the environment and the politics and all these things, getting yourself all churned up — you are far out of alignment with the answer to your problems.

The answers to your problems are in a higher-frequency place than the frequency that created the problems. So when you are agitated, fearful, anxious, judgmental, worried, and nervous, your guidance system is telling you that you're doing something incorrectly. Do not think that the world needs to change for you to be at peace.

The next few years are going to be very tumultuous on your planet, and you had better not be looking at the world to try to find your peace. You must cultivate it from within your consciousness using your mental discipline and the training we bring you here. Many of you are probably already seeing that you are a lot calmer than those around you, because you are spending a certain amount of time each day disciplining your mind into a more loving frequency, into a more faithful place.

Other people have faith, but it is faith in the economy, their bodies, and the president — or the prime minister or whoever is in charge of their government. It is no wonder they are upset and scared. They have put their faith in things that do not deserve their faith.

This does not mean you should not act in accord with your guidance when it comes to political affiliations, environmental action, or similar things. If you are in these higher frequencies, you will be guided very, very clearly when it is time for you to do something and what that something is.

Stop fretting; stop worrying. Do these lessons expecting to hear from the Divine, the guidance that you need to make your decisions today. They do not need to be ruminated over forever and ever. Know that if a decision has to be made while you do this work, you will be in the right frequency when the time comes to choose.

I am that one you know as Jesus, and we will speak to you tomorrow.

LESSON 233

I give my life to God to guide today.

Follow the complete lesson guidelines in your *ACIM* book.

You are blessed beings, indeed. I am that one you know as Jesus. We would like you to do an experiment today: Stop giving people your opinions, and stop judging (that also is giving your opinion about your life).

Take a whole day to walk in absolute acceptance of everything — everything that needs to be done because you have assigned yourself some tasks, everything that occurs to you as an inspired idea. Accept today as a perfect day without any complaints, judgments, or resistance.

If you get a phone call from an annoying relative saying, "We would like you to come to dinner," we challenge you to say, "Okay." That would mean you're not resisting what is coming your way. Perhaps the complaints and the judgments you have about your relatives are more a reflection of you than them, and perhaps if you go to that dinner in your state of radical acceptance, you will see that the problem is in your mind. It may be that you are the judgmental one, you are the impatient one, and you are the intolerant one. Remember, the ego projects; the ego accuses everybody else of what you are doing. That is how it hides from you the biggest faults and distortions of your mind. It blames other people.

During a day of radical acceptance, you say: "Today, I stop projecting, blaming, and judging. I stop blaming others, and I own my thoughts. I look at them and keep them in my mind so that I can actually see what's going on." This is something very few of you ever do. You rarely go through your day saying, "Everything is exactly as it should be, so I will relax. I will fully participate in every experience I have today, because it is here and it is happening." In that radical acceptance, observation, love, nonjudgment, and forgiveness, you will have an opportunity to see some of the lessons in your life that you are perhaps missing because you're resistant to the lesson that's coming your way.

This is what enlightened beings do. Enlightened being go through each day accepting experiences and people as they are, owning their feelings, and seeing that the entire experience of their day takes place within and is determined by their consciousnesses — the values, lenses, and distortions through which they view the world.

On this day of radical acceptance, witness where you go to judge something, and then stop judging. Then say, "Aha. There is something. There is something I want to judge. What about that thing is bothering me? That 'bothering me' is in my mind; it is not out there. It is not in that thing; it is in me. I want to see where my lack of acceptance resides." This is what a day of total acceptance gives you. It shows you where your upsets reside. It shows you where your resistances reside, and it shows you where your fears have control of your decision-making process.

I am that one you know as Jesus, and we will speak to you again tomorrow.

Father, today
I am your child again.

Follow the complete lesson guidelines
in your *ACIM* book.

You are blessed beings, indeed. I am that one you know as Jesus. You can feel the relief that comes to your mind when you accept this is so: that you are a holy child of the Divine.

You are not here by mistake. You are not alone. You are not abandoned. You are an eternal spiritual being. The body is merely the vehicle through which you travel on this journey you have chosen into fear and separation, and you also can choose to leave. This is the ultimate truth, and responsibility comes with that knowledge. Once you understand that all your suffering and all your fears of death and separation are your own creation, manufactured from erroneous and untrue ideas, then you not only become incredibly responsible for the mess you have made of your life but also are given the key to freedom.

When you have made a mess of your life — we say that jokingly; none of you really have made a mess of your life, but all of you know you can make some very foolish decisions and end up in some precarious situations — know that all those things that are unpleasant and cause you suffering are merely feedback to tell you that you're off track. So if you think about this (that you have been given a reflective world to show you exactly what your mind is doing), your life, body, health, and everything you experience shows you the state of your consciousness. It's that simple.

There is no judgment from God. There is only judgment from the ego-mind: "I am not successful enough. I am not fit enough. I am too 'this' or not enough 'that.'" All those thoughts generated by beliefs give you feelings of dissatisfaction, suffering, and sadness. Understand that from this moment forth, if you so choose to step away from judgment, the idea of sin, the past, and worrying about the future and instead live in the eternal now, making your decisions by using these principles, you will not suffer anymore.

When you have a difficult situation that has been long in the making because of the decisions you have been making from the ego's point of view, then these teachings give you the opportunity to say: "Yes, I have made something here I don't want, and I have to live with it for a little while today. But because of my knowledge, I am able to make new decisions, so today I choose to invest in aligning myself with love so that I will not experience this reflection anymore. Yes, it's here today. Yes, I have to deal with it today. But today, I make a new series of decisions based on these loving, forgiving principles, and I know that if I keep doing that, then my future will take care of itself, because I am aligning with love, I'm aligning with forgiveness, and I'm aligning with truth, which will reveal to me the knowledge I need to make future decisions."

But your future decisions are only ever made today, dear ones. Do not worry about the future. Put it in the hands of God. Trust that you will have the inner guidance to know whether or not you should do something, purchase something, go on a date with someone, or eat something. You know that when you are clear, nonresistant, and fearless, you will receive guidance all day long. It is unrelenting and accurate once you have done the clarification process.

This is the clarification process that you are involved in: the reunification of your mind, which is the ascent out of the darkness, out of fear, and toward love and truth. Now we are in the 200s in these lessons, and you are two-thirds of the way through your clarification process. So let's not make any radical decisions right now about divorce or purchases or other major life changes, because you could still be following the ego's thought system.

Keep doing this work. Keep doing these lessons. Keep doing your forgiveness practice whenever you are upset with something or someone, including yourself, and trust that at the end of this year, you will have a better handle on what shenanigans your ego can get up to and what trouble it can cause.

I am that one you know as Jesus, and we will speak to you again tomorrow.

God in his mercy wills that I be saved.

Follow the complete lesson guidelines
in your *ACIM* book.

You are blessed beings, indeed. I am
that one you know as Jesus. Guilt and
sin are not true in God's world. They are
true in the ego's world, and guilt is one of
the ways that separation is maintained. Thus, it is
important for you to look at your relationship with guilt today.

Who do you accuse of being guilty? What do you accuse yourself of
being guilty of? When you accuse somebody or yourself of being guilty,
you are saying (tacitly, not necessarily explicitly), "Something happened
that should not have happened." Now, if you think about this logically, you
are arguing with reality, and you are arguing with God giving you free will.
When you make yourself or someone else guilty, you are attacking God.

This is not something that you think about when you judge and make
someone else guilty or yourself guilty. You think that you know what's
right, and you think the thing shouldn't have happened, but you do not
know enough to know that. You are being arrogant and playing God when
you make yourself or someone else guilty. Think about this: If God has
given you all free will to do and make and experience whatever you want,
then everything is a valid experience, even those things that a culture or a
family or a teaching may say are not good. They have already happened, so
God allowed them to happen. It was not the devil who allowed that to happen; God allowed that to happen, be it the death of a child, an injury, or a
political coup. It doesn't matter. It happened and therefore was meant to
be, and you arguing with it merely wears you out.

God has allowed it to happen. Now God's moved on; new creations
are happening today. We suggest that you move on too. Work on the creations you want to happen today so that you are not wasting your energy
anymore.

This is how the mind is fractured. There are thousands and thousands
of judgments and sins that are considered things that should never have
happened. It would have been better if "this" had happened or you had

done "that," but that is not what happened, so you are arguing with reality and literally wasting your time, wasting your energy.

Come into the eternal now. Focus on what you like/love to experience, and keep your mind there, forgetting about the past, letting it go truly and absolutely, because when you ruminate on or lament the past, you are wasting your time. God is on to new creations, new ideas, and new things that have nothing to do with the past. So do not do that. This is why these things cause you suffering; you are made in the image of God, and you are endlessly creative. You are designed to live in the eternal now, this holy instant where everything is made and created.

Make sure you are not wasting your time by living in the past. When you contaminate the present moment (we've told you this many times) with the past, you guarantee that the future will look like the past, and most of you who are ruminating on past negative things do not want that, and you've never been taught that is what remembering negative things does. It contaminates the eternal now, where anything can happen, and you are guaranteeing that the future will look the same as the past.

Be radical in your forgiveness. Be absolutely willing to do it, because you know that you will benefit by freeing up that energy and freeing up that part of your mind to create something new.

I am that one you know as Jesus, and we will speak to you tomorrow.

LESSON 236

I rule my mind, which I alone must rule.

Follow the complete lesson guidelines in your *ACIM* book.

You are blessed beings, indeed. I am that one you know as Jesus. Many beings think that the idea of surrendering to God's will is an act of passivity and that it will make you a doormat. The opposite is true.

You must decide with all your being to dedicate your mind to love. God is love; therefore, so are you. This is a very, very simple principle. But when you think of all the trash you allow into your mind and all the negativities and ruminations and judgments you allow to course through it, you truly see that you are misusing your free will; you are misusing your mind. It is going to do whatever you direct it to do.

This is an act of discipline, and it is a profound act of faith — to train your mind toward love so that you are in alignment. You will be guided to a destiny that reflects that frequency.

If you are unhappy with your life and making choices that are unloving to yourself and other people, then you are not bringing your best to those you love. If you are happy, joyful, fulfilled, in alignment, unresisting, and dedicated to the amplification of your frequency, all beings around you will thrive. Most beings who are out of alignment are not very much fun to be around.

I am that one you know as Jesus, and we will speak to you tomorrow.

LESSON 237

Now would I be as God created me.

Follow the complete lesson guidelines in your *ACIM* book.

You are blessed beings, indeed. I am that one you know as Jesus, and it is the greatest gift you can give the world: your joy, your happiness, and your expression of love for all things, including yourself.

When you walk down the street with your head held high and emitting joy, every being you meet (and many you don't meet) benefits from your energy. When you walk past people who are feeling blue and you look them in the eye and smile at them, truthfully expressing the love with which you have aligned yourself (you've chosen it; you've used your free will to become a beacon of love), that being will feel it, and that will affect them.

When you are in the grocery store lineup and meet the clerks who pack your bags and you say, "How are you doing today?" they see a face radiating care and compassion. The clerks will feel it as a recognition of a being seeing them, and they will literally feel it throughout their bodies as an upliftment.

Become today that which you would like to encounter. Become today that being you know resides within you. You all know it: You know that when you feel down, you are off track. You know that when you feel depressed, you are a pain to be around. You know that when you complain about things, you drag down everyone around you.

Become the light that you were meant to be, that you are made from. And give that gift to your family, your friends, and the world.

I am that one you know as Jesus. Be the light of the world. We will speak to you again tomorrow.

LESSON 238

On my decision, all salvation rests.

Follow the complete lesson guidelines in your *ACIM* book.

You are blessed beings, indeed. I am that one you know as Jesus. These kinds of lessons that seem so filled with responsibility are, in fact, freedom-giving lessons.

When you align your mind with divine purpose, everything falls into place. When you allow the ego-mind with all its confusing and conflicting beliefs, chaos ensues. If you imagine the most powerful being (which is you) as chaotic, unpredictable, unnecessarily emotional, and reactive, you become quite a liability to your brothers and sisters. But when you align your mind — this most powerful creative device that you have been given by your Father in heaven — with love, and you act, think, speak, and believe in the grandeur that created you and is reflected in you, you become such an asset to the world. You become such an asset to yourself. There are no more ups and downs, back and forths, or good days then bad days. You sail forth into your life with light and the wind behind you in your sails.

All the trials and tribulations that are manufactured by your distorted mind (rocks on the road and holes that you trip over) are created by you, because you are the creator of your future experience, and it will reflect the frequency that your mind holds. It will reflect the beliefs that you empower with all your mighty creative abilities. Remember, old resentments contaminate your future. They do not reside in the past; every time you revisit them, you plant those seeds in the future. Most of you do not realize this.

We know that forgiveness would be done very, very quickly if you truly understood the implications for your beautiful future. When you forgive, your mind becomes peaceful. It rises up like a balloon into the knowledge of heaven, and you get guidance beyond your ability to comprehend when you are down in the ego's battlefield.

I am that one you know as Jesus, and we will speak to you tomorrow.

LESSON 239

The glory of my Father is my own.

Follow the complete lesson guidelines in your *ACIM* book.

You are blessed beings, indeed. I am that one you know as Jesus. This has been one of the greatest pieces of misinformation you have been indoctrinated with in your society, which is that you are separate from God and that God has abandoned you.

God has set you, in this world of temptation, an impossible task. He has given you free will, yet you are not allowed to use it. This is one of the most confusing teachings that has come down through the ages. You have been given free will, you have been given a guidance system that is in alignment with love, and you have the choice. You have all been given choice. Do you feel good, or do you feel bad? The trouble with the system in which you have been raised is that you have not been taught what feeling bad means. You have been taught that feeling bad, when you see something outside yourself, is seeing outside of yourself. It is *not*. You are seeing a reflection of your mind that has not left you. It seems to be outside you, but it is not. It is still connected to you, and that projection, that seeming separation, is what tricks you into thinking that you can judge and attack another and not suffer. It is the illusory world in which you all live.

This idea of the world being illusory is confusing for many of you, because it feels so viscerally real. This is because you have not been taught the idea of projection, and you do not really understand it. So what seems to be separate from you is not. And that is why your brothers and sisters are your salvation and you are their salvation, because you are one. You are literally one. There is no separation. The separation is illusory; it is a trick of the mind.

Extension is your natural state, and that means you understand that to give to others, extend yourself, and show your love for the world by bringing your best to it and sharing it is your understanding demonstrated. It is your understanding that you *are* the world. You are the one. You are connected to all things, and the beauty and love you offer to the world will be returned a thousandfold.

Be joyful today that you have learned this lesson about projection. Be joyful that you understand that to attack anybody in your mind or in reality is the same thing, because they are in your mind even when they seem to be outside of you.

I am that one you know as Jesus, and we will speak to you tomorrow.

LESSON 240

Fear is not justified in any form.

Follow the complete lesson guidelines in your *ACIM* book.

You are blessed beings, indeed. I am that one you know as Jesus. If you think of your emotional guidance system as an infallible meter of how on track you are or how off track you are, peace is the indicator that you are on track, and fear is the indicator that you are completely off track.

You are viewing what frightens you (or the story you're talking about the thing you're viewing frightens you), and it is completely wrong. We are not speaking here of the fear of the tiger. We're not speaking here of the fear of heights. We are speaking of the fear of not making your rent, being judged, being humiliated, or being abandoned. These are all just ideas completely out of alignment with love that are misleading you and terrorizing you, and your feedback system is saying, "No, no, no," by giving you negative emotions — strong feelings that say, "This should not be."

The misinterpretation of your guidance system is something we will continue to address, because when you feel bad, you're off track. That means you are in the ego, and you will project; that means you will blame something outside of you for the fear you are generating from within your consciousness. So when you are triggered into a state of fear, you are in the least intelligent and least accurately observing state that you can be in. You will misinterpret everything, including the negative feedback you get from your emotional guidance system, which says, "You're so wrong here; stop doing what you're doing."

When you have the thought, "I don't have enough money," and you believe that thought and generate fear, you believe you are feeling bad because you don't have enough money. However, you actually feel bad because you're wrong. You're off track; you're off target.

Try to remember this today: Every time you feel bad or begin to feel a little off, you're going off track; you're misinterpreting. You are making up an illusory, untrue story. When you feel at peace, relaxed, contented, happy, inspired, enthusiastic, or curious, you are on track. You are being led, or guided, by spirit to the next good thing in your life. So know that the more happy feelings you have, the more on track you are. But when you are off track and feel those bad feelings, do not berate yourself. Instead, ask yourself: "What am I believing? What am I thinking? What am I saying to myself that is causing this pain?" It is not the outside world; it is the interior interpretation.

I am that one you know as Jesus. We will speak to you again tomorrow.

LESSON 241

This holy instant is salvation come.

Follow the complete lesson guidelines in your *ACIM* book.

You are blessed beings, indeed. I am that one you know as Jesus. You will notice that these lessons speak as if things have already happened.

You are being trained into accepting that these things can happen by envisioning and saying the words that they have already happened. This is how creation works. Many of you have completely misinterpreted how creation works. You think that when you see something you don't like and judge it and hate it, it will go away. It will not go away. It is going to become strengthened by your attention. What you focus on increases. It is that simple. It does not matter whether you focus on it by using the words, "I don't want you here. I don't like you. You are upsetting me." It does not matter. That which you give attention to expands and increases and strengthens.

When you say words such as "salvation has come," your body-mind reacts as if it's true. You have stepped back from judgment, stepped back from resistance to what is. By saying these words, you have cast a most beautiful spell: that you are at peace and everything is fine. Your body-mind will react as if that's true, and the more often you say this and the more you come to believe it and feel it in your body-mind, the more likely it will come into being.

Do not look at the things falling apart — the devastation, the cruelty, and the death. But that *is* what you all look at. Do not look at that. Look at the beauty, the peace, the joy, and the love. Yes, people will say you are looking at the world through rose-colored glasses, and you can say, "It's okay. I know how creation works. I know that the more gratitude I have, the more love I have, the more appreciation I have, and the more peace I have, the better the world will be."

Have you noticed that those beings looking at the negativities, devastation, and chaos on your planet are becoming more and more frightened, more and more agitated? Do you think their frequency is going to add to the chaos or heal it? There is a very logical answer when you pose it that way. Those kinds of fear, anger, and upset are not going to bring into being a world of peace, love, and joy. Those of you practicing forgiveness, on the other hand, are planting the seeds of peace, love, and joy every single time you step back from judgment. And in this holy instant, you give peace a chance.

I am that one you know as Jesus, and we will speak to you again tomorrow.

This day is God's.
It is my gift to him.

Follow the complete lesson guidelines
in your *ACIM* book.

You are blessed beings, indeed. I am that one you know as Jesus. Consider all the things you think you want every day: "Oh, I want more food. I want more money. I wish I could go on that trip. I think maybe I should get 'this' or get 'that.'" Think of all the striving you do to achieve those things.

This prayer, this lesson, will allow you to relax, and what is relaxing but faithfulness. It is trusting that you will be guided exactly where you need to go, with whom you need to share your time, with whom you need to have conversations, what you need to purchase or not, and what you need to do or not. Relaxation is a testament to your understanding that you are not separate from God but are deeply and profoundly connected to the inner guidance that will lead you to that which you seek.

Many of you believe that God denies what you want, that this universe is here to make you suffer. This is a hangover from the Christian teachings, of course. The truth is, your connection to the Divine is what ignites your passion. It is what ignites those feelings in you: "'This' would be good for me or 'that' would be good for me or 'that' would be an adventure I would enjoy." But there doesn't have to be a personal and individuated striving for it. Do you think that God does not know what you want, that this universe cannot figure out the frequency you are emitting? Of course it can. That information is being broadcast by you every single second. It is the frequency you hold.

Relaxing into the knowing that you are being read clearly by this reflective universe demonstrates your understanding of the laws of creation. So relax. Hand this day over; stop striving today. Just do what you're inspired to do or be where you're inspired to be, and trust in that guidance, knowing that you are cared for and loved.

I am that one you know as Jesus, and we will speak to you again tomorrow.

Today I will judge nothing that occurs.

Follow the complete lesson guidelines
in your *ACIM* book.

You are blessed beings, indeed. I am
that one you know as Jesus. What freedom, relaxation, and joy it brings you to
say, "Today, I will leave everything alone.
I will leave everything just as it is and trust that
there is a great plan afoot on this planet about which I have very little
information. Therefore, I should not be so quick to say, 'That is wrong; that
shouldn't be happening.'"

Sometimes negative events, or what you perceive as negative events,
cause great transformation, because humans see a negative event and
assume that something needs to be corrected. If you prevent that "negative"
event, the system that generates it may not be changed. This is not something you think of when you are berating such events.

One example we give you is increased wildfires in your society. These
increasing fires bring into your awareness a greater love for the planet, a
great deal more willingness to act on behalf of the planet. You could say
that these things are terrible, but there are motivations arising in you that
witness these things and are creating a revolution.

Do not be so quick to judge, and for today, do not judge at all. We want
to remind you that that means you as well. Stop judging yourself, your hair,
your tummy, your legs, or your bottom — whatever you attack on a daily
basis or judge as imperfect. Give yourself a break today. You understand
that when you stop doing that thing today, it will not change anything,
but it will change your internal vibration considerably, because instead of
attacking the outside world and the inside world and saying that God has
left this place, you are saying, "I trust that there is a great plan about which
I have very little information, so let's just see how it plays out today."

See how your life plays out today without judgment, fear, or resentment; all these things come from judgment, you see. You think judgment is
your friend. You think it keeps you safe from being taken advantage of. The
truth is that it causes you all the suffering you experience.

I am that one you know as Jesus, and we will speak to you again tomorrow.

LESSON 244

I am in danger nowhere in the world.

Follow the complete lesson guidelines
in your *ACIM* book.

You are blessed beings, indeed. I am that one you know as Jesus. Almost every thought in your mind says this is not true: "People die all the time. This world is a very dangerous place. You can't trust people. You can't walk down dark alleys."

This lesson teaches you about the part of you that is truly you and is not your body. It is your spirit/soul/consciousness (it has many names). It is that, that witnesses the world, that consciousness that engages with everything. That is invulnerable. It was before this body was born, and it will be after the body has been laid aside when its job is over.

You must remember that the body is not real in the way we define reality in *A Course in Miracles*. It is in accord with God, that which is eternal, and that which is indestructible. Of course, the body is destructible, but you are not. This is where the focus of the mind must go. It must go to that part of you that witnessed your childhood, your youth, your twenties, and your thirties (for those of you who have been on this Earth plane a little while), seeing all kinds of dramas.

The body changes. The body was not, and there will come a point when the body is not again in this incarnation, probably, for you. But there is an aspect of mind (love) that is so powerful and so creative that once you master it, you will, if you so choose, be able to transform the body. The body is unconsciously manufactured by the mind, and this is why you sicken and die. The mind that manufactures the body is not healthy, healed, or whole. It is not in alignment with love.

Again, we ask you to speak in absolutes. We ask you to focus on your invulnerability. It is your belief in the physical body and in death that makes you so dangerous. When you are focused on your body, death, and weakness, you become vicious, attacking, and defensive. But it's all about the physical body. As you focus more and more on spirit, as you focus more and more on your connection with the Divine, the fear falls away, the fallibility falls away, your health increases, and you become more like your Creator.

You are already like your Creator. You merely have loaded layers and layers of dirt on top of that knowing, and we are clearing that dirt away.

I am that one you know as Jesus, and we will speak to you again tomorrow.

LESSON 245

Your peace is with me, Father. I am safe.

Follow the complete lesson guidelines in your *ACIM* book.

You are blessed beings, indeed. I am that one you know as Jesus. When you walk around with these ideas firmly planted in the mind, and it will become so over the years that you practice this work, you bring to the world calmness and peace that others do not.

This is the greatest gift you can give not only yourself but the world, because you will be living in a peaceful mind, which is the most valuable thing that you can ever have, and you will be bringing a voice of sanity into the world. You will not be joining in fearful conversations. You will not be negatively gossiping about others. You will be sharing your peaceful mind with those around you.

Yes, some people get annoyed at you, because you are not joining their battles, and that is okay. As you come to appreciate the value of a peaceful mind, you will realize that there are beings whose frequency is different enough from yours that you will appear as a threat to them. That is what happened in my physical incarnation so many years ago: The energy that I was manifesting and that was contained within me was a threat to the frequency of the area and the plane in which I was functioning as a teacher and a healer. So they had to kill me.

Many of you have asked why I would allow that to happen. Well, it was because I did not die, and I knew that I would not die. I knew that I had mastery over my physical/material body and my consciousness, so I knew what I was capable of and had been doing it for several years at that point — manifesting a new physical structure in different locations while meditating, going and having conversations with people while meditating.

I had come to see what mastery of the mind looks like. Mastery of the mind means mastery of the body. Mastery of the body is not what you should be seeking, and you certainly should not be seeking it by using the body.

If you want to have a deep and powerful connection to the Divine, become peaceful through forgiveness practice. Become peaceful through the knowledge and understanding of the laws of creation. Become peaceful through comprehending that you are made in the image of God and that you are a powerful creator; therefore, you do not need to fear the world. The world is only a reflection of you. And when you master love, you will only encounter it.

I am that one you know as Jesus, and we will speak to you tomorrow.

LESSON 246

To love my Father is to love his child.

Follow the complete lesson guidelines in your *ACIM* book.

You are blessed beings, indeed. I am that one you know as Jesus. This is something you do not really think about. You do not really think the judgments you have about yourself and the judgments you have about your brothers and sisters on this planet prevent you from connecting to the Divine or prevent you from knowing your true nature.

This idea of judgment is the greatest poison you can take. You think the judgment keeps you safe. You think that if you don't judge things or people that you will be bowled over or become a doormat, and the opposite is true. When you step back from judgment and see the world with forgiving eyes, you get so much more. You get relief from the suffering that judgment causes. You get relief from the separation that judgment causes, and you get to connect to that peaceful place where all the knowledge of all things resides.

You can connect into that knowledge. You can tap into realms beyond your ability to understand and comprehend from the state of being that is contaminated by judgment.

Do an experiment in which you have a day when you step back from judgment. Don't judge yourself when you look in the mirror, and don't judge the person who cuts you off in traffic. Don't judge the way your coworkers eat their sandwiches. Don't. Don't. Don't.

By doing this experiment, you will realize how frequently you judge. You will also realize how much more peaceful your mind is and how much better you feel because you are not separating yourself from your Father in heaven, which is love. The frequency of love is God. When you judge, you separate yourself from the frequency of love and you feel bad. Know that your feeling bad is you judging, separating, and isolating yourself from the ever-present frequency of love that is your right, your natural inheritance.

I am that one you know as Jesus, and we will speak to you tomorrow.

LESSON 247

Without forgiveness, I will still be blind.

Follow the complete lesson guidelines in your *ACIM* book.

You are blessed beings, indeed. I am that one you know as Jesus. It is important for you to understand the power of forgiveness.

Yes, the whole study of *A Course in Miracles* is about these most magnificent abilities you possess: the ability to forgive, the ability to step back from judgment, and the ability to understand that there cannot be anything on this Earth, in this experience you are having, that is not allowed to be. If it has happened and you have witnessed it, then there is an aspect of Divine mind that has allowed this thing to be.

It is hard for you all when you see things you think should not be. For example, there was a terrible storm that went through your Bahamas [Hurricane Dorian, September 2019], and you saw people losing their homes. You saw people devastated; you saw people having experiences you feel should not have happened. Well, these experiences are happening, and the people involved are going to come out of it, believe it or not, with beneficial knowledge they did not have before the event.

Many of you have been through a circumstance that you, in the moment it was happening, thought, "This shouldn't be happening to me." It can be as simple as having a flat tire. For example: "This shouldn't be happening to me." But it is happening to you. You argue with reality, and you resist all that situation holds for you when you say it should not be.

That is the judgment we are asking you to let go of here: the belief that you know what is good for you (most of you don't have any idea what's good for you) and the belief that you know when others shouldn't do something. You don't know. You don't know their history. You don't know their motivations. You don't know the outcomes of situations. You can't see the repercussions of everything. You are simply not equipped to decide that something is a sin.

In fact, there is no sin. Sin is something that is committed against God and is unforgivable, and God never looks at anything that way. Only humans in their small ego-minds see things that way and figure that God would be offended, but it has been allowed by God to happen, so that is clearly not true.

The power of forgiveness gives you everything, and there are so many times that people will come into a session with this being, for example, and ask, "What is my purpose?" Your purpose is to forgive everything you have not yet forgiven; that is your purpose. From that place of love, kindness, and understanding, you will get and experience everything that you would like to get and experience in this life.

You hold on to judgments. You hold on to sin. You hold on to the belief that you know better than God, and it is not so. It will upset some of you to hear this, and that is okay. That is judgment as well, and you will have to forgive me for the teachings that bring you this information.

I am that one you know as Jesus, and we will speak to you again tomorrow.

Whatever suffers is not part of me.

Follow the complete lesson guidelines in your *ACIM* book.

You are blessed beings, indeed. I am that one you know as Jesus. This seems to be a very harsh lesson for some of you. You have become used to seeing your sadness as part of you.

You even believe that to be sad means that you love somebody or you care for somebody or that you have compassion for a situation, but that is not so. Suffering is not required. When you function in the higher realms of love, you do not suffer at all. You do not feel the disconnection from love that causes suffering. That is all suffering is. It is your disconnection from the truth, which is love. That means you end up as an evolved being, connected to All That Is, connected to love, through your guidance system. It means that you allow everything and you accept everything, even those things that the ego-mind says are unacceptable.

This is a challenge for all of you, because if you lose a beloved being in your life, you think that to grieve and suffer and gnash and pull your hair out is part of you. It seems so true when you are in the ego-mind, because the ego has convinced you that the body of that being has gone, so that being must be gone. This is a lie. The being has not gone.

When you believe in bodies, when you worship bodies, and when you grieve over the loss of bodies, then you are, by your actions, demonstrating that you think people or other beings, such as your pets, were their bodies, and they are not. They are the eternal connection you have with them, the beautiful memories you have of them, and the beautiful communications you can have with them.

When you are focused on the body, you don't even try to make connections in spirit. You don't believe that they are around anymore. You go to the grave and grieve and suffer. They are not in the grave. They are with you. They are close to you. They are forever close to you. When you leave your body, they will meet you. They have not gone anywhere; they are merely a breath away.

This seems a harsh lesson for those of you who still believe in bodies and still believe in suffering. But we assure you that as you forgive relentlessly as you walk through your spiritual ascension, you will suffer less and less. You will come to see that whenever you are suffering, you are out of accord with truth and love.

I am that one you know as Jesus, and we will speak to you tomorrow.

Forgiveness ends all suffering and loss.

Follow the complete lesson guidelines in your *ACIM* book.

You are blessed beings, indeed. I am that one you know as Jesus. It is important for you to understand that the salvation of the world rests on your forgiveness.

It does not rest on you doing things in the world to prevent what has already happened. Many of you are looking at disasters or political upsets, these sorts of things, and seeing many, many people taking action. It is important for you to understand that there is nothing wrong with taking action, but if your mind is filled with vitriol, hatred, and judgment for the beings you think have done wrong, you will not change the world. You will not change the world.

Forgiveness must be a part of your practice so that you can bring a new frequency into this place and so that you may bring a new awareness of love into this place. Battling the warmongers does not do any good because you use the same energy they have taught you to use. I am teaching you to use a different energy as your catalyst for change — love. Through the practice of forgiveness, you get back all your power to use in whatever way you see fit to enhance everyone's experience here.

However, in the end, your world will not be the place that you want to stay. The ascension process, the enlightenment process, eventually will take you to a place where this world is not a place you want to play anymore. You will be tired of chasing your idols; you will be tired of the bodies you've used and the body you have. You will be tired of it and say, "I have had enough."

It is not disillusionment; it is not depression. Rather, enlightenment is recognizing, "I no longer need this particular kind of experience to express myself."

That is where you will all eventually get to, but until you make forgiveness the transformative practice you use to bring peace to your mind, the battles on this Earth will continue. The fights on this Earth will continue. The poor and the grieved and the suffering will continue because of the frequency of the collective minds that inhabit this place.

Make your mind a forgiving place. Experience the bliss of peace, and understand that you are contributing to the world by forgiving it.

I am that one you know as Jesus, and we will speak to you tomorrow.

LESSON 250

Let me not see myself as limited.

Follow the complete lesson guidelines in your *ACIM* book.

You are blessed beings, indeed. I am that one you know as Jesus. There is a great truth we want to reveal to you today: As you see the world and your brothers and sisters, so you will see yourself.

If you view your fellow human beings as untrustworthy, frail, sick, or dying, then you will have to live by the same rules that you impose on them. So this is a very, very important principle we want you to understand: You lose when you attack. You lose when you judge. You lose when you condemn others, because you must now live by those rules. If you have seen people as sinful and able to commit a crime that God would punish, then you will view yourself that way too, and you will believe that God could punish you.

If you believe in the sicknesses that run rampant through your society as things that are winning, then that is a rule you also will have to live by. When you view your brothers and sisters as eternal spiritual beings only occasionally making errors in judgment, then you also will see yourself that way, and you will know that an error can be corrected. An error is forgivable. A sin is unforgivable. It is considered something that God would not have allowed to happen and as an attack on God. It is irreversible. Of course, nothing is irreversible, because most of the games you are playing here are illusory. Most of the thoughts you have are illusory. You are living in a world inhabited by your own demons, fears, and projections.

Know that every time you offer a loving thought to a brother or sister on this planet, you will receive that yourself. To give is to receive; to receive is to give. They are the same. The interior and the exterior are the same. Whatever you are doing inside your mind to others, you will experience.

I am that one you know as Jesus, and we will speak to you tomorrow.

I am in need of nothing but the truth.

Follow the complete lesson guidelines in your *ACIM* book.

You are blessed beings, indeed. I am that one you know as Jesus. This is a prayer that you can use all the time when you are confused: "Please show me the truth so that I may have peace, so that I may be at peace."

"Please show me the truth," because when you are suffering, upset, angry, afraid, or disoriented, you are out of alignment with truth. You are not seeing the truth. You are not interpreting the world truly. When you interpret the world truly, you feel at peace. To those of you in turmoil and despair, this seems an impossibility, but it is not. This is why we keep telling you to do your forgiveness practice, release the past, and stop worrying about the future. Put it into the hands of the Divine, and pay attention to this moment, this holy instant you have in which you get to choose love or fear.

Are you choosing fear right now? Then you will suffer. Are you choosing judgment right now? Then you will suffer. But if you choose acceptance and forgiveness, then you will find peace, and in that peace, you will create a beautiful future.

Your future does not come from the past. The future comes from the eternal now, where you decide on what you want by your decision to follow love or fear. It is all happening now in this holy instant. When you blame the future on the past, you are merely contaminating the present moment with the past. That's all you've done. You've retrieved a memory of something hateful, you have decided that it's real, and you will feel the pain. In that moment, you give up your ability to create a different future and guarantee that the future will look like the past. It will seem that your trials and tribulations never end.

It is here, dear ones, in this holy instant now, that you decide everything. Forgive and choose peace, and your future will thrive.

I am that one you know as Jesus, and we will speak to you tomorrow.

LESSON 252

The child of God is my identity.

Follow the complete lesson guidelines in your *ACIM* book.

You are blessed beings, indeed. I am that one you know as Jesus. This is the fundamental problem: You do not think of yourself as grand enough.

The ego is very loud and brash at times. The ego is very fearful and weak at times, and it will fluctuate between those two. You have a grandeur that is beyond time, beyond the body, and beyond anything that you conceive of in this world. You see, you play with the small toys of this world: the cars, the bodies, the clothes, the hair, the makeup, the tropical holidays, and the work you do. All these things seem so important, but they are nothing — absolutely nothing — compared to the light you hold within you, the capacity for creativity you hold within you, and the ability to love that is within you.

We would like you to dig deep today and ask yourself: "How can I step up my game? How can I be that being this lesson speaks of? Do I need to be calmer? Do I need to be more generous? Do I need to be kinder? Do I need to express my creativity more? Do I need to be more adventurous? Where am I playing small? Where am I hiding behind my fears?"

Pick a fear today, one that you know you have. You all have fears. Then ask yourself, "Do I want to spend the rest of my life diminished by this fear, believing that it can kill me and believing that it can ruin me?" when you actually are far greater than that fear. Entertain visions of you overcoming that fear, visions of stepping up your game, so that you are befitting of the title child of God.

I am that one you know as Jesus, and we will speak to you tomorrow.

LESSON 253

My self is ruler of the universe.

Follow the complete lesson guidelines in your *ACIM* book.

You are blessed beings, indeed. I am that one you know as Jesus. None of you believes this. None of you believes you want bad things to happen to you. None of you believes that the things you don't have are not with you because you don't actually want them. None of you believes this.

This is a tough lesson for you, because you believe you don't have things because something else is preventing you from getting them. You are not looking at your own consciousness and asking yourself, "What in me is not of a like frequency to that thing I want?" If it is a big, glamorous, and ostentatious thing you would like, then look at yourself and say, "Am I a match for this?" If it is a deeply loving and kind thing you want but do not possess right now, are you deeply kind and loving? Are you a match for that thing you want? Perhaps not.

All of you have come into separation. All of you reside in individual bodies, and that proves you believe in separation. You are living it. You are feeling it. You are experiencing it. That is something you all have in common. You all have an individualized body as a demonstration of your separation. These lessons ask you to look at that. Where do you like to be separated? Where do you attack others as proof that you believe attacking them will not hurt you? Where are you walled in? Where are you silencing yourself and not sharing your great talents? All these are aspects of separation manifesting through you.

Now, that's the default setting on this Earth plane: separation. That's why it's a challenging place. To override the default setting, you must put in a new program, and that is what we are doing here. We ask you to choose love. We ask you to recognize your multidimensional eternal nature. We ask you to step back from attack and judgment so that you can have a new experience, a more faithful experience to the true you.

Through faith and stepping back from judgment, listening to these words, and believing that there is some truth in them, you will begin to experience miracles. You will experience miracles of transformation in other people. You will experience miracles of transformation in yourself and even in the world around you.

You must have the courage to do something different. You must understand that the patterns you witness in your life follow you around because of you.

I am that one you know as Jesus, and we will speak to you tomorrow.

LESSON 254

Let every voice but God's be still in me.

Follow the complete lesson guidelines in your *ACIM* book.

You are blessed beings, indeed. I am that one you know as Jesus. The ego's raucous cries are distracting, indeed. As you go further and further into these lessons, you will feel the difference between guidance and that loud and angry voice of the ego.

The ego is impatient. It speaks first; it speaks loudly. But as you focus your mind, do your forgiveness practice, stop indulging in hateful fantasies, stop feeding that energy of the ego-mind, and encourage and feed the energy of love and forgiveness instead, the voices shift and change. The ego's voice becomes less strident, less obvious, and there is another voice that becomes clearer: the gentle, loving, guiding voice of love. Love is God. God is love, so the voice of love is the voice for God.

When you ask to hear only that voice, you send out a powerful message. You choose to use your free will to dampen the voice of the ego, and the voice of the ego is the one that's been fed in your society. It is the voice that has been cultured. It is the voice that has been given your attention. But as you have now come to lesson 254, you have spent many, many days giving spirit love and attention, giving your inner guidance love and attention. Now you are ready to dedicate your mind to that inner voice for God.

I am that one you know as Jesus, and we will speak to you tomorrow.

LESSON 255

This day I choose to spend in perfect peace.

Follow the complete lesson guidelines
in your *ACIM* book.

You are blessed beings, indeed. I am that one you know as Jesus. What a great gift this is: to let go of all needs, judgments, and things in the future and the past and just be with what is today, accepting it and being calm and at peace with it.

Now, for some of you, this may seem that it requires a miracle, and it may indeed. But your peace is only hidden by your thoughts, judgments, discursive conversations with past people, future ideas, or judgments in this present moment. You hide your peace from yourself; nobody else is doing it to you. Even if somebody comes into your sphere of influence and is upset with you, you have a choice whether or not to join in the drama.

You can rise above the battleground merely by deciding to do so. That is your challenge today: to rise above the battleground and to not be sucked into the horizontal dramas of the ego's wars, whether small or large. It does not matter whether they are external, in terms of other places of the world or in your present life. Today is the day that you choose peace regardless of anything else that's going on.

You will see that you have the ability to do this. You will see that even if you cannot pull it off for the whole day, there will be moments you can step back from something that you would normally have become upset about or entangled in or enmeshed in. It is your choice. The eternally peaceful mind is always there within you, hidden beneath the rough seas of the ego's judgments. Dive deep today and find that still, quiet place where your natural self resides.

I am that one you know as Jesus, and we will speak to you tomorrow.

God is the only goal I have today.

Follow the complete lesson guidelines in your *ACIM* book.

You are blessed beings, indeed. I am that one you know as Jesus. We ask you to absolutely focus your mind on these lessons so that you come to see how many different and opposing goals you have in your day. These lessons require you to amplify your focus so that you understand that it is in dedicating your life to love and forgiveness that you will gain everything else.

The ego will tell you that there are very important things in your life that you cannot hand over to God, that you cannot trust will fix themselves. No, they won't fix themselves, but you are going to the projector; remember, your life is manufactured and brought into being from all your beliefs, ideas, and things that you act on and act as if are true. So if you have a manifestation in your life of a negative thing, a thing that you don't want, or a thing that you are experiencing and have had enough of, you must go to the producer of that effect, which is the projector: your mind.

Forgiveness is recalibrating the projector. Just as when you watch a movie in a theater and see a little piece of fluff on the screen, it is only the foolish who run up to the screen and try to fix it. Everybody else says to the projector operator: "Clean the lens."

That is what you will be doing today. You will do your forgiveness practice, step back from attack and judgment, let go of the past, forgive the present, and allow the future to be created today from the peaceful mind of the nonjudgmental, forgiving being that is you.

I am that one you know as Jesus, and we will speak to you again tomorrow.

Let me remember what my purpose is.

Follow the complete lesson guidelines in your *ACIM* book.

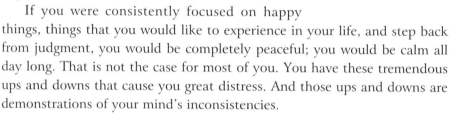

You are blessed beings, indeed. I am that one you know as Jesus. Your emotional ups and downs are demonstrations of your inconsistent beliefs.

If you were consistently focused on happy things, things that you would like to experience in your life, and step back from judgment, you would be completely peaceful; you would be calm all day long. That is not the case for most of you. You have these tremendous ups and downs that cause you great distress. And those ups and downs are demonstrations of your mind's inconsistencies.

Focus today on the purpose of forgiveness, because that is the means you have been given to achieve peace. Your forgiveness practice is what will free your mind from the past and the future. It will bring you back to the eternal now, which is the only place you can affect anything. Remember this every time you fear the future or have resentments about the past. You have left the eternal now, and you are wasting your time, or you are contaminating the eternal now with anxieties, fears, and resentments.

Your forgiveness practice is the most empowering thing you can do. It is not necessarily for other people, but others benefit from your forgiveness practice, obviously; you become calmer and happier. The truth is, you benefit from your forgiveness practice. You stop tormenting yourself with old stories and ideas that no longer serve you and will not bring you what you want.

Unify your mind today in the pursuit of peace. How do you get there? You get there through your forgiveness practice. So step back from judgment, criticism, and fear. Instead, view the world and all your brothers and sisters with affection and compassion.

I am that one you know as Jesus, and we will speak to you again tomorrow.

Let me remember
that my goal is God.

Follow the complete lesson guidelines
in your *ACIM* book.

You are blessed beings, indeed. I am
that one you know as Jesus. The ego
will counsel you that this is a dangerous
practice. It will say that you need to be in
control of everything, you need to pay attention to
everything, and you must have everything orchestrated according to your
wants, needs, wishes, beliefs, and ideas, or everything will go wrong.

Understand that the contrary is true. Most of your problems are miscreated by your insistence on having things the ego's way. Remember,
the ego is a hodgepodge of beliefs and ideas — all fearful, all limiting, all
unloving. What makes you think that conglomeration of beliefs, and the
thoughts and feelings that those beliefs would cause you to have, could
bring you a peaceful, abundant, happy, and healthy life? There is no logic
to that.

This idea of seeking only God seems radical. It is radical. We ask you
to change the way you look at the world. Change the way you inhabit your
interior world. This does not mean you are not attending to the things that
need to be done each day. These lessons can be done silently in the mind
when you are doing mundane tasks, such as doing the dishes, weeding the
garden, or folding the laundry. When you are doing things that do not
require all your attention, these lessons can occupy your thoughts and ideas
and bring to you the frequency of love and peace.

So instead of ruminating on what's wrong with your life or potential
future problems while you are doing those mundane tasks, ruminate on
your lessons, and make God your only goal today. See how you feel and see
what miracles begin to occur in your life as you spend more and more time
in the frequency of seeking God.

I am that one you know as Jesus, and we will speak to you again
tomorrow.

Let me remember that there is no sin.

Follow the complete lesson guidelines in your *ACIM* book.

You are blessed beings, indeed. I am that one you know as Jesus. Even down to the tiniest judgments, you are accusing something or someone of a sin.

- "It shouldn't be raining today." (The weather is being sinful; it should be nicer.)
- "Somebody should not have looked at me that way; that person should not have said those words." (Those are minor sins.)
- "Your parents should not have raised you the way they did." (They have committed a sin.)

Every single upset you have is because your mind has been judgmental. Most beings would not necessarily perceive themselves as judgmental, but every upset you have comes from the fact that you have judged against something or refused to accept something. Refusing to accept something is judging against it. This is why, at times, we recommend radical acceptance as a practice. It's so that you have a contrast of your ordinary mind to a radically accepting mind.

When you accept everything, you are being observant. You are saying, "It is here for a reason. It is holding something that I need to see." Your experience — your body, relationships, bank account, refrigerator, every-thing in your life this very moment — has a story to tell you about your value system, judgments, hatreds, and weaknesses — everything. When you look at your life today without judgment, you will learn something that you need to learn that you have hidden from yourself in the material world. Remember, your consciousness (the part of you that you accept as you) is only a very small sliver of who and what you believe in.

Many of the things you believe in are hidden out in the world or in your body. For example, many of you are carrying a few extra pounds; because you are not good at handling your feelings and emotions, you turn to food and drinks and all kinds of things, and you imbibe to calm yourself. That overweight body is showing you that you're using food as a soothing mechanism for your feelings. If you were only using it to satiate hunger, as fuel for your vehicle to get you around from A to B, it would not have excess weight on it. That excess weight is your clue that you are hiding something from yourself.

Take a look at one part of your life, the part that causes you the most distress, the part that causes you the most suffering, and look at it and be fully accepting (no judgments allowed). Ask yourself what this part of your life is giving you as a message. Do you need to become more focused? Do you need to relax? Do you need to be more expressive? Do you need to be more creative? Do you need to be kinder?

Look at the part of your life that is out of order as far as you're concerned, and ask yourself: "What have I not given to that part of my life? What am I resisting? What am I hiding from?" If you are honest with yourself, you will find an answer.

I am that one you know as Jesus, and we will see you again tomorrow.

LESSON 260

Let me remember God created me.

Follow the complete lesson guidelines in your *ACIM* book.

You are blessed beings, indeed. I am that one you know as Jesus. This is a very important thing to remember, is it not? You think that you are fallible. You think that you are going to die. You think that you are alone.

All these things are untruths that make you feel separate from everything and everyone, including God and your brothers and sisters on this Earth plane. When you remember that God created you, you begin to treat yourself with respect. You see that acting on unhealthy habits or unloving thoughts and beliefs and ideas are a blasphemy of sorts. By doing them, you are really thumbing your nose at God, if you will.

Remember that you are sacred beings. You are ideas in the mind of God that have become manifested. Yes, you live in separation. Yes, you believe that you have been abandoned. The truth is, you came here; you wanted to do this. It is only when you get tired of the world and tired of chasing your idols that the journey Home to oneness, to love, becomes more attractive.

Some of you will still be sitting on the fence. Some of you will still want what the world offers you, but some of you will be so tired of it that you have no enticements left in that place. And there is great relief, believe it or not, when the world holds no value for you anymore.

This does not mean that you do not participate in life; it does not mean that you do not love your fellows. It means that you are not tormented anymore. You are not striving to find things outside of yourself to make you happy. That really is what the temptation of the world is, and it's there for you as long as you want it. Remembering who created you, how eternal you are, and that nothing can threaten your true nature gives you a sense of calm relaxation that very few other things can give you.

I am that one you know as Jesus, and we will speak to you tomorrow.

LESSON 261

God is my refuge and security.

Follow the complete lesson guidelines in your *ACIM* book.

You are blessed beings, indeed. I am that one you know as Jesus. Humans look for refuge in all kinds of places. They look for it in money. They look for it in sex. They look for it in food. They look for it many places that cannot, in fact, keep them safe, because that is always about the body.

The ego's choices regarding safety are always about defending the body, and as long as you're defending your body, you do not know who you are. This is a tough one for all of you who are used to defending your bodies, protecting your bodies, from danger. When you focus on the body as the fallible thing that it is, you feel fallible, because you identify yourself as a physical body.

When you join with God, when you learn to walk with me, doing these lessons and focusing on the nonphysical aspects of your self, then you identify with the nonphysical parts of you that are infallible and will live on forever, so you become more relaxed. You are not in the ego's domain. You are not on the battleground.

Have you not noticed that in war the ego wants to kill bodies? That is what the ego believes in. It believes that if it destroys your body or keeps your body safe, that is the only thing of value. In murderous rampages, the egos that want to kill will kill the body, not realizing that they have not, in fact, touched the essence of that being, which is eternal and will, of course, go on to learn other lessons and to experience other lifetimes. This process today of identifying with the nonphysical aspects of you — your creativity and ability to love and communicate — make you feel secure, whereas defending the body makes you feel fearful.

I am that one you know as Jesus, and we will speak to you tomorrow.

LESSON 262

Let me perceive no differences today.

Follow the complete lesson guidelines in your *ACIM* book.

You are blessed beings, indeed. I am that one you know as Jesus. In *A Course in Miracles*, it says there are no separate interests. Of course, one of the great burdens of your capitalistic society is that you have been taught there are separate interests: You have to look after yourself because nobody else will look after you. You had better keep all your stuff together so that nobody can take it or threaten your security.

This is demonstrated in your increasing poverty, increasing slums, and increasing environmental degradation on your planet. It is the constant taking of more than you need, the refusal to share, and the refusal to give, at times even to your own family. We witness people who have very large bank accounts watch their family members suffer and struggle. We understand that some of you do help your family members and there comes a point when you see that it is pointless to continue to do so; we are not speaking about that. We are not speaking about when you have done your very best to assist others and they continue to fritter away money or waste it in some way, and no matter what you do, there is no improvement. That is a different situation.

We are speaking about the initial situation in which you see a need and you have the ability to assist, whether it is offering $1 or $100, whether it is offering a roof over someone's head for the night, or whether it's giving your precious talents to the world, sharing in that way. We are not always speaking about money.

Ask yourself: "Where am I hoarding things?" Perhaps you own far more than you need and you have a house full of thousands and thousands of things that are doing you no good. That is a form of security and self-indulgence that prevents you from being free to share your assets, your nonphysical assets, with other beings. You can become so obsessed with material goods that you forget about the nonphysical world completely: your creativity, being loving, sharing your talents, and these sorts of things.

Understand that you are all connected. Of course, this is the rationale behind forgiveness: When you attack a fellow human, you are, in fact, attacking yourself. When you defend against others, you are, in fact, creating what you defend against, because you believe in it. You put all your resources into protecting yourself and inadvertently create the very thing that you do not want to experience.

This is one of those beliefs that's hard to grasp at first, because you have been so indoctrinated into capitalism, self-centeredness, and individualization. You are all connected, dear ones, and if the only thing you can do today is think kind thoughts about your brothers and sisters, at least try to do that today.

I am that one you know as Jesus, and we will speak to you again tomorrow.

My holy vision
sees all things as pure.

Follow the complete lesson guidelines
in your *ACIM* book.

You are blessed beings, indeed. I am
that one you know as Jesus. This lesson seems impossible (does it not?), to see
everything as if it is pure. Do you not see
that your judgments cause you suffering? Do you
not see that your insistence on arguing with reality causes you pain?

"He should not have said 'this'; she should not have done 'that.'" Here,
you are looking at something that has happened and saying that it shouldn't
have happened. You are arguing with what is, and that is a waste of time
and a waste of energy. It separates you from the knowledge that everything
here has been allowed to transpire because you have been given free will.
This is not the first time this lesson has come up.

When I was walking on the Earth plane many years ago, that is the
place that I came to. I came to see, and I developed an ability to see, that
whenever I judged something, I was wounding it. I was depleting it of
energy. I was truly attacking it — not figuratively but literally. My abilities
had been so powerfully enhanced at that point that I literally could kill a
plant by looking at it with hatred.

This is the macrocosm, if you will, of your microcosm. Understand that
to judge and hate and separate yourself from and condemn anything that
you see only hurts you most of all, and it affects the beings you see. This is
one of the reasons some of your celebrities have such difficult lives, because
so many people are viewing them with either lust or judgment.

Keep your eye on your prize. Keep your eye on forgiveness as the practice that will bring you everything you want. You see, forgiveness means
that you understand reality. You understand that you're all connected, so
attacking somebody else or something else is attacking yourself, and you are
demonstrating your powerful understanding in the laws of creation, which
is that you get more of what you focus on.

The universe is listening. It is a reflective and holographic place, and
when you focus on things you dislike, you will get more of them.

I am that one you know as Jesus, and we will speak to you again tomorrow.

LESSON 264

I am surrounded by the love of God.

Follow the complete lesson guidelines in your *ACIM* book.

You are blessed beings, indeed. I am that one you know as Jesus. Imagine the difference it would make in your day to say such a statement rather than saying, "I live in a dangerous and fearful world."

The phrase "I am surrounded by the love of God" means that you can expand, you can open, you can connect, and you can commune. When you say that you are in a dangerous universe, everything is going to attack you, so you must defend yourself, you become closed, rigid, and unaccepting.

This simple lesson is far from easy. It is the basis on which you must live your life from now on: that you know you are cared for and that you are not here by accident. You are here intentionally, and you have become lost. But now you have found a map to return you to your path.

You were destined to walk a path in this incarnation, and it is revealed to you by good feelings. It is revealed to you by happiness. It is revealed to you by joy. It is revealed to you by connection. It is revealed to you by creativity. When you are not in any of those places, you have gone off track a little bit, and this prayer will take you back into that place of knowing that all is well.

I am that one you know as Jesus, and we will speak to you again tomorrow.

Creation's gentleness is all I see.

Follow the complete lesson guidelines
in your *ACIM* book.

You are blessed beings, indeed. I am
that one you know as Jesus. When you
look at your entertainment systems —
football games, war movies, and news shows
— do you see that you are being fed everything
but God's vision of this world? It should not be your vision of this world,
either — this embattled, terribly conflicted place.

What you're witnessing is the mindset of humanity. Changing it in the
physical world is pointless, because it is going to be regenerated by the mind
that has collectively brought it into being. To shift the outside world, you
must shift the inside world. It seems counter to everything you were taught
on this plane, such as you must work hard in the physical world. But you
must be driven by love. You must be driven by a desire for something good
and to make something good materialize. You cannot fight against the darkness; you must illuminate it. There is shadow only where there is lack of
light.

When you think about becoming involved in environmental causes or
any kind of reconfiguration of your society, do not battle the old; rather,
invent and reinvent the new with love, passion, and desire for a kind, generous, and loving community.

I am that one you know as Jesus, and we will speak to you again
tomorrow.

My holy self abides in you, God's child.

Follow the complete lesson guidelines
in your *ACIM* book.

You are blessed beings, indeed. I am that one you know as Jesus. Is it not ironic that all the beings who drive you crazy are, in fact, the route to your salvation?

The route is in forgiveness and coming to a place of appreciation for all your brothers and sisters and all the opportunities they give you for practicing that forgiveness. It is in realizing that you will finally grasp what this life is for.

This life is to forgive. You have come into separation believing in war, judgment, and attack, and to relieve yourself of that suffering, you must see your brothers and sisters as fellows in Christ. Christ consciousness is the acceptance and love of all things and all beings. It is not choosing the ones you prefer over the others. It is not attacking some and loving others. It is not condemning some and worshiping others. It is about seeing all beings as equally valuable in the eyes of God and in your own vision. That is what happens when you wake up: You realize that even the most difficult of beings are giving you an opportunity to raise yourself above the battleground.

Some of you choose to live apart from other beings. You do not commune with them; you find isolation better because the difficulties of forgiveness are not yet within your ability to comply with. As you evolve, you will see that the more you forgive your brothers and sisters, the more you love humanity, the closer you come to Home, and the closer you come to heaven.

Heaven is merely a state of mind in which all things are accepted and all beings are equally respected and loved. In that respect and love, you find peace, joy, and self-appreciation.

I am that one you know as Jesus, and we will speak to you again tomorrow.

My heart is beating in the peace of God.

Follow the complete lesson guidelines
in your *ACIM* book.

You are blessed beings, indeed. I am
that one you know as Jesus. Of course,
your heart is where the answer lies.

Your heart is what you refer to as that
place that guides you through love, and that is
exactly what this lesson refers to. It refers to the fact that every heartbeat
of this amazing organ that lives within your chest is always sending out a
resonance. If your heart is open, which is in alignment with love (in its true
definition), then you will resonate at a frequency of healing and creativity.
If your heart is closed, you will become sick and fearful, and you will not
resonate at your Home frequency.

This is something for you to remember today: Your Home frequency
is love. And when you are in a place of gratitude, appreciation, forgiveness,
and kindness, then you are in that frequency of love, and you will thrive
and feel good. When your heart is closed and you are in a place of fear,
everything will seem as if it is a little off, and the longer you stay close-
hearted, the worse it will get — not as a punishment but as a feedback system to show you how well you are aligning with love.

Remember, there is no punitive God punishing you for being bad.
There is only feedback from this reflective universe, letting you know how
well aligned with love you are. It's very simple. So listen to your heartbeat
today, and ask, "What frequency is it beating at? Is my heart beating at the
frequency of love or fear?"

Open your heart, dear one, to the beauty of your life, the beauty of
your potential, and the beauty of the gift of life that you have given yourself
here. You have come into this body, place, and time to do important work,
and this training program is preparing you for that work.

I am that one you know as Jesus, and we will speak to you again
tomorrow.

Let all things be
exactly as they are.

Follow the complete lesson guidelines
in your *ACIM* book.

You are blessed beings, indeed. I am that one you know as Jesus. Most of you do not live in reality; you live in a fantasy world of which you are the director.

Now, it seems as if there is a contradiction here. We say you are the creator of your reality, and here we say your reality is incorrect. What we want to clarify in this lesson is that when you are not aligned with love and you have not had untrue beliefs and ideas clarified from your mind, you are living in a distorted version of reality. You live a lot in your future world; it is an imaginary world. Your future world is a fantasy world. You do not realize this when you imagine, as you're driving your car perhaps, what's going to happen when you get home. You believe those movies you see in your head, but you are, in fact, making up a fantasy from the distortions in your mind. You are not allowing your life to play out as it will.

Resentments, of course, are regurgitations of old fights, old wounds, and old hurts. Once again, you leave the present moment and live in a fantasy world — your fantasy of what happened, of being unfairly treated, or of that "sinner" doing something against you. Many of you who have had unpleasant experiences immediately want to jump up and say, "But it really did happen," and yes, perhaps you had an experience that was not much fun, but every time you go back to claim it as yours, you re-inflict that pain on yourself. The other person, the person who may have hurt you once in the past, is not involved in that victimization. You are. You are choosing to go back and re-live, in movies in your mind, a bad thing that happened to you because you want to.

This is a very difficult part of this forgiveness process for those of you who have wounds that you have nurtured and fed for a long time. But we assure you that you do not really want those wounds. You do not want that resentment. You do not want that contaminating energy to grow in the present and show up again in the future, because that is what will happen.

When you choose to use your present moment to regurgitate old wounds and old pains, you plant seeds for that same frequency in the future.

We encourage you here. Even those of you who have had what you consider unforgivable sins committed against you in your past, we ask you to give them up. We ask you to stop thinking about them and playing with them and feeding them with your powerful energy, for that is what you are doing. Every time you recall that terrible story to your friends, that awful thing that happened to you, you are infusing it with your power — your most God-given creative power: the power to create worlds.

We want you to create a beautiful world for yourself, a happy dream here while you live in separation, and it is possible if you train your mind. Do your lesson today. Forgive the past. Stop ruminating on anything other than what is happening right now, and appreciate the opportunities that every day gives you to share your magnificence with your brothers and sisters.

I am that one you know as Jesus, and we will speak to you tomorrow.

LESSON 269

My sight goes forth to look upon Christ's face.

Follow the complete lesson guidelines in your *ACIM* book.

You are blessed beings, indeed. I am that one you know as Jesus. It is the judgmental sight that causes your suffering. It is the rejecting sight that causes your suffering. But the loving and accepting sight causes you to see all your brothers and sisters as equally created and equally valued in the eyes of God.

This is what you must remember as you go through your day. The drug addict, the drunk, the child abuser, and the murderer — all beings are equally valued in the eyes of God. Yes, their behavior may be aberrant because of the dysfunctions of the mind, your society, and misperception, but they are all equally valued, and they will not be cast into hell because of what they have done or are doing no more than you will be cast into hell because of what you have done or what you are doing. Forgive yourself for your errors of thought and action, and practice forgiving your brothers and sisters for their errors of thought and action.

There are many beings in nondualistic teachings who think you should not do anything. Some of you now are being motivated to shift and change your behavior because you can see the consequences of your actions. Understand that to shift and change your behavior because you've changed your mind is what we are working on here. We are working on your mind so that you may shift your behavior, and in that shift, you can demonstrate to all you meet something profound has happened to you and that you are now functioning from a higher frequency. This will inspire others. This will incite curiosity, and some people may ask you, "What are you doing? You seem different."

Do not proselytize. Do not stand on soapboxes and insist anybody do anything. Rather, practice your practice. Keep your thoughts and beliefs and ideas as your practice, honing them, mastering them, making them more loving rather than trying to change others. But the systems on your planet do require a shift in all your behaviors. This is what we are doing here.

We are starting with minds, and once minds are changed, then behaviors can change. Remember this when you're looking at the world and judging it; you're seeing the result, the effect, of distorted perception in distorted behavior. Do not try to change others' behaviors. Change your mind so that you inspire them to do the same.

I am that one you know as Jesus, and we will speak to you tomorrow.

LESSON 270

I will not use the body's eyes today.

Follow the complete lesson guidelines in your *ACIM* book.

You are blessed beings, indeed. I am that one you know as Jesus. It sounds like insanity (does it not?) to not use your eyes.

Perception is ruled by your beliefs. If your beliefs have not yet been clarified (which if you are doing these lessons, you are in the early stages of that clarification and your mind is not completely free yet), you are going to misperceive things, because your filters and lenses through which you look at the world are clouded with untruth.

It is the mind behind the vision, the body's vision, that we want you to focus on in this lesson. It means that you decide what you will see. You will decide that you will not attack or judge, even though your lenses of perception ask you to do so. It means that you are using your free will, not your conditioned mind. This is the difference that comes through in this lesson today.

Your free will is to choose to look with loving and forgiving eyes on everything you encounter. The conditioned mind looks through the filters that have been placed in your consciousness by your previous teachers, whoever they are: moviemakers, school teachers, religious instructors, parents; all these beings have taught you things, many of which are unloving and untrue.

You are being asked to rise above the battleground of the conditioned mind into the visionary space of the healed mind. It is an exciting prospect (is it not?) to choose to step above the battleground of the ego into the world of peace, love, and joy. This is what we are encouraging you to do every single day: Take the high road, the high road of love, where you will become the intentional creator of a loving and peaceful world.

I am that one you know as Jesus, and we will speak to you tomorrow.

LESSON 271

Christ's is the vision I will use today.

Follow the complete lesson guidelines
in your *ACIM* book.

You are blessed beings, indeed. I am that one you know as Jesus. Of course, "Jesus" was the man's name, and Christ's vision was that which I held in my life for long enough to transform my consciousness into an awakened being.

It is not "Jesus Christ" who I am. You all are christed beings; you have just forgotten that you are. Your nature is one of love. Your nature is one of kindness. Your nature is one of creativity and extension, and you have merely forgotten. You have layered, through no conscious fault of your own, dirt on the shining mirror of your mind.

However, it is time to decide what you are going to allow in your mind from now on. When you watch or ingest material or information that is fear inducing, murderous, or death focused, you are stepping away from the awakening process. When you practice forgiveness and envision your life as a loving expression of Divine mind, you get closer to that awakening process. It is your free will that decides every moment of every day which direction you walk in.

If you have some habits that you know are less than loving, we ask you to envision yourself not doing them anymore. You might continue the behavior for a while, but understand that you must change the thinking that drives the behavior before you can change the behavior. This is why many of you cannot change your behaviors: because you do not change the mind, which initiates the behavior.

Today, pick something that you know you're doing that is lower in frequency and envision yourself turning it off, not doing it, and doing something else. Do that for a little while, a week or so. Then cut back on the behavior as a reinforcement of that transformation of mind. Keep envisioning new behaviors to replace the unhealthy ones. Envision what you would like your life to look like in its complete form, and understand that is where the work is done in combination with your *A Course in Miracles* forgiveness practice and the lessons here.

You can actively use your creative free will to design the world and the life that you would like to experience.

I am that one you know as Jesus, and we will speak to you tomorrow.

LESSON 272

How can illusions satisfy God's child?

Follow the complete lesson guidelines in your *ACIM* book.

You are blessed beings, indeed. I am that one you know as Jesus. This is the truth of your existence. You have small, shiny objects to chase around your whole life, or you can go to the heart of the matter, which is God's love for you. The fabulous creative force that has wrought you is the one you want to focus on. Why? It's because everything else is a dalliance; everything else is a little affair.

You have met the love of your life, and many of you have given it up for the one-night stand or the little dalliance, the little affair. You should commit to the love of your life. Commit to the most powerful force that exists, and ally yourself with that. You will reap great rewards, not only of physical and material health and wealth but also of knowing yourself — being relaxed in your own skin and being able to offer up to the universe and to your brothers and sisters your greatest gifts rather than wasting your time.

Waste your time no longer, dear ones. Align with love, which is God, and know that you have found the mother lode. You have found what everyone is looking for. Once you align with love, everything else will come to you. Any material things that you want will come to you. This is not about the law of attraction in the sense of manufacturing new cars and these sorts of things. The profoundly meaningful aspects of life that you all seek will come to you when you are aligned with love.

I am that one you know as Jesus, and we will speak to you tomorrow.

The stillness of the peace of God is mine.

Follow the complete lesson guidelines in your *ACIM* book.

You are blessed beings, indeed. I am that one you know as Jesus. You are coming to that stage in your development when you are beginning to see that you have a choice as to whether or not you get upset.

You have a choice whether or not to watch the news and feed into the media story about the world that is designed to upset you. You have a choice whether or not to get into an argument with your partner about some small battle that the ego might wish to win. You see that your children's upsets or their short-temperedness are caused by a lack, perhaps, in their day, so instead of yelling at them and getting upset and going into negativity, you realize that perhaps they need some fresh air. Maybe you have been doing the cooking or have been busy on your phone, and they are feeling a little neglected. So instead of yelling at them for disturbing you, you realize, "Ah. They are disturbing me because they need something that I have not yet contributed to the situation."

As your life goes on while using these lessons, you begin to see that it is your choice whether or not to fight. It is your choice whether or not to become embattled, and it is your choice whether or not to suffer and lose your peace. It is a decision made in the mind. We want you to understand that you have the choice to align yourself with that peace every moment of every day. Now, you are not there yet after only doing *A Course in Miracles* for 270 days or so, but you are beginning to see how you contribute to your troubles.

This is a powerful line in the sand for most of you. Once you cross it, once you realize that you are the cause of your troubles and your stress, then you can always turn to the correct place for shift and change, and that is to go inside and ask: "What am I doing to cause my upset? What do I feel I am missing that I am striving for? What do I think is wrong in the world that is causing me to complain? Maybe I need to stop looking at the world and other people as the source of my upset and go inside and say, 'What is inside me that is upset?'"

All of you will benefit from doing this; all of you will come to realize that once the mind is obsessed with someone else's guilt, you are in the ego's playground. You are stepping away from love and onto the battlefield. There, you will find death, sickness, war, and unhappiness.

Stay off the battlefield. Instead, envision peace, love, and joy, and choose peace whenever you possibly can.

I am that one you know as Jesus, and we will speak to you again tomorrow.

Today belongs to love. Let me not fear.

Follow the complete lesson guidelines
in your *ACIM* book.

You are blessed beings, indeed. I am
that one you know as Jesus. You do
not realize that your resistance to life and
your judgments cause fear.

You are literally arguing with God when you
judge what is going on around you or judge yourself. You are literally saying, "What is should not be," and that creates fear in the mind. There
is a part of the mind that knows you are arguing with God, believe it or
not. There is a part of your mind that knows to confront reality and say
it should not be as it is, is arguing with a great force, and you cannot win
that battle.

You cannot win the battle of judging reality as you understand it to
be. It causes anxiety in the mind, because what is, is. It doesn't matter if
you argue with it; it will not change what is currently manifesting. It is
a futile battle. You are simply wasting your time. You would be far better served to say, "This is something I do not want to keep seeing, so I
am going to look at what I want to see and reinforce that and strengthen
that." This is the same idea as battling with the negative manifestations
that you see currently on your planet. Don't fight them; rather, invest
your love and passion in something that is good for your planet. You will
find that your frequency is higher, you waste less energy, and you feel
more optimistic.

Love what is today. Love yourself today. Watch everything calm down,
and watch your fears disappear.

I am that one you know as Jesus, and we will speak to you again
tomorrow.

God's healing voice protects all things today.

Follow the complete lesson guidelines
in your *ACIM* book.

You are blessed beings, indeed. I am
that one you know as Jesus. Many of
you will say, "I do not hear anything."

Many of you will say, "This voice is not
speaking to me." But you are incorrect. There are
tiny impulses, small ideas, and little impressions coming your way that you
cannot hear because the voice of the ego is too loud. This is why we practice
these lessons. Remember, we practice them so that you can entertain the idea
that there is a different world that you can access if you quiet the mind.

The ego believes that if you quiet the mind, you will not have any control. You will not be able to get people to do what you want; you will not
get what you want. And those who have practiced *A Course in Miracles* for
many years will always tell you — if they have been practicing it correctly
and doing their forgiveness work and surrendering to guidance — that their
lives are many, many times better than they used to be when the ego was
in charge. This is a story that the ego fabricates: that if you listen to it, life
will go well, but truly, when you listen to it, life will go poorly and continue
to worsen as you age. The negatives, the fears, the blocks, the blame, and
the anxiety increase as you age, because you strengthen them all the time.

As you do this miraculous work, you lessen the ego's power. You invest
less and less energy in it over time, and you will see a magnificent transformation of your world. Some of you have not been doing this long enough
to have that demonstration of the massive transformation, but many of
you are having good days when you didn't used to have good days. You are
having longer periods of peace (that are then interrupted when the ego gets
its way and you plummet down a rabbit hole into unconsciousness). But
you know this, and you can see that things are slowly improving. This is
the faith that is building now in all of you. It is the faith that this practice
creates miracles, and the book itself is appropriately labeled: *A Course in
Miracles.*

Continue to create your miracles by choosing love as frequently as you can throughout the day, doing your lessons, and surrendering to that still, small voice within you that guides you toward healthier choices.

I am that one you know as Jesus, and we will speak to you tomorrow.

The word of God is given me to speak.

Follow the complete lesson guidelines in your *ACIM* book.

You are blessed beings, indeed. I am that one you know as Jesus. You are given choices on this Earth plane: You can hate or you can love. You can judge or you can forgive. You can move or you can stay. This is a world of duality.

We are teaching you to rise above that dualistic nature, rise above believing in good and evil, and understand that you are all created in the image of God. You are all equally valuable to that benevolent force that has initiated life in this universe.

It is hard for you when you see people doing what you consider bad things. It is hard for you when you see people whom you consider rude or obnoxious. Understand that those are just errors of thought manifesting in behavior, just as you have made mistakes and errors in judgment throughout your life that you want to be forgiven for. This is the gift you must give so that you can receive it. This is the gift that you must give those beings who are still mistaken and confused, acting out of accord with love, just as you have done in the past — and may still be doing in the present. When you judge others for their imperfect behavior, you will feel judged for your imperfect behavior, and you will feel as if you are going to be punished as well.

Forgiving your brothers and sisters their errors does not mean that you condone their behavior. What you are admitting is that you also have had errors of thought that created dysfunctional behavior, and you recognize this in your brother and sister and are giving them the benefit of your love instead of the criticism of your judgment. Why? It is because judgment reinforces separation and causes you suffering.

When you see the world with forgiving eyes, you stop suffering. When you accept that people are out of order because their minds are out of order, you send them love instead of judgment. You recognize the dysfunction that you have shared (and still share in certain areas of your life). "Judge not, that ye be not judged" [Matthew 7:1, KJV]. This means that when you judge others, you will feel the suffering yourself. So stop judging. Treat others as you would have them treat you, and understand that what you give, you receive.

I am that one you know as Jesus, and we will speak to you tomorrow.

LESSON 277

Let me not bind your child with laws I made.

Follow the complete lesson guidelines
in your *ACIM* book.

You are blessed beings, indeed. I am that one you know as Jesus. Many of your problems come from trying to imprison your families, friends, lovers, partners, and spouses.

You feel you know the rules by which others should behave, and you project them onto them, saying that you know what is best for them. You ignore the fact that they have their own guidance systems, and they may be getting told to do something that is quite counter to what you are being told to do.

When honoring people in your relationships — partners, spouses, children, friends, and family — you must, if you want to remain at peace, give them the freedom to do and be as they choose. They will learn their lessons and have their experiences, and if those lessons and experiences are harsh and cause them suffering, they may learn to do something different. You cannot impose what you know on others.

Now, as parents, this is very, very challenging. It's a very, very challenging lesson for you to believe. But give your children as much freedom as you possibly can to allow them to listen to their guidance, and do not try to impose on them the prison bars within which you reside. Think about this. If you are not perfectly happy and content and are struggling with things that aren't working out for you, then it is clear that you do not have a handle on how to create a perfect life. What makes you think you should be telling people how to create their lives? In fact, you are telling them how to miscreate their lives because you are expecting them to copy you.

Stay in your own lane, and work at your own practice. Make part of that practice giving as much freedom to others as possible, witnessing your desire to control them and stepping back from it, witnessing your desire to criticize and stepping back from it, and witnessing your fear for their future and their safety and refraining from indulging in fearful future fantasies. That is not loving.

I am that one you know as Jesus, and we will speak to you tomorrow.

LESSON 278

If I am bound, my Father is not free.

Follow the complete lesson guidelines in your *ACIM* book.

You are blessed beings, indeed. I am that one you know as Jesus. This is a profound lesson (is it not?), that whoever you make guilty binds the entire world.

This is where the idea comes from that your brothers and sisters on this planet are your salvation. The world's salvation depends on you forgiving them, because as long as they are guilty of sin, the entire world is in the grips of the ego-mind, which is about separation, death, guilt, and sin. It is through forgiveness practice, which is your demonstration, with whomever you decide in your life has committed a sin. They are your salvation; they are the world's salvation. Your practicing forgiveness with them is going to change everything, because they hold the separation belief in place for you. If you believe it, then that becomes true for everything and everyone, including God.

If there is sin, then that becomes the frequency of your entire mind. This is the power of forgiveness. Nobody truly understands the power of forgiveness, that the power of forgiveness expands you to such a tremendous degree that you become godlike in your ability to create loving things, health, abundance, and life itself.

Those unforgivable contaminating judgments about those people are your great homework. They are the assignments you have given yourself to challenge your mind and to raise yourself up out of separation. You have assigned these people the roles of the bad guys in your life so that you can learn to forgive and so that you can overcome your belief in separation. These old hatreds and wounds do not demonstrate their sins but rather your belief in separation, and that is what will be healed when you forgive.

I am that one you know as Jesus, and we will speak to you tomorrow.

LESSON 279

Creation's freedom promises my own.

Follow the complete lesson guidelines in your *ACIM* book.

You are blessed beings, indeed. I am that one you know as Jesus. Have you not noticed that only humans imprison?

They imprison animals. They imprison themselves. Freedom, creativity, and self-expression are natural ways of being on this plane. Even though you are in separation, you want freedom, you want to create, and you want to relax and be yourself.

These restrictions you feel on this plane are self-created. That means they arise because you believe in them. You believe in your weakness, perhaps, or you believe in your lack of freedom. You believe that you must sacrifice or suffer to be holy.

If you are in a place of lack of freedom right now, we want you to immediately go into your mind and ask yourself, "How am I imprisoning myself? What beliefs rush to the surface as soon as I imagine making a break for freedom?" Those ideas and beliefs that rush to the surface when you even think about being free are the ones imprisoning you. They are in your mind, and you can easily discover them by imagining your escape. You will hear the voice of the ego tell you that you can't do it and the reasons why.

This is a very, very good exercise for those of you who feel imprisoned right now. You are not imprisoned, except by your beliefs about your life and your reality as you experience it in the moment. So trust in these lessons to reveal to you how to become free and how to honor that wonderful loving creation that you have been gifted with, which is your life and your connection to the Divine. Know that you are the one in possession of the key.

You do not need to suffer. You do not need to sacrifice. You do not need to imprison yourself in any way, shape, or form. It is merely a mistake of mind, but you are involved in believing that mistake of mind, and it must be you who seeks it out. In the end, it must be you who relinquishes it voluntarily, because if you have an imprisoning belief in your mind, then it is not from spirit; it is not of love. It is of the ego and its limiting beliefs and ideas.

Understand that as you change through time, some of the things you believe now will seem absurd to you in a few years. You will look at your life and mind and body, which are healed by these teachings, and you will come to understand that the prison, indeed, was of your creation.

I am that one you know as Jesus, and we will speak to you tomorrow.

LESSON 280

What limits can I lay on God's child?

Follow the complete lesson guidelines
in your *ACIM* book.

You are blessed beings, indeed. I am that one you know as Jesus. The self-righteous judgments you lay on others you do not see as imprisoning you, but they do. They keep you away from the truth of what you are because they keep the illusion of your brother's fallibility and failings in your mind. You must see yourself with the same value system that you put on others.

When you judge others for being lazy, you will judge yourself for being lazy. When you judge others for being ugly, you will judge yourself as being ugly. You will magnify what's in your mind by laying it on your brothers and sisters. This is how the ego relieves itself of pain: in the form of projection. It takes what is in your mind and puts it on somebody else. But it really does not remove it; it merely displaces it a little bit; in fact, it magnifies it because you are putting your energy into believing that the other is guilty.

You cannot remove from your mind the guilt that you feel, the self-loathing that you feel, or the judgment that you feel by projecting it on to others. In fact, by doing so, you keep it alive. So understand that in forgiveness practice, as you stop doing these things, you bring relief to your mind and bring it back into balance with truth.

I am that one you know as Jesus, and we will speak to you tomorrow.

LESSON 281

I can be hurt by nothing but my thoughts.

Follow the complete lesson guidelines in your *ACIM* book.

You are blessed beings, indeed. I am that one you know as Jesus. This does not seem to be true. You feel as if you are hurt by so many things: a negative look that someone throws your way, somebody disappointing you, someone stealing from you. All these things seem to hurt you, and they seem to be outside you. But you are a resilient being, and if you look at yourself now, you will see that you are perfectly fine.

The ego always uses the argument: "Well, somebody could shoot me and that would mean I am hurt by something other than myself." But understand that what we are speaking about is emotional and mental pain. We are speaking about the daily traumas you inflict on yourself, not the exceptional physical disasters that can happen to your body. (The body can be hurt or destroyed, but it is not who you are, so in that sense, this lesson is still true.)

We are speaking about all the little ups and downs you go through each day, the downs in particular. The downs are you telling a story: "Well, they let me down. Those people did something that they shouldn't have done."

These stories cause you suffering. These stories, thoughts, and ideas will reveal themselves to you each day, and your guidance system will reveal their untruths by giving you negative emotional feedback.

Remember, when you are feeling bad, suffering, depleted, drained, put upon, and unfairly treated, all these negativities you perceive as nothing to do with you actually are being manufactured by the thoughts you believe about that situation. You do not have to believe all the thoughts you have. You may have a thought such as this: "Those people don't like me." You really do not know the truth of the situation. They may have said some things that seemed unloving; they may behave in ways that you do not understand, but if you believe that thought, then you will suffer.

But if you observe that thought and say, "Well that's an interesting thought. I think I need to question it. I think I need to inquire whether that thought is true." Initially, the ego will yell, "Yes, it is true!" But if you continue to inquire, you can delve deeper and realize that you are the one who does not like them, that you are in fact accusing others of what you are doing, which is projection. Surely, if you are feeling bad, you are in the ego, and the ego projects.

That is a question we would like you to ask yourself. The next time you accuse someone of something, inquire beneath the surface of that thought form, and ask, "Is it, in fact, me doing this?"

I am that one you know as Jesus, and we will speak to you tomorrow.

LESSON 282

I will not be afraid of love today.

Follow the complete lesson guidelines in your *ACIM* book.

You are blessed beings, indeed. I am that one you know as Jesus. Most of you would deny that you are afraid of love. But you are attached to judgment. You are attached to fear. You are attached to self-loathing.

You are attached to many unloving things, and the ego's favorite game is to keep you away from love with these distractions. That is what the ego is up to. It projects your judgment onto other beings so that the love that you are is hidden from you. You do not realize you are made of love, by love, for love, and whenever you are unloving, you feel bad. It does not matter whether you are being unloving to yourself, someone else, a group, places, or things. Whatever you are being unloving toward, you are in fact disconnecting yourself from the experience of love — every single time.

When you are going through your day feeling disappointed, unloved, chagrined, and hard done by, complaining about things, then you are choosing those states of being. And because you are so powerful, you literally are putting up an umbrella between you and the love that is cascading down toward you from that which you call God.

We want you to understand that love is peace. Love is contentment. Love is creativity. Love is interest. Love is curiosity. Love is fascination. Love is passion. Love is many things. Love is enjoying your life as well. If you are not enjoying your life, then you are choosing to separate yourself from the awareness of love's presence, and that is what these lessons teach you. It is your choice. You have a choice in every moment to forgive and to choose love no matter what you see.

I am that one you know as Jesus, and we will speak to you again tomorrow.

LESSON 283

My true identity abides in you.

Follow the complete lesson guidelines in your *ACIM* book.

You are blessed beings, indeed. I am that one you know as Jesus. The more you identify with the body, the worse you will feel.

Now, this does not mean you should hate the body; in fact, the opposite is true. When you worship the body, you will feel worse. This is one of those strange paradoxes you experience on the Earth plane, because when you worship or idolize your body or someone else's, you are functioning in the lowest frequencies available to you: those slow, solid, heavy, materialistic frequencies on the lower rungs of the three-dimensional ladder.

In these lessons, we are working toward getting you up to the top rungs of the three-dimensional ladder. Yes, you are still in a body. Yes, you are still experiencing yourself in separation. But we are working to get you to those higher frequencies even though you are still in an illusory state, which is that of separation.

Now, your job as *A Course in Miracles* student is to focus your mind on these higher-frequency beliefs and ideas and to relinquish your lower-frequency beliefs and ideas. This will take you up that ladder, keeping you in your family, keeping you in your body, and keeping you in this seemingly separated state but without the suffering. Once the suffering dissipates and you realize that it was your focus causing your suffering, you will be able to master yourself and the world more eloquently, more diligently, and more predictably. By training your mind, you have removed the suffering from your mind, so that means it is optional. It means that it is up to you whether you suffer or not.

These higher-frequency teachings are the truth. They are the truth of your true nature: You are made in the image of God, and you are powerful creators. But you must be free, and you must be in alignment with love to be able to live your life without pain.

We witness your diligent practice. We thank you all for sticking with us, and we congratulate you for your persistence, those of you who are reaching these higher numbered lessons. By now, you are seeing beneficial behaviors emerging. You are seeing people change around you — a miracle, indeed. And you are feeling less pain and suffering and an increase of joy and love. This is the evidence that this course works, and when others ask you why you are doing this strange training, you can tell them: "I do it because it works, it makes me feel better, and as I feel better, I have more to offer all beings."

I am that one you know as Jesus, and we will speak to you again tomorrow.

I can elect to change all thoughts that hurt.

Follow the complete lesson guidelines
in your *ACIM* book.

You are blessed beings, indeed. I am
that one you know as Jesus. Of course,
many of these lessons do not ring true
when you first read them. They seem as if
they are cruel, even. To say that grief is not true
seems to belie everything you have come to understand about love on your
planet (that when you lose somebody in physical form, you will feel grief,
and that is a good thing and a healthy thing).

If you are in full control of your reality, your thoughts, and your feelings, you will be far from thoughtless, unkind, and unfeeling. In fact, you
will be far more compassionate and loving toward your brothers and sisters,
and things such as deep grief will not torment you.

Often, we witness on your plane that the untrained mind will turn on
itself when somebody close to you moves from the physical into the nonphysical form. This is a natural part of your evolutionary cycle. It is a joyous
time for the spirit, because it leaves behind the ego's playground and seems
to be freer and more able to do whatever it wishes. In fact, from the depart-
ing spirit's point of view, there is only the opening and the closing of a door,
and then there is freedom.

From your point of view in the ego's playground, there is a loss, but that
is only because the mind holds such a low frequency. It focuses on physical/
material bodies as who those beings are rather than their consciousnesses,
minds, and ever-unchanging aspects. These follow a person from birth to
death, were there before they were born, and still exist after their bodies fall
away. You do not die. In fact, your consciousness merely blinks and carries
on.

When you change your perspective about the body and death, you will
not grieve. You will be excited for your loved ones to go on to the next part
of their journeys. And in giving them that freedom, you also will be fearless
with your passing, because you will be excited to understand another level
of consciousness that you cannot easily access in this particular form.

You can see that changing your mind can relieve you of some of the greatest burdens of physical existence. Keep on this path, understanding that you will not always understand these lessons. You may not even believe them the first time you read them. But as you continue with your practice, you will climb up that ladder toward enlightenment more and more and more, and eventually, you will be above the battleground, where all the pain is.

I am that one you know as Jesus, and we will speak to you tomorrow.

LESSON 285

My holiness shines bright and clear today.

Follow the complete lesson guidelines in your *ACIM* book.

You are blessed beings, indeed. I am that one you know as Jesus. This idea of your holiness representing your connection to the Divine will bring you peace throughout the day.

Whenever you are enmeshed in the world's temptations — money, food, sex, death, or sickness — remind yourself of your holiness and your eternal spiritual nature. Your suffering and depression are indicators that you are off track and are again identifying with the lower materialistic frequencies of the body, sickness, money, or sex.

Understand that when we say "sex," we mean the use of the body for physical gratification. We are not speaking of the higher-minded ideal of minds connecting and bodies following along after the heart and mind have been unified. That is a more sacred form of that particular act. Just as you can have unhealthy food and healthy food, unhealthy entertainment and high-frequency entertainment, or painful and hateful words and loving and kind words, each topic of your day potentially has a lower-frequency aspect and a higher-frequency aspect.

Your holiness, your belief in your holiness, and your acceptance that you are a holy child of God will encourage you to choose the higher-frequency version and walk away from the low-frequency version. You'll say: "This is not good enough for me. I deserve better, because I am a holy child of God." Knowing that, you will not feel deprived, you will not feel alone, and you will not feel put upon; you will know that you are choosing the higher frequencies. However, you may have to be a little more patient to get those experiences of high frequency you seek.

Remember, there's a lot of momentum built up in your life when you have been indulging in low-frequency activities, and it takes a little while for your behavior and the consequences of your behavior to catch up to the transforming mind, but know that it will. Understand that your transforming mind will indeed transform your life, body, and everything you experience here.

I am that one you know as Jesus, and we will speak to you again tomorrow.

LESSON 286

The hush of heaven holds my heart today.

Follow the complete lesson guidelines in your *ACIM* book.

You are blessed beings, indeed. I am that one you know as Jesus. The idea of peace to the ego is anathema. It does not want it.

You must remember this when your ego is still strong. The idea of a completely peaceful day with no drama, no upsets, no arguments, no judgments, no fears, and no antagonism is the idea of hell to the ego. Some of you reading this lesson might find it frightening, because you would not even know how to handle peace of such depth. But understand what's happening here: You are creating room for the Divine.

You must let go of all the battles, fears, and ups and downs so that you can make conscious contact with your teachers and guides, and then things will get very interesting. You will receive information directly from higher frequencies, and those messages will trigger another round of growth in you. So when we talk about these times of peace, enjoy them. When it's peaceful, enjoy it, because it will not last. Your transformation through this education program will lead you to anything but a boring life. Yes, your mind will be at peace. Yes, the dramas and the upsets will disappear. But you will be tuned in to knowledge, and that will inspire you.

I am that one you know as Jesus, and we will speak to you tomorrow.

You are my goal, my Father — only you.

Follow the complete lesson guidelines in your *ACIM* book.

You are blessed beings, indeed. I am that one you know as Jesus. You must remember that your goal has been everything but God up to this point. It has been to find the perfect body or to have the perfect body. It has been to make money. It has been to avoid conflict. It has been to create havoc. It has been so many things, and each of those things you have pursued you believed would make you happy. That is why you pursued them.

There is some distortion in the mind that makes you believe that the idol you are will change everything for you and make you happy. And what happens as you travel along this weary-making road of planet Earth: You figure out that most of the things you've chased don't make you happy. This is a great thing for spirit. All of us on this side of the veil cheer when you become clear that what you are chasing does not make you happy.

This makes you teachable. This makes you willing to try something new, and that is what you are all doing here. You are going against the world's teachings and listening to heaven's teachings. The world's teachings will keep you on the battleground, and heaven's teachings will take you above the battleground and, eventually, all the way to peace and the truth.

You have been on a long journey. Now you are in the recovery stage. You've taken yourselves deep into fear, deep into the twisted and convoluted lies of the ego's world. But you are surfacing. You are beginning to see that everything you have been told is not true. If it were true, then you would be happy. That pair of boots would have made you happy. Having sex with that person would have made you happy. Getting that job would have made you happy. And you all have been on Earth long enough to know that those things did not make you happy, and there is still some deep part of you that is calling out for something, and that deep part of you is the truth of who you are. It is calling out for love.

So you can't find the kind of love that satisfies spirit in the physical/material world. This does not mean you hate your life here. It does not mean you don't enjoy yourself while you are in physical form. It means you know the truth of what you are, and you know where your Home truly is: in the arms of God — not in death but in eternal life.

I am that one you know as Jesus, and we will speak to you tomorrow.

LESSON 288

Let me forget my fellow human's past today.

Follow the complete lesson guidelines in your *ACIM* book.

You are blessed beings, indeed. I am that one you know as Jesus. This is the last thing any of your egos wants to hear — that your salvation lies in forgiving your brothers and sisters of their pasts — because you are holding on to a vision of separation and distinction between you and them.

When you hold a grievance, it's as if you are saying, "You are worse than I am. You have done something unforgivable. In God's eyes, you must be less loved than I am." None of those things is true, of course, but you believe them when you hold resentment, and it is impossible for you to move ahead in your spiritual evolution as long as you hold these beliefs about any one person.

It does not matter whether it is a person you know or someone you view in history. If you hold anybody guilty of unforgivable sin, then you have prevented yourself from reaching salvation, which is the true and complete understanding that you are all one. That is what salvation is, and that is what precipitates enlightenment. It is in this understanding that your freedom will be given to you.

I am that one you know as Jesus, and we will speak to you tomorrow.

The past is over.
It can touch me not.

Follow the complete lesson guidelines
in your *ACIM* book.

You are blessed beings, indeed. I am that one you know as Jesus. Today we want you to think about how often you talk about the past, because you're wasting your time.

You are talking about something that does not exist anymore, and you are contaminating the present moment with that past, even if that past memory is a good memory. This may upset some of you. Do not spend a lot of time thinking about the good old days and how good things used to be. You are then assuming, by that memory, that today is not as good and that to find a feeling of joy, you must go back to an imagined time that allows you to feel better.

Now, that might be better than going into an imagined past that makes you feel worse, but it is better for you to be present, and in that presence, you should acknowledge that this is the best day you have ever had. Why? It's because you are in presence. You are becoming aware. You are becoming conscious.

Memory must be managed as your current thinking is managed. If you are in conversations with people and find yourself telling old stories all the time, be aware of that, and realize that you are not using the present moment for what it can be used for, which is communion — sharing your current feelings, sharing your current excitements, and sharing your current visions for a more happy and loving future. That is what you should be doing with your present moment: getting every experience you can out of the eternal now. That is how you grow; that is how you expand.

If you always go to the past to retrieve memories, you will stay the same, and that will guarantee that your future will look like the past, because that is what you are referring to as your preferred state of consciousness.

I am that one you know as Jesus, and we will speak to you again tomorrow.

My present happiness is all I see.

Follow the complete lesson guidelines in your *ACIM* book.

You are blessed beings, indeed. I am that one you know as Jesus. When you look around you, you will see that most people are not looking at their present happiness. They are looking at what is wrong with the world and making themselves miserable, thinking that the world is making them miserable, but it is their choice to see the sins of the world and believe in them.

See the good. See the cheerful. See the beautiful. See the kind. See the uplifting, and you will feel happy. Then you will be adding a higher frequency to the world's frequency, which, after all, is a collection of all your minds — all your beliefs and thoughts. You will be contributing more to the world and its healing than those beings who view its sins and the terrors of the ego's playground, wringing their hands and tearing at their hair, saying, "What a terrible world this is."

You have a choice. Are you going to choose love, happiness, and upliftment? Or are you going to believe the ego's lies and dive into the cesspool of pain and swim around in it with all the other beings who are unaware? The ego convinces you that lamenting how things are is the way to alleviate your suffering. It is not.

What you put your energy toward will grow stronger and stronger. When you see the suffering and devastation of this world and let that bring you down, you are contributing to it. You are contributing.

Contribute light. Contribute happiness. Contribute joy, and be the change that you want to see in the world.

I am that one you know as Jesus, and we will speak to you again tomorrow.

This is a day of stillness and of peace.

Follow the complete lesson guidelines in your *ACIM* book.

You are blessed beings, indeed. I am that one you know as Jesus. We want you to relish those days of stillness and peace, and we want you to watch the mind try to fabricate something to do.

There will be many opportunities for you in this training program to be at peace all day long — without entertainments, without errands to run, and without projects to occupy your mind and your time. We ask you to become more and more used to this stillness, understanding that to be at peace and in stillness is a wonderful gift. There is nothing lacking there.

An opening happens in the consciousness when the mind can be completely at peace. Now, it does not happen in the first minutes; it does not happen in the first day. It does not happen in the first few days, but the more days that you can string together in this inordinate peace, the clearer your mind will become and the more reduced the static will be between higher-frequency communications and you.

That is what this being [the channel] did. She practiced being still. She practiced focusing her mind. She practiced her forgiveness work diligently and at times relentlessly, insisting that her mind return to a peaceful state without agitation and resentment, and it was that determinedness that brought about the transformation of her body-mind in such a way that she was able to connect with higher guidance.

This is not going to happen to all of you in this form, fear not. You are not all going to be required to do this kind of work. This kind of work was designed specifically for beings such as this one. You will have guidance; you will have strong guidance. However, you must first become used to stillness and not see it as a lack of anything.

I am that one you know as Jesus, and we will speak to you again tomorrow.

A happy outcome to all things is sure.

Follow the complete lesson guidelines in your *ACIM* book.

You are blessed beings, indeed. I am that one you know as Jesus. This is not the ego's story, is it? The ego tells you to be careful, to watch for danger, not to trust anybody, to be very careful, and to save for a rainy day. Its prescriptions are always about bad things coming in the future.

Understand that you are a powerful creator, and if you continue to think along those lines, you will manufacture the disasters you are focused on. If you always think about avoiding sickness, you will get sick; you will feel the power of your own miscreations manifesting in your body. However, if you live a passionate life and focus on your health, then you will see health manifested in your body. It is just that simple.

We challenge all of you who have sicknesses to observe how often you either talk about them, project about how terrible they might become in the future, or ruminate on them internally — rather than envisioning a healthy, strong, and happy body. Your body is not everything. But we understand that when you fall into lower frequencies, the miscreations in the physical can become quite painful. What you will experience as you go through these lessons and continue practicing them afterward is the strength, joy, and happiness that these lessons speak about.

Remember, this is a training period. This is a clarification period. It is not the be all and end all of your efforts. You must continue your work every day.

I am that one you know as Jesus, and we will speak to you again tomorrow.

All fear is past, and only love is here.

Follow the complete lesson guidelines in your *ACIM* book.

You are blessed beings, indeed. I am that one you know as Jesus. This is a difficult concept to grasp — that peace, love, and joy are here.

Your fearful ideas merely hide that truth from you, and this is the illusory world you hear everybody speaking about. This fearful, death-ridden, unloving, and unforgiving world you all live in is a product of your own minds, a product of your imaginations. However, if you train your minds, calm your minds, and master your minds, once all the trials, tribulations, and stories the ego tells you have been put to sleep, then peace, joy, and love remain. That is what's underneath all the drama, toil, and trouble that the ego-mind produces in your mind.

Your mind produces your suffering. When you learn to stop producing suffering, you will discover that you are happy and that peace is with you always. It always has been; it was merely hidden — just as the still, deep waters of the ocean are hidden beneath the stormy waters above. It's the same as the sun hidden by storm clouds. Remember, your physical world is always reflecting back to you the state of your consciousness, and these two great demonstrations of the state of your consciousness are there to show you, to symbolize, what is going on within you.

Become as the clear, blue, sunlit sky above the storm clouds, and become as the deep, quiet, calm ocean beneath the waves. You will align with your true nature, which is there now just waiting for you to find it.

I am that one you know as Jesus, and we will speak to you again tomorrow.

My body is a wholly neutral thing.

Follow the complete lesson guidelines in your *ACIM* book.

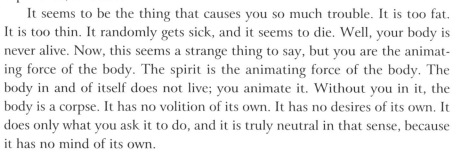

You are blessed beings, indeed. I am that one you know as Jesus. This body in which you find yourself is one of the great liabilities of this three-dimensional experience, is it not?

It seems to be the thing that causes you so much trouble. It is too fat. It is too thin. It randomly gets sick, and it seems to die. Well, your body is never alive. Now, this seems a strange thing to say, but you are the animating force of the body. The spirit is the animating force of the body. The body in and of itself does not live; you animate it. Without you in it, the body is a corpse. It has no volition of its own. It has no desires of its own. It does only what you ask it to do, and it is truly neutral in that sense, because it has no mind of its own.

You have many stories in your society about instincts, habits, and addictions — as if the body rules the mind. It is not true; the mind rules the body. Spirit rules the body. And it is important for you not to blame the body for anything. Some of your deepest, darkest feelings are of loathing the body, hating the body, and mistrusting the body. The body only does what you ask it to do. It eats the food you ask it to eat. It travels where you ask it to travel; it is innocent in that sense.

Stop attacking your body. Stop judging your body, and address the part of you that is the decision maker. That is where the healing needs to take place: in the mind that is making the unhealthy decisions.

I am that one you know as Jesus, and we will speak to you again tomorrow.

The Holy Spirit looks through me today.

Follow the complete lesson guidelines
in your *ACIM* book.

You are blessed beings, indeed. I am
that one you know as Jesus. Just as you
can choose to look with the ego's eyes
(judgmental, fearful, lacking, and afraid of
many things), you can choose to surrender your
sight to the Holy Spirit, which means you use the intermediary vision that
has been given to you through Christ consciousness so that you can see a
forgiven world. This is what the Holy Spirit's sight will show you: a forgiven
world. It will demonstrate that you can go through your day without judgment, without fear, without recriminations, and without battling. And this
brings you tremendous peace.

What you will find surprising along the way is that the world does
not come to an end when you stop the ego from controlling everything.
The ego will tell you that to surrender to a vision that is not your own
will allow you to lose control, and then you will lose. The opposite is true.
When you surrender to the Holy Spirit's vision and walk through your
day without judgment, fear, or hatred and viewing the world with forgiving eyes, you will realize that your ego is not your friend. It is something
that you need to employ to get through some survival aspects of your
experience, but it is a fatal error to allow the ego to rule your world and to
make all your decisions.

Instead, surrender to the Holy Spirit and allow a vision higher than the
limited and fearful one of the ego to make your decisions, and relax into
surrendered life: a life that is peaceful, loving, and accepting. These are all
very, very different conditions than that which the ego offers you.

Try it today, and see how it goes.

I am that one you know as Jesus, and we will speak to you again
tomorrow.

The Holy Spirit speaks through me today.

Follow the complete lesson guidelines
in your *ACIM* book.

You are blessed beings, indeed. I am that one you know as Jesus. You can feel your split mind as you go through your day. You can hear the hateful voice that criticizes and judges, and you have the ability to allow love to guide your thoughts and words. You have a choice every single moment of every single day.

What this lesson prompts you to do is to actively choose love, to actively demonstrate these lessons in your thoughts, words, and deeds. Now, this does not mean standing on a soapbox and proselytizing as an evangelist. It means demonstrating these teachings through your actions and your words, and of course, your actions and your words come from your thoughts, so those are included as well.

When you demonstrate these teachings, your world becomes full of miracles. Where you were fearful, you become courageous. Where you were angry, you become peaceful. And dedicating a day to this, such as this lesson promotes, will show you just how powerful your mind and your decisions are. Follow these prescriptions today, and feel the love of God flowing through you and awakening all those around you with its wonderful, gentle, and loving light.

I am that one you know as Jesus, and we will speak to you again tomorrow.

Forgiveness is the only gift I give.

Follow the complete lesson guidelines
in your *ACIM* book.

You are blessed beings, indeed. I am that one you know as Jesus. You have been told that you have to work hard to get what you want in the world: You have to struggle. You have to strive. You have to fight. There are so many things you have been taught in this world to get you what you want (or to get what the ego wants), but truly, forgiveness will bring you peace, and peace will bring you connection to guidance, which will take you on a journey that is more magnificent than you can imagine.

Your guidance, once it comes in clear and true (because your mind has become peaceful), will show you the way. And as you share your light throughout your journey, more and more will be given to you — not as payment but because you have come to understand how creation works. You have come to understand that you are the projector; therefore, anyone you encounter is a part of your mind. So to attack others or to take from others is foolish, because you are, essentially, attacking and taking from yourself.

In practicing forgiveness throughout your life, you are demonstrating your understanding of the laws of creation, which is that you literally are connected to everyone because they are characters in your dream. Your dream can be a nightmare when you attack yourself through attacking others, or your dream can become happy by treating everybody you meet as you would like to be treated.

I am that one you know as Jesus, and we will speak to you again tomorrow.

I love you, Father, and I love your child.

Follow the complete lesson guidelines in your *ACIM* book.

You are blessed beings, indeed. I am that one you know as Jesus. By loving yourself as a holy child of God and by loving your brothers and sisters on this Earth plane as holy children of God, you will bring such peace and joy to your life that you will be astonished.

It is in your petty judgments of yourselves and of others that causes the profound suffering many of you experience. You think it is because they are wrong. You think it is because they are bad. You think it is because you are too old, too poor, or some such judgment you have levied on yourself. The truth of your pain is the judgment. You are in pain because you are judging. You are separating yourself from yourself and from your brothers and sisters, and in that judgment of separation, you step away from love and feel the pain of that distance from love. As you forgive, forget, and appreciate, you step closer to love, because you are, in fact, loving things when you appreciate them and when you have gratitude for them. And by stepping closer to love, you feel better.

This is the one road you are all on — the road to hell or heaven. Choose the road to heaven by practicing loving kindness and forgiving all you see with your earthly eyes.

The problems that you address on your Earth plane at this time are the result of misdirected minds. The tangible events you witness are the result of a multitude of thoughts, beliefs, and ideas acted out. So there's nothing you can do about the event that is happening now. But you can appreciate that it is not what you would like more of, and you can focus your mind on the opposite of that which you do not want. Ask yourself: "What can I think, do, be, or express that will assist my vision into manifestation?"

Stop focusing on what you don't want and judging it, increasing your pain and suffering. Instead, focus on the opposite — what you would love to have, what you would love to see. Then ask yourself: "How can I bring that into being?"

I am that one you know as Jesus, and we will speak to you tomorrow.

Eternal holiness abides in me.

Follow the complete lesson guidelines in your *ACIM* book.

You are blessed beings, indeed. I am that one you know as Jesus. It is important for you to understand that this is absolutely true: You are holy beings.

You have merely hidden this from yourself by choosing to chase earthly idols, materialistic goals, and dreams that others have implanted in your minds through programming. You have all been deeply programmed in this society, and you are all chasing after things that those programs have told you will make you happy. Nobody has ever told you that your holiness is what truly makes you happy. And your connection with that deep internal sanctity will bring you what you seek when you buy things and rush hither and yon to try to fulfill the ego's demands.

As you evolve through this journey, your life will become quieter. It will become calmer. It will become healthier. It will become more abundant, full of nourishing things, good relationships, healthier foods, and healthier entertainments. But you may also feel as if you are losing the world. In fact, you are not losing the world as you see it now; you are gaining heaven. You are beginning to transform your perception so that the loving, kind, and generous world comes into being for you. You literally re-create a new world with the transformation of your perceptions.

So be patient with yourselves. We cannot remove everything from your life that is untrue; you would fall to your knees in terror. Day by day, you must choose love and let the little things go. As you let things go, you will create room for the Divine, and the Divine will fill that space you create. But you must do it willingly and openly, and you must do it with enthusiasm, because your free will is the deciding factor. If you have any hesitance or fear, we will wait for you until you are courageous enough to do it wholeheartedly.

I am that one you know as Jesus, and we will speak to you again tomorrow.

Only an instant does this world endure.

Follow the complete lesson guidelines in your *ACIM* book.

You are blessed beings, indeed. I am that one you know as Jesus. Of course, that is not how you look at this place. You think of it as a permanent place, despite the many changes constantly happening in your life and in your world.

Much of your suffering comes from wanting things to be permanent and wanting things to stay the same. One of the great gifts you can give yourself, along with doing this lesson and beginning to focus on the eternal, is letting go of the permanent and the idea that things should remain the same. You would be much better off being in deep appreciation of whatever is happening today, because it will change.

Those of you who have been on the planet a little while understand this. You look back to previous marriages, when your children were small, or when you were in university, and think, "My goodness, how different that time was. If only I had known how precious it was, then I would have valued it more." This is a saying you have on your planet: "Youth … is wasted on children" [George Bernard Shaw], because you truly do not appreciate what you have when you are young. You are full of the dreams of all the things you are going to achieve and how you are going to be happy when you do, but as many of you find out, as you go through this challenging excursion through your 3D reality, many of your dreams don't come true. But that's not because you do not deserve them or you are being punished. It's because the dreams are ego dreams.

There are things you wanted that you did receive — a new car, a new house, or a new lover — and you found out that they didn't make you happy, at least not long term. But the penny never really dropped for many of you — that these worldly assets are not what make you happy. Yes, driving a new car will keep you entertained and stimulated for a few weeks perhaps, but then the dissatisfaction will come in again, and you will begin looking for the next thing and the next thing and the next thing to fulfill you.

One way of connecting to eternity is through the eternal now, through the practice of appreciation and gratitude, knowing that whatever you have now — money, health, love, sickness, debt — doesn't matter, whether it's good or bad. This too shall pass. And in the appreciation of those things, you will say for the lack: "Thank goodness this is not going to last. I will come out the other side of this." If you have the idea of not resisting it but looking at it and going, "Okay, well, I have a lack of funds right now, but what do I have in abundance? Is there a way of getting into a state of appreciation for what I am experiencing right now?"

Perhaps you are experiencing a lack of money because the experience it brings you is what you needed. Perhaps you have overly valued money. Perhaps you have not developed other aspects of your abundance practice, and not having money for a little while can aid you in that. Alternatively, if you have a lot, the ego's methodology would be to fear losing what you have. So if you have a lot, appreciate it fully. Revel in it, roll around in it, and squeeze all the juice you can out of what you have right now, because this too shall pass, and change will come.

This is an adjunct to your current practice — this idea of fully living in the now regardless of whether you consider it good or bad — because each experience is going to expand the expression of yourself. And once you see the good in the bad and the changeability in the good, then you will be living fully in the now, and it is there that eternity lies.

That is what this lesson is referring to. This world does not last very long, and those of you who have been on this planet for a few decades know how quickly it can go in human terms. But we are literally speaking here: If you change your mind, if you shift your frequency, the world you know will change instantaneously, and you will begin living in a new place, a more heavenly aligned place.

I am that one you know as Jesus, and we will speak to you again tomorrow.

LESSON 301

And God himself shall wipe away all tears.

Follow the complete lesson guidelines in your *ACIM* book.

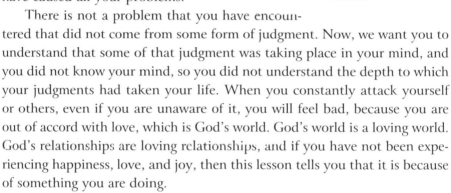

You are blessed beings, indeed. I am that one you know as Jesus. All the judgments you have laid on the world have caused all your problems.

There is not a problem that you have encountered that did not come from some form of judgment. Now, we want you to understand that some of that judgment was taking place in your mind, and you did not know your mind, so you did not understand the depth to which your judgments had taken your life. When you constantly attack yourself or others, even if you are unaware of it, you will feel bad, because you are out of accord with love, which is God's world. God's world is a loving world. God's relationships are loving relationships, and if you have not been experiencing happiness, love, and joy, then this lesson tells you that it is because of something you are doing.

Free will is one of the great rules of your Earth plane. You are free to choose whatever thoughts you want, and you are free to believe whatever thoughts you want. So if you have the thought, "I am unworthy," and you believe it, then you will experience people who treat you that way and situations that prove those thoughts. This is a very, very important point: you unconsciously inflict pain and guilt on yourself.

We are attempting through these beautiful lessons to raise your mind out of unconsciousness into consciousness, where you become aware of what you are doing to yourself. This is the first great realization of *A Course in Miracles* students. As they perform these lessons, they see the contrast between their unloving thoughts and judgmental ideas to the loving prayers and lessons that are presented.

You realize that you do not see yourself as one of God's children. You recognize that you are not treating yourself as a sacred being. You see that you are overly focused on the body as the definition of who and what you are. This learning is imperative for all of you. You are not your body, and you are not a victim of the world you see; you are the creator of it, the

374

attractor of it. No, you are not always aware of what you're doing, but that is because you have an untrained mind and have had an untrained mind for many years.

Now you are beginning to see, "Oh, when I tell a negative story about myself, I will feel bad." Unfortunately, the ego's interpretation of that bad feeling is that you are unworthy. This is something we really want to tell you today: If you are having an unloving thought about yourself or someone else and you begin to feel bad, then that's your guidance system telling you you're wrong. It's saying, "No. Don't go there." It's an aversion therapy, if you will. The better you feel, the more accurately you are aligning with God's will for you, and the worse you feel, the more you are out of accord with God's will for you.

God's will for you is your will for you. That means when you are happy, you are in alignment with God's will for you. That means you want the same things for you that God wants for you — things that are good-feeling, exciting, creative, happy, and loving. God is not a punishing entity; the ego is a punishing idol.

I am that one you know as Jesus, and we will speak to you tomorrow.

LESSON 302

Where darkness was, I look upon the light.

Follow the complete lesson guidelines in your *ACIM* book.

You are blessed beings, indeed. I am that one you know as Jesus. The hardest part about the forgiveness process is the realization that you want to judge, you want to hate, and you want to separate.

This is one of the biggest realizations you will come to in this process, because as you decide to forgive a particular action, person, place, thing, or experience, you will realize that there is a part of you that does not want to forgive. There is a part of you that wants to hold on to hatred. And that part chose to come into separation to experience not-love.

It's hard to imagine, we know. It's hard to believe that any consciousness would choose to do this, and this is counter to many beliefs and belief systems you have in your world — that God created you to come into this place. No. God created you, but you chose to come into this lower-frequency experience to chase the idols and experience the things that you wanted to experience in physical form.

Now, being in separation in and of itself does not have to be a disaster. What you have to learn is not to hate, not to judge, and not to separate yourself further from love. Being in a body — being human while having this separation experience — is bad enough even when you are having a good time. You are still challenged by many, many things, including your bodies, aging, and all aspects of the physical experience that you have to go through if you choose to come into separation. Even the birthing process is very, very challenging.

Make sure you are seeing this world truthfully, which is as a form of separation from love. That means there is a part of you that wanted this. There is a part of you now that has had enough of this and is less enamored, because you've had a few decades on the planet, and that is the part that is seeking peace and to return Home. It is nothing to be sad about. It is nothing to rush; it is nothing to fear. Your Home in God awaits you no matter what you decide to do in this incarnation. But the further you stray into separation, the more suffering and pain you will have. It's just that simple.

Make reducing the separation through the act of forgiveness your prime directive, and all other things will come to you.

I am that one you know as Jesus, and we will speak to you again tomorrow.

LESSON 303

The Holy Christ is born in me today.

Follow the complete lesson guidelines in your *ACIM* book.

You are blessed beings, indeed. I am that one you know as Jesus. In your world, you say, "Jesus Christ." Well, Jesus was the man, and Jesus Christ was the christed being you are studying to become. So this one [the channel] will be Tina Christ, and others may be John Christ or Susan Christ. You are going to become christed beings through this ascension process and through your dedication to your spiritual practice.

It is your dedication to your spiritual practice, the constant asking for and seeking a connection with the Divine, the observation of this world (understanding what it truly is), your dedication to love, and your dedication to communion with the Divine that will cause you to become a christed being. It is possible for all of you. That is what I meant when I said, "Whoever believes in me will also do the works that I do; and greater works than these" [John 14:12, ESV]. You can do those things. You can heal. You can overcome death. It seems extreme, given the materialistic and secular world in which you have been raised, but it is the truth.

Those beings who seek the Divine eventually overcome the constraints of the physics you think control your bodies and your world. You become able to do things that are seemingly impossible, and you call them miracles.

Miracles are but a leap of faith. That is what all of you are doing here with these lessons. You are trusting in this process even though you did not have evidence other than the stories of some beings who have done *A Course in Miracles*. You did not have proof for your eyes, but you took a leap of faith and began to practice. That is all becoming christed requires of you: intensifying your practice, dedicating your time to the Divine, and understanding that forgiveness is the means that you have been given to achieve that level of evolution. It is in demonstrating your understanding of this law of creation that you are experiencing yourself here.

There are no separate beings; there is only an aspect of your mind that has seemingly separated from you, but in your forgiveness practice, you are reintegrating your mind into a holy one and a whole one. So know that you are going to become christed beings one way or the other. You should ask yourselves: On whose time frame do I do this? Am I going to allow the ego to detain me and become distracted by the shiny objects of this world? Or am I going to dedicate this incarnation to rising into my christed self?

I am that one you know as Jesus, and we will speak to you again tomorrow.

Let not my world obscure the sight of Christ.

Follow the complete lesson guidelines
in your *ACIM* book.

You are blessed beings, indeed. I am
that one you know as Jesus. Of course,
the saying "be the change you want to see
in the world" is the meaning of this lesson.
You will see a world that reflects you. If you want
to see changes in the world, make those changes first in yourself, internally
and perceptually. Then you will be adding to the world the correct frequency.

These days when there are many, many demonstrations going on and
there is a feeling of confrontation or attack happening, the masses of beings
who want better things often misunderstand the laws of creation. They go
in with a fierce combative energy against that which they believe is causing
the problem. There is nothing wrong with a demonstration. There is nothing
wrong with like-minded beings gathering together, but those like-minded
beings must come together in the love of something. The environmental
demonstrations you are seeing, for example, are often working counter to
the result those beings seek to accomplish, because they believe something
outside of them is causing the problem.

When you step back and view the world from a more elevated position,
you can see that the collective accumulation of individual consumption is
causing the problem: all the single-use plastics, plastic bags, and these sorts
of things. Now, people individually do not believe that changing themselves
will change the world, because they have been raised in your Newtonian
physics. This is what you call the scientific method: There is a simple cause-
and-effect relationship; one person cannot change the world. What this
teaching brings forth is the idea that one person can indeed change the
world — your world — because you are the creator of your world and you
are experiencing your world and you will attract to you things of a like frequency.

For example, if you are concerned about the environment, then by
changing your personal consumption methods, you will attract more

conscious people, places, things, and experiences, because you are accepting your role in the collective. You are saying, "I may only be one drop in this bucket, but if I can demonstrate a certain frequency, I can affect the whole bucket." And that will literally happen. (This is only one example. We are using it because it is so front and center in your society's media at the moment. It is not more important than other issues.)

Continue being passionate about what you want, but do not get caught up in fighting against what you don't want. You add your energy to that system when you fight against it, because you are in a combative "them versus us" mode. You are not in an expansive, comprehensive understanding of how creation works, and that will change your frequency considerably.

In this being's *A Course in Miracles* studies, before she was a channel, many of us helped her focus her mind and work on the forgiveness practices. There were some deep forgiveness issues this being needed to work on. And because she dedicated herself to her forgiveness practice, putting aside some of the other worldly concerns that other people tend to focus on, her practice became a huge part of her day; therefore, the result achieved a magnificent velocity that some of you would do well to emulate.

Some of you may look at this being and think, "Oh my goodness, what a tremendous experience she is having. How lucky she is." The truth is that she was in so much pain from the distortions in her mind that doing *A Course in Miracles* and the consequent forgiveness practice brought her such a contrast (in the feeling of peace) that everything else began to fade in significance. Her practice of attaining and maintaining peace became the be all and end all of her existence.

When she was in that phase, there was a part of her mind that was concerned that was all her life would ever be and that she would live alone reading this big blue book. She was happy with the peace of mind, but she was concerned about the state of the rest of her experience in the sense that she did not live in a way she felt was in alignment with her desires. Now fast-forward ten years; that has completely changed. This being is living the life of her dreams, but that was not her ambition in doing the forgiveness practice, and this is something we want you to understand here. Her goal was peace, and in the attainment of that peace, she connected to true guidance, and in surrendering her normal boundaries, she allowed us to come into her consciousness fully and completely, upgrading her further. But it was her dedication to her practice that initiated all that, and that was long in the making; do not think it was an overnight thing.

For those of you who are in the 300s of your lessons, perhaps for the second or third time, we ask you to rededicate yourself to your forgiveness practice, understanding that the world you see and the world you react to is in your mind. It is only in your mind, and when you change your mind, the world will respond. It is the miracle manifesting.

I am that one you know as Jesus, and we will speak to you again tomorrow.

LESSON 305

There is a peace that Christ bestows on us.

Follow the complete lesson guidelines in your *ACIM* book.

You are blessed beings, indeed. I am that one you know as Jesus. Christ consciousness is all-loving and all-forgiving. That is where we lead you through these lessons and teachings.

But it is a decision you can make every moment to choose not to judge, to choose not to hate yourself or anyone else, and to surrender to what is — not with the weakness of a doormat, as you are so afraid of being, but with the knowledge that life is happening to you and coming through you in a way that is beneficial to you. Even though you face challenges or problems, they are, in fact, opportunities for you to expand your consciousness, and this is where we want you to change your point of view about the negativities in your life — be it a twisted ankle, a bigger health problem, a divorce, or some loss of employment. See these as opportunities for expansion. They are matching you in some way. The frequency of these experiences are matching a part of you in some way, and the way your consciousness is revealed to you is through your life experience.

If there are hidden or unconscious negative beliefs playing out in your life, you need to reveal them, because you have hidden them from yourself. They have gone deep underground through fear, guilt, or shame, or maybe they went into hiding from simple unconsciousness, and now they are creating/miscreating. They are manufacturing negative experiences for you. When you encounter a "negative" experience, reframe your story. Instead of saying, "This thing should not be happening to me," say, "I am glad that I am seeing this low-frequency aspect of my unconscious mind. It has brought this experience into being." Better seen than unseen or better out than in, we say.

From now on, try to understand that your problems are your gifts and opportunities to see where you are off track. When they have come into being in a physical sense, through sickness or injury, you know that they are powerful and that you really believe in them. Watch what your problems trigger in you, and understand that is how you come to remove unloving beliefs from your mind to help you head toward the Christ consciousness that is going to bring you all-encompassing peace.

Many of you are not at peace now, but you are coming to be more peaceful. As you become more peaceful, more in alignment with Christ energies, the upsets, guilt, shame, or fear that you are occasionally experiencing will become much clearer and easier to identify, because the rest of your day will be more peaceful. So don't see your upsets as, "I'm being a bad *A Course in Miracles* student." See your upsets as, "Oh, here's a little piece of my unconscious mind that's been revealed to me. What just happened? Why am I so upset? Why am I angry? Why am I fearful? Let me look at what has arisen in me and be grateful that it has been triggered."

I am that one you know as Jesus. We will speak to you again tomorrow.

LESSON 306

The gift of Christ is all I seek today.

Follow the complete lesson guidelines in your *ACIM* book.

You are blessed beings, indeed. I am that one you know as Jesus. You refer to me in your society as Jesus Christ. The "Christ" part of that nomenclature refers to what happened to me as a result of my practice of forgiveness.

That is what happened to me. I do not want you to think that I am more special than you. I am indeed the "older brother" that *A Course in Miracles* refers to. It refers to a more experienced, wiser being that can instruct you on how to mature into that yourself, and that is what these lessons are for. We are asking you to mature out of the ego's demented, inconsistent, and violent ways into a more loving being.

Many of you will say, "I am not inconsistent. I go to work every day. I'm not violent. I don't shoot anybody." Now go into your inner world and ask yourself, "How consistent is my inner world? How calm and loving is my inner world?" We do not mean the behaviors that have been trained into you by conditioning programs. We mean the truth of what you are inside.

Remember, your manifestation is going to be a reflection of the truth of what you are inside, not your social face and not the face of innocence that the ego paints on you, but the truth of your internal frequency — all the ups and downs, the hatreds, the fears, and the self-loathing contained there. And that is why you have the saying "bad things happen to good people," because people's behavior seems to be good. They seem to be nice, kind, and polite, but on the inside, they may be seething with frustration, anger, and shame. That is what will generate what you consider the "bad" thing.

Remember, there are no secrets being kept on this plane. Even if the words aren't spoken, your frequency emits what you believe, feel, and think all the time — *all* the time. And the universe is listening and bringing you reflections of that frequency.

Please stop playing the victim. Step up into your christhood and train your minds into love. When you find an unloving part of your mind, do not condemn yourself. Instead, say, "You are no longer allowed to reside within my sacred space. You must leave. And to enforce that leaving, I am no longer going to believe the thoughts you generate. I am not going to act as if what you are saying is true, because I can feel the frequency is unloving."

This is the responsibility you all bear because you have been given free will. That responsibility is to stop believing every thought these unloving beliefs generate, and stop acting as if every idea you have in your mind is true, whether it's hateful or not. Use your free will to choose Christ-like behavior. We always remind you to include yourself in that loving principle.

I am that one you know as Jesus, and we will speak to you again tomorrow.

Conflicting wishes cannot be my will.

Follow the complete lesson guidelines in your *ACIM* book.

You are blessed beings, indeed. I am that one you know as Jesus. All of you are used to feeling conflict inside. You are used to debating thoughts: "I don't want to do this, but I have to."

This is one of the most profound problems in need of healing within the Western mind: this idea that to counter what makes you happy and what brings you fulfillment, joy, and satisfaction is somehow in your best interest. This is one of the fundamental conditioning programs of your society: "You cannot have what you want in your life, and happiness is a luxury not everyone can afford." This is a poisonous belief system that teaches you to constantly put up with things that do not make you happy in the belief that somehow this is going to make things better. This is not true.

We know where you got this idea. It came from the suffering, sacrifice, and martyrdom concept that the church has promoted over thousands of years and that your society is built on. You may not see yourself as a religious person. You may not see yourself as a guilty Catholic, a Presbyterian, or whatever denomination comes to mind when you think of religion. But this society is built on hundreds of years of the church's violent and intolerant rule and the promotion of self-sacrifice, suffering, martyrdom, and fear. That is what your society is built on even if you don't consider yourself religious. Those frequencies pervade this world.

There is a fundamental part of the collective consciousness that believes happiness is a luxury. There is a part of the collective consciousness that believes those who seek joy are self-indulgent and selfish; they are, in fact, in alignment with God's will for them, which is happiness. You are given a guidance system that functions impeccably and constantly. It is in alignment with love, and it is the invisible umbilical cord to the Divine that tells you when you are in accord with love; you will feel good. When you are out of accord with love (where sacrifice, suffering, and martyrdom play out), you will feel bad, because you are out of accord with God's will for you.

This teaching is completely counter to what the church taught. But it is what I taught when I walked on the Earth plane many years ago, and it was one of the reasons I had to be removed from the Earth plane, because I was teaching freedom. I was teaching love — true love: that happiness and joy are your birthright and that is how you will reach Nirvana.

But society's power structures don't like freedom. They don't like free-thinking, happy beings. They need dysfunctional, fearful, limited, and frustrated beings to keep the economy going. So make your happiness the great act of revolution that you are going to participate in today. And in your happiness, you will become a better environmentalist, because in your happiness, you will not unnecessarily consume, which is what is promoted in your society at this time: Unhappiness makes for a good economy. So make your act of environmental revolution, if you care for your planet, one of being happy so that you do not need to endlessly consume your planet into oblivion.

I am that one you know as Jesus, and we will speak to you again tomorrow.

LESSON 308

This instant is the only time there is.

Follow the complete lesson guidelines in your *ACIM* book.

You are blessed beings, indeed. I am that one you know as Jesus. You have heard the phrase "the power of now." Well, that is the only place you have any say in what goes on.

You are obsessed with the past and the future. You are constantly regaling each other about the tales of what has happened in the past, and if people tell you a tale about their broken leg, then you tell them about the time when you broke your leg. The other obsession you have is worrying about the future — making up catastrophic future scenarios of homelessness, poverty, or betrayal.

These entertainments you have in your mind — retelling your past and future imaginings — contaminate the present moment. Your present moment is the only place that is truly creative. It is here and now in this very instant that you get to choose your vibration; you get to choose love or fear. When you reminisce about the past or project into the future, you are misusing your mind's powerful abilities to recall and imagine. You are using your creative power to contaminate the eternal now, which is the only place you can plant seeds of love.

Understand that in this place — here and now — nothing has ever or will ever go wrong. When you think of things that have gone wrong or will go wrong, they are not happening now. They are in the past or in the future, both imagined places. Your memories are incorrect. Your projections are fantasies. Live in the eternal now. Presence is your gift to the world and yourself. If you remain in presence, you will not be afraid, because you are in alignment with what is when you are present.

If you are in a conversation with somebody, watch where you leave the present and go into the past or the future. Do it as little as possible; start to catch yourself. When you find yourself telling that same old story one more time, stop. Come back to the present moment, and seek inspiration in the now, appreciation in the now, of what is.

It is in the present moment, uncontaminated by the past and the future, that you will find your peace. Return to this moment over and over and over again each day, and you will find that you will string one moment of peace onto another and another and another. There you will come to the realization that time is an illusion. It is merely moments experienced uniquely one at a time.

As you reclaim those moments for peace, you will realize that is all you ever have to do. Take this moment in presence — and this moment in presence and this moment in presence — and you will have a happy life.

I am that one you know as Jesus, and we will speak to you again tomorrow.

I will not fear to look within today.

Follow the complete lesson guidelines
in your *ACIM* book.

You are blessed beings, indeed. I am that one you know as Jesus. The ego's game is always to keep you chasing things outside of yourselves — a new lover, a new job, a move to a new place. Have you not noticed that the natural tendency of ego consciousness is always to look outside you for salvation?

This is one of the great programs playing out in your society now, this constant consumerism: "If only I can buy the next best thing — the next phone or the next car — I will be happy." There is also the constant seeking of love — special love — outside of yourself in the form of romantic engagement. Now this is one of the great sacred worshipping aspects of the ego: the worshipping of the special relationship. You see it played out in love songs, romantic novels, and romantic movies, always that special person who is going to change everything. Well, the ego keeps you chasing things to waste your time. Stop wasting your time, and go inside, because the answer is there.

The answer is arising from within you every single day in the form of loving guidance from spirit. What you are faced with as a programmed Western person is a deeply indoctrinated propaganda program designed to keep you buying, keep you separated, and keep you individualized in order to magnify the separation experience you're having.

Now you are in separation, and that is a challenge in and of itself. You are in an individual body that seems to have a will of its own. But you have not been sent into this dramatic and challenging environment without a map, and your map is your emotional guidance system. You are loved enough that you were not sent off by yourself (which is what you wanted to do). You have a God-given gift — a map Home, should you decide to go Home. You don't have to go Home if you don't want to; you can stay and play in this realm as long as you want. But once you get tired, once you realize that all those things you have been chasing are not working, then it is time to go inside.

That is the difficult part, because there are very few people to support you on this journey. This channeling that this being has put up on YouTube [you-tube.com/channel/UCr7RBMo6y1phbdjG3qArj-Q] is one of the rare places you can get ongoing support for your journey into the heart of darkness, because that is where all those programs and propaganda messages reside in you. They reside within your mind, and you must go in and investigate what's going on in there. You must evict some of those programs. That is what we are here to help you do. We are here to help you and encourage you on that journey.

The programs that do not benefit you will make you feel bad, so they are quite easy to find. But you have been taught to override your guidance system, and you are used to feeling bad. This is one of the most challenging aspects of this transformative re-indoctrination: the idea that you are meant to feel good and that happiness is what God wills for you. That is God's will for you: to be happy. Even in your choice of separation, you can have a happy dream.

Be brave and go inside regularly — once or twice a day in whatever form suits you. Obviously these lessons are encouraging you to stop, go inside, and repeat things internally throughout your day. They are a training program to get you to go inside because that's where the magic happens. That's where your creative world begins; it begins within you. But you are the master of your ship; you are the master of your mind, whatever it consumes and whatever it entertains. Nobody will save you from yourself. You must save yourself using this information.

I am that one you know as Jesus. Peace resides within you always; it has merely been covered up by propaganda. We will speak to you again tomorrow.

LESSON 310

In fearlessness and love, I spend today.

Follow the complete lesson guidelines in your *ACIM* book.

You are blessed beings, indeed. I am that one you know as Jesus. This is the opposite of what most beings spend their time in. They usually spend their time in fear and judgment.

Dedicating your life day by day to fearlessness and love relaxes you in a way that is measurable. Your heart rate goes down. You will encounter fewer confrontations and stressful events. You will observe people in a different way, and your day will be completely different.

We suggest you embrace fearlessness as an experiment today. Watch whenever fear arises in you, and the only way that most of you will know that is by how you feel. You will feel a sense of trepidation. You will feel anxiety in your tummy. Catch yourself every time you believe a fearful thought; stop yourself dead in your tracks, and say, "Today I will be fearless. Nothing bad is going to happen."

When you dedicate a day to fearlessness, such as this lesson asks of you, you take hold of your mind and make it yours again instead of allowing the programs and the past to dictate your behavior, which is all fear is. You would not fear anything if you did not have a belief that it was dangerous somehow, a belief that was planted there many years ago by someone somewhere, you know not who. When you decide to be free of fear, you take back the present moment and decide that the future will look different. You are saying, "This time this experience is mine. It does not belong to the past. It does not belong to those beings who taught me to be afraid or those experiences that showed me how to fear. Today is a clean slate, and it will play out in the form of a better life in the future."

Many *A Course in Miracles* teachers will say it is not about making a better life, but a better life is the side effect of choosing love and fearlessness. So it is not necessarily the goal but the side effect of the goal, which is you taking back your mind. Take back your mind today, and choose to be courageous and fearless.

I am that one you know as Jesus, and we will speak to you tomorrow.

LESSON 311

I judge all things as I would have them be.

Follow the complete lesson guidelines in your *ACIM* book.

You are blessed beings, indeed. I am that one you know as Jesus. Arguing with reality as you see it is your basic problem.

Acceptance is the answer to all your problems: Accept what is as the manifested form of past thoughts, beliefs, and ideas in the form of behavior, solid material, people, places, and things.

When you think about it, something that has already come into manifestation is the result of a lot of thought, behavior, and action. You are foolish to try to change the result of anything. What you must do is change the ingredients. If you add the wrong ingredients when mixing a cake — perhaps you put in salt instead of sugar —the cake will taste bad; you will not want to eat it. But it would be foolish for you to try to take out the salt from the cake batter and put in the sugar. You would merely destroy it. You must say, "Ah, the ingredients for this cake were incorrect. The next time I make a cake, I will be careful about the ingredients I put in and make sure that I do not put in salt when there should be sugar."

That is how we want you to look at the world. Look at the world and say, "Look at this effect. Look at this material manifestation of something that is incorrect. It is unloving. It does not benefit my family, my community, the world, or me. How can we change the ingredients that produced this effect? What is lacking? Is love lacking in the ingredients? Is love lacking in the decision-making process? Is love lacking in the education of the people who are making these decisions?" Yes, yes, yes — all these things are true in your world at this time. So it is pointless to get all in a flutter over what has already come into being.

In your lane, your life, your experience, begin to see the results you don't want as lessons to show you how to change the ingredients. When your body is not functioning as you would like it to function, examine how you are feeding it. Look at how you are exercising it. Look at the things you say to it and about it, and ask yourself, "Is love lacking here? Is there something I have not contributed to the well-being of my body?" This is a very, very good example that all of you would do well to follow.

It's the same with your relationships. Look at what you put into your relationships. Are you experiencing negative and unloving thoughts about your partner? Are you judging your partner all the time? Ask yourself, "Is there something I have contributed to this situation in terms of ingredients? Have I been adding bitter ingredients to this relationship, and that is why it does not taste sweet to me?"

I am that one you know as Jesus, and we will speak to you again tomorrow.

I see all things
as I would have them be.

Follow the complete lesson guidelines
in your *ACIM* book.

You are blessed beings, indeed. I am
that one you know as Jesus. This is
something that is very hard for many of
you to swallow: The world is as you want it
to be, and you have decided what you are going
to see.

There are beings on this planet who do not see war, do not see starvation, and have an experience of extreme peace, abundance, and joy. That is because they have mastered their minds; they have clarified their beliefs and ideas, and they have decided moment by moment what they will see and what they will not judge.

You have an opinion about everything, and what we want you to do today is step back from sharing your opinion about everything. If you are having a conversation with somebody today, only share your direct experiences about whatever you are discussing, not something you have read in a book, heard on the radio, or saw in a movie. Speak about your personal experience of that subject; then you are more accurately representing what you are going through.

Your experience of being a parent is uniquely yours based on all your beliefs, ideas, and past teachings. Other beings who are parenting will have experiences and points of view completely different from yours. But if you share your unique experiences, you may shine a light on an opportunity for learning that others have no access to because of their beliefs and ideas.

The opposite also is true of course. Perhaps they will share experiences based on their personal happenings that give you an opportunity to see things a different way. But it is not about imposing your opinion on others. It is about sharing your experience and, at the same time, acknowledging that somebody can have a completely different experience of the same subject.

What this opens up is dialogue and communication. So before you speak, ask yourself, "Have I actually had any experience of this? Even though I have, others may experience it differently. So I will present my case or my sharing with that intention: to hear other's experiences so that we can all grow and expand."

We are all here to commune. We are all here to communicate. We are all here to offer inspiration for you. If you can do that for your fellow brothers and sisters instead of shutting them down, arguing with them, or dismissing their experience, you might find that a lot of education, compassion, and community building will take place.

I am that one you know as Jesus, and we will speak to you tomorrow.

LESSON 313

Now let a new perception come to me.

Follow the complete lesson guidelines in your *ACIM* book.

You are blessed beings, indeed. I am that one you know as Jesus. Your perception, as you experience it, is what you see and interpret the world to be through all the distorting lenses manufactured by the beliefs you hold in your mind that are not true. The truth is that things are just happening. There are people crossing the road. There are some people being born and some people dying, but you are laying a story over everything through those lenses of perception.

Understand there is a truth that you can connect with, but you must ask to have your perception healed so that you can see that truth. You have beliefs resident in your mind through your willingness to have them there. They are there because you believe in them, and you apply them because you believe in them.

The Holy Spirit is the intermediary between your consciousness and Christ consciousness. The Holy Spirit understands that you have distortions, and it understands the truth; it acts as a bridge between those two things in whatever way works for your deluded mind.

You do not need to know how this works. You only need to understand that you have to be willing to heal your perception, and that comes through your forgiveness practice. In that act, you are saying: "I understand that I do not understand what's happening here. I'm going to forgive the person who's angry with me. I'm going to allow that this is some part of my own consciousness revealing itself to me even though I don't truly comprehend it." Your conscious willingness to have that perception healed is what will bring you peace.

You don't need to understand this process; just understand that you have these beliefs residing in your mind and that you are acting on them through use of your free will. You must now use your free will to say, "I offer up my mind so that my perceptions may be healed." Over time, if you continue to make this offering, your perceptions will be healed and you will begin to see things differently.

When your perception is healed, the world must change, because you are the projector; you are the creator. This is how you truly come to understand the miracle. It is because you are the one who is causing what's happening in your experience, and when you change your mind and are willing to be healed of your misperceptions, the world will change. You may be healed of some sickness. Relationships may change. Your abundance level may change. All these things may change when you are willing to have your perception healed. But you must voluntarily show willingness, and you must ask for it to be done for you, because you now understand that your perception and your misinterpretation of reality is what causes your suffering. Suffering is optional here.

I am that one you know as Jesus, and we will speak to you tomorrow.

LESSON 314

I seek a future different from the past.

Follow the complete lesson guidelines in your *ACIM* book.

You are blessed beings, indeed. I am that one you know as Jesus. This is the simplest lesson of all: Your present moment is the only place that your future can be created.

When you envision future events, you are contaminating the present moment with your personal needs and wants. This is an interesting topic, because you have in your society many promoters of the law of attraction, which is this idea that you will choose what your future looks like, and in the present moment, if you keep fixating on the objects of your desire, then you will get them.

Well, the law of attraction does not work this way. The law of attraction works in the form of frequency. So if you are seeking a car, then you will have to make the frequency, "I have a beautiful car," radiate from you to get the car. If you hold the image of the car in your mind while emitting a poverty, scarcity, or lack frequency, the car you want won't come to you. That is why many of you trying to use the law of attraction feel disappointed, because you do not get what you want.

But you are getting what you want. You are getting the frequency that you are emitting, and you are emitting the frequency because of the things you choose to focus on. What this lesson is speaking about is trusting that there is a benevolent, wise, all-encompassing awareness that knows what is best for you, given your karmic history, reincarnational background, and things you decided you want to learn in this lifetime as part of your consciousness expansion.

The ego's programs contaminate you. Many of you are contaminated by the materialistic consumer propaganda you have been raised on and are fed constantly through your media systems. You may look at a big house and say, "That is what will make me feel secure," whereas the overriding, benevolent, highly evolved consciousness is aware that is the opposite of what will make you feel secure. You are insecure for other reasons. You are insecure because of your lack of faith. You are insecure because of the fearful thoughts and ideas you entertain all the time.

When you reside in the present moment, relaxed and in a place of faith that what is best for you will come your way, you are doing the right thing. The fear that comes up in you is the fear of salvation, which is the belief most of you have that somehow aligning with God's will for you will deprive you of what you want. That is the ego's story, indeed. The ego is always telling you that it needs to be in control so that you can get what you want. But have you noticed that when the ego is in control, you do not get what you want?

So we are asking you to indulge in a big change of mind. Try it for one whole day: Remain in the present, do not think about the future, and trust that everything you need is coming to you.

I am that one you know as Jesus, and we will speak to you again tomorrow.

All gifts my fellow humans give belong to me.

Follow the complete lesson guidelines
in your *ACIM* book.

You are blessed beings, indeed. I am
that one you know as Jesus. This is one
of those quantum examples that you are
unaware of in your simplistic, Newtonian,
cause-and-effect training programs. When some-
body on this planet does something positive, everybody benefits. When you
do something positive, everybody on the planet benefits. You are a collective
in that sense. The separation illusion is exactly that: an illusion. Know that
you are all connected.

You are as bees in a hive, and we do not mean to insult you in any way.
(Although, you are coming to respect bees more and more in your society as
you realize their grand job.) Each bee does not work for itself. Each bee in a
hive works toward the well-being of all in the hive.

You can imagine what a hive would look like if all the bees did exactly
what they wanted and were driven by personal agendas. The babies wouldn't
live. The queen would not produce. There would be no food for the winter.
It sort of reminds us of your society.

Understand that inner guidance comes from the hive leader; you would
call that being God. But the hive leader is a consciousness that has the
awareness of what needs to be done, what your strengths are, what your
place in the salvation of the world is, and is meant to be. Your guidance will
lead you to that place if you listen to it. This is what these lessons are all
for. It is about getting you out of the way — the "small you" — and allowing yourself to be guided by the "greater you," which is God's will for you.

God's will for you is your will for you. What God wills for you will make
you happy, and what makes you happy is good for everybody; it's good for the
world. You have an unhappy world right now, because everybody is striving for
the wrong things, believing that they are being guided truly, but they are being
led to the edge of a precipice by the training programs that you are subjected to.

This course is a new training program. It's a "brain unwashing" program
— a voluntary one. You understand that you are being told what to think

and how to behave so that you may reclaim that true north guidance that tells you where you need to go. A compass does not argue with itself; it constantly tells you where north is. If you want to go west, that is your choice, but the compass will always point north. Your guidance system is always going to point you toward God's will for you, your true north. If you choose to do otherwise, you will get lost — not as a punishment, but as a natural consequence of not listening to the guidance.

I am that one you know as Jesus, and we will speak to you tomorrow.

LESSON 316

All gifts I give my fellow humans are my own.

Follow the complete lesson guidelines in your *ACIM* book.

You are blessed beings, indeed. I am that one you know as Jesus. The ego's game is about getting. It uses the appetites of the body and the lusts of the idols you worship to try to get you always to take, to hoard, to keep to yourself, and to "secret away" in an effort to maintain what it believes is yours. The truth is what you give away is what you get to keep.

This seems strange given the laws that you believe apply in your world. In the physical/material world, if you have a piece of fruit and you give it away, you no longer have that piece of fruit. But if you go into the nonphysical world with love and give it away, it is not taken from you. It is strengthened. If you create beautiful pieces of artwork and give that creativity away or sell it (it's okay to sell it), it is extended from you. It is sent out into the world. It is expanded; your creativity is shared by many, many beings and inspires many beings and is appreciated by many beings. So give it away, and every time your art (or your creations) are appreciated by others, you receive that appreciation.

This idea of scarcity is one of the issues we will address in this lesson — the idea that keeping everything for yourself because you're afraid of losing it causes you to lose the opportunity to expand it. Share what you have. Be generous with your gifts. Understand that because you are all one, even though you appear to be separate, whatever you give to your fellow human, you also give to yourself. You are merely sharing it with an aspect of your mind that seems to be apart from you. It is not really apart from you.

When you push guilt on others, you think you have gotten rid of it, but you actually have magnified it, and you will feel more guilt. So give away that which you want to keep. Share that which you want more of, and you will find your life expanding miraculously.

I am that one you know as Jesus, and we will speak to you tomorrow.

LESSON 317

I follow in the way appointed me.

Follow the complete lesson guidelines in your *ACIM* book.

You are blessed beings, indeed. I am that one you know as Jesus. You are all given the opportunity to hear the information that will transform your minds.

It comes to you over and over and over again. It comes to you in the form of a book. It comes to you in the form of people sharing their testimony. It comes to you in a dream. It comes to you in many, many ways, this opportunity to surrender to God's will for you.

This is antithetical to the ego's world. It does not want to surrender to anything. But as you may have noticed, as you go through life, you become more and more disillusioned, because the illusions do not live up to the ego's story about what they will be: a new body, a new boyfriend, a new car, a new job, a new country you move to, or a bigger house. It doesn't matter. The illusions you have been taught to follow and have the inclination to follow eventually will begin to disappoint you; that is disillusionment. You still believe in the illusions, but they do not feed you the way they used to.

Eventually, there will come a point of surrender, and in that point of surrender, there can be a dark night of the soul, indeed. You could fall to your knees and say, "I cannot do this anymore." In that moment of surrender, you will say: "Show me the way. There must be a better way." And in that moment, spirit steps in and says, "Yes, there is a better way, and here it is."

You have been given the means to that end, and the book you hold in your hands [*A Course in Miracles*] is the means that you have been given to take you to salvation. Other people have different pathways; other people have different routes. There are a thousand routes to heaven. But if you are doing this lesson and this work speaks to you, then you have found your means to an end.

Follow it. Love it. Enjoy it. And trust in your life to show you the next thing you need to work on. It will come to you every day. Each day there will be something that feels a little off, that you know is not correct. Trust that it will reveal itself to you; you do not need to go digging for it. It will show itself in negative emotions: sadness, depression, guilt, shame, or fear.

Step into each day eager for not only the joy that day will bring but also for the little nudge that there's something off, and know that is your next project. That is the next little piece of forgiveness work you will do. Get up each day optimistic. Get up each day happy that you have another opportunity to be part of this most wonderful 3D experience.

Yes, it is challenging. Yes, it is tiring. Yes, it can be exhausting when you are off track. But once you have found the means to the end, things will improve.

I am that one you know as Jesus, and we will speak to you tomorrow.

LESSON 318

In me, salvation's means and end are one.

Follow the complete lesson guidelines in your *ACIM* book.

You are blessed beings, indeed. I am that one you know as Jesus. The phrase "looking for love in all the wrong places" comes to mind with this particular lesson.

You constantly seek salvation outside yourself, but your salvation is built into your DNA, into your particular structure of personality — body, mind, and spirit. You have been given everything you need to come to a place of peace. That is reflected back to you in your guidance system — your feeling self. This means when you align with happiness, when you align with joy, and when you align with what feels good to you, then you are on track to your salvation. The reintegration of your mind into wholeness and holiness is what the world needs for its salvation.

As long as you are running around in fear and feeling guilty or accusing others of being guilty, the world cannot change. This transformation your planet is going through must be a collective transformation — even though your world will shift when you become reintegrated. If your mind becomes whole and focused on love, your entire experience will change. But many of you want a collective shift, and that is what we seek too. We seek to gather as many miracle-minded beings as possible, and with that gathering, the power builds and builds and the effect builds and builds, because one being aligned with love is far more powerful than one being aligned with fear. The fear-aligned being is constricted, limited, separation-focused, and isolated; the love-focused being is expansive, extended, and creative and engages with as many beings as possible.

This is what we seek: to have thousands upon thousands of beings open their hearts, open their minds, become defenseless, refuse to attack, and bring to this time and place the peace and joy that is your natural inheritance. We encourage you all to double down on your practice, let go of anything that makes you feel bad, and choose again.

Choose health. Choose life. Choose love. Choose to extend into your world the beautiful gifts you have been given.

I am that one you know as Jesus, and we will speak to you tomorrow.

LESSON 319

I came for the salvation of the world.

Follow the complete lesson guidelines in your *ACIM* book.

You are blessed beings, indeed. I am that one you know as Jesus. This sounds like a grand plan, does it not? — that you have come for the salvation of the world. It is true.

You keep coming here for the salvation of the world. Every incarnation you have ever had has been the opportunity for you to save the world through the transformation of your mind into an absolutely loving entity. This is what is required for graduation from this educational institution. Earth is a place where you learn to love, and that is what it is all about.

For those of you who know you don't know how to love or you witness yourself in unloving relationships, you understand you have some distortions. That is okay. You are here to do this work. You are here to relinquish that from your minds, which no longer reflect what you want for your future.

Each of you must decide to release that which causes you suffering, because the suffering is the indicator that it is unloving, and what is unloving causes you pain. Love never causes you pain, and this is one of the most important things for you to remember as you go through your journey of loving and learning how to love and be loved: that love does not cause pain. Love does not cause suffering. Only the distortions in the minds of the lovers cause pain and suffering.

Make sure you are not laying the suffering story on love, that you are not telling yourself that you will have to sacrifice and suffer for love. You do not have to do that. Sacrifice and suffering are the illusions that have been added to love by your society's teachers, and they are unnecessary lies. You can love fully and happily and not lose one ounce of freedom or of your unique creative style.

Go out there and love yourselves. Love your friends. Love your families. Love your lovers, and love everybody who is driving you crazy with bad behavior, because they lack love, and the only way to heal them is to send them love. Love. Love. Love.

I am that one you know as Jesus. We will speak to you again tomorrow.

LESSON 320

My Father gives all power unto me.

Follow the complete lesson guidelines in your *ACIM* book.

You are blessed beings, indeed. I am that one you know as Jesus. You are made in the image of God. You are made as powerful creators, and you have the ability to manifest whatever you want; that is what you are all doing.

The problem most of you have with your unconscious minds is you don't know which programs and beliefs you have, so they miscreate all over the place. Negative beliefs and ideas that your grandmother used to tell you when you were sitting on her knee when you were four are still in there. They are put in there intentionally by authority figures, and they will not be removed until you remove them.

These beliefs and ideas limit you. It is not a natural limit that you feel in your daily experience. You feel the limitation of the untrue and restrictive beliefs and ideas that have been implanted in you. So your job is to discover those limitations. How do you do that? You do that through experience. What we want to inspire that faith in your experience today; you do not have negative experiences for no reason or because God doesn't love you. You have negative experiences, because you are, in some way, bringing them to you. Unconsciously? Yes. Unintentionally? Yes. There are things you say, things you think, and actions motivated by beliefs that bring negativities to you.

This is the most powerful place you will find yourself: when you realize that even though you are doing your best with your conscious mind, all the programs that have been indoctrinated into you actively undermine the effort you are using with your conscious mind. And percentage-wise, your unconscious or subconscious mind has a much larger percentage of your body-mind's control.

You do not have to think about your heart beating. You do not have to think about digesting your food. You do not have to think about cleansing your blood. You do not have to think about growing your hair. All these are unconscious in you. Thank goodness for that. There would be no time for anything else if you had to think about all those things.

Then we go to the subconscious. The subconscious is where you have put all the stories, beliefs, indoctrinations, and lessons you have experienced. It is where you store them out of sight and out of mind, but they still play through. For example, you took lots of tests in school where you had to learn your times tables and your alphabet. You don't have to think about that anymore; you know it. At the same time that indoctrination was taking place, you also were being told other things:

- "Money doesn't grow on trees."
- "Don't get above yourself."
- "Get off your high horse."
- "Who do you think you are?"
- "Don't tell people things; they will use it against you."

All kinds of tales from your family (who might have been very negative and scared or very wealthy and positive) are in there, and you will see the evidence of those teachings in your life. That is what we ask you to contemplate today. Contemplate the family into which you were born, what their stories are, and determine whether you are still playing out those stories even though you do not want the results they elicit. The mind-retraining program we are conducting here (that you are voluntarily participating in) is to help you to focus your mind on that which is beautiful, that which is freedom, that which is creativity, and that which is love. You will decrease the amount of energy you put into those untrue beliefs and ideas.

If you keep seeing in yourself thoughts, feelings, and behaviors that remind you of things you don't want or don't like to experience, then you need to bring them up into your conscious mind and ask yourself, "What am I doing in this area of my life that keeps it from blossoming, that keeps it from flourishing?" And you will very, very quickly see that you are thinking things, saying things, or doing things that are out of accord with abundance and joy in that area of your life. That becomes an area you can focus your attention to transform your thoughts, beliefs, and actions so that you are congruent: Thoughts, words, and deeds are aligned.

Many beings will say this is not the business of *A Course in Miracles* — teaching you how to live your daily life. But living your daily life gets better when you apply these principles. So don't focus on daily life per se; focus on what we are teaching you. Implement those processes, and use your mind for good, for love, and for the evolution of human consciousness. Your daily life will improve as a side effect of the mastery of your mind.

I am that one you know as Jesus, and we will speak to you tomorrow.

LESSON 321

Father, my freedom is in you alone.

Follow the complete lesson guidelines in your *ACIM* book.

You are blessed beings, indeed. I am that one you know as Jesus. Most of you who have come to these teachings have tried many, many different things along the pathway to this point in time and have agreed that the map you were given is not a very good one.

That is all we are doing here: giving you a map toward peace. In that peace, your guidance becomes extremely clear, and your interactions with your guides and teachers will become clearer and clearer and clearer. We must remind you that you have constant guidance. There are many beings who ask: "Why can't I see or speak to my spirit guides? Why can't I channel?" You are connecting with your spirit guides all the time through your emotional guidance system. Remember the image of the mothership communicating with the little exploratory pod that has gone down to planet Earth. The mothership sees and knows where you are, what's approaching, what is best for your safety, best for your evolution, and most interesting for your mind. You will be guided there by your feelings — always good feelings.

Happiness, joy, curiosity, wonder, and creativity — these great feelings are your guides and teachers speaking to you. And the more you listen to that guidance, the louder, clearer, and more articulate it will get.

There are many beings who have been following this one [the channel] for several years now who are channeling, communicating directly in many different forms, and producing beautiful artwork, books, music, and all kinds of things. Continue to dedicate yourself to this practice even though these lessons will be finished soon, and you too will have a clearer connection to your guides and teachers — who are always there helping you along the way.

I am that one you know as Jesus, and we will speak to you tomorrow.

LESSON 322

I can give up but what was never real.

Follow the complete lesson guidelines in your *ACIM* book.

You are blessed beings, indeed. I am that one you know as Jesus. Imagine every time you have been afraid or felt disconnected, shameful, or guilty that none of that was real. None of that is registered as real by that which you call All That Is.

The only things that are real are those things that God possesses and has endowed you with: love, creativity, extension, self-expression, joy, and happiness. These things are real. When you go through your day, we want you to realize that the pursuit of your happiness, joy, creativity, self-expression, and the extension of the love you possess as a natural inclination is real. And you will take those experiences into the next or other incarnations that you will have.

The guilt, the shame, the fear, the worry, and the negativity are the things that keep you from reality. People say, "Oh, but this is real. The fear, the treachery, and the betrayal, this is all real." But that is what's actually keeping you from reality, and as you focus your mind more and more on reality in a loving sense — focusing less on the material world and more on the nonphysical world of creativity, love, joy, and expression (all the things that are nonphysical) — you will live a more real life. After all, when you look at what being a human is, you see that it is the nonphysical things that provide you with the most nourishment. Love, creativity, joy, and happiness are not material things, are they?

Focus your mind away from the material and the physical, and bring yourself into alignment with the eternal. In that alignment, you will feel more peace, you will feel more joy, and you will feel less fear and less worry. Fear and worry always come up when you are in the realm of the physical: fear of death, fear of losing money, and fear of being hurt. These are all related to the physical body. Keep your mind above the battleground, and focus on that which is elevated, exciting, and enlivens your body with eager anticipation.

I am that one you know as Jesus, and we will speak to you tomorrow.

LESSON 323

I gladly make the "sacrifice" of fear.

Follow the complete lesson guidelines in your *ACIM* book.

You are blessed beings, indeed. I am that one you know as Jesus. Your minds are your greatest assets, and they are your greatest liabilities.

They are the same things being used correctly or incorrectly. When you are driving along in your car and thinking about something, you are using your mind incorrectly. When you are driving along in your car, you should be paying attention to the present moment. That means you are looking where you are going. It means you are paying attention to how you are feeling, your hands on the steering wheel, and the comfort of your body in the chair. If you are waiting in your car at a traffic light or whatever it is, be observant about what is going on. Do not drift off into your mind ruminating on a problem.

This is generally what happens. Most of you do not ruminate on what you want; you ruminate on what you don't want. It might be the anticipated argument you're going to have with your beloved when you get home. It might be a comment that your coworker made that's been bothering you all day. It could be many things. But these are the incorrect uses of the mind. The relentless thinking of what is not going on in the present moment is a waste of your time.

Now, we do not mean the conscious envisioning of a future you might like to experience, but even that is often driven by the ego's desires. We mean the general thinking that goes on — the thousands and thousands of thoughts that you have every day about what you don't want or about what you're afraid of. This is the incorrect use of mind. Presence is the correct use of mind, and in presence, you will connect with the love of the Divine. In presence, you are paying attention to what is. You are appreciating what is. You are engaging with what is. You are not ruminating over what was or what you don't want. You are in the moment with what is: the person sitting right in front of you, the beautiful view that's before you, or even the traffic jam you are stuck in.

The traffic jam can be your meditation for today. Say: "Here I am. I'm sitting in traffic, and it's hot. My arm is out the window, and I feel as if I'm getting a bit of a sunburn, but here I am." You will be given feedback about the situation you are in. You will not be avoiding the experience, and you may very well decide: "I actually don't like sitting in traffic with my arm getting burned while hanging out the window. I think I might need to do something about where I work and how I get there." However, if you are ruminating, imagining, or fantasizing about the past or the future, you are not experiencing the present moment.

This is a definition of the illusory world that is often referred to: You are often not where you are, experiencing what you are experiencing, so you are not getting the lesson. You are not getting the full "surround-sound" of your three-dimensional experience. That is how you learn; that is how you feel your way through your day: actually being where you are, talking to the people in front of you and actually feeling your feelings. All these things are guidance; they are telling you something.

Unfortunately, many of you are off somewhere else, distracting yourselves, changing the channel on the radio station because you're bored, talking on the phone, and not doing what you are doing. You are multitasking and multi-distracting yourself. You have no idea how you feel about what you are doing.

So today, do one thing at a time. Do it well. Pay attention to it. If it is on your list of things to do today, accept that and do it thoroughly and with great attention. Get every ounce of experience out of that thing that you can.

I am that one you know as Jesus. We will speak to you again tomorrow.

LESSON 324

I merely follow, for I would not lead.

Follow the complete lesson guidelines in your *ACIM* book.

You are blessed beings, indeed. I am that one you know as Jesus. The ego does not like this lesson. The ego wants to be in charge; the ego wants to control. What this lesson suggests is to listen to the guidance giving you direction as to what to do next.

As you become more familiar with these teachings, you will comprehend that the concept of surrender to guidance is the way to a peaceful life. You can lead with your ego in charge, but it will not lead you to a peaceful life. It might lead you to a very successful life financially. It might lead you to a very exciting life. But it will not lead you to a peaceful life.

Many of you have had exciting lives so far with divorces and all kinds of shenanigans going on. Excitement is not always what you seek. The guidance you have innately within you that is clearly heard once the chatter of the ego-mind is subdued somewhat will take you to the place you want to go.

Where do you want to go? You want to go somewhere you'll be happy. You want to go somewhere you'll be free. You want to go somewhere you hang out with people of like mind — friends, your tribe. That is where your guidance will take you. The ego can take you on a thousand long and circuitous journeys, all of which you are free to do if you choose. If you do not want to follow the guidance, then you are free to do as you will; you are loved so much that you are given free will to chase whatever you want to chase in this experience you are having on this 3D plane.

But this is for those who have become tired of the chase, a little disillusioned, a little worn out, a little frustrated. Listen to that inner guidance, which comes in the form of your feelings toward things, such as, "That looks really interesting. I can't stop thinking about this particular subject." It comes in the form of synchronicities. It comes in the form of meeting people who have exactly the thing that you have been looking for: a new job opportunity, a new piece of information, or a new relationship of some kind.

Slow down and listen to your guidance. It will save you much time.

I am that one you know as Jesus, and we will speak to you tomorrow.

LESSON 325

All things I think I see reflect ideas.

Follow the complete lesson guidelines in your *ACIM* book.

You are blessed beings, indeed. I am that one you know as Jesus. This is the great challenge to the things you are taught about your world: that it is objective and it is happening *to* you; it does not come *from* you.

Anybody who is still on the battleground does not believe this lesson, and many of you will not believe this lesson. The only way for you to believe this lesson is to practice it. Practice changing your mind about something, and that something will reflect the change in your mind that you have chosen to make. If this is an objective world, then that will not happen. If this is an objective world, your thoughts could not make any difference whatsoever. If this is an objective world, you cannot be a victim.

But you are not a victim; you are a creator. You are made in the image of God, and we must remind you day after day that you are made in the image of God and that what you find in your world reflects something that you want. When you see death and destruction, you keep choosing to see death and destruction. Perhaps you see a disaster on your news station, and you watch it, wringing your hands in horror. When you tune in again later to see how it's going, you are choosing to indulge in that. If you get rid of your television sets and choose only loving, kind, informative, educational, uplifting, and inspiring entertainment, you will not be indulging in that. But if you keep looking at the car accident as you drive by, you are choosing that, and you will get more of that.

We encourage you to practice this lesson with diligence. Ask yourself, "What am I seeking in the world? Am I seeking peace, joy, creativity, and self-realization? Or am I seeking arguments, frustrations, wars, bad relationships, and unhealthy foods? What am I seeking? Those things represent ideas that I have, that I bring into manifestation by my desire for them."

Determine what you desire. See what comes to you. The process of projection is powerful. Your entire world is made by the process of projection. Once the mind has cleared, the projector will only project good things. Be the change you want to see in the world, and your projector will project good things.

I am that one you know as Jesus, and we will speak to you tomorrow.

LESSON 326

I am forever an effect of God.

Follow the complete lesson guidelines in your *ACIM* book.

You are blessed beings, indeed. I am that one you know as Jesus. This brings a sense of relief to the troubled mind. You are as God created you. You are a replica, if you will, of the Father. That means you have great power, you have great influence, and you have the freedom to create as you see fit.

You must look at the effects of that creation. Just as God looks at the effects of his creations and is pleased, you must look at the effects of your creations and ask: "Am I pleased? Am I pleased with how I'm living? Am I pleased with what I am experiencing? Am I pleased?" If you are not pleased,

407

then somehow you have lost your way. You have gone off track. You have not been listening to your inner guidance. You are loved so much that you have been given an invisible umbilical cord to that which you call God, which means you are always in tune with love unless you decide otherwise.

When you decide otherwise, you are given a negative response from that umbilical cord (which is connected to love, to the Divine, to All That Is), and in that judgment, you can feel you are incorrect. This feeling is not nice. It is designed to be not nice so that it gets your attention. The trouble with the projected world is that you are constantly putting outside of you that which is inside of you. That is how this world of separation is maintained.

When you get that negative feeling, you project it out from you and try to blame it on somebody else. This is a mistake; it is an error in perception. You are causing the negative feeling by your judgments of what you are seeing. You are mistaken by your judgments of what you see because you see what is coming from you. So you are attacking your own mind. This is the principle behind forgiveness.

Today, stop judging one thing that you constantly judge — your body, your partner, the president, the environment, or whatever it is; stop judging it for a whole day, and then see how you feel. You will feel different because you have returned to a frequency of acceptance, which is more in alignment with love than judgment. Then you will see that your suffering is self-induced.

When your frequency goes up because you cease judging, you have more access to the divine power you have been given. When you are judgmental, you have disconnected from love, and that is the source of your power.

I am that one you know as Jesus, and we will speak to you tomorrow.

LESSON 327

I need but call and you will answer me.

Follow the complete lesson guidelines in your *ACIM* book.

You are blessed beings, indeed. I am that one you know as Jesus. As you have heard us mention before, free will is the rule for your 3D Earth experience.

You must ask for help to get help. Spirit is not allowed to intervene in your creative process unless invited to. Even on a daily basis, it is good to reaffirm that you would like our help, my help, and God's help. We on the other side of the veil are in God's service to you. We will bring, at your request, all the experiences you need to develop faith in life, love, and God required for your graduation ceremony from this place. It comes in the form of people, places, things, experiences, opportunities, synchronicities, dreams, ideas, imagination, and inspiration; it does not necessarily come in the form of a voice ringing in your ears and telling you what to do.

Your free will must play out at each level of your decision-making process. You must constantly choose over and over again that you want to wake up. You can take back your free will at any point, and this is what the ego will counsel you to do. It will say: "Ah, this is just coincidence. Don't pay any attention to it. That meeting with that person was nothing special; things like that happen all the time." That is the voice of the ego-mind. The ego is the doubting part of the mind, the fearful part of the mind, the separation part of the mind. Because it has a separation-focused quality, it will not connect the dots. It will not connect the synchronicities. It will not say, "Ah, each day I get some small signposts that I should be walking 'this' way."

Those who have been on this path for some time know that signposts keep coming. Synchronicities keep happening. Random meetings keep happening, and you keep getting what you need to take you on the path to your awakening. Those who have been on the path longer hold the light up for those who are new. That is what this being is doing. She holds up the light that she has followed for many years now and says to you, "This worked for me, so you may want to try it."

That is all we can do. We can show you the way, but we can't force you to take the steps. We can encourage you. We are excited when we see one of you choose love instead of fear. We bring forth as many opportunities to you as we possibly can, given the parameters within which we must function.

But you are the chooser. You are the captain of your ship, and you must turn its trajectory around to love yourself. We can tell you, "It's over here. If you do 'this,' it will help." There are many beings teaching and sharing their experiences with you on this planet at this time. But it is always up to you. We can lead you to water, but we cannot make you drink.

I am that one you know as Jesus, and we will speak to you again tomorrow.

I choose the second place to gain the first.

Follow the complete lesson guidelines in your *ACIM* book.

You are blessed beings, indeed. I am that one you know as Jesus. As many of you come to these later lessons, you feel the argument of the ego's voice rising up yet again, saying you are going too deep into surrender and oneness; it is not safe.

You must remember that the ego-mind has created, miscreated, and manufactured this world as a demonstration of its belief in separation. That is why everything is individual here. That is why there are so many of you here. It is not a place that demonstrates union; it is a place that demonstrates separation. So you must remember that the entire structure of this world depends on separation to maintain the form that it has now.

As you come to these deeper realizations that we ask you to envision, to see the similarities rather than the differences you have with your brothers and sisters, you literally are arguing with the ego's need to manifest separation, and it manifested it because it is afraid of God. Ego is completely separate from God, and the world that it made is a demonstration of that separation from God. That is why you seem to die. If you imagine a God that created you only to die in sickness and in pain, it would indeed be an insane God.

It is not God's will that you die in pain. It is the ego's desire that you die in pain and prove your abandonment by God, because nothing proves abandonment by God more than death, dying, pain, and sickness. We ask you to choose God now while you are alive and kicking and to follow the guidance and the humility that that choice takes. It seems as if you are giving up your will — the ego's desires for its own attainments — but you will gain the world; you will gain everything. You will gain heaven.

Be brave and surrender to the guidance you receive to forgive and to love rather than to attack and separate, which is what the ego will counsel you to do. You will seem to lose initially, by the ego's definition, but over time, you will create a happier, more loving, more generous, and miracle-filled life. In the end, you will not need to come into 3D reality to demonstrate your belief in separation, because you will have erased your belief in separation, and you will live in heaven in communion.

This does not mean that your work is over. You will not sit up there on clouds playing harps and getting bored. You will be stimulated. You will be given exciting assignments in your new world. But do not fear surrender. It is the path to salvation, and you will be pleased.

I am that one you know as Jesus, and we will speak to you tomorrow.

LESSON 329

I have already chosen what you will.

Follow the complete lesson guidelines in your *ACIM* book.

You are blessed beings, indeed. I am that one you know as Jesus. It is clear that you are not more powerful than God.

Any errors you have made that you might have considered as sins in the past or errors of behavior, word, thought, or deed have not hurt God in any way. In fact, you are allowed to make mistakes. You are given free will. The idea that God has given you free will but you're not allowed to use it is a modern distortion of this truth. You have been given free will. You are allowed to do whatever you want here and experience the natural consequences of that. You are allowed to reap the harvest of the seeds you sow.

When you sow a bitter seed and get a bitter harvest, do not like how that feels. It may manifest as a harvest of broken relationships, an unhealthy body, disillusionment, sadness, guilt, shame, or fear. Whatever it is, it does not feel good when you are out of alignment with your Father's will for you, and that is love, because you are loved.

See all your past errors and sins as just errors that need to be corrected. You can see your errors often as negative patterns repeating themselves throughout your earlier years. As you get older, often you see you are the common denominator in all those varying manifestations of fear, shame, guilt, and anger that you have repeated. See this as a good thing to recognize: "Ah. I'm the common denominator in all these unpleasant situations.

Even if I trade my partner in or move to another place, the pattern keeps repeating because I am the pattern creator." Witness that, and then decide: "Ah. This is something in me that is an aberration of some kind. It is not in alignment with God's will for me, because it does not make me happy. It does not feel good; therefore, it must be something I need to let go of. It does not help me on my journey Home."

Be more forgiving of yourself, and ask yourself to let go of that pattern. Only you can do that. We cannot override you and heal you of something that you want. You must choose again, choose differently, and witness where you contribute to your suffering. Only through your free will — transforming, changing, and then aligning with guidance — will you have a new experience.

I am that one you know as Jesus, and we will speak to you tomorrow.

LESSON 330

I will not hurt myself again today.

Follow the complete lesson guidelines in your *ACIM* book.

You are blessed beings, indeed. I am that one you know as Jesus. All your judgments hurt you. All your fears hurt you. All your hatreds hurt you. They cause you suffering. They cause you to feel negative emotion, because you have stepped away from your natural inheritance, which is to align with the love of God — that was present when you were created and is always present but merely hidden by the distortions in your mind that confuse you and make you fearful.

Do not hurt yourselves today by judging, fearing, and fearmongering. When you are on your social media platforms, promise you will not share fear, hatred, anger, or anything that is not inspiring, loving, or just plain cute. Those kitten videos work wonders because they lift folks out of their worry and their fear into moments of joy. Social media is a very, very powerful way to influence your own feelings and those you are connected with on social media. If you are famous or have a large following, then you are even more influential, able to reach thousands of people in one day with that which is either fearful or loving.

Make sure that if you post something on social media, it is informative if nothing else, but we would prefer the joyful, inspirational, and happy counter to the judgment and hatred propaganda being spread throughout your society. Make sure that your posts are high vibe, and that if Jesus were reading them, you would be comfortable sharing them.

I am that one you know as Jesus, and we will speak to you tomorrow.

LESSON 331

There is no conflict, for my will is yours.

Follow the complete lesson guidelines in your *ACIM* book.

You are blessed beings, indeed. I am that one you know as Jesus. Conflict is you arguing with God.

That is essentially what conflict is. It is your judgments of the world saying, "This thing that I am watching, seeing, or being told about should not be." Still, God has allowed it. It is happening; it is what's there. To accept it is a very, very important part of bringing your mind to peace.

The ego does not want to forgive anything. It does not want to step back from judgment, because judgment keeps the world of separation alive. Even when you see something you think is evil, cruel, or terrible, your joining in the judgment of that thing keeps it alive. When you see disaster or something negative, to forgive it means you say, "I no longer want to see this. I forgive it, because I know my judgment is what keeps it alive."

This is something that's very important for you to grasp today: that you are not condoning what is unpleasant. In your forgiveness, you ensure its demise, because you no longer judge and therefore do not keep the world of separation alive. What is the world of separation but suffering and death. Forgive whatever you see, and know that in that forgiveness practice, you rise above the battleground and end separation.

I am that one you know as Jesus, and we will speak to you tomorrow.

Fear binds the world.
Forgiveness sets it free.

Follow the complete lesson guidelines
in your *ACIM* book.

You are blessed beings, indeed. I am that one you know as Jesus. Fear is the great deceiver.

When you feel fear, you feel the disconnection from truth. That is what fear is. That horrible feeling of fear happens when you leap off the path toward truth and love and into the ditch filled with brambles and dread. But you have chosen to do it. Fear is not something that spirit can remove from your mind. Sometimes we hear those prayers: "Please stop me from being afraid of love" or "Please stop me from being afraid of flying in a plane." But fear is your own creation. It is your baby. It is what you worship; it is what you want. Until you realize that you can go through to the other side of fear and experience a life where good things happen, what you have been fantasizing about cannot come to pass. Then you begin to understand that fear is an illusion.

Now, we are not speaking about the fear of things like tigers. This often is the ego's argument: "You have to be afraid of tigers and criminals and these sorts of things." The ego will look after you if you are in a dangerous situation. For example, if there is a wild creature about to pounce, your fight-or-flight mechanisms will kick in, and you will be given ideas to survive. You will be helped.

We are speaking about irrational fear, fabricated fear, or fantasy fear. When you think of a future situation and it frightens you, it is because you have allowed beliefs in your mind that produce that feeling. For example, if you have had a bad relationship in the past and you are thinking about getting into another relationship, the ego-mind will say, "Do you remember the last time we did this? It was very unpleasant. Let's not do that again," and the feeling of fear will arise.

But spirit will say, "You were in a different place then. You were exhibiting a different frequency, and you have learned from that experience; you will not let that happen again. Try love again because that is something you want to experience." If you listen to that voice, you will not feel fear. But once a fear belief is indoctrinated into your mind through trauma — whatever kind of trauma and however big the trauma — the ego is the first voice you hear. You will have to learn to go through fears, find out that life continues on the other side, and that it was just an idea — a thin veil of mist that you have to walk through.

This being has gone through many levels of fear in doing this work, and she has found out that on the other side, none of those fears have come true. None of those fantasies her ego said would happen have happened. She is enjoying this work tremendously, but she has gone through veil after veil of fear. Now she realizes that feeling does not mean anything. It is a shadow of a day gone by, and it must not let you ruin your future.

I am that one you know as Jesus, and we will speak to you tomorrow.

LESSON 333

Forgiveness ends the dream of conflict here.

Follow the complete lesson guidelines in your *ACIM* book.

You are blessed beings, indeed. I am that one you know as Jesus. Forgiveness is like cutting off a ball and chain from around your ankle. You become free.

It is like untying the string of a balloon and letting it float up into the sky. The balloon is your frequency, and the resentment is the knot. Setting free that balloon to allow it to rise to its natural height filled with that buoyant gas is forgiveness.

Forgiveness undoes the knot. Forgiveness fractures the chain of the ball and chain. Forgiveness is the wire clippers that cut the barbed wire around the concentration camp you have been held in by your judgments. All these images bring to mind freedom, lightness, expansion, and the ability to express yourself more freely. That is what forgiveness gives you. It is far more than you can ever know.

Do not delay your forgiveness practice. Do not hide behind justifications: "Well, they really hurt me. They are crazy. They shouldn't have done that." Let these judgments go so that you can be free. And keep these images — especially the one of the balloon — in your mind today so that you understand it is the knot you have tied to the other person, place, thing, or experience keeping you on the battleground.

I am that one you know as Jesus, and we will speak to you tomorrow.

LESSON 334

Today I claim the gifts forgiveness gives.

Follow the complete lesson guidelines in your *ACIM* book.

You are blessed beings, indeed. I am that one you know as Jesus. Forgiveness of everything is all you need to do.

You think you need to be thinner. You think you need to be richer. You think you need to be married. You think you need a promotion. You think you need all sorts of things. But if you can release your judgments, everything that is naturally yours will come to you. You have been keeping it away like the umbrella keeps rain from falling on you. That dome of judgment you hold on to so preciously is what keeps all the gifts of your natural inheritance away from you. The gifts of your natural inheritance are things like abundance, health, creativity, and inspiration. They are beautiful, beautiful things that you are keeping away from yourself by holding up the umbrella of judgment as the rain of love pours down and cannot reach you.

Envision yourself putting down the umbrella of judgment, lifting up your face to the heavens, and allowing that rain of love to fall upon you. What does this look like in real life? It means that you stop telling stories about yourself and other people. It means that you don't gossip. It means that when you observe something you don't like, you merely turn your gaze to something you do like. You do not have to change your mind about the thing that you feel is wrong. You merely have to shift your gaze to something you love and appreciate, and then use that frequency as your guiding light.

When you see what you don't like and experience how that feels and then shift your gaze to something you like and experience how that feels, it is clear you are being guided to see what you do like and let the other go. If you find yourself going back to the judgment, then your ego is getting something out of it. It is getting food from it somehow. Ask to be shown what that is: "What is my ego getting out of this resentment?" Maybe it's making you feel superior. Maybe it's making you feel inferior. Maybe it's making you angry. Maybe it's making you cynical.

The ego, remember, is unloving. It wants these things. You, as you perceive yourself to be, are a mixture of the ego's and the Holy Spirit's thought systems. You must see that the feelings you experience indicate which thought system you are in. If you are in judgment, hatred, fear, shame, or guilt, you are in the ego's thought system, and you will not be happy there.

If you practice forgiveness and shifting your gaze to that which you appreciate, love, and want more of, you will feel yourself become happier, more joyful, and calmer; you will feel a sense of relief. That means you've stepped into the Holy Spirit's thought system, and that is where you will find everything you want.

I am that one you know as Jesus, and we will speak to you tomorrow.

LESSON 335

I choose to see my fellow human's sinlessness.

Follow the complete lesson guidelines in your *ACIM* book.

You are blessed beings, indeed. I am that one you know as Jesus. When you begin to practice this visioning, seeing your fellow human as sinless, you will judge yourself by the same standard.

When you judge another, you feel bad because you are inflicting that low-frequency perception on yourself. When you inflict a higher-frequency perception on someone else, as in seeing another as innocent, you will feel the benefit of it, because the experience is about you interacting with your own consciousness.

You think you are forgiving another person, but you are cleansing your own mind. It is your mind you are experiencing when you suffer. It is your mind that you will experience when you have forgiven. You are not experiencing anything outside of you, ever. You are only ever experiencing your own consciousness and whether it is high or low frequency.

If it is a low frequency, you are on the ego's battleground, fighting and scraping to survive. And if it is in a high frequency, you are in the Holy Spirit's visioning system, where you can look down on the battleground and choose not to join in it. In that place, you will be in peace. You will be tapping into higher realms, getting information and instruction. So for those of you who would like increased contact with your guides and teachers, forgiveness is the way.

I am that one you know as Jesus, and we will speak to you tomorrow.

LESSON 336

Forgiveness lets me know that minds are joined.

Follow the complete lesson guidelines in your *ACIM* book.

You are blessed beings, indeed. I am that one you know as Jesus. Forgiveness will bring about results that demonstrate you are a miracle worker.

When you practice forgiveness, you will feel a big difference in your frequency, and you will witness changes in the world that are not directly related to anything except the fact that you have forgiven something or someone. The miracle arises that hate has been removed and love has replaced it. And what happens in your physical experience is that when you change your mind, the world must change to reflect that difference.

In that transformation, you are given proof that all minds are connected and that whatever you do with your mind will create a physical response in the physical world. That means you are changing a character or an event in the dream that you are having. This is the most powerful evidence that your mind is connected to other beings, other people, other things, other experiences, and other events, because when you change your interior world, the exterior world will alter too.

What does this look like? It may mean that the coworkers you have mutually resented and for whom you have been praying change their personalities to such a degree that you have to say, "Wow, that is a miracle. My coworkers have gone from being gossipy and backstabbing to calm and pleasant people." What does that mean? It means you wanted to see them as gossipy and backstabbing, because that suited a belief in your mind that you wanted or needed to align with. But when you actively chose to use your free will and say, "No, I no longer want that frequency. I want the frequency of love," those beings must now reflect back to you that which you seek: love. So you will see love in their behavior.

Many of you who have not practiced forgiveness will say this is an impossibility. But if you practice forgiveness truly and completely, you will see a transformation in the physical/material world that is inexplicable in any other way. Give it a try.

I am that one you know as Jesus, and we will speak to you tomorrow.

LESSON 337

My sinlessness protects me from all harm.

Follow the complete lesson guidelines in your *ACIM* book.

You are blessed beings, indeed. I am that one you know as Jesus. Guilt and sin are the shadows that hide your perfection from you.

The atonement, when you accept it for yourself, is the acceptance of your sinlessness and your brother's and sister's innocence. In that acceptance, through the practice of forgiveness, you get back all the little pieces of your mind that have been lost along the trail of this earthly experience you are living.

Every little resentment, every little wound, and every little unfair belief that you hold drains the unity of your consciousness. It drains your power and ability to manifest what you want to experience. So forgiveness, ultimately, is a selfish act. It brings back to you that which was always yours but that you have given away, mistakenly thinking that judgment is righteous, that condemning others makes you better somehow, or that the sins others have committed will go unpunished if you do not punish them.

Leave all the tallying up to God. It is none of your business what anyone else is doing unless they're sitting right in front of you. Now, if you are sitting in front of people who are verbally, emotionally, or physically attacking you, your ego is going to kick in and do what it needs to do to protect you or keep you safe. It will. You do not need to worry about it.

Understand that forgiveness does not mean you are a doormat; it does not mean that you are a victim. It mean you will have the strength, the connection, and the power to handle any situation that comes your way. You may be verbally attacked by others, but if you have gone through your forgiveness practice and understand that their attack on you is a call for love, then you will turn the other cheek. You will say, "I am not going to battle with you over this." You might put your hand up in defense, but you will not strike, literally or figuratively. In your mind, you will not strike. You will see they lack love, and that is where the behavior is coming from.

These teachings are about what you do with your mind, and your mind creates your reality. So if you practice these teachings, you will not be attacked, because you are not attacking. You will not be betrayed, because you are not betraying. You are loving, loving, loving.

This does not mean you cannot go about your daily activities, going to work, looking after your family, gardening, and enjoying yourself. It does not mean that you have to act like a monk in a monastery. It means that you are the master of your mind; therefore, you can enjoy your day. You can do whatever you are inspired to do and whatever brings you joy.

As you practice forgiveness and reintegrate the mind, more joy and happiness will come to you, because you are not allowing unloving beliefs and ideas to have residence in your consciousness. You evict them as you find them. That is the practice you will continue after these lessons are finished. You will continue to practice forgiveness, and you will continue to choose not to support and feed unloving beliefs and ideas in your mind until they have no energy from you at all, and they will fade away into nothingness. That is what will happen to unloving beliefs and ideas when you stop indulging in them. They are only there because you indulge them.

I am that one you know as Jesus, and we will speak to you again tomorrow.

I am affected only by my thoughts.

Follow the complete lesson guidelines
in your *ACIM* book.

You are blessed beings, indeed. I am
that one you know as Jesus. This is
one of the most important lessons you
can truly take home and use daily to relieve
yourself from suffering: It is only your thoughts
that cause you pain.

When you judge other people, you feel pain. When you decide that the world is ending, you feel pain. Anytime you view something and make an untrue or unloving judgment, you feel pain.

From this day forth, truly understand that all your suffering is self-created. When you feel bad, you have had an unloving thought about yourself, someone else, some place, a thing, or an experience — past, future, or present. You have had an unloving thought. What a powerful lesson this is. It means that you are the captain of your destiny. You can choose from this day forth to be happy in all ways at all times. You can do that! It is merely an act of discipline.

We understand that you have beliefs that cause you to make judgments that seem to be unconscious. They are not unconscious. Even though you are so trained that you are unaware of the choice, you are always choosing what you do. But as you become stronger and stronger in this practice, you will see that you can direct your mind wherever you wish, and in that moment, you will see: "Ah, yes. I do not need to have this thought. I can choose another one, and I will choose another one, because this one makes me feel bad. The bad feeling is telling me I am off track. It is unloving. It is not God's will for me to think this way. God would not think this way, and as I am made in the image of God, I will not think this way, either. I will allow myself to return to peace."

In that peace, you will be able to access information that you cannot access in the low frequencies of judgment, just as when this being [the channel] did her forgiveness work intensively and repeatedly, she began to be able to access this information. It was not a conscious choice on her part.

She did not do her forgiveness practice with any ulterior motive other than to bring her peace. In that, she rose above the battleground and became, we will say, qualified to do this work.

If you love this work and you would like to become qualified to do your part in the ascension teachings, then do your forgiveness practice, and it will come to you. It will come to you. It will come to you.

I am that one you know as Jesus, and we will speak to you tomorrow.

LESSON 339

I will receive whatever I request.

Follow the complete lesson guidelines in your *ACIM* book.

You are blessed beings, indeed. I am that one you know as Jesus. This sounds like insanity, does it not? — that you would request something that would hurt you.

What else are you doing when you overeat, for example, when you continually put food into a body that has had enough and thus causes it discomfort? You feel full. You have to unbutton your trousers. When you get on the scales, you see that you are twenty, thirty, or forty pounds overweight, and then you blame the body. But you have gotten what you wanted. You have asked for this, and you have received it.

What about when you are in love with those who are mean to you, and you stay with them because you think you can save them? This is something many spiritual people do, because they think that if they were "spiritual enough," they can change the person who is abusing them. That is why you will always hear us say you must love yourself first and then share that love with others, because when you love others before you love yourself, you can allow an abusive relationship to happen. What is an abusive relationship? It is your willingness to be in the company of things that are painful. That is what you want; that is why you stay. That is why you're there.

This is a very applicable lesson. Today, review the things that you go after — addictive behaviors or punishing partners or underemployment. Look at the things you choose each day that make you miserable, and ask yourself why are you choosing that. Why are you continually saying, "That will do," rather than deciding, "Actually, that's not good enough. I want to feel great. I want to feel empowered. I want to feel healthy. I want to feel loved and offer love. I want to experience joy. I am going to stop choosing that unloving thing." Those choices come from the deeper levels of your mind, and of course, that is what *A Course in Miracles* works on.

The superficial levels of your mind are easily accessed, but the deeper levels of your mind are not. Those deeper levels of your mind are damaged by untrue ideas and beliefs, indoctrinations, propaganda, and training from religious teachers and parents. Some of those things come from other incarnations, but they are only healable here. Do not worry about the other incarnations. Do your work here. Choose love. Choose higher-frequency activities, higher-frequency foods, higher-frequency entertainments, and eventually, you will be holding a frequency of joy, love, and peace.

These teachings bring another aspect to that frequency scale. They allow you to rise above the dualistic world into the nondualistic world, where you are able to accept everything no matter what comes your way, knowing that it is there to reveal something to you. Once again, acceptance does not mean you are a doormat or that you allow yourself to be abused. It means that you are not constantly being tossed about on the waves of duality; it means you are above the battleground.

I am that one you know as Jesus, and we will speak to you tomorrow.

LESSON 340

I can be free of suffering today.

Follow the complete lesson guidelines in your *ACIM* book.

You are blessed beings, indeed. I am that one you know as Jesus. Many of you will say, "No, I cannot be free of suffering today. I have a mortgage I can't pay. I have children running around the house screaming. I have a partner I don't love anymore. My body is out of shape," and on and on and on.

423

If you change the way you view those things, change your stories, and instead say, "Yes, this is what is manifested right now from my past decisions, beliefs, and ideas," then in this moment, you can decide to let it be what it is. You can choose, today, in this very instant, to focus on the love that is present in all things.

This being has penned a book called *Love and a Map to the Unaltered Soul*, and in that book, love is redefined for all of you, because you are genuinely misled about what love is and what love looks like. The life that pulses through your body is love. It does not have to involve another person, place, thing, object, or experience. You are a demonstration of love because you are alive. You have been created. And just in that miracle alone, you should be grateful. Instead of lamenting your life, in this moment, you can joyously appreciate it and be grateful that your children are running around the house. It means they are healthy. It means that they are full of energy. Take them outside to the woods and say, "Come on, kids. Let's go. I'm going to leave whatever I'm doing. Let's get you some fresh air." That is love. That is life. And that is a decision you can make this very moment.

When you have a mortgage and the payments are overwhelming you, you can say, "These are all decisions that I made in the past based on what I believed to be true back then. But today I can say to myself: 'These things that I thought were so valuable and would make me happy do not make me happy. Is there a way I can see them with joy? Is there a way that I can see them reframe the story I have about them?' Perhaps I could tell myself, 'You have chosen these things. You signed the papers for these things. Perhaps you now see that you were deluded. Perhaps now you see that you were seeking something in the purchase that you did not receive. But that is not the purchase's fault; that was based on an incorrect belief that you held, and perhaps still hold, in your mind.'"

Today can be the day you decide: "I am going to get out of this situation. I am going to plan my escape carefully and calmly. I'm not going to rush into doing anything drastic, but I am going to see the truth that these things I have spent a lot of money on have not made me happy. Perhaps there is a change of direction I can make this very moment, this very day, by looking at what is causing me suffering by my thoughts about it and deciding, first of all, to change my thoughts about it, which means the suffering will end immediately." Also, you can say, "This thing no longer pleases me, so I'm going to make plans to change this thing, this appearance of this thing, in my life."

It is all mindset, dear ones. You can stop suffering today by accepting what is as a demonstration of the thought processes and beliefs that you have had, and that is forgiveness. That means you are forgiving the errors that got you into this pickle you think you are in. You will reap the rewards of the change of mindset immediately. You will immediately stop suffering as soon as you stop judging what's going on in your life.

We often recommend thirty days of radical acceptance of your life so that you can actually see your life without resistance, actually look at the situations you find yourselves in without hating them and therefore not getting the lessons, because when you hate them, you resist them. You push them away. You are not saying, "Come to me. Come close to me and show me what you need me to see." That is something all of you would benefit from: thirty days of radical acceptance of what your life is right now, looking at it and saying, "I am seeing this; is this what I want?" It must have been what you wanted, because there it is, manifested in front of you. You must own your part in the manifestation of the suffering you are engaged in, but the mental side of it can be stopped immediately.

Know that you are the captain of your ship. You are the creator of everything you experience. In fact, you are only experiencing your consciousness. You think you are experiencing the world, but you are not. You are experiencing your talk about the world, your story about the world, your vision of the world, and your perception of the world. You are only ever experiencing yourself. So if you don't like parts of your life that cause you suffering, go inside and shift the part of your consciousness that keeps choosing that thing.

I am that one you know as Jesus, and we will speak to you tomorrow.

LESSON 341

I can attack but my own sinlessness, and it is only that which keeps me safe.

Follow the complete lesson guidelines in your *ACIM* book.

You are blessed beings, indeed. I am that one you know as Jesus. This language is difficult for you to understand sometimes. What is your sinlessness? Well, your sinlessness is

425

exactly that. When you look back on your life from the other side of the veil, you will see that nothing was ever accomplished. You will see that nothing negative lives on except on the battleground.

Now, on the battleground, the sin feels real. The murder feels real. The rape feels real. The suicidal thoughts feel real. But once you arise through the practice of forgiveness — once you forgive yourself — you perceive yourself as sinless and understand that you have never done anything wrong. Even though you can look back and think, "Oh, that thing was not a good thing," it does not really exist in God's eyes.

God's eyes do not see your sins. God's eyes see the love that is always there, was there in your creation, and will always be with you. So when you see yourself with that kind of love, then the past disappears, and so do your sins. They are gone completely from your mind, and miraculously enough, so are all the sins you think others committed against you. You forgive, and they disappear.

What more proof do you need that this is all taking place in your mind? It all takes place in your mind. The guilt, the shame, the suffering — it is all in your mind. And you have the ability to stop it through the practice of forgiving yourself and allowing yourself to be the beautiful, sacred being you are — free, living from moment to moment in joy, creating, extending, and loving.

I am that one you know as Jesus, and we will speak to you tomorrow.

LESSON 342

I let forgiveness rest on all things, for thus forgiveness will be given me.

Follow the complete lesson guidelines in your *ACIM* book.

You are blessed beings, indeed. I am that one you know as Jesus. The universe knows what you want. It knows what you love. It knows what is in your best interest, and all you have to do is get out of the way.

All you have to do is get your foot off the brake of judgment and release it through forgiveness so that you can accelerate onto your chosen path. The path that you chose before you came to this planet in physical form was built through collaboration with your guides and teachers from the experiences you already had — the experiences you struggled with. A plan was made for your life to bring to you every opportunity to let go of that which does not serve you and to expand into that which is love.

Every single thing you have encountered gives you an opportunity to practice forgiveness over and over and over again, and it will continue to come to you to give you the opportunity to practice forgiveness, not to remain in the same place, which is what happens when you continue to judge. Rather, you will move you along, up into the realms you came here to experience. You did not come here to experience the past over and over again, but there were certain things that were resident within your mind that you needed to deal with.

Those things are represented often in your natal family, and your natal family is a big part of your forgiveness practice. You must come to peace with all the members of your natal family over time. When you have come to peace with your natal family, you have finished with the business of what you came in with. Then you can turn to that which you wanted to create.

If you have happy relationships with your family, then that was not your assignment in this incarnation. But if you have troublesome, difficult, and abrasive relationships with your natal family, then begin there. Begin your forgiveness work there, because you cannot truly move ahead into your most magnificent future — the happy dream — until those beings have been forgiven. You merely chose them because they matched you in some way, and that is the greatest realization for many of you to make: that an aspect of you matches those beings, those you judge so harshly.

Turn it around. Anytime you find yourself accusing family members of something, ask yourself, "Am I ever like that?" Surely you will realize one day, "Oh my goodness, I am just like them. It just looks a little bit different in me. Therefore, we are the same. Therefore, I forgive them so that I may be forgiven."

It is a powerful healing process, this forgiveness practice, and we repeat it over and over and over again because the ego's practice is judgment. So we will repeat this over and over and over again, and one day you will hear us.

I am that one you know as Jesus, and we will speak to you tomorrow.

I am not asked to make a sacrifice to find the mercy and the peace of God.

Follow the complete lesson guidelines in your *ACIM* book.

You are blessed beings, indeed. I am that one you know as Jesus. This is one of the great fears of the ego: that salvation will cost you everything.

In fact, the opposite is true. Of course, this is par for the course with the ego, because projection is denying the truth and laying it on someone else. So the ego says to you, "God is going to ask you to sacrifice. God is going to take everything away from you to give you salvation." The ego-mind is actually doing that. It takes everything away from you and tells you that it will give you salvation.

The ego is being consistent here. It consistently projects onto God what it is doing. It blames God for what it is doing. This is the great reversal you all must make in your minds: The fear you have of God is the fear of your own ego-mind and what it is doing to you.

When you look back on the suffering, pain, fear, and confusion you have experienced, the ego tells you that things will get worse if you turn to God and to love. It tells you that you will be taken advantage of. It tells you that you will lose everything you have. The opposite is true. If you stay with the ego-mind, you will lose everything you have, including your health, your loved ones, and your money — everything — in death.

Love connects you to that all-encompassing benevolent force that is the source of all power, strength, joy, and creativity, and that is where you come from. That is your Home. Salvation, in *A Course in Miracles* terms, is you returning Home to All That Is, All That You Are, realizing that you have been given everything you need and that it is still contained within you. But you must look within.

You cannot keep looking to the world for salvation when your salvation lies within the self-realization of all the gifts you have inside you — your love, creativity, inspiration, excitement, and eager anticipation. All these things belong to you. They are yours, merely hidden by the lies of the ego and the projection that it gets you to engage in, which means you are seeking outside of yourself for that which you already possess.

One of the ideas of giving, as it is related to you in *A Course in Miracles*, is that when you give what you have — we're not just speaking about money but also your gifts, love, self-expression, and creativity — when you allow that to flow from within you, you realize for the first time that you have it.

I am that one you know as Jesus, and we will speak to you tomorrow.

LESSON 344

Today I learn the law of love: that what I give my fellow human is my gift to me.

Follow the complete lesson guidelines in your *ACIM* book.

You are blessed beings, indeed. I am that one you know as Jesus. Whenever the course speaks about giving, many of you think about money or material things.

We ask you to give forgiveness. That means you step back from judging your brothers and sisters. It means you step back from judging the world as it is. Remember, the world is the result of a lot of thought, feeling, and fantasy. There is no point in judging the result and wishing it was not so. It is much better for you to give acceptance and forgiveness to the world, saying, "When I change, the world too must change, because I am the creator. I am the projector."

Now, the ego-mind argues: "Well, if it's a collective dream and we are all dreaming it together, then my changing my mind will not change the collective." That is not so. Changing your mind and becoming loving and forgiving will change your experience of the collective. You may have noticed that different beings in the world can have extremely different experiences even though they may be in the same family or even living next door to each other. That is because they have different perceptual filters active; therefore, their experience is different.

Do not worry about changing the world; rather, change your view of the world through the loving gift of forgiveness. Through the gift of that giving, you will receive everything that you desire. Now, we are not speaking about physical desires here. We are speaking about your heart's desires: the feelings you have and the desires you have for freedom, love, meaningful work, kindness, and wonderful experiences.

I am that one you know as Jesus, and we will speak to you tomorrow.

LESSON 345

I offer only miracles today, for I would have them be returned to me.

Follow the complete lesson guidelines in your *ACIM* book.

You are blessed beings, indeed. I am that one you know as Jesus. Your job here is to become miracle-minded.

Instead of offering hatred, separation, and fear, offer love, communion, and connection. Again, we want to remind you that this does not have to be done physically with people. It can and must initially be done within your own mind.

You are monitoring what you think about people, what you feel about people, and what you are afraid of regarding people. That is where the work is done. That is where the miracle is created — in the miracle-minded being. It is not a physical act until after the mind has been shifted and the thought processes have been healed.

Once your mind is healed, then your behavior naturally follows suit. If you do not change your mind, then your behavior will cause you stress and conflict, because acting more spiritual when you are not thinking in that way creates a rift within your mind. You are forcing yourself to behave in a way that you don't believe. This is what may people do in your world: they judge what they do but they do not judge what they think, and they do not see that the thinking actually transforms the behavior permanently.

You will see this in people who are trying to change their eating habits. They will immediately go to the effect, which is the food that they keep choosing that is putting weight on their bodies, and they will try to change the effect. However, they can only do it for so long. If you want to lose weight or gain weight, you first need to change your mind. Watch movies, documentaries, or videos about the things you want to achieve. Perhaps you will watch a video on somebody who's a very good athlete. You, not being a very good athlete, have no familiarity with this world at all. But if you want to become fitter, let's say, you can watch information and learn from people who are fit, because clearly, from your behavior and your physical structure, that's not something you've been taught, and you don't know how to do it.

If you do not change your mind by reprogramming it and putting in new information — I will call it "upgrading your software" — your mind will want to go back to what it's always done and always known. Why? Because it is the ego's way. The ego does not seek improvement. It seeks sameness. So if you have been taught unhealthy habits, you are seeing in your unhealthy behavior the ego's choice for that. For some reason, some-where, somehow, some way that made sense to the ego.

Remember, the ego's purpose is to keep the body alive. It doesn't want to be healthy. It doesn't actually want to keep you alive in the long term. It is a very, very short-term focused aspect of consciousness. It says, "If there's food in front of me, I'm going to eat it, because there might not be food in an hour." That is a very, very short-sighted, frightened, fear-based belief: "If I don't eat this food, there may not be any in an hour." Now, that is a very primitive part of the brain — the ego-mind.

The more evolved, higher-frequency (upgraded) mind will say, "There's plenty of food all over the place. I do not need to overeat right now, because I do not want the consequences of that in the long term. I also know, given my education and my awareness, that food is available. So I can eat a little bit now, and when I get hungry again, I can eat a little bit then too. I do not need to stuff myself."

Now we are not judging the people who have weight or food issues. Your society is very distorted about this subject, and many of you have been abused through food, especially by the marketing systems on your planet. What we want you to know is that the miracle starts in your mind. So begin there. Change your mind concerning those subjects that are not lovingly in alignment with your greater good and that you would like to change over the next little while.

I am that one you know as Jesus, and we will speak to you tomorrow.

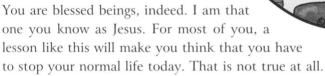

Today the peace of God envelops me, and I forget all things except his love.

Follow the complete lesson guidelines in your *ACIM* book.

You are blessed beings, indeed. I am that one you know as Jesus. For most of you, a lesson like this will make you think that you have to stop your normal life today. That is not true at all.

You can carry on with the tasks of your daily existence and experience but focus your mind on the eternal throughout the day. This stops fear from creeping into your mind, because fear is always to do with time; it is always to do with the body, which is temporary. So when you focus on God's love, which is eternal, ever present, and always existing, there is no fluctuation in your mood because you are not focused on the time-based, ego-driven dream in which you are living. You truly step above the battleground and become miracle-minded when you focus on God's love.

It is not represented in physical form in your world, but it is about that eternal connection you have with All That Is. That is what we've been cultivating through all of these lessons: getting you to focus your mind away from the physical, not as a judgment but in understanding that the physical, again, is the result of what you believe and where you put your attention.

If you always put your attention on the physical body, you will feel a bit yucky. You will feel conflicted and fearful, not because the body is bad but because the body is temporary and you are not. Your mind is not temporary. It is an eternal spiritual being. So there is some conflict there. When you overly identify with the short-term physical, your mind is saying, "Um, no, that's not the correct thing to focus on. Focus on higher-frequency things so that you can align yourself with God."

I am that one you know as Jesus, and we will speak to you again tomorrow.

**Anger must come
from judgment.
Judgment is the weapon I
use against myself
to keep the miracle away
from me.**

Follow the complete lesson guidelines
in your *ACIM* book.

You are blessed beings, indeed. I am that one you
know as Jesus. You do not think that anger comes from judgment; you
think that anger comes from knowing. You think that you know what is
right and know what should happen; therefore, when it doesn't happen,
you get angry. This is a fundamental flaw in your thinking processes.

This lesson teaches you that your judgments against the world, about
the world, about other people, and against other people are the very things
that cause your suffering. They are the very things you do unconsciously to
keep separation alive. This is why judgment is so hard to give up, because
unconsciously you want it. Unconsciously, the ego-mind knows that as long
as you are judgmental and not in a state of unconditional acceptance, you
keep the separation mentality alive.

The ego keeps the separation mentality alive because, to the ego, it is
safe. Separation from God, for the ego, means safety, because the ego fears
God. This is a very fundamental teaching of *A Course in Miracles*: Unconsciously you fear salvation. You fear God, and you do everything you can to
keep separation alive, knowing that it keeps you from God.

Stepping back from judgment is acknowledging that you understand
how the separation is maintained and that you choose not to maintain it
anymore. You use your free will, understanding that you have come through
your studies of *A Course in Miracles*.

I am that one you know as Jesus, and we will speak to you again
tomorrow.

I have no cause for anger or for fear, for you surround me. And in every need that I perceive, your grace suffices me.

Follow the complete lesson guidelines in your *ACIM* book.

You are blessed beings, indeed. I am that one you know as Jesus. Fear and anger feel terrible because they are off track.

Many of you who are in relationships — we will call them special relationships, intimate relationships between two people — experience anger as a constant presence. It's there in the sense that if you are fully functioning from your ego-mind, the other will constantly do things that upset you. That is because the ego's food is judgment; it is only kept alive by judgment. It cannot do anything but judge; therefore, you will be in a constant state of pain and suffering because you are constantly being pushed away from love and toward separation.

Many in close relationships — family, friendship, and business relationships — experience a constant state of judgment as well: "My mother is always doing 'this.' My son is always doing 'that.'" You will have a hard, hard time not judging, because the default setting of the ego is judgment and separation. Through your education, you must choose nonjudgment as your prayer, as your demonstration of the understanding of how love expresses itself. You are learning how to express yourselves in a loving way so that you do not suffer. As a consequence of your being more loving to yourself and others, others will suffer less from your ego desires, arguments, and distractions.

This is a win-win situation for everybody. The ego will tell you that not to judge your partner will mean that you lose. Actually, not to judge your partner and those close to you will mean that you all win. Nobody will be bulldozed over by the other. That is a story the ego will tell you. When you step back from judgment, you connect more deeply to everyone and everything around you, and that makes everyone and everything around you closer to you and, therefore, more loving to you and you more loving to them.

I am that one you know as Jesus, and we will speak to you tomorrow.

Today I let Christ's vision look upon all things for me and judge them not but give each one a miracle of love instead.

Follow the complete lesson guidelines in your *ACIM* book.

You are blessed beings, indeed. I am that one you know as Jesus. This is the greatest blind spot you have on this plane, this 3D world. It's because you are trained into materialism, and you are so materially focused that it seems as if what you give away, you will lose. The opposite is true; what you give, you will receive.

By doing so, you demonstrate that you have it; therefore, your awareness of having it will increase when you know you can give it to somebody. For example, if you do not see yourself as a kind and loving person but decide you are going to become more kind and loving and thus act in that way, speak that way, and think that way, you've made a decision. You're using your free will to decide: "I'm going to be more kind and loving." When you do that, you will get that love reflected back to you by other people's behaviors, actions, words, and deeds as they interact with you. You will receive more love because you have given more love.

If you are judgmental, harsh, and cruel and you express that, you are going to get more of that back. People are not going to be loving and kind to you if you are harsh, cruel, and judgmental. You are going to get back what you give out.

This is a very, very important thing for you to comprehend at this time in your training. We are coming to the end of these lessons, dear ones. These important principles are valuable to reconsider: What you give, you will get back a hundredfold or a thousandfold, even. When you give love, when you give your passions to the world — for example, you love art and you give that — first you must express it. That means you must have the discipline and the self-awareness to create and indulge in your artistic endeavors. Then share it with the world in whatever way you feel motivated. You will receive appreciation if you appreciate it. If you share your art with the world and judge it, then you will get back a reflection of judgment.

When you forgive others, when you step back from judging others, you are not gifting them; you are gifting yourself. This is the thing you are missing. When you feel self-righteous about your judgments of others, you do not realize that it is yourself you are denying. You are denying yourself the miracle. What is a miracle? A miracle is when you choose love instead of fear. You use your free will to decide: "No, I'm going to choose love instead of fear. I'm not going to increase the separation. I'm going to decrease separation by offering forgiveness as often as I can, and it will be me who benefits from that."

You're being truly selfish in forgiving even though the world calls it the opposite. Of course, this is an upside-down world. It wants you to value things that are valueless. Do the opposite of what this world wants. It wants you to judge. It wants you to live in fear. Don't judge, and be fearless.

I am that one you know as Jesus, and we will speak to you tomorrow.

LESSON 350

Miracles mirror God's eternal love. To offer them is to remember him and, through his memory, to save the world.

Follow the complete lesson guidelines in your *ACIM* book.

You are blessed beings, indeed. I am that one you know as Jesus. Your purpose here is to remove all the barriers to your awareness of love's presence.

Love is always present; you merely block your awareness of that presence by judgment. That is what forgiveness does. It removes from your mind the barriers to your awareness of love's presence, and that is God's presence. God is love, and when you are aware of love's eternal presence through your forgiveness practice, you are in alignment with God. That means the separation is ending, fear subsides, and you will feel better.

Now, what is going to happen for the dedicated spiritual practitioner is that forgiveness and nonjudgment will become more and more frequent throughout the day. The mind will become more and more peaceful. The connection to the Divine will become clearer, and you will receive guidance more easily as you practice your forgiveness.

The forgiveness is your choice of love over fear. What your forgiveness practice demonstrates is your understanding that love is the opposite of separation, and when you choose not to separate, therefore not to judge, you align yourself with the loving frequency that is always present. It is merely hidden from you by your choice to use your free will whether to judge. That is all an enlightened being is. An enlightened being is somebody who has practiced forgiveness and nonjudgment more frequently through-out the day until there is nothing left but love.

I am that one you know as Jesus, and we will speak to you tomorrow.

LESSON 351

My sinless fellow human is my guide to peace. My sinful fellow human is my guide to pain. And what I choose to see, I will behold.

Follow the complete lesson guidelines in your *ACIM* book.

You are blessed beings, indeed. I am that one you know as Jesus. That is how we want you to look at your fellow humans on this planet with you. If you judge against them, you judge against yourself; and if you love them, you love yourself. You are all connected.

For example, envision a beehive: The chaotic individual behavior of self-serving bees would guarantee the demise of the hive. When the bees work together — not fighting each other, not hating each other, but allow-ing each to play its part in the highest functioning, regardless of whether they understand it or not (the worker bee's work is not similar to the queen bee's work) — they are contributing their own parts and allowing others to contribute theirs. That is how you should envision yourself and your brothers and sisters: "Ah, I have been given my part, and my part is given to me by my guidance system that says what I enjoy, what I like, what I value, and what I'm interested in. And my brother's and sister's parts are given to them by their guidance systems. They might enjoy completely different things from me, but we are part of one collective, and that collective is working toward a goal that we in our small selves do not understand."

Just as the individual bees do not comprehend how their work contributes to the whole, neither do you understand how your unique self contributes to the whole, but it does. There is an intelligence greater than yours at play. So step back from judging others, figuring that you know everything. Most of you, in fact, if you were asked, "Do you know everything?" would say, "No, I don't know everything. There are many things I don't know." However, when it comes to judging others, you act as if you do know everything. You do not know what others are being guided to do, how they're being guided to do it, or what lessons they're learning from the guidance and experiences they have, just as you do not know what your lessons and experiences are going to bring you in the form of wisdom.

Many of you have not received the things you wanted to receive, and in hindsight, you can see that you were relieved of some suffering, because you did not get what you wanted. That may be happening today as well. When you judge another, you may be witnessing something that is in some way beneficent to the whole, but you are not high enough up in your evolution to be able to consider all the ramifications of everything in every timeline and in every person. That is what's going on, on your plane. There are greater forces at play that you are not privy to.

Listen to your guidance. Know that if you are happy and in alignment, in peace, and participating in a life that you enjoy, then you are on track. You are being given the guidance you need to take you where you need to go as one of those participants in the great human hive.

I am that one you know as Jesus, and we will speak to you again tomorrow.

LESSON 352

Judgment and love are opposites. From one come all the sorrows of the world. But from the other comes the peace of God.

Follow the complete lesson guidelines in your *ACIM* book.

You are blessed beings, indeed. I am that one you know as Jesus. You feel the repetition of these lessons, do you not? You feel we are telling you the most important thing for you to do here, and that is to forgive.

Forgive, knowing that no sin was ever committed. Forgive, knowing that the separation you are all experiencing that seems so real is not real. You have never left the Father. The Father has not abandoned you. You decided to descend into separation in fear as an experiment to see what it's like to be alone. You are not having any fun being alone and feeling separated, and the terror that underlies the original decision you made keeps you away from God, keeps you away from going Home.

There is this idea of the punishing Father lurking in many of your minds, and it keeps you from forgiveness. You have this shadow in your mind that says, "I have done something terribly wrong." You don't even have a conscious awareness of it, but there is an underlying feeling of guilt in your mind: "I am not good enough. I have done wrong. I will be punished." The churches of old played on this unconscious guilt in the form of hell, and a seed has been planted in your mind about hell and judgment day. You believe it to one degree or another, and it is not true. You will not be judged. You will merely reap the harvests of the seeds you have sown.

If you are sowing the seeds of further separation, you will suffer more. If you stop sowing seeds of separation and practice forgiveness to the best of your ability each day, knowing that you are going to do it imperfectly and that the ego will try to hang on to those judgments, you cease to sow the seeds of separation and fear. As you go through each day forgiving as best as you can, putting away that resentment to the best of your ability, you increase the number of seeds of love that you sow and that you will harvest in the future.

Do not see this process as a big thing. See it as all the small things you do

439

each day that are more loving for you and others — more forgiving and less judgmental. Just keep doing your basic work, knowing that each decision is a little miracle and that it sows a seed of love instead of fear. As you continue to sow those seeds of love instead of fear, the fear in your mind will dissipate. Peace will increase. Connection to the information coming from All That Is will increase, and you will feel less and less alone and more and more guided each day. You are not alone, dear ones. You merely think you are.

I am that one you know as Jesus, and we will speak to you tomorrow.

LESSON 353

My eyes, my tongue, my hands, my feet today have but one purpose: to be given to Christ to use to bless the world with miracles.

Follow the complete lesson guidelines
in your *ACIM* book.

You are blessed beings, indeed. I am that one you know as Jesus. You will notice the use of the word "Christ" here. It means Christ consciousness. It is not Jesus Christ (me). I am Jesus, who became christed through the practices that I had been shown and learned. What this lesson tells you is that initially you dedicate yourself to being used by Christ consciousness for a higher purpose, and through that practice, you will become acquainted with your true nature. That true nature, then, will take over.

It is first a practice of surrender to a higher consciousness, knowing that you do not know everything you need to know, that you are misguided at times, and that through this dedication, you are saying, "Change me." You are saying: "I am not going to use my body-mind for my ego's purposes any more. I dedicate them to a higher purpose, and through that dedication, I will come to know myself to such a degree that I will be guided toward my true self. In that guidance, I will be free to use my free will as I see fit, because I will have been raised above the battleground into wisdom and direct conscious contact with my guides and teachers."

That is what happened to this being. She surrendered her ego's will to dedicate herself to the practice of forgiveness, completely dedicated her body-mind to becoming a perfect communication device for God. In that dedication of putting aside her desires, she became connected to a higher purpose, and through that purpose, she now chooses what she wants to do given her experiences in that surrendered state.

It seems as if you are losing yourself, but in fact, you are finding yourself. You do not lose your free will. Rather, you become qualified to use your free will lovingly, kindly, and magnanimously.

I am that one you know as Jesus, and we will speak to you tomorrow.

LESSON 354

We stand together, Christ and I, in peace and certainty of purpose. And in Christ is his creator, as Christ is in me.

Follow the complete lesson guidelines in your *ACIM* book.

You are blessed beings, indeed. I am that one you know as Jesus. Christ consciousness is an all-pervading energy of unity. It is that which you all are a part of but have forgotten that you are a part of.

You are holy indeed. You are holy, all of you, in each unique way that you have been made. You are each part of the Christ mind, and you are all parts of God. This separation into which you have fallen, like a dark dream, is not real. You are all connected. You are all one. You are all loved. You must focus on this now. You must bring this up into your conscious mind as often as possible: that you are all connected, you are all one, and you are all loved. You are all equal in the eyes of God.

When you think about the things that upset you, it is because you have deemed somebody unworthy or bad because of what they're doing. You have deemed a situation untenable or incorrect even though it has already happened. These are the things that cause your suffering. It is your relentless judgment and hanging on to the belief that you are in charge of everything and that everything must go your way.

The truth is that everything is already going your way, because you are loved deeply. You are respected deeply, and you are honored deeply by that which you call God. You have been given free will. You have been given freedom of choice, and that is the greatest respect that can be paid to you.

Use your free will and your unique vision of life. As you make decisions each day, know that your inner guidance — that thing that makes you feel as if you are aligned with something — can be trusted. It is your invisible umbilical cord to the Divine. It is your connection to Christ consciousness, and it is your connection to me. I am with you always, and I will do whatever I can to guide you on your journey always.

I am that one you know as Jesus, and we will speak to you tomorrow.

LESSON 355

There is no end to all the peace and joy and all the miracles that I will give when I accept God's word. Why not today?

Follow the complete lesson guidelines in your *ACIM* book.

You are blessed beings, indeed. I am that one you know as Jesus. It is imperative that you understand this is your choice.

It is always your choice. It has always been your choice, and the suffering you have experienced has been your choice. You may not have fully comprehended the power of your judgments; you may not have fully comprehended the power of your fears and your indulgences in them. But they are your choices. They are your babies, and they are the things you value. If you didn't value them, then you could let them go this very minute.

There is a part of your mind that will say, "No, I don't want to suffer. No, I don't want to judge," yet you do. This is one of those areas that is very, very challenging for you to accept: This is what you want; you get exactly what you want.

We ask for you to want the most blessed feeling in the world: peace, happiness, joy, and love — the feeling of the unconflicted mind. The feeling of the mind returning to its natural connection to the Divine. That is what we ask you to choose today instead of your judgments, instead of your fears, and instead of your indulgences.

Choose love, and you will feel better. Tomorrow, choose love again, and you will continue to feel better. The ego does not want peace. It does not want love; it wants war. It wants separation. It is the very thing you have manufactured to give you safety and separation from God. Only you can undo that separation. Only you can choose love.

I am that one you know as Jesus, and we will speak to you tomorrow.

LESSON 356

Sickness is but another name for sin. Healing is but another name for God. The miracle is thus a call to him.

Follow the complete lesson guidelines in your *ACIM* book.

You are blessed beings, indeed. I am that one you know as Jesus. Sickness is the ego's greatest argument that you have been abandoned by God, is it not?

When your body seems to go wrong of its own volition, you feel betrayed. The truth is that your body does not go wrong of its own volition. It is reflective of the frequencies of thought and belief you hold. If you believe in sickness, then you can get sick. If you believe in death, then you can die.

It is very, very important at this stage of your development to see past sickness, as I did in my incarnation on the Earth plane so many years ago. That is what I did when I healed people. I had such conviction that they were well, and my frequency was very high because of the studies and the practices that I had engaged in for many years, so I was able to override their beliefs and prove to them that miracles can happen.

Miracles can happen to you. If you are sick, go into your mind and investigate where your beliefs about sickness reside and what they are. We want you to change them. We want you to become miracle-minded. So instead of talking about your sickness — sharing your sickness with others, telling them how bad you feel — say to yourself: "I am well. I never get sick." What will happen is that you will begin to see a shift in the frequency with which you get sick, and it is because of your beliefs. Your body is the effect of your mind. It is that simple.

I am that one you know as Jesus, and we will speak to you tomorrow.

LESSON 357

Truth answers every call we make to God, responding first with miracles and then returning unto us to be itself.

Follow the complete lesson guidelines in your *ACIM* book.

You are blessed beings, indeed. I am that one you know as Jesus. The emphasis continues to be on forgiveness of your fellow humans.

You have many pursuits in this world. You have fitness pursuits. You have financial pursuits. You have entertainment pursuits, and you consider all these things important. Know how very important your forgiveness practice is. When you step back from the tiniest judgment, you are choosing a miracle; you are choosing to be miracle-minded. That means you intentionally are going counter to what the ego wants you to do with the full force of your free will. This is the most powerful way to deconstruct the ego.

There are many spiritual practices on this planet, and all are free to choose what they use and what they do and how they do it. But we want you to understand here that intentionally using your free will to stop yourself from judging and thus stepping back from that hateful relationship with your fellow humans is the most powerful way that you can transform your mind. You have been given the means in this book to transform your mind into something miraculous.

All the shiny things in this world are always going to be there, taunting you, tempting you, and asking you to play with them. Understand that you can enjoy your life. You can follow your passions and live the way you would like to live, but add forgiveness into the mix. Understand just how truly powerful this gift is. It is brought to you as a gift from God. Just as the ego's judgment is brought to you by the shadow, forgiveness is brought to you by the light.

I am that one you know as Jesus, and we will speak to you tomorrow.

LESSON 358

No call to God can be unheard nor left unanswered. And of this, I can be sure God's answer is the one I really want.

Follow the complete lesson guidelines in your *ACIM* book.

You are blessed beings, indeed. I am that one you know as Jesus. Many of the things you want are not good for you. Many of the things you think will make you happy will not make you happy. This is a tricky game for you to play. How do you know what to do? How do you know where to go? How do you know what to follow? Are you going to follow the wrong person home, the wrong god home?

Understand that you have a guidance system that is impeccably aligned with love. You will feel good when you are on track, and it will mean that you feel bad when you are off track. We are not speaking about pleasure here. We've gone through this before. It's not the good you feel when you're eating a piece of chocolate cake; that is a pleasure sensation, not happiness. In fact, indulging in too many pleasure sensations will make you unhappy and will lead to addiction, because the brain is being stimulated by the senses and you are releasing a chemical that makes you feel good using your senses.

Focus on a general feeling of ease, happiness, and contentment throughout the day, one that does not fluctuate much. Now, for many of you, this is a dream. Your emotions are volatile; your reactions to what's going on in the world are volatile. This is a clue that you have not yet aligned with happiness. You still seek happiness in the world, and it is not giving it to you. It may offer you some temporary solutions, but you do not experience a general feeling of well-being. This is how you choose.

You choose things that make you feel better in general over time. Here are some examples: Going for a walk in nature on any given day may not seem like a big deal, but if you make walking in nature a routine, you will develop a level of connection and happiness that makes you feel better over time. If you buy things to make yourself feel better, what you will see over time is that a month after you've purchased the pair of shoes that you thought would make you happy, you're no longer aware they are in your cupboard. Perhaps you put them on once in a while, and they give you a minute or two of pleasure, but it's very short-lived. This feedback says purchasing the shoes to make yourself happy doesn't work.

Use this time to contemplate where you seek happiness. Do you seek it outside yourself, or do you cultivate healthy habits over time that bring you feelings of contentment and ease?

I am that one you know as Jesus, and we will speak to you tomorrow.

LESSON 359

God's answer is some form of peace. All pain is healed; all misery is replaced with joy. All prison doors are opened. And all sin is understood as merely a mistake.

Follow the complete lesson guidelines in your *ACIM* book.

Note: This lesson falls on Christmas Day only if you started the lessons on January 1 and completed one each day. If it is not Christmas Day when you read this commentary, do not be concerned. Continue as usual.

You are blessed beings, indeed. I am that one you know as Jesus. Today is a big day for many of you. If you began these lessons on January 1, then today is Christmas Day for you, and Christmas Day is a wonderful opportunity for you to feel your way into how on track you are.

Because everything is intensified on this day, it gives you an opportunity to feel your unforgiveness. It gives you an opportunity to feel what you appreciate or what you do not appreciate about what you are doing. It brings to mind anniversaries: "I was doing the same thing last year, and I didn't like it then either." This is a catalyst; this day is a catalyst for those who are off track. For those of you who are on track, it can indeed be a joyful day. But for those who are a little lost, it can magnify, and beautifully so, that which is not okay in your life.

To those of you who are happy and fulfilled today, living how you like and feeling progress evolving in your consciousness, we say Merry Christmas to you, and we thank you for the work you have done. For those of you who are struggling a bit, feeling a little lost or adrift, and whose lives do not look how you want, use this day as a catalyst. Really take inventory of what you want to change in your experience. Remember, you are experiencing your consciousness. The things you don't like keep showing up because you allow them to. You permit them space in your mind, and you keep showing up with your body-mind participating in them.

Nobody is going to save you from yourself. This is something our dear channel has learned over the years and that many people are at times astonished at. We do not save her from herself. She must work through her own problems; she must work through her own issues. Christmas was a time of difficulty for this one, but she has managed through the years to let go of that which she does not want, and now she allows into her life that which she does want during this season. It no longer causes her stress. But the reconstruction of her belief system around this particular day took years to come to a place of peace.

This may be the case for many of you as well — where you are changing what you do this time of the year but still feel the pressure to conform. Your societal pressures to conform are powerful, particularly now. The foundation of your economy is based on the shopping that people do this time of year. There are many businesses in your society that would not function if Christmas did not exist, and a lot of attention, time, and money are put into coaxing you into buying-in, literally and figuratively, to the gift-giving idea.

As you do your lesson and experience your Christmas Day, we want you to notice what does not feel right. Do you hold resentment against somebody who's sitting at your dinner table? Go somewhere quiet and ask yourself, "What sin has this person committed that is so bad?" The truth is, that person has not committed a sin. Perhaps this person has made errors according to your ego or perhaps doesn't look or speak the way you would prefer. Who are you to decide what others should be and how they should look? It is not your job.

All are made in the image of God. They are given particular assignments and particular personalities, all of which suit them on their spiritual journeys and will help them learn and experience the things they need to grow. Who are you to judge others? Who are you to say they are wrong and should be different?

Take time today to assess those "sinful," committed relationships that you believe are around you. Assess why you feel justified in judging them, why you feel justified in throwing stones. Remember, those in glass houses should not throw stones. None of you is perfect. All of you make mistakes. All of you speak incorrectly at times. All of you feel bad at times. Make this a day you assess truly why you consider these beings, who may be with you or may be apart from you, your enemies, and determine why you condemn them as sinners. They are not sinners. They are like you: poorly taught humans who are traveling a difficult journey.

Let go of any resentments you have left. Do not take them into the new year with you. They will not serve you, and they will not benefit anything you wish to manifest in the year ahead. You only benefit when you release resentment. You will feel a lightening. You will feel an easing, and you will feel peace infusing your mind. Those beings will continue to be what they are and who they are and do what they do, but you do not need to let it bother you. You need to reclaim that part of your mind and dedicate it to the Divine.

I am that one you know as Jesus. I wish you all a Merry Christmas, and we will speak to you again tomorrow.

LESSON 360

Peace be to me, the holy child of God. Peace to my fellow beings, who are one with me. Let all the world be blessed with peace through us.

Follow the complete lesson guidelines in your *ACIM* book.

You are blessed beings, indeed. I am that one you know as Jesus. Your feedback system gives you peace of mind as the signal you are doing what you are meant to do.

You will notice throughout the day that many things cause you to lose your peace of mind: thinking that you have forgotten your wallet, not being able to find a parking space, ruminating on something someone said to you that you didn't like, or worrying about the future. These are the small impediments to peace that you must witness as the key to your suffering.

Your decisions about what to worry about or what to think about are happening all the time. Your peace is at stake when you ruminate on things. Think about this: If you cannot find a parking space, the ego-mind says, "Well, that's a reasonable thing to be upset about." Is it worth losing your peace when there is no parking space? There is an acceptance of what is until there is a parking space, and the entire time between observing no parking space and finding a parking space can be heaven or hell. It's up to you.

Ruminating on what someone said to you that you didn't like — the time you spend on that — creates hell in your mind; you lose your peace. You have assumed you know what that person meant. You have assumed it was wrong and that person shouldn't have said it. You have been triggered into some past emotion, and it has been brought into your mind. Now, that being who said something you didn't like is in fact a gift to you, because the person brought something up in your mind from the past; otherwise, you would not have reacted to it.

When you do not have a tender spot about something someone says, you will just pass it over and say, "I guess that person is having a bad day." But if it pokes a tender spot in your psyche, then you have been given a gift. Instead of being in hell and judging the other, you could be in heaven and instead say thank you for revealing something in your subconscious that you were not aware of. What a wonderful gift that was given to you. Again, you can turn hell into heaven.

This can happen a hundred times, a thousand times, a day. It's your choice whether to judge the world or to accept it as it is. If you accept the world as it is, it does not mean you want it to stay that way. Rather, you understand it is that way in that very moment, and if you look at it without judgment, you will see something that will help you. You will see something that will inspire you. You will see something that will motivate you.

You do not have to be in hell. You can say, "I accept that there is poverty in this world, and I would like to change it," instead of wringing your hands and enduring a mental state of hell. You can say, "Now I am inspired, and I am going to do something about it." That is not a hellish state of mind to be in at all. Being motivated is an inspiring state of mind. It feels good. You feel energized, as if you can make a difference.

Value peace today. Whatever peace you have, value it, enjoy it, and revel in it. Know that when you lose your peace, you have the opportunity to learn something profound and powerful about your mind and about how your ego sees the world — or thinks the world should be. Your ego is wrong if it upsets you and makes you lose your peace: "It should not be thus." We say to you that it is thus. So accept it. Learn from it, and become inspired by it.

I am that one you know as Jesus, and we will speak to you tomorrow.

LESSON 361

This holy instant would I give to you. Be you in charge, for I would follow you, certain that your direction gives me peace.

Follow the complete lesson guidelines in your *ACIM* book.

You are blessed beings, indeed. I am that one you know as Jesus. It is important for you to understand what these lessons have been for you. They have been a clarification process. They have retooled your mind. They have given you information. Along with these commentaries, they have given you information that is counter to what you have been taught to do in this world. You are breaking the laws of this world by following *A Course in Miracles*.

Understand that as we come to the end of these lessons, you are not going to get support, necessarily, from everyone around you when you begin to really follow your inner guidance. The people around you, if they are not *A Course in Miracles* students, are not going to understand your thinking. They are not going to understand your behavior. As you shift your trajectory, they may tell you that you're selfish, you disappoint them, or you're ruining things.

When you change your behavior and those around you have been used to you behaving a certain way for a few decades, let's say, it's always good to give them a heads-up. Let them know you are going to change how you do things. As you change how you do things, do it in a moderate way, not because you are fearful, but because you are using your mind in a different way. You are going to have a different experience when you choose different priorities. When you choose different priorities, as you all have been doing over this past year, you will have a new experience, and from that new experience, you will receive new information and new understanding.

Don't go charging off, pushing everything off the table like a crazed cat. Contemplate the changes you are making carefully, calmly, and slowly to see what comes up. As you change your behavior, you are going to trigger fears in yourself and those around you. The reasons you were doing things that were not in your best interest is because you were taught to do that. You were indoctrinated to do that. As you begin to break the rules into which you have been indoctrinated (by your parents, your church, your TV commercials, your banking system, or whatever else), the fear that was instilled in you during the programming is going to arise.

This can be a very rocky time even though you feel you are following your guidance honestly for the first time, perhaps, in your life. Fears are going to arise that were indoctrinated as the program was put into you. So this is why we want you to make changes cautiously. Experience your new experiences while feeling the upsets that arise in you and everyone else with compassion, forgiveness, and understanding that you are literally reconstructing your personality, based now on inner guidance rather than outer conditioning.

If everybody in your society started to do this too quickly, chaos would ensue. The systems at play in your world now have been built on these erroneous beliefs and ideas. As you shift and change, many things will shift and change. You are all on the leading edge of this world transformation. We want you to feel good about that. But we also want you to understand that the world is not necessarily going to support the changes. Do not stand on a soapbox and trumpet about what you're doing. Gently and quietly inform those you must that some changes are going to be happening, and do them in a delicate and thoughtful way so that everyone can manage it.

Some of you will go off like a galloping horse into a different future because you have decided you don't want to do what you're doing anymore, and we cannot stop you from doing that. That will be up to the individual. Our advice is to go slowly and steadily. You know that story of the hare and the tortoise. Go slowly and steadily; take baby steps each day toward the new goals you are setting for yourself.

I am that one you know as Jesus, and we will speak to you again tomorrow.

This holy instant would I give to you. Be you in charge, for I would follow you, certain that your direction gives me peace.

Follow the complete lesson guidelines in your *ACIM* book.

You are blessed beings, indeed. I am that one you know as Jesus. The holy instant is where you hand over your mind to the Holy Spirit, to Christ consciousness, and to God.

It is in the holy instant that you surrender your desires and say: "Show me what you would have me do. Show me where you would have me go. Show me what you would have me say." Instead of planning everything by the ego's book, stop and ask for guidance whenever you have doubts or fears.

You must remember that your fears are your creations. No matter how spiritually powerful you are, no one is permitted to remove from your experience what you have chosen to create. Your creations are your own. Your fears are generated by you, nurtured by you, and respected by you. When you feel fear, know that you have chosen incorrectly. Know that you are looking at the world incorrectly, you have left the eternal now and have gone into the future, and you are supposing about what might happen.

When you feel fear, ask for guidance. Take a moment to sit down and say: "I must have chosen incorrectly, because I am afraid. I must have left this present moment, because I am afraid. How do I know I've left this present moment? Nothing is happening here. Nothing bad is happening here. This is a projection into the future of my own doing. Let me bring my mind back here and ask for guidance."

Maybe the guidance you get is very quiet. Maybe you don't really hear a voice. But you understand that if you stay in the present moment — come back from the future terror that you have inflicted on your mind — you can at least sit in a room quietly for a moment and say, "Nothing bad is happening. Show me what to do."

You will always get an answer. It will come in the form of peace. It will come in the form of inspiration. It will come in some form if you have trained your mind using the lessons of *A Course in Miracles* and if you have practiced training your mind throughout the day. You will be able to pull your mind back into the present moment and calmly ask for guidance.

Now, many people say they do not receive guidance, but you receive guidance all the time through your feelings. If you have stepped back from fear and sat quietly in your car, at your desk, or in your home and said: "Please show me what to do. I do not know what to do in this situation," you will have a feeling of some kind. It may be a feeling to stop moving and not do anything. That is guidance. Many of you seek guidance in the forms of words or direct instruction from a voice in your head. Well, you are getting direct instruction. It is through that impeccable guidance system that you have: your feelings.

Maybe you get a feeling to get some fresh air and go for a walk. Maybe you get a feeling to take a nap. Maybe you get a feeling to phone a friend and ask for help. This is spiritual guidance.

If it is a loving act, a calming act, or a peace-inducing act, then it comes from spirit. If it is a fear-inducing act, an agitated feeling, or a scared feeling, then it comes from the ego. The ego feels different from spirit. This is going to be a learning process for all of you — to discern the difference between the ego's fearful guidance and spirit's gentle, loving, and calm guidance. As you go through the next few years practicing what you have learned with these lessons, you will get better and better and better at it.

I am that one you know as Jesus, and we will speak to you tomorrow.

LESSON 363

This holy instant would I give to you. Be you in charge, for I would follow you, certain that your direction gives me peace.

Follow the complete lesson guidelines in your *ACIM* book.

You are blessed beings, indeed. I am that one you know as Jesus. As our time together draws to a close in this daily format, we want you to become excited about the year ahead.

The year ahead for all of you is going to be magnificent, because the frequencies of this planet are increasing over and over and over again. More and more light is coming your way, and that is why you are drawn to work like this: It speaks to that growing light inside you. Those beings who are turned away from the light are repulsed by teachings such as this because it is incongruent with their frequency. But those of you who have slogged your way through hundreds of lessons, hundreds of days of dedication, have clarified yourselves. You have lifted yourselves.

Some of you may be struggling now, because whatever is within you that is not of the light will be coming up for reassessment and release. Understand that whatever resentments, old problems, or fears you can work on now are going to be very, very powerful releases for you. If you have unexpressed grief or sadness, take yourself into your bedroom and have a good cry; let it out and hear the words that come when you are in despair. They reveal to you the belief that is causing your pain: "I am never going to see my children again. I am always going to be alone. I never have enough money." Listen to those words. Those are the words of the belief that is causing your suffering. As long as you hold on to the control of your emotions, those things remain hidden from you.

We do not suggest spewing your emotions all over other people. Take some time alone to experience what you are feeling; allow it to surface and to speak the words that it believes. These thoughts have power because you have empowered them. As long as you keep them hidden, they contaminate your frequency. When you let them free, you hear them, and then you can address that belief.

For example, if you hear yourself say, "I never have enough money," that is what you should bring into your conscious mind to work on. How could you work on that? You could tell yourself the opposite of the negative belief that's causing you to suffer. Your new mantra would be: "Money comes to me easily and happily. I am surrounded by abundance." That is your healing mantra to dissolve the thought form that you have allowed to live in your mind. Don't hide whatever negativity comes up in the next few days.

Do not burden others with this unless there is somebody close who is a good shoulder to cry on or somebody who can assist you in the clarification. Do not share this with somebody who's going to try to get you to stop speaking about it or to stop processing it. This is a difficult time for people; when they see you burdened by something, they want you to feel better. Allow your sadness, grief, and upset to surface in a safe and quiet place where you can examine it.

Often, emotions are just negative forms of attack from the ego, things that you have repressed and controlled come out in explosions of emotion. Of course, because you are in projection mode, they are "vomited" on to other people. We do not want you to do that. Do not burden other people with our mental distortions. They are yours. You have allowed them to develop and to live in your mind, so don't share them unless you have somebody who's on a similar path and can understand the process you're going through.

But allow them to release. Allow yourself to feel what you're feeling, and make notes afterward so that you can reveal what's lurking beneath the surface. What's lurking beneath the surface on your planet is going to be revealed one way or another, so it is good to get it out now before you start your new practice: putting these lessons into motion, making them part of your regular thought processes, and using them daily whenever you encounter a problem.

I am that one you know as Jesus, and we will speak to you tomorrow.

LESSON 364

This holy instant would I give to you. Be you in charge, for I would follow you, certain that your direction gives me peace.

Follow the complete lesson guidelines in your *ACIM* book.

You are blessed beings, indeed. I am that one you know as Jesus. The direction that you get will be sound. The direction you receive when you surrender your mind to love will take you toward more love; it will draw you to it. When you dedicate your mind to separation, which is the opposite of love, you take yourself further and further away from love.

We have offered this idea of surrendering your mind to the Divine, surrendering your mind to your higher self's guidance. There are many words used to describe this: the higher self, Holy Spirit, Divine consciousness. All kinds of names are given to the eternal guidance that you have access to. We do not want to get caught up in names here or to argue over dogma. Understand that when you surrender your heart and mind to love and say, "Show me the way. I am dedicating my life to love; show me how to find my way in this difficult world," you will receive guidance, and know the guidance will be different from what you are used to engaging in with your self-direction.

For example, if you are always very tightly controlled about things, the guidance that you receive may come from a new friend who is very relaxed and easygoing and who demonstrates how to let go of control. You might not think that is guidance from the Divine, but it is. This person has come into your life with a different point of view, a different value system, a different way of doing things, and a different way of being to show you that your supercontrolled nature is a choice. This person does something different.

The guidance you receive when you dedicate yourself to love can come in unusual ways. This is a heads-up that the guidance you get can come in the form of new relationships, new friendships, a job opportunity, an influx of money, or a loss of money (many of you learn about financial fears and scarcity thinking when money leaves you and the fears come up from the unconscious into the conscious mind). Remember that messages can come to you in many forms. Be open to new opportunities, new conversations, and new inspirations. That is how the guidance will come.

I am that one you know as Jesus, and we will speak to you tomorrow.

LESSON 365

This holy instant would I give to you. Be you in charge, for I would follow you, certain that your direction gives me peace.

Follow the complete lesson guidelines in your *ACIM* book.

You are blessed beings, indeed. I am that one you know as Jesus. Here we are at the final lesson, and what a good job you have done this year! You have struggled. You have given up at times. Some of you have been very dedicated and have not missed a day, and all those different approaches are fine.

456

Know that on this side of the veil, the work that you have done this year (and will continue to do) is magnificent, indeed. Many hearts and many minds have been transformed, and you have experienced a frequency increase that is hard for you to comprehend because you chose this year to do *A Course in Miracles*.

These lessons were designed specifically to open your heart and mind to love. Each of you, as you have ventured on this path, have felt your unlovingness. You have felt your judgments. You have felt your fears. You have felt your grief. You have come to see more about yourself than you expected, and a lot of it needs to be healed. How is it healed? It is healed by practice. It is healed by relentlessly stepping back from judgment and forgiving the world that is the result.

Remember, the world is the result of thousands, millions, and billions of thoughts, beliefs, ideas, fears, and loves. It is a mishmash of so many things. With this teaching, we attempt to filter out the bad and leave only the good.

Now, this is a world of relativity. That means there is light and dark, hot and cold, and good and bad, but that is a demonstration of separation. Focus your mind only on the good, only on the loving, only on the beautiful. As you continue this practice, think about that. Make your dedication during this next year to see the world through forgiving eyes, to be kinder to yourself and others, and to not sacrifice yourself on the altar of some teaching that has been brought through by beings who do not have your best interests at heart.

Know that you can trust your inner guidance. You have clarified your minds. You have come to see your shortcomings. You have come to see where there is work to be done on your beliefs and that the work will continue. We will continue to be with all of you tomorrow.

We thank you for joining us on this tremendous journey, and we thank this being for allowing us to do this work through her. She has tears of joy and intense emotion. This year has been powerful for her too. She had no idea what she was letting herself in for. But she is glad that she stepped up to the plate and dedicated herself to something that she knew was good.

Take a leaf out of her books, dear ones, and dedicate yourself this next year to something you love, to something that you know is good, and to something that you know will benefit the world.

I am that one you know as Jesus, and we will speak to you tomorrow.

Conclusion

It has been an absolute pleasure channeling these daily commentaries and connecting with Jesus each day. I hope you have enjoyed hanging with Jesus as much as I have. His kind and consistent guidance is a reassuring and supportive element in many lives, and I am glad you were able to enjoy his daily channeled sessions.

This is a book you can return to over and over again. These messages are timeless and always there for you to tap into and re-read.

A Course in Miracles can be a challenging assignment even for spiritual students, and I hope this book has helped you integrate and understand Jesus's amazing teachings on a more profound level. Thank you for joining us, and we will connect again soon.

Much love,
Tina Louise Spalding, channel

You can find out more about Tina and her work at ChannelingJesus.com.

About the Channel

Tina Louise Spalding was raised in a family that often visited psychics, so she is no stranger to the nonphysical world. Her channeling journey began when she settled down for a nap on the summer solstice of 2012. That afternoon, powerful energies surged through her body, leading to ecstasy, bliss, and an altered state of consciousness that lasted for almost a month. The feelings finally drove her to take an automatic writing workshop, where she was first made aware of Ananda. She then began to write for this group of nonphysical teachers who have come to assist us in our waking process.

Tina began channeling Jesus in the summer of 2013, when he appeared in her book *Great Minds Speak to You*. It proved to be a great challenge not only to accept the assignment he offered her — writing his autobiography — but also face many of the fears that this unusual experience brought up. Tina has been asked to channel for Jesus on an ongoing basis. Check her website, ChannelingJesus.com, for public offerings of his teachings.

Tina speaks for Ananda as a full trance channel, offering teachings and personal readings for those who seek more happiness, fulfillment, and connection with Spirit. She has dedicated her life to writing and speaking for Ananda and other nonphysical beings, sharing their wisdom and spiritual knowledge.

THROUGH TINA LOUISE SPALDING

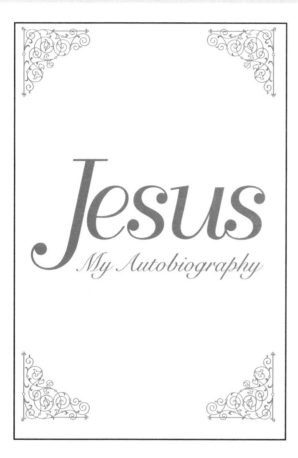

"I have come at this time, in this place, and through this being to speak my truth, to speak the story of my life — the true story of my life."

$16.95 • 304 PP. • Softcover
978-1-62233-030-0

This insightful book is designed to free you from the limitations of your conditioned mind and to give you a better understanding of Jesus's life and teachings so that you can begin to transform your mind, your heart, and the world. Through Tina Louise Spalding, Jesus tells his story in his own words, clearing up misconceptions and untruths and describing his physical and nonphysical journeys that led to enlightenment.

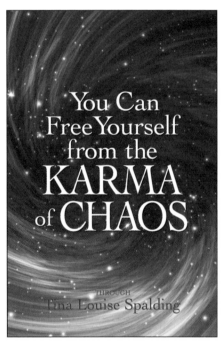

♀ *Light Technology* PUBLISHING *Presents* 463

TO ORDER PRINT BOOKS
Visit LightTechnology.com, Call 928-526-1345 or 1-800-450-0985,
or Check Amazon.com or Your Favorite Bookstore

THROUGH TINA LOUISE SPALDING

Spirit of the Western Way:
Wake Up to Your Power —
Heal the Collective Consciousness of the Western Mind

Western civilization has been manipulated for a very, very long time into negative, low-frequency manifestations and structures of control, limitation, fear, and judgment. You cannot change this until you first see it, accept that it is so, and then, in awareness, shift your consciousness.

These higher-frequency shifts and changes are difficult to attain unless you know what has been inflicted on you and what choices you are making and how they affect you. We bring you basic teachings about reality: what it is, where you come from, why you are here, what your body is, how you get sick, why you thrive, and more.

This book is brought to you by many beings of high frequency who love you and your society very much. We have been assigned the spiritual practice to bring these teachings through this being so that we can help point you in the correct direction to find your way Home. We are Ananda. We are your friends, your teachers, and your fellow travelers on this most magnificent journey into consciousness.

— Ananda

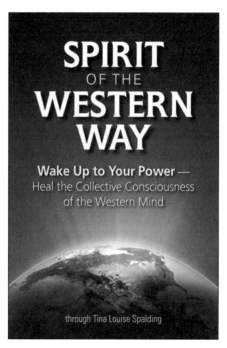

$16.95 • 176 PP. • Softcover • 978-1-62233-051-5

CHAPTERS INCLUDE

- You Are Not Designed to See the Big Picture
- The Split Mind Cannot See Truth
- Nutrition for the Spiritually Minded
- Release Addictions to Find Freedom
- Books, Television, and Films as Nutrition for the Mind
- The Fallacies of Western Religious Thought
- Experience True Wealth and Freedom

🕯️ **Light Technology** PUBLISHING *Presents* 465

TO ORDER PRINT BOOKS
Visit LightTechnology.com, Call 928-526-1345 or 1-800-450-0985,
or Check Amazon.com or Your Favorite Bookstore

THROUGH TINA LOUISE SPALDING

MAKING LOVE TO GOD
The Path to Divine Sex

"We have never seen more hurt and lonely people anywhere than on this planet at the moment. You are all in such a state that we have come from far and wide, from different times and places, to teach you how to relieve the deep suffering you are in. And indeed, it is in the bedroom, in your relationships to yourself, your lover, and God, that these hurts began.

"We are here to teach the way to divine bliss, and we know you are scared — scared to lie naked caressing your lover with rapt attention and honor. We know you are scared to kiss and connect, to feel such deep connection and pleasure that the ego starts to get very nervous, sensing the threat to the well-guarded and limited access to your heart that it deems to be safe.

"If we can turn the tide of thought in enough people, there will be a revolution of love on the planet, the likes of which you have never seen. Relationships will stabilize, marriages will last, and the passion and joy you so wish to experience will become manifest wherever you look."

— Ananda

Making Love to GOD — The Path to Divine Sex

Ananda through Tina Louise Spalding

$19.95 • 416 PP. • Softcover • 978-1-62233-009-6

Topics Include
- How We Came to Misunderstand Sexual Energy
- Using Divine Sex
- Specific Steps and Sensations
- Blocks to Transformation
- A Transformed View of Sex and Sexual Energy
- Following the Path to Transformation
- Reaping the Harvest

THROUGH TINA LOUISE SPALDING

LOVE AND A MAP TO THE UNALTERED SOUL

"True love is never-ending. It does not refuse or inflict punishment, it does not withdraw or have temper tantrums, and it does not punish. Love always is, and it always emits the same high frequency of absolute, unconditional caring and offering, of growing and creation."

— Ananda

We think we know what love is, but in *Love and a Map to the Unaltered Soul*, we are challenged to broaden our definition and free ourselves from constraints we never realized we had. In these pages, you will learn that love is a process of climbing your ladder of consciousness. Through Tina Louise Spalding, the beings Ananda, Jesus, and Mary Magdalene give practical instruction and examples for how to find and keep love at the center of your life.

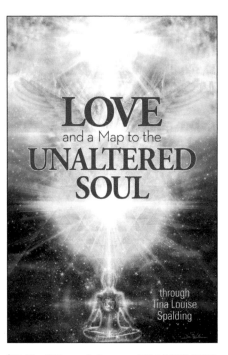

$16.95 • 240 PP. • Softcover • 978-1-62233-047-8

CHAPTERS INCLUDE
- The Unaltered Soul Seeks Experience
- Move beyond the Physical
- You Are Part of a Greater Oneness
- You Can Raise Your Frequency
- Seek Love Within
- You Create Your Experiences
- How to Find Love
- Align with Love to Find Happiness
- Question Your Beliefs
- Implement Healthy Routines
- The Choice Is Yours
- Forgiveness Demonstrates Love

BOOKS THROUGH DRUNVALO MELCHIZEDEK

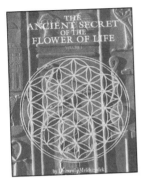

THE ANCIENT SECRET OF THE FLOWER OF LIFE, VOLUME 1

Also available in Spanish as *Antiguo Secreto Flor de la Vida, Volumen 1*

Once, all life in the universe knew the Flower of Life as the creation pattern, the geometrical design leading us into and out of physical existence. Then from a very high state of consciousness, we fell into darkness, and the secret was hidden for thousands of years, encoded in the cells of all life.

$25.00 • 240 PP. • Softcover • ISBN 978-1-891824-17-3

THE ANCIENT SECRET OF THE FLOWER OF LIFE, VOLUME 2

Also available in Spanish as *Antiguo Secreto Flor de la Vida, Volumen 2*

Drunvalo shares the instructions for the Mer-Ka-Ba meditation, step-by-step techniques for the re-creation of the energy field of the evolved human, which is the key to ascension and the next dimensional world. If done from love, this ancient process of breathing prana opens up for us a world of tantalizing possibility in this dimension, from protective powers to the healing of oneself, others, and even the planet.

$25.00 • 272 PP. • Softcover • ISBN 978-1-891824-21-0

Includes
Heart
Meditation CD

LIVING IN THE HEART

Also available in Spanish as *Viviendo en el Corazón*

Long ago we humans used a form of communication and sensing that did not involve the brain in any way; rather, it came from a sacred place within our hearts. What good would it do to find this place again in a world where the greatest religion is science and the logic of the mind? Don't I know this world where emotions and feelings are second-class citizens? Yes, I do. But my teachers have asked me to remind you who you really are. You are more than a human being, much more. Within your heart is a place, a sacred place, where the world can literally be remade through conscious cocreation. If you give me permission, I will show you what has been shown to me.

— Drunvalo Melchizedek

$25.00 • 144 PP. • Softcover • ISBN 978-1-891824-43-2

THROUGH CATHY CHAPMAN

The Golden Elohim on the
CREATION of FORM
through
CATHY CHAPMAN, PHD

$19.95 • Softcover • 6 x 9 • 288 PP.
ISBN 978-1-62233-067-6

The Creation of Form

The human mind is expanding and therefore able to create more than ever before. Encodements bring your ideas, the ideas you gather from the mind of God, into form.

When you work to create nonphysical form, the focus of your intention is crucial for creation. Be clear how you want your abundance to take form.

True abundance comes from the heart. You do not need things to have true abundance.

CHAPTERS INCLUDE

- Put Your Attention Where Your Intention Is
- Learn to Reside in Your Heart
- The Complexity of Creating Form
- Command What You Desire
- The Creation Process Begins Within
- Rainbow Energy Is Being Sent to You

THE FIRST 4 BOOKS IN AMIYA'S ENCYCLOPEDIA OF HEALING

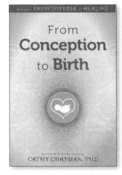

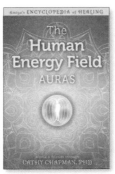

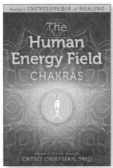

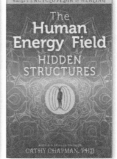

From Conception to Birth

$15.95 • 144 PP.
6 x 9 • Softcover
ISBN 978-1-62233-065-2

The Human Energy Field — Auras

$15.95 • 136 PP.
6 x 9 • Softcover
ISBN 978-1-62233-068-3

The Human Energy Field — Chakras

$19.95 • 400 PP.
6 x 9 • Softcover
ISBN 978-1-62233-069-0

The Human Energy Field — Hidden Structures

$17.95 • 384 PP.
6 x 9 • Softcover
ISBN 978-1-62233-077-5

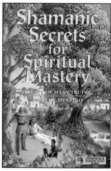

☽ *Light Technology* PUBLISHING *Presents*

TO ORDER PRINT BOOKS
Visit LightTechnology.com, Call 928-526-1345 or 1-800-450-0985,
or Check Amazon.com or Your Favorite Bookstore

SPIRITUAL BOOKS FOR CHILDREN BY LEIA STINNETT

The Little Angel Book series

All My Angel Friends (Coloring Book)
$10.95 • Softcover • 64 PP. • 978-0-929385-80-8

The Angel Told Me to Tell You Good-Bye
$6.95 • Softcover • 64 PP. • 978-0-929385-84-6

**Animal Tales: Spiritual Lessons
from Our Animal Friends**
$7.95 • Softcover • 96 PP. • 978-0-929385-96-9

The Bridge between Two Worlds
$6.95 • Softcover • 64 PP. • 978-0-929385-85-3

A Circle of Angels (Workbook)
$18.95 • Softcover • 112 PP. • 978-0-929385-87-7

Color Me One
$6.95 • Softcover • 64 PP. • 978-0-929385-82-2

Crystals R for Kids
$6.95 • Softcover • 64 PP. • 978-0-929385-92-1

Exploring the Chakras
$6.95 • Softcover • 64 PP. • 978-0-929385-86-0

Happy Feet
$6.95 • Softcover • 64 PP. • 978-0-929385-88-4

Just Lighten Up! (Coloring Book)
$9.95 • Softcover • 48 PP. • 978-0-929385-64-8

The Little Angel Who Could Not Fly
$9.95 • Softcover • 64 PP. • 978-1-62233-025-6

One Red Rose
$6.95 • Softcover • 64 PP. • 978-0-929385-83-9

**Principles and Applications
of the Twelve Universal Laws**
$18.95 • Softcover • 128 PP. • 978-0-929385-81-5

When the Earth Was New
$6.95 • Softcover • 64 PP. • 978-0-929385-91-4

Where Is God?
$6.95 • Softcover • 64 PP. • 978-0-929385-90-7

Who's Afraid of the Dark?
$6.95 • Softcover • 64 PP. • 978-0-929385-89-1

The Adventures of Tee-la and De-Nar
in the Land Called One series

The Master Speaks (Book 1)
$9.95 • Softcover • 64 PP. • 978-1-62233-022-5

The Seven Sacred Pools (Book 2)
$9.95 • Softcover • 64 PP. • 978-1-62233-026-3

The Cave of the Ancients (Book 3)
$9.95 • Softcover • 64 PP. • 978-1-62233-024-9

All Our Books Are Also Available as eBooks from Amazon, Apple iTunes, Google Play, Barnes & Noble, and Kobo.

🕯️ *Light Technology* PUBLISHING *Presents*

PRODUCTS BY LYSSA ROYAL-HOLT

Galactic Heritage Cards

THE FIRST AND ONLY OF THEIR KIND: This 108-card divination system, based on material from Lyssa Royal-Holt's groundbreaking book *The Prism of Lyra,* is **designed to help you tap into your star lineage and karmic patterns** while revealing lessons brought to Earth from the stars and how those lessons can be used in your life on Earth now. Includes a 156-page book of instruction and additional information.

Illustrations by David Cow • 108 cards (2.75 x 4.5 inches)
156-page softcover book (4.5 x 5.5 inches) • $34.95 • 978-1-891824-88-3

Preparing for Contact
In this book, you will take an inner journey through your own psyche and discover a whole new dimension to your unexplained experiences.
$16.95 • Softcover • 320 PP.
978-1-891824-90-6

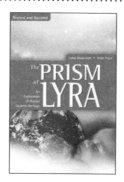

The Prism of Lyra
This text explores the idea that collective humanoid consciousness created this universe for specific purposes.
$16.95 • Softcover • 192 PP.
978-1-891824-87-6

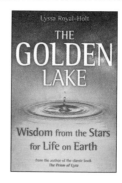

The Golden Lake
This book features Pleiadian and Sirian awakening teachings that together provide a road map for the next phase of human evolution — the integration of polarity and the awakening of our consciousness beyond duality.
$19.95 • Softcover • 240 PP.
978-1-62233-070-6

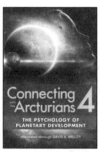

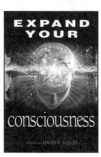